DEDICATED TO THE SOUL

The Writings and Drawings of Emma Jung

FRONTISPIECE.
[Girl with birds].
Painting by Emma
Jung, undated.

Dedicated to the Soul

The Writings and Drawings of Emma Jung

Emma Jung

EDITED BY

ANN CONRAD LAMMERS (LEAD EDITOR)
THOMAS FISCHER AND MEDEA HOCH (COEDITORS)

TRANSLATED BY

ALISON KAPPES-BATES
WITH ANN CONRAD LAMMERS

PRINCETON UNIVERSITY PRESS
Princeton & Oxford

Foundation of the Works of
C.G. Jung

recollections
LLC

Published by Princeton University Press
41 William Street, Princeton, New Jersey 08540
99 Banbury Road, Oxford OX2 6JX

press.princeton.edu

All Rights Reserved

ISBN 978-0-691-25327-5
ISBN (e-book) 978-0-691-26243-7
Library of Congress Control Number: 2024942761

British Library Cataloging-in-Publication Data is available

Editorial: Fred Appel and James Collier
Production Editorial: Karen Carter
Text and Cover Design: Heather Hansen
Production: Steven Sears
Publicity: Kate Hensley and Kathryn Stevens

Jacket/Cover Credit: Courtesy of the Jung Family Archive

Published in cooperation with: The Foundation of the Works of C. G. Jung, the exclusive owner of all copyrights on the literary and visual artistic works of Carl Gustav Jung and Emma Jung-Rauschenbach; The Jung Family Archive Küsnacht, the owner and administrator of the Emma Jung-Rauschenbach papers collection; and Recollections LLC, devoted to promoting and supporting the publication of materials related to the early development of analytical psychology.

This book has been composed in Sabon Next

Printed in China

10 9 8 7 6 5 4 3 2 1

CONTENTS

FIGURE XX.
[Color wheel mandala].
Painting by Emma
Jung, undated.

ILLUSTRATIONS

Figures

All figures © Foundation of the Works of C. G. Jung.

Plates

*With the exception of plates 21 and 26, all plates
courtesy of the Jung Family Archive, Küsnacht.*

Table

Drawings

Miscellaneous drawings by the author, Chapters VI and VII.

FIGURE 1A.1.
Several notebooks
and portfolios of
Emma Jung at the
Jung Family Archive,
2023. Photographer:
Fabian Feigenblatt.

PREFACE AND EDITORIAL NOTE

Preface

AS EARLY AS 2012, representatives of the Foundation of the Works of C. G. Jung began to think about publishing the previously unpublished lectures and presentations of Emma Jung-Rauschenbach. It had long been known that, aside from her two published books, *Animus and Anima*[1] and *The Grail Legend*,[2] a set of her papers had survived in the archives of the Psychology Club Zurich and the Jung Family Archive, Küsnacht.[3] Initially, it appeared that this additional material might only be substantial enough to justify a slim, stand-alone publication.

A question that has long concerned those interested in Emma Jung's contribution to the literature of analytical psychology is whether her volume on the Grail, published posthumously and coauthored by Marie-Louise von Franz, faithfully reproduced all the drafts she left at her death in 1955. An internal study, commissioned by the Foundation of the Works of C. G. Jung in 2013 to address this very question, found that, indeed, the substance of Emma Jung's manuscript material, her lectures and presentations on the theme of the Grail, had been incorporated almost verbatim in the final volume. Marie-Louise von Franz was found to have faithfully arranged Emma Jung's material into a single book, adding mainly transitions between chapters and pertinent passages on the subject of alchemy, her own area of specialization. Thanks to this study, it was decided not to reprint the body of the author's Grail writings. We are fortunate, however, that Emma Jung's abstracts of her Grail lectures in 1940 and 1944 (Appendix A, 363ff.) have never before been published in English. These lecture abstracts not only summarize the author's central themes but also illustrate her mature mastery of central psychological concepts.

---

1   Emma Jung, *Animus and Anima*, translated by Cary F. Baynes ("On the Nature of the Animus") and Hildegard Nagel ("The Anima as an Elemental Being").

2   Emma Jung and Marie-Louise von Franz, *The Grail Legend*, 2nd ed., translated by Andrea Dykes.

3   Distinct from the C. G. Jung Papers Collection at the ETH Zurich University Archives, which contains materials pertaining to Carl Jung's work, the Jung Family Archive contains the personal papers of Carl and Emma Jung. It is still run by the family and has its own rules. This private archive has not yet been fully indexed and, for reasons of capacity, cannot be publicly consulted. For scholarly purposes, however, and with oversight by the archivist, a visitor may inquire about access to specific documents and information from the archive.

By 2013, the Foundation was aware that biographical studies of Emma Jung's life and work had now appeared in Italian and French, followed by a fictionalized account in English of her early married life.[4] While sympathetic, the authors of these works were dependent on the incomplete picture available at the time, reflecting mainly the perspective of Carl Jung and the accounts and information provided by third parties. Still missing from this material was Emma Jung's own voice.

Within the Jung family, and particularly among her grandchildren, Emma Jung was and is fondly remembered as a mindful and generous grandmother. She is often pictured at home in Küsnacht, typically reading at a desk near the living room fireplace, but always ready to turn her attention to the children's troubles, play games with them, read stories, or help with homework. In contrast with their grandfather, so busy with work and not to be disturbed, she seemed immune to indignation. She was regularly sought out for her experience of life and appreciated for her wit and humor in family conversations. Yet, for all their love and reverence toward their grandmother, the family history told by later generations still lacked a full account of Emma Jung's inner life.

By the late 1990s, the Society of the Heirs of C. G. Jung (predecessor of the Foundation of the Works of C. G. Jung), copyright owner for the writings and works of Carl Gustav Jung and Emma Jung-Rauschenbach, had established a first overview of Emma Jung's literary deposit, that is, the papers that were left at her death in the Jung Family Archive. A proper inventory of Emma Jung's papers was only undertaken, however, by the new head of the Family Archive, Susanne Eggenberger-Jung, with assistance from the Foundation of the Works of C. G. Jung, after the start of the new publication project.

Initially, the editors for this volume believed that Emma Jung's surviving papers would include mainly the manuscripts and typescripts from her Psychology Club lectures and possibly her courses at the C. G. Jung Institute. Family legend had it that, apart from these, she herself had destroyed or discarded most of her personal material during her final months, when she knew that she was suffering from a terminal illness. To the great surprise of those editing her work, however, the case proved otherwise. In addition to lecture material, a whole series of Emma Jung's personal notebooks had been preserved in the Jung Family Archive, containing her records of dreams and commentaries, fantasy drawings, and other writings.

---

4   Nadia Neri, *Oltre l'Ombra: Donne intorno a Jung*, 63–82; Imelda Gaudissart, *Emma Jung, Analyste et écrivain*; Catrine Clay, *Labyrinths: Emma Jung, Her Marriage to Carl and the Early Years of Psychoanalysis*. Emma Jung is also the subject of a creative play, written by Elizabeth Clark-Stern, titled *Out of the Shadows: A Story of Toni Wolff and Emma Jung*; and she is discussed in a number of biographies of her husband. While the early biographical memoir by Barbara Hannah, *Jung: His Life and Work*, provides valuable firsthand information, some of the later biographies, in particular Deirdre Bair, *Jung: A Biography*, contain factual misinformation that has inaccurately informed subsequent accounts of Emma Jung's life.

An intriguing collection of her poems was also discovered. Together with two rich portfolios of her drawings and paintings, these opened a vista on her remarkable psychological development, evidence of which had lain dormant for decades, away from anyone's interest or knowledge.

Finally, a substantial number of Emma Jung's correspondences came to light. These letters, written by private acquaintances, friends, and professional colleagues, contradicted the assumption that, except for early letters to her husband and a few other family members, all of her private correspondences had been lost or destroyed. After inventory, her correspondences filled several archival boxes. The editors and partners of this project now realized the full potential of a publication showing all the facets of Emma Jung's creative and intellectual life.

The evidence that has surfaced from recent archival research gives new substance to the existing view of Emma Jung from contemporary witnesses, who had recorded her deep personal wisdom, compounded of keen intellect, curiosity toward the fundamental questions of human existence, and profound psychological understanding. This book introduces Emma Jung's voice into the literature of the early psychoanalytical movement, the development of analytical psychology, and the history of women in the early twentieth century. The primary material provides glimpses into what it meant to be the wife of one of the most unusual thinkers of his time, a world-renowned founding figure of modern psychology, and leads us closer to understanding what it took, under the circumstances, for Emma Jung, née Rauschenbach, to become a full personality in her own right.

Editorial Note

This volume presents a rich, carefully selected multitude of primary materials. It provides an overview of crucial developmental points in Emma Jung's personal work and her psychology. True to the Foundation's editorial policy, the scholarly apparatus and editorial introductions of this volume focus on offering sufficient contextual information to situate the primary material within Emma Jung's intellectual and social setting, so that readers can understand her texts and images in relation to their historical context. Two biographical essays compose the volume introduction, together with a reader's guide to the author's themes and methods. Appendices include Emma Jung's Grail abstracts and a list of essential dates in her life.

THE AUTHOR'S NOTEBOOKS AND PORTFOLIOS

In addition to her typewritten lectures, Emma Jung left behind a substantial collection of handwritten notebooks in various formats and sizes, including bound books, manila folders, art portfolios, dream journals, and so forth. The lectures in Chapter I are based on the author's typescripts. Other chapters in the primary text are based on materials in her handwritten notebooks.

The author gave titles to a few of her notebooks, leaving the rest untitled. For identification purposes, the editors have assigned informal, descriptive names to some of the untitled sources. Frequently consulted notebooks are named below.[5]

Marbled book. A well-crafted, bound notebook, whose cover design led the editors to call it the marbled book, is the source of many writings and a few paintings published here. The pages of the marbled book, hand-numbered 1 to 180,[6] contain writings dated from 1911 to 1917 and an important painting probably executed in 1919.[7] The marbled book is an especially important source for the present volume, since the author evidently used its pages to record her most-valued dreams, fantasies, commentaries, poems, and paintings. It contains the polished versions of a number of writings; consequently, it is the source for many of the texts published here.

Manila poem folder. Many of Emma Jung's short poems are found in a manila folder bearing a penciled title, *Gedichte Mama* (*Mama's poems*), perhaps added by one of the Jung children. The poems appear to date from 1915 to 1924. Because the papers in the folder are loose, and not all poems are dated, their original order is not always certain. Some poems clearly exist in earlier and later versions. Some also exist in typed copies.

1921 poem booklet. An additional source of poems, the 1921 poem booklet is a short, handwritten booklet, softbound in green and white fabric, containing 22 poems. It is inscribed on the first page as a gift and dated 31 August 1921.[8] The booklet was discovered by chance at a late stage in the editorial process, in the former house of Lill Hoerni-Jung (Carl and Emma Jung's youngest child, deceased in 2014). The poems in the booklet are dated from September 1915 to New Year's Day 1921. By comparing poems in this booklet with other versions of the same poems, we determined that the texts of five poems in Chapter V should be updated. The 1921 booklet also supplied titles or dates for a few poems in the chapter.

---

5   Only the notebooks discussed in the editorial apparatus are listed here. Since Emma Jung's notebooks are unpublished, their titles are printed in roman type. The author's titles for her notebooks are printed with quotation marks. Informal, descriptive names, provided by the editors, are printed without quotation marks.

6   Emma Jung made a few errors in hand-numbering. The true page count of the marbled book is 184.

7   Cf. Chapter VII, 315, 361 and notes.

8   The inscription lacks a name, but this booklet was very likely a gift to Hans Trüb, a family friend with whom Emma Jung corresponded and with whom she was in an analytic conversation. Its date, 31 August 1921, marks the end of a shared summer vacation that included the Jungs and the Trübs.

"Night Voices." Raw material for Emma Jung's cosmology, as discussed in the introduction to Chapter VII (314ff.), is taken from a dream journal with a gold-embossed black leather cover, which the author titled "Stimmen der Nacht" (Night Voices). The first page bears the dates February 1914–July 1915. This notebook contains the dream texts and fantasies from April and May 1915, whose lengthy commentaries, including ink and colored-pencil drawings, led the author into her cosmological reflections. The notebook ends with a journal entry, dated 30 July 1915, devoted to her reading of Schopenhauer.[9]

Diamond-cover notebook. This dream journal, dated March 1917, has a white cover painted with a full-color diamond design. It includes handwritten copies of two dreams published here: the dream of "the animal enclosure" (287) and of "the world turned upside-down" (289).

Black notebook. The longer version of Emma Jung's cosmology, printed in Chapter VII as "System I," is found in a notebook with a black cover, whose text and drawings are devoted to her first effort at putting these symbolic materials into coherent form. Although the writings and drawings in the black notebook are undated, internal evidence dates them to 1915 or 1916.

Brown leather notebook. A more condensed version of the same cosmology, published in Chapter VII as "System II," is found in the middle section of a notebook covered in brown leather, whose front page is dated by the author "February 1915–June 1924." Pages devoted to cosmology are in an undated middle section of the brown leather notebook, bracketed by entries dated 1918 and 1919.

Green linen notebook. The first page of this notebook bears the dates February–July 1921. It contains two long writings. An undated first draft of the narrative poem, "Do you see the sea?" is followed by a copy of the extended fantasy, "Journey to the underworld," dated January 1919.

Diamond portfolio. The white parchment cover of this portfolio is painted by the author with a colorful diamond design. The diamond portfolio contains symbolic paintings by Emma Jung, mostly dated from January 1917 to January 1918, many of which were selected for publication in this volume. It also includes a dream image dated September 1928.

Blue portfolio. The cover of this portfolio is blue cardboard. Its many undated drawings, mostly naturalistic in style, include one of a tree in Bollingen, dated 1930. The blue portfolio also contains the symbolic painting of a little girl facing the gate in a stone wall.

---

9   See Chapter VII, 337.

Emma Jung does not seem to have prepared most of her poems, dreams, active imaginations, and dream commentaries with publication in mind. A comparison of various versions, however, shows the writer's attention to the literary quality of these private writings. The marbled book, as mentioned, includes pieces that were clearly copied from other notebooks. A comparison between versions shows that she revised her writings for style, and sometimes also for content. Stylistic revisions show her writerly attention to detail. Significant revisions of content are identified by the editors.

Where the author left multiple versions of a given writing, our policy has been to print the most final version available. In undated texts, or those that were copied more than once, dating is not always easy to determine. Sometimes we rely on external evidence; for example, typewritten copies are presumed to be later than handwritten. Internal textual evidence includes passages where the author has made corrections, later incorporated into a fresh copy. As noted, textual comparisons show that the marbled book contains minor revisions of many writings originally recorded elsewhere; thus the writings in that source are often presumed to be the author's final versions.

A number of dreams by Emma Jung have been anonymously discussed in the works of her husband.[10] For reasons of volume length, the dream texts previously published in C. G. Jung's *Collected Works*[11] are generally not republished here. One exception was made to this policy, however. The author's dream of 19 September 1915, previously published in *CW* 9.i, §354, is republished here (275ff.). Emma Jung's original record of her dream includes information, significant for this volume, that was omitted by Carl Jung in his summary. Several of her paintings reproduced here in color (75, 77, 292, 361) are also discussed in C. G. Jung's published work, although she is not named there as the source.

With few exceptions, the editors have made it a policy to publish the author's texts *in toto*. An exception was made when we chose to print only an excerpt from the long, poetic fantasy, "Journey to the underworld" (294ff.). We judged that this fantasy was too long to print in full; but the chosen portion is extraordinarily important and sheds light on the author's major themes.

Chapter VII represents another special case. A chapter introduction, laying out the author's first, raw materials for her cosmology, is followed by both completed versions of her System. In this case, we abandoned our policy of printing only

---

10 Five of the author's dreams are presented anonymously in *CW* 9.i, §340, §342, §349, §§352–53, and §354.

11 Citations to the *Collected Works of C. G. Jung* are conventionally abbreviated, as here, to *CW* and volume number. The twenty volumes of the *Collected Works* are published in both German and English. To facilitate locating passages in both editions, references are commonly made to paragraph numbers rather than page numbers (see Bibliography, 384).

the latest version of each piece of writing. Emma Jung's "System" begins with personal experience but soon moves to a high level of abstraction, extending into philosophy, physics, and archetypal psychology. The latest version (System II) is more accessible when one approaches it in stages, using the author's raw materials in "Night Voices" and her first completed version (System I) as stepping stones, allowing the reader to follow her developing thought.

TRANSCRIPTIONS

Texts selected for translation and eventual publication were transcribed by the editors, working from complete photocopies and photographs of the original documents in the Jung Family Archive.[12] In translating the transcriptions and preparing translations for publication in the English edition, abbreviations were spelled out, and missing punctuation was added. Crossed-out words were omitted from the primary text but sometimes reproduced in footnotes. Corrections added above the line were integrated into the text. Any remaining obscurities are printed within square brackets and footnoted. A few mannerisms, such as *Sperrdruck* (spaces between letters), characteristic of German writing at the turn of the twentieth century, were silently changed to reflect more modern conventions.

In addition, all quotations from letters and notebooks used in the introductory essays to this volume have been transcribed and translated from German following the same principles as above, with the exception of passages originally written in English, including a letter by Emma Jung, written in 1942 (55). No stylistic revisions were made in such quoted passages, and the writer's original punctuation was allowed to stand.

TITLES

Many pieces of Emma Jung's creative output were titled by the author; but a good number of her writings and paintings were left untitled. To avoid confusion, anticipating that the contents of this volume will be widely discussed and cited, the editors have supplied working titles for the previously untitled elements. These include paintings, poems, dreams, fantasies, and the stages of Emma Jung's cosmology (Chapter VII). Our policy in creating titles was to identify each piece as simply and descriptively as possible, in a style consistent with the author's titles, while avoiding interpretation. For both textual elements and illustrations, the

---

12 The guidelines of the Foundation of the Works of C. G. Jung state that transcriptions are to be as faithful as possible to the original texts: spelling and punctuation are to be reproduced exactly; author's abbreviations to be transcribed as written; legible errors to be allowed to stand, etc.

author's original titles are printed without special punctuation. Editors' working titles are marked by square brackets.

STRUCTURE OF THE VOLUME

As far as possible, the chapters of this book were designed to reflect the author's multifaceted use of genres—lectures, thoughts, narrative poem, verse drama, poems, and so forth. As she focused on her inner process, Emma Jung seems to have deployed whatever literary and artistic forms best met her needs. Accordingly, her types of self-expression flow from one to another: prose, poetry, painting, and back to prose. What begins as a dream narrative extends into a pages-long fantasy, ending with a poem (268ff.). A painting is elaborated by a poem (231); a fantasy is accompanied by a painting (292ff.). Fantasy shifts into poetry, then returns to prose (279ff.). The unifying principle is the writer's faithfulness to the voices and images of her psyche.

Since many of Emma Jung's writings and paintings reflect her inner life and growth as an analyst, we have tried to choose materials that also reflect this essential dimension of her development. Within each chapter, we have followed the author's chronological sequence as far as possible. The chapters, however, are not ordered chronologically but follow a sequence that we think will best allow readers to take in and understand Emma Jung's artistic, intellectual, and psychological experience. Our concern overall is to show the full range of ways in which the author expressed her inner world, her relationship to the artistic and intellectual currents of her era, and her developing knowledge of depth psychology.

The first biographical essay, "Emma Rauschenbach: Portrait of Her Childhood and Youth," was written by a contributing scholar, the director of the Jung Family Archive, Susanne Eggenberger-Jung. She has exclusive access to the private papers in the Jung Family Archive, a unique degree of access, which allows her to present this part of Emma Jung's biography for the first time to the public. The other introductory essays are written and signed by the volume's editors. Chapter introductions for Chapter III, "Narrative Poem" ("Do you see the sea?") and Chapter VII, "The System: A Cosmology," and the textual summary introducing "Journey to the underworld" (294), in Chapter VI, are by the editor of the English edition, Ann Conrad Lammers, in collaboration with the editorial team. Footnotes were written by Ann Conrad Lammers and Thomas Fischer.

SELECTION OF ARTWORKS

The visual elements in this volume were chosen, out of a multitude of Emma Jung's drawings and paintings, to demonstrate the power and importance of images in her interior life. Many of the paintings reproduced here have both a representational and a symbolic character. A few of her most striking symbolic paintings are published and discussed in the "Reader's Guide" (67ff.). Several others are published with the texts they illustrate. Free-standing images, or image-series, are located between chapters.

The final chapter of this work, exploring the theme of cosmology, includes a great number of abstract and symbolic drawings, reproduced here in facsimile, as the author generated them in her notebooks. It concludes with a powerful painting combining many of her symbolic motifs to depict the emergence of a world.

Thomas Fischer and Ann Conrad Lammers
June 2023

ACKNOWLEDGMENTS

EDITORIAL WORK ON this volume started in 2019 with the negotiation of a formal cooperation agreement, titled "Publication of Selected Papers and Drawings by Emma Jung," between the Foundation of the Works of C. G. Jung Zurich, Recollections, LLC, Carpinteria, and the Jung Family Archive Küsnacht, which set the framework for this project and guided the work of the editors and translators. After four years of intense collaboration, the editors would like to thank all three institutions for their continuing support and trust. We especially thank the Foundation of the Works of C. G. Jung Zurich and its board members for initiating this project, clearing the selected material for publication, granting copyrights to the Emma Jung-Rauschenbach material, and financially supporting the editing and publication of the book. The editors are also grateful to Ulrich Hoerni, former president and member of the board and longtime director of the Foundation and its predecessor, the Society of the Heirs of C. G. Jung, for participating in early conceptual discussions of a possible Emma Jung publication project. At an early stage, too, Bettina Kaufmann reviewed all the Emma Jung material available at the Foundation.

Decisive financial support and backing was generously given by Nancy Furlotti through Recollections, LLC, which is devoted to promoting and supporting the publication of material related to the early development of analytical psychology. The editors are specifically thankful to Recollections for covering the costs of Ann Lammers's editorial work and the translations produced by Alison Kappes-Bates.

The collaboration of the Jung Family Archive was indispensable to the realization of the project. For full access to the Emma Jung papers in the Jung Family Archive, the editors are grateful to Andreas Jung, owner of the archive, and his daughter Susanne Eggenberger-Jung. We especially thank Susanne Eggenberger-Jung, archivist of the Jung Family Archive, for her cooperation at every stage of the project. It was only through her systematic inventorying of the Emma Jung papers during the project that the editors were able to realize such an encompassing publication and extract the necessary contextualizing information.

Besides these three main partners in the project the editors and authors of the book would like to thank a number of individuals and institutions for their help and support. At the ETH Zurich University Archives, Dr. Yvonne Voegeli and Claudia

Briellmann gave us access to copies of Emma Jung's letters from the C. G. Jung Papers collection. Other libraries and archives whose help we wish to acknowledge include the Zentralbibliothek Zürich, Handschriftensammlung; Universitätsbibliothek Basel, Handschriftensammlung; the library of the Psychology Club Zurich; the Peterborough (NH) Town Library, Ann Harrison at Interlibrary Loan.

Many individuals assisted the editors in this project. Rali Neumann allowed us to see the letters from Emma Jung to Erich Neumann. Ernst Falzeder helped with transcription of letters from Sigmund Freud to Emma Jung. Ursula Nussbaumer gave information on the titles and dates of Psychology Club lectures and provided guidance to Club library sources. Andreas Schweizer allowed us to access the protocols of meetings of the Verein für Analytische Psychologie and the Psychology Club Zurich. Nadir Weber and Felix Naeff allowed access to copies of Jung-Trüb family correspondence. Florent Serina brought to our attention a letter of Emma Jung to Lucie Heyer-Grote in the Basel University Library, the Lucie Heyer-Grote bequest. Corina Fisch gave us access to Erika Schlegel's diaries. Petra Brem at the C. G. Jung Institute Zurich in Küsnacht provided access to the early lecture programs. Sonu Shamdasani consulted with us regarding Jung's discovery of the concept of *anima* and the origins of Jung's cosmology (*Systema mundi totius*). Niklaus Largier gave historical and linguistic consultation on passages by Meister Eckhart.

Susanne Eggenberger-Jung thanks Vreni Jung-Gerber for transcribing letters written in the old cursive form of German handwriting. She would also like to thank Andreas Jung, Brigitte Merk, and Adrian Baumann for their personal family memories of Emma Jung. Thomas Fischer would like to specifically acknowledge Helene Hoerni-Jung, Ulrich Hoerni, Marianne Fischer-Hoerni, and Andreas Jung for sharing details of family history.

For assistance with the English text, we would like to thank the following. Shannon Ashlyn helped decipher handwritten passages in the original materials. Tak Kappes consulted regularly on German-English translations. While he lived, Richard Corney identified biblical passages, commented on biblical translations and ancient Near Eastern history, and advised on poetry translation and English style. Riccardo Bernardini consulted on the source and meaning of "vis ut sis." Barbara Davies and Michel F. Juillerat consulted on the French text and approved the English translation of "Mystery of the Crusade."

For historical and linguistic advice, we are indebted to the following. Arthur Holder consulted on writings by Tertullian, Augustine, and other Patristic writers. Robert Segal advised on the use of the word "primitive" in early twentieth-century writings. Diane Finiello Zervas gave us information about Emma Jung's early presentation on the Grail at C. G. Jung's Sennen Cove seminar, 1920. Ursula Kiraly made available her lecture and paper "The Club Problem, 1920–1924."

As we prepared to approach publishers, Hope Singsen helped us frame the book proposal. In further preparing the manuscript for submission photographer Fabian Feigenblatt produced all the image material for this volume.

We are grateful to Fred Appel, James Collier, and Karen Carter at Princeton University Press for taking on the publication and working with us through production of the manuscript. We are particularly grateful for the in-house designer's attention to detail with the illustrations, and for Jenn Backer's excellent work in copyediting the manuscript. Finally, we thank three anonymous peer reviewers who gave valuable support and critical feedback on the first draft of the manuscript.

Introductory Essays

Emma Rauschenbach
Portrait of Her Childhood and Youth

SUSANNE EGGENBERGER-JUNG

The following text is not a biography in the true sense of the word. Rather, it sheds light on Emma Rauschenbach's background and what she brought with her, in terms of preconditions, characteristics, talents, and interests, as a starting point for her later work. Accordingly, the essay focuses mainly on her early years, concluding with a brief summary of events and circumstances in her later life. Unless otherwise stated, all citations and information are from sources found in the Jung Family Archive,[1] primarily private correspondence.

The world is full of the enigmatic and the mysterious, and people just live their lives without asking many questions. … O who could know much, know all![2]

Background and Childhood

EMMA MARIA RAUSCHENBACH was born in Schaffhausen on 30 March 1882, daughter of Bertha Rauschenbach (1856–1932), née Schenk, and Johannes Rauschenbach (1856–1905), known as Jean. She spent her childhood years together with her

---

1   The Jung Family Archive is not yet open to the public. See "Preface and Editorial Note," xiii, note 3.

2   Emma Rauschenbach to Carl Jung, private correspondence, 5 February 1902.

parents, her sister, Marguerite, who was fifteen months younger, and her paternal grandmother in the spacious house "zum Rosengarten" on the banks of the Rhine. The rooms of this historical house were furnished with Jonc furniture and mirrors, and there were plenty of toys for the children.[3]

Emma Rauschenbach's father was the owner of the Rauschenbach Machine Factory and the watchmaking firm International Watch Company (IWC). Her grandfather Johannes Rauschenbach (1815–81) had founded a mechanics workshop in Schaffhausen in 1842 and had soon become a leader in the manufacturing of agricultural equipment and machinery, which he sold throughout Europe. Five years later, with his brother Conrad Rauschenbach, he also founded a nail-making and cotton wool factory. He had been quick to recognize the significance of the Rhine being dammed for the industrialization of Schaffhausen. In 1879 he took over the bankrupt Schaffhausen watchmaking company, the International Watch Company, and turned it, too, into a successful company. He was also a member of the Schaffhausen City Council for twenty-three years and, for a time, a member of the Cantonal Council, the Building Commission, and the Constitutional Council, and he initiated the Trade Association in 1881. "Rauschenbach was also a rich man within himself: he had a serious, deep and gentle disposition," the *Schaffhauser Intelligenzblatt* wrote in 1881 upon the death of the richest Schaffhausen citizen at that time.[4]

With his sudden death, his son Jean, Emma's father, had to step in at only twenty-five years of age and take over the management of his father's businesses. Fortunately, he was not completely unprepared, for he was already working in his father's employ. After high school, he had studied at the Polytechnic University in Dresden (1875–78), followed by an internship with one of his father's business partners in Limoges. Thanks to his foresight and a great deal of entrepreneurial skill, Jean continued the success story of the two factories. He made many business

---

3   Gertrud Henne-Bendel, *Jugend-Erinnerungen einer Grossmutter* (privately printed, 1960). Gertrud Bendel (married Henne) and her sister Hedwig Bendel (married Sturzenegger) were cousins of Emma Rauschenbach on her father's side.

4   In the 1880 census, the small rural canton of Schaffhausen in the north of Switzerland counted a population of 38,241, which was 1.4 percent of the total population of Switzerland. The city of Schaffhausen in 1880 was a small town of 12,557 inhabitants. Cf. Bundesamt für Statistik, ed., *Eidgenössische Volkszählung 1990: Bevölkerungsentwicklung 1850–1990—Die Bevölkerung der Gemeinden*. The canton of Schaffhausen in the years 1850 to 1900 suffered a significant overseas net migration loss, mostly from poor rural areas. Johannes Rauschenbach was one of the first to build up some wealth in the area. He set up his machine factory, taking advantage of the opportunity created by a first hydroelectric power station, constructed in 1850 on the Rhine in Schaffhausen, a place where not much international trading, business, or banking tradition had previously existed. See Joseph Jung, *Das Laboratorium des Fortschritts* (The Laboratory of Progress), 226–28 (net migration loss), 453–57 (industrialization of Schaffhausen), 486ff. (Rauschenbach agriculture machinery and watchmaking production). As a result, Emma Jung and her sister inherited substantial wealth when their father, who had taken over the factories, passed away. The Rauschenbach estate still bore no comparison, however, to other categories of wealth that abounded at the time in the large Swiss industrial and financial centers, such as Zurich, Geneva, Basel, and Winterthur.

trips to the surrounding countries or to the Budapest branch of the Rauschenbach Machine Factory, a journey on which his daughters were once allowed to accompany him.

In 1881, Jean Rauschenbach married Bertha Schenk, with whom he had a good marriage. Emma's mother grew up in the inn "Hirschen" in Uhwiesen, as the daughter of both governor and colonel Johann Jakob Schenk and his wife, Elisabetha, née Müller. Bertha's mother died postpartum, when Bertha was seven years old, and the children were brought up by a maid. Bertha Schenk had a good relationship with her father. She had an open, generous, interested personality, and to a large extent was probably self-taught. The only known fact about her education is that after her years of obligatory schooling, she learned French in the Romandy.

Initially a religious, rather pious woman, Bertha became a broad-minded, well-rounded personality over the course of her life. Despite the great wealth she married into, she remained down-to-earth, interested in her fellow human beings and active in charitable work. She was a social-minded employer, who sometimes took her employees to theater and concert performances in the evenings.

Bertha Rauschenbach had many interests: she was a birdwatcher and an astronomy enthusiast—an enthusiasm later passed on to Emma and Carl[5]—and took pleasure in literature and music. She cultivated contacts with various artists, supported writers and musicians—also financially—and often allowed guest musicians in Schaffhausen to stay at her large house. The latter repaid her kindness in turn with house concerts.[6]

Emma Rauschenbach was a bright, versatile, and extremely interested girl, who wrote her first letter when she was only four and a half years old. She also enjoyed making things and painting, as well as collecting flowers to dry. Many longer and shorter family trips were undertaken in the surrounding areas with Rupert, the coachman. Emma very much enjoyed being out in the fresh air surrounded by nature, in which she took great delight.

She enjoyed going to school and passed with flying colors. She had lessons in both dance and piano and practiced so diligently that by the age of ten she could already play piano pieces from the opera *Der Freischütz* by C. M. von Weber. In October 1896, at the age of fourteen, she passed her music exams in Schaffhausen and, three years later, a further one in Paris. She also devoured books with a

---

5   Bertha Rauschenbach made regular celestial observations. She owned a telescope and a large celestial globe, which also included a small planetarium. How far back her interest in astronomy went, and where she got her enormous knowledge from, cannot be determined. From the memories of her grandchildren Franz Jung and Helene Hoerni-Jung, it is known that Bertha was friends with the president of the Astronomical Society of Schaffhausen and invited him to lecture several times at her house, the Oelberg. In 1906, Emma wrote to her: "The more we read, the more enthusiastic we [Emma and Carl] become about astronomy."

6   Helene Hoerni-Jung, "Memories."

passion. During a stay in Baden (Canton Aargau), where she was accompanying her mother, who was there for treatment, she wrote to her sister[7] that, because of the bad weather, she was lying in bed until noon, reading one book after the other.[8] One girls' novel which she found to be, in her own words, "terribly fine" was *Der Trotzkopf* by Emmy von Rhoden.[9]

With Anna Stokar von Neuforn, their governess from an old Schaffhausen family, the two sisters practiced various skills and the etiquette of high society. Their mother also regularly took the two girls to the theater, opera, and concerts. Emma was fascinated by these cultural events and vividly described her impressions in letters to her father, who was often away on business. From a young age, she was involved with art and artists, collecting art postcards and writing out poems by great masters into her notebook. Evidently, she was inspired not only by her art- and literature-loving mother; her father, too, played the violin in his youth and enjoyed poetry. His drawing portfolio, which still exists, shows us that he also enjoyed being creative. During summer vacations in Normandy, where the mornings were often spent drawing, Emma was grateful that the very talented daughter of her Parisian host family explained all that she wished to know about drawing. A further role model may also have been her older cousin Hedwig Bendel,[10] who was artistically gifted and close to Emma.

Compared to her sister, Marguerite, Emma Rauschenbach was an introverted child. She was reticent, rather reserved all her life, and extremely discreet. Nevertheless, she was able to enjoy herself to the full and reported exuberantly on her pleasant experiences, whether it be day trips into the countryside with her sister and her two cousins Hedwig and Gertrud Bendel, hours spent with her sister ice-skating or playing tennis, vacations in the Swiss mountains (Churwalden, Engelberg), or later, her first beach vacations in Belgium, which she spent with her aunt Anna Bendel-Rauschenbach and her two cousins.

Unlike Marguerite, who was a passionate swimmer, Emma Rauschenbach preferred to have solid ground under her feet and enjoyed long walks and hikes. She wanted to be able to do and know everything, and she was always setting new goals for herself. Emma was ambitious and wanted to demonstrate her strong points. When her father did not permit her to climb the Titlis,[11] she was disappointed. In a letter to him in 1896, she described how she was determined not to avail herself of

---

7 Emma Rauschenbach to Marguerite Rauschenbach, 20 April 1892.

8 Books still extant from her childhood: Marie Beeg, *Lust und Leid der Kinderzeit: In Wort und Bild* (received for Christmas 1886); Brigitte Augusti, *Im Banne der freien Reichsstadt* (cultural-historical stories from old and recent times).

9 Emmy von Rhoden, *Der Trotzkopf* (girls' novel). Quotation: Emma Jung to her cousin Gertrud Bendel, 31 October 1896.

10 Emma's cousin Hedwig Sturzenegger-Bendel was the mother of Hans Sturzenegger, founder of the Sturzenegger Foundation, whose aim was to collect works of art and historical objects of significance for Schaffhausen (curriculum vitae Fritz Sturzenegger-Bendel).

11 Mountain in central Switzerland (10,623 feet above sea level).

the option of sitting on a donkey when she was tired. This was her way of signaling that she was capable of doing the hike under her own steam.

Emma Rauschenbach had a very close relationship to her parents and her sister, and when either she was on vacation or her parents were away on one of their various spa or business trips, she shared her life with them by letter almost daily. She described her observations in detail and always inquired about the well-being of her loved ones. When writing letters, she was not very particular about her handwriting or her choice of words. She felt it was more important to recount her feelings and experiences "hot off the press" than it was to wrap them in beautiful words and phrases. Even ink blots and deletions were countenanced.

Illness of Her Father

In the early 1890s, her father fell ill. It is thought that he contracted syphilis while on a business trip to Budapest. Family members attributed his declining health to the consequences of a childhood accident. In 1894, Jean went blind, which was almost unbearable for him. He lost his independence and was reliant upon the care provided by his wife and daughters. Emma supported him as best she could and regularly read aloud to him as a diversion. She welcomed this task, for it enabled her to further her knowledge. She read both literary and scientific works.

Emma Rauschenbach felt ineffable compassion for her father, who was so full of drive. But she also had respect for his illness-related unpredictable temper and emerging sarcasm, which only subsided after a certain time. With the father's illness, family life changed. Care of Father was in the foreground. Social occasions and visits were kept to a minimum, and the management of the companies was delegated. The tragedy of human fate gave Emma pause for thought. She attributed her own reticence in part to her father's illness.[12] She had been twelve years old when her mother traveled with her father to an eye clinic, and her governess, Fräulein Stokar, came to take care of the girls. At first Emma rebelled, thinking that at her age she no longer needed a governess. Furthermore, she was jealous and felt that she was being "distanced" from her mother by Miss Stokar's familiarity with her. Since her mother was already otherwise heavily burdened, Emma was reluctant to further distress her with her feelings, and she withdrew. Looking back, however, she realized that she owed a lot to Anna Stokar.

Emma was mostly surrounded by women. Apart from her father and grandfather Schenk, to whom Emma was allowed to go on vacation for a few days, there were not many men with whom she had a close relationship. Her few male cousins were much younger.

---

12   Emma Rauschenbach to Carl Jung, 25 February 1902.

A Year Abroad in Paris

After finishing school brilliantly, Emma Rauschenbach expressed a desire to study. Her wish, however, was not supported by her father. At that time, only a few women, mostly from other countries, studied at Swiss universities. Women of Emma Rauschenbach's standing were expected to prepare themselves for the management of a grand household. Instead of university, once she had left school, her parents sent her to Paris for a year to live with a distant relative, Madame Lavater, who lived in an elegant apartment block at 139 Avenue Malakoff. As her husband had died, Madame Lavater secured her livelihood by allowing girls from upper-class European families to stay on her premises, where they were taught by tutors. This provided Emma with the opportunity to take French, Italian, English, history, literature, and piano lessons, of which, unlike the other female boarders, she took full advantage. She felt very much at home with Madame Lavater and especially enjoyed socializing with her daughter Louise, who was four years older. Contact with the Lavater family and with most of the boarders persisted beyond the time they spent together in Paris. She subsequently formed a lifelong friendship with Ida Sträuli, from a family of soap manufacturers in Winterthur.

On weekends and free afternoons, joint excursions were organized. The girls visited museums and galleries, went to theaters and concerts, and made visits to the Sèvres porcelain factory and a workshop for young blind people. They also enjoyed relaxing picnics and reading time in the surrounding parks. On Sunday, church was the order of the day, but for the girls it was not mandatory. In the evenings, people played music, studied, read aloud, or played cards in the salon. Emma Rauschenbach also attended lectures on modern literature or opera. She was particularly thrilled about a performance of *Faust*. She wrote to her parents:

> I wish you could enjoy all these fine things with me, and I feel sorry for Schwöri-li, who is floating around at home so alone.[13]

During the summer vacation of 1898, she was allowed to travel with the Lavater family and two other girls for four weeks. They had a beach vacation in Carteret (Normandy) and traveled back to Paris via the Channel Islands of Jersey, Sark, Guernsey, Saint-Malo, and Mont-Saint-Michel.

During the vacation, Emma Rauschenbach changed the language of her letters to French. She was overwhelmed by so many new impressions, and she described her experiences to her parents in detail and vividly. She was thrilled to get to know yet another country through the Channel Islands, and she was impressed with how

---

13   Emma Rauschenbach to her parents, Bertha and Jean Rauschenbach, 16 July 1898, sent from Paris. "Schwörili" is her sister Marguerite. The pet names she used in various forms for her family suggests great familiarity: Papali, Muttingli, Schwörrel, Gerrili, Emmerich, etc.

very English everything was. But what she liked best were the rocky cliffs, against which the waves broke.

> I have found a good way to avoid getting seasick: gazing at the sea and the horizon and thinking of the good Lord.[14]

She thoroughly enjoyed her time in Paris, but she was looking forward to her brief return home for Christmas. In the meantime, her parents' new villa on the Oelberg had been completed, and the family—in Emma's absence—had moved from the "Rose Garden" to their new home on the hill overlooking Schaffhausen.[15] The two daughters were given a floor of their own, and they were allowed to design and decorate their rooms according to their own taste.[16] Emma had competently expressed her views on building issues from Paris and had shared her opinions with her father.

After a further four months in the French capital, at the end of April 1899, Emma was collected by her mother and her aunt Anna, and she took the opportunity to show them all the places she had grown fond of.

Making the Acquaintance of Carl Gustav Jung

After her return in May 1899, the stimulation Emma Rauschenbach had received up to that point from school and her stay abroad fell by the wayside. She helped her mother, went to Zurich now and again on errands, took care of her father, or visited friends. We do not know why a correspondence between Emma Rauschenbach and Carl Jung started in the middle of 1899. It is possible that Ernst Jung occasionally took his nephew and godson Carl to visit Villa Oelberg, which he had built for the Rauschenbach family.[17] Carl's parents, Paul Achilles and Emilie Jung, already knew Emma's mother from the time when Carl's father was pastor in Laufen-Uhwiesen (1876–79). As a young woman, Bertha Rauschenbach had looked

---

14   Emma Rauschenbach to her parents, 30 August 1898, sent from Sark.

15   Initially, the estate was rented by the family as a summer residence and was purchased by Jean Rauschenbach in 1896. In 1897, it had to make way for the new building Villa Oelberg, which was designed by the architectural firm Jung & Bridler Winterthur (co-owner Ernst Jung was Carl Jung's uncle and godfather). Like the garden at "Haus zum Rosengarten," the new gardens, made in the style of an English country-house garden, were designed by Evariste Mertens, the husband of Bertha Rauschenbach's cousin. The name Oelberg goes back to a medieval depiction of the Mount of Olives. For a long time, until it fell victim to the Reformation, the Chapel of St. Wolfgang stood on the site (Frauenfelder, *Siebzig Bilder aus dem alten Schaffhausen*, 57).

16   Hoerni-Jung, "Memories."

17   A further connection was through Hedwig Bridler, the wife of Ernst Jung's business partner Otto Bridler. She was the sister of Emma Rauschenbach's friend Sträuli, and a friend of Carl Jung's.

after the pastor's little son, Karl,[18] or taken him for a walk.[19] After the Jung family moved away to Kleinhüningen near Basel, Bertha Rauschenbach and Emilie Jung had stayed loosely in touch with each other. But the very first encounter in person between Carl Jung and Emma Rauschenbach, which Carl never forgot, took place in 1896 at Emma's parents' house. While staying in Schaffhausen, and at the request of his mother, Carl was paying his respects to the family. Emma was standing at the top of the stairs in the Rose Garden house, wearing a blue dress—an image that would stay with him for years.

> Whenever I have thought about my future over the last five years, she has always come to mind. I cannot and could not imagine marrying any other girl, no matter how many I have met. [...] She has no idea what I'm feeling.[20]

Subsequently, Carl Jung visited the Rauschenbach family many times and maintained a sporadic correspondence with Emma's mother, Bertha. They regularly exchanged ideas about art and shared mutual recommendations or impressions. He often also sent Bertha Rauschenbach books or small pictures, thereby maintaining indirect contact with Emma. After Emma's return from Paris, in 1899, Carl Jung was finally able to stay in touch with her directly, initially by postcard and then by letter. He always addressed her courteously with *Sie*, the polite form of address.

In March 1901, the two met at a ball in Winterthur. Carl felt somewhat jealous, for Emma's beauty made her the center of attention. He nevertheless believed she was interested in him. He felt this even more when he received an invitation from the Rauschenbach family to attend the festival of the Centenary Celebration in Schaffhausen in August. After these encounters, Carl was sure that Emma returned his feelings.[21] Nevertheless, he had an uneasy feeling that there might be something standing between them. In mid-August 1901, the tension became too much for him; and so Carl, who in the meantime had accepted the position of assistant physician to Professor Eugen Bleuler[22] at the "insane asylum Burghölzli"[23] in Zurich, revealed his feelings to Emma. He eagerly awaited her reply. But Emma turned

---

18   Carl Jung changed the spelling of his first name around 1900 from Karl to Carl.

19   Carl Jung mentions this encounter in his memoir, *Memories, Dreams, Reflections*, 9.

20   Personal note, Carl Jung, March 1901.

21   Carl Jung to his mother, Emilie Jung, 6 October 1901.

22   Eugen Bleuler (1857–1939): Swiss psychiatrist and humanist, most notable for his contributions to the understanding of mental illnesses, in particular his works on schizophrenia (dementia praecox). As the director (1898–1927) of the Burghölzli psychiatric clinic in Zurich, he was the first state clinic director in Europe to become interested in Sigmund Freud's method of psychoanalysis. Bleuler implemented psychoanalytic treatment and research at the Burghölzli, making it the leading institution in the field in the early twentieth century.

23   The clinic was founded in 1870 under the name "Irrenheilanstalt [insane asylum] Burghölzli." In 1915 the Zurich clinic was renamed "Kantonale Heilanstalt [cantonal asylum] Burghölzli," and in 1966 was given the name it bears today, "Psychiatrische Universitätsklinik Zürich" (Zurich University Psychiatric Clinic). It is often referred to simply as "the Burghölzli."

him down, in a letter the wording of which we do not know. Carl, who thought he had perceived that she had feelings for him, was deeply shaken.

Then, at the beginning of October, Emma's mother intervened. She summoned up her courage and wrote Carl a letter, asking him for a meeting. She wanted to clarify the situation by explaining the confusing situation to him.[24] She told him that Emma had thought she was promised to a childhood friend, even though she had developed feelings for Carl in the meantime. Only a few days after Emma Rauschenbach had turned Carl Jung down, she was informed by this same childhood friend that she was terribly mistaken. Her mother, Bertha, then arranged a further meeting with Carl. And on 6 October 1901, in the garden of Emma's parents' villa in Schaffhausen, their secret engagement followed.

In a letter to his mother, Carl wrote of a fairy tale in which he was the prince:

> She is uncommonly beautiful. [...] Her spiritual qualities are far above the ordinary, she is of a delicate form and the most amiable character.[25]

Closest family members and friends were informed individually. Official announcement of the engagement had to wait, however, until Carl's dissertation had been accepted. The influential industrialist Rauschenbach was known far and wide, and Carl wanted to avoid any talk of this connection before he handed in his thesis.

Although Emma repeatedly assured Carl both of her love and of how she looked forward to their future together, even after their engagement Carl was plagued by doubts as to whether she might not have been mistaken in him. Why would a daughter of her rank, who had received many other proposals, want to share her life with him? He felt the only future prospect he could offer her would be that of an unsettled life. She, on the other hand, assured him:

> You must not, under any circumstances, renounce your present profession, for which you were born, and which fulfills you. There is no rush with the announcement. [...] I would rather beg and starve with you than sit alone in plenitude.[26]

Emma enjoyed getting to know Carl, his family, and his friends. She took a lively interest in the problems that arose in the course of Carl's stressful daily routine at the clinic, as well as in his numerous questions about his own state of mind. Emma found the philosophical and psychological questions she could discuss with Carl absorbing, along with their discussions on art and literature. These were all topics that immensely stimulated her mind. Outward appearances and material

---

24 Bertha Rauschenbach to Carl Jung, 2 October 1901.
25 Carl Jung to his mother, Emilie Jung, 6 October 1901.
26 Emma Rauschenbach to Carl Jung, 30 December 1901.

things, on the other hand, were not so important to her. Thus, even in later years, she adapted easily to the simple lifestyle she was not accustomed to: for example, camping on an island in Zurich's Upper Lake or later staying in Carl's tower in Bollingen, where she fit in effortlessly and lent a hand as a matter of course.

> For you see, I am not marrying an illustrious position or a fortune, but a human being. My soul needs a soul and not outward appearances.[27]

An intensive period followed for Carl Jung. Unlike his colleagues, he could not afford to take time off to write his dissertation and, for financial reasons, he had to reconcile his writing with the daily routine at the clinic. He was correspondingly frugal with his time and, not infrequently, he worked late into the night. His enormous workload and the fates he was confronted with on a daily basis, as well as the dreary fall, all weighed on him. He was troubled by whether or not he would be able to finish his dissertation and whether anyone would be interested in it at all. Furthermore, he was concerned if, as a simple assistant physician and scientist with poor career prospects, he would be able to offer his beloved a future worthy of her rank.

Emma, on the other hand, exuded endless optimism. The feeling of being able to support him boosted her spirits. Emma truly flourished. Through his reassurance and encouragement, she was able to come out of herself more and found that she had shed some of her shyness.

> It is as if a curtain has been pulled back from before my eyes and I look out into vast, undreamed-of distances that open up to my astonished gaze, still somewhat veiled and blurred, like a morning landscape, but in such a way that one senses the outlines, almost perceiving them.[28]

At certain times, however, Emma was so fascinated by Carl's open, honest manner and his extensive knowledge that her self-confidence temporarily faltered.

> I have the unpleasant characteristic of holding on to those thoughts that want to hop by as unremarkably as possible, and of scrutinizing them from all sides. But this is very likely to dampen one's self-confidence.[29]

Doubts arose as to whether she might fall short for Carl, as a woman without a degree. Her sense that she might be found wanting in knowledge and skill weighed upon her.

---

27 Emma Rauschenbach to Carl Jung, 26 October 1901.
28 Emma Rauschenbach to Carl Jung, 22 January 1902.
29 Emma Rauschenbach to Carl Jung, 22 October 1902.

I sometimes felt terribly cramped here, like a caged bird that tries in vain to spread its wings and fly out, free and uninhibited, over all the small confines and ugliness. I love my childhood home very much, as you know, and yet I sometimes dread a fate like that of most local women.[30]

He, on the other hand, was impressed by her dauntlessness, her strong will, and her enormous thirst for knowledge. Together, they freed themselves from unnecessary doubts and built one another up. This was just the beginning of their mutual shaping of each other, and of a lifelong dialogue.

Philosophy and Psychology

Even as a child, Emma Rauschenbach enjoyed immersing herself in a wide variety of subjects. She marveled at the book about Australia that her grandmother Rauschenbach gave her when they were learning about that country at school. In her family home, people read a lot, and literature was also very important to Madame Lavater in Paris. While there, Emma read, for example, *Les Femmes Savantes* by Molière and, after seeing the performance, she bought *Cyrano de Bergerac*. In 1899, after her return from Paris, Carl Jung recommended the author Carl du Prel to Emma Rauschenbach:

I highly recommend you read du Prel's writings, dear lady. It will perhaps require a little study: but your gain will be great. For explanations of any kind, I am always at your service.[31]

At Christmas in 1901, she was given a book of poems by Theodor Storm. She studied the biography and poems of Friedrich Nietzsche and learned a lot from what she read aloud to her father. Emma read a book by Leopold Loewenfeld with great interest[32] and thought that it provided a counterbalance to Justinus Kerner's *The Seeress of Prevorst*.[33] Carl encouraged her to delve into different topics and to come up with her own thoughts on them:

But I am driven by the desire not only to kindle the fire of love in you, but also the highest spiritual life; it alone is the true life and provides the most intense delight in being.[34]

---

30 Emma Rauschenbach to Carl Jung, 2 December 1901.
31 Postcard, Carl Jung to Emma Rauschenbach, 27 July 1899.
32 Presumably Loewenfeld, *Somnambulismus und Spiritismus*, read early in 1902.
33 Emma Rauschenbach to Carl Jung, 5 February 1902.
34 Carl Jung to Emma Rauschenbach, 5 February 1902.

Carl Jung recommended further readings: Johann Peter Eckermann's *Conversations with Goethe in the Last Years of His Life* and the authors Joël and Landsberg.[35] If she were able somewhat to digest the ghost and somnambulist stories that Carl was preoccupied with as part of his dissertation, and if she took delight in Landsberg's philosophizing, then she should read Nietzsche's *Schopenhauer as an Educator*. In addition to spiritualistic writings, he also introduced her to other literary works previously unknown to her.[36]

In connection with his dissertation, *Zur Psychologie und Pathologie sogenannter Okkulter Phänomene* (On the psychology and pathology of so-called occult phenomena), Carl asked Emma for assistance with difficult English texts, which, in 1902, she pledged to give in order to support him in his professional research. She offered to read and translate French as well as English books for him.[37] From then on, Carl not only drew increasingly on his fiancée's good language skills for his work but, at the same time, by drawing her attention to further specialist literature within the context of his dissertation, promoted Emma's interest in the field of psychology. Thus, in January and February 1902, he discussed with her, among other things, the works of Camille Flammarion,[38] Théodore Flournoy,[39] Carl du Prel,[40] and the Italian medium Eusapia Palladino.[41] In June, Emma picked up *Crime et anomalies mentales constitutionelles*, the latest book by the former Burghölzli director, Auguste Forel,[42] which the *Allgemeine Schweizer Zeitung* in Basel[43] had sent to Carl Jung, asking for a review. She also immersed herself in Möbius's *Über das Pathologische bei Nietzsche*[44] and carefully read her future husband's dissertation, which, in the meantime, had been published.

Emma was also reading French novels at this time, for which, from her stay in France, she had a special fondness. In a letter to her fiancé, she described how she had been gripped by Emile Zola's *Lourdes* and how it had cast a strange spell on her.[45] After Carl completed his dissertation in the fall of 1902, and while he prepared for a language and study trip to Paris, it is probable that Emma further

---

35 The C. G. Jung library catalog lists the following two titles by these authors: Joël, *Philosophenwege, Ausblicke und Rückblicke* (Paths in philosophy, perspectives and retrospectives); Landsberg, *Friedrich Nietzsche und die deutsche Literatur* (Friedrich Nietzsche and German literature).

36 To name but a few: Förster-Nietzsche, *Das Leben Friedrich Nietzsches* (*The Life of Nietzsche*); Dostoyevski, *Raskolnikow's Schuld und Sühne* (*Crime and Punishment*); Tolstoy, *Auferstehung* (*Resurrection*); Viebig, *Das tägliche Brot* (*Our Daily Bread*).

37 Letters between Carl Jung and Emma Rauschenbach, early 1902.

38 Flammarion, *L'Inconnu et les problèmes psychiques*.

39 Flournoy, *Des Indes à la Planète Mars*.

40 du Prel, *Der Spiritismus*.

41 Eusapia Palladino (1854–1918): Italian psychic and medium.

42 Forel and Mahaim, *Crime et anomalies mentales constitutionelles*.

43 Swiss daily newspaper, founded in 1873, merged in 1902 with the *Basler Nachrichten*.

44 Möbius, *Über das Pathologische bei Nietzsche*.

45 Emma Rauschenbach to Carl Jung, 23 June 1902.

encouraged him to read French literature. She sent him works by Bourget and Loti[46] about which they subsequently exchanged letters. From his stopover at Château d'Oex, he asked her, among other things, to send him sequels of Zola, *Rome* (1896) or *Paris* (1898). Carl, in turn, sent her a book about the facts of life by a Russian physician. It was important to him that his future wife be informed, and that he could talk openly with her about everything. Rather than being indignant, as he feared, she was pleased and admitted to him that she was not as ignorant as her mother, and perhaps even he, thought.

> Why should a young girl not know anything about the world, about things that are only natural? At first, you are brought up as if wrapped in cotton wool, and then, sooner or later, you are thrust into the rough and tumble of life, which does not, after all, hold only sweet things in store.[47]

Carl's Dissertation and Engagement

Carl Jung's doubts as to whether his dissertation would find favor were dispelled by the praise of his doctoral advisors, Dr. Ludwig von Muralt[48] and Professor Eugen Bleuler.[49] After its submission, the dual burden of job and dissertation dropped from his shoulders, on the one hand, while on the other, nothing now stood in the way of announcing his engagement to Emma Rauschenbach. On 1 May 1902, the couple sent out the announcement of their engagement.

However, the publication of his dissertation was by no means met only with recognition. Despite changing the initials of his test person, it was easy to deduce that it concerned his cousin Helene Preiswerk, and this caused an uproar among Carl's Basel relatives. He himself took it calmly, knowing that Emma stood behind him, saying that psychiatrists were always threatened by arguments. "After all," he wrote, "nothing good and new can be achieved without a struggle."[50]

Religious Point of View and the Meaning of Life

> I read a chapter or two in the Bible every night. I have already read the Gospels, and now the Epistles to the Corinthians.[51]

---

46 Bourget, *L'étape*; Loti, *Pêcheurs d'Islande*.

47 Emma Rauschenbach to Carl Jung, 20 February 1902.

48 Ludwig von Muralt (1869–1917): senior physician at the Burghölzli psychiatric clinic in 1898–1903. Suffering from tuberculosis, he gave up this position and changed specialization, becoming chief physician at the pulmonary sanatorium in Davos, in the Swiss Alps.

49 For Eugen Bleuler, see p. 8, note 22.

50 Carl Jung to Emma Rauschenbach, 31 July 1902.

51 Emma Rauschenbach to her mother, Bertha Rauschenbach, 12 October 1898.

Emma Rauschenbach grappled with the meaning of life from the start. She was tormented by injustice and wondered if there was a higher purpose behind people's fates, behind happiness and unhappiness. She was convinced that life had to have a purpose, and she believed in an afterlife. If everyone is supposed to be good, why do some people have it easier than others? And why, despite our most diverse starting points, is the same expected of everyone? Emma was agonizing over this and seeking explanations before she met Carl Jung. Not even her mother, with whom she discussed almost everything, understood what was really going on in her mind. Thus, Emma initially had to settle this question on her own. After reflecting upon it for some time, however, she had the redeeming insight:

> I said to myself every person is appointed their proper place; every person is given certain abilities with which they have to make as much as they possibly can out of themselves, advantageously using all circumstances and eventualities. Thus, every person has their own special task; everyone must achieve their own result, be it greater or lesser, which emerges out of the interplay of the most diverse factors.[52]

As generous as Emma's mother was in many ways, she remained strict about religion.[53] In order to justify only a single visit to church during her summer vacation with Madame Lavater, Emma explained to her mother that she read the Bible every evening and talked a lot about religion with Madame Lavater's daughter, Louise. In an exchange of letters in early 1902, Emma set forth her points of view to Carl. It was with her fiancé, then, that she was finally able to immerse herself in this subject matter.

> Mama misjudged both of us a little when she asked you not to tamper with my religion. For me, religion, or how it is understood, is individual, and I know that Mama and I are different in this respect. To my mind, everything is rather a parable. In all humans, both those who are and were, dwells the longing and the need for a higher being. They may call it so or so, or worship it in this or that way, but basically, they all mean the One God, whom everyone understands according to their own nature.[54]

For Emma Rauschenbach, it was more important, crucial even, to have one's own convictions, and to come to grips with them, rather than allowing oneself to drift

---

52 Emma Rauschenbach to Carl Jung, 12 February 1902.

53 When the church of Laufen, where Carl Jung's father, Paul Achilles Jung, was pastor from 1876 to 1879, was rebuilt in 1895, Emma's parents were the donors of the new church window, in which the two coats of arms Rauschenbach & Schenk are integrated (*Schweizerische Bauzeitung* 1948, vol. 66, no. 52).

54 Emma Rauschenbach to Carl Jung, 12 February 1902.

along without reflection. To her, going to church and reading the Bible did not make one religious. The many conversations Bertha Rauschenbach had with Emma and her son-in-law played no small part in opening up her own narrow religious mindset over the years.

A Common Interest in Art

> Does not the artist speak to us through his work? […] Art is also a language, only much more inward, much subtler than our everyday language, and therefore not everyone understands it.[55]

It was not only in psychology, philosophy, and literature that Carl Jung and Emma Rauschenbach found a common denominator. Both were also equally interested in art and music, especially opera. Even prior to their engagement, Carl gave Emma two paintings: *Two Puttis in Flight* attributed to François Boucher and *The Guardian of the Valley* by Hans Thoma. She in turn gave him an Arnold Böcklin album. From time to time, he sent Emma and her mother little pictures, art prints, and the magazine *Jugend*. Initially, they often met at the Künstlerhaus[56] in Zurich, where they exchanged views on different works of art; or they visited antiquarian bookstores. To Emma's mind, her childhood home and later her own home became more and more beautiful with pieces he selected, such as the *Venus de Milo*, the bust of Niccolo da Uzzano, and the bas-relief *Madonna and Child* by Desiderio da Settignano.

> As all of this went through my mind, it suddenly became clear to me that there are not earthly and heavenly things and an unbridgeable gulf between the two, but that everything earthly is the initial stage, a higher or lower step on the great ladder that everything and everyone must climb, and which leads to perfection—Could it be thus?[57]

After his military service in the fall of 1902, Carl went to Paris for a study semester. He wanted to further his professional training at the Salpêtrière psychiatric clinic and to establish contact with Professor Pierre Janet.[58] Emma, meanwhile,

---

55 Emma Rauschenbach to Carl Jung, 28 January 1902.

56 Behind the Künstlerhaus on Talstrasse in Zurich, which operated from 1895 to 1911, were two associations that merged in 1896 to form the Zürcher Kunstgesellschaft, the sponsor of today's Kunsthaus.

57 Emma Rauschenbach to Carl Jung, 28 January 1902.

58 Pierre Janet (1857–1947): French philosopher, physician, and psychologist. While teaching philosophy in Le Havre he began studying hypnosis and suggestion, continuing his research under the leading French neurologist, Jean-Martin Charcot, at the Salpêtrière hospital in Paris, completing his medical degree with a dissertation, *The Mental States of Hysterics*, in 1893. Head of a newly established psychological laboratory at the Salpêtrière in 1902.

strongly encouraged him also to visit the museums and galleries in Paris, and not to forgo them out of frugality. Thus, through language, art, and culture, his time in Paris and then in London became more of an educational tour. His visits to museums and galleries far outweighed those to the Salpêtrière. He also pursued his own artistic endeavors. In these months of separation, his exchange of letters with Emma was mostly about the painting technique of works that had impressed him, which he had seen in the Louvre and other museums, and the evaluation of operas, theater, and music pieces, as well as various literary works. Together, they also decided with what furniture and art works they would furnish their future home, and they discussed which paintings Carl should have copied for their own four walls, and at what price.

Meanwhile, in preparation for married life, Emma diligently practiced cooking at home in the mornings and expanded her homemaking skills in other areas in the afternoons. In between, she painted and often played the piano. In addition, she and her mother planned her wedding for the following February. Carl and Emma's original plan to visit the archaeological sites of ancient Egypt for their honeymoon was rejected by her father, Jean. For one thing, a trip of that nature was inappropriate for a young woman, and, for another, their allocated budget was insufficient.

Burghölzli and the First Years of Marriage

Their wedding took place in Schaffhausen in mid-February 1903, within days of Carl Jung's return from his study tour. On 14 February there was a grand ball at the Hotel Belle-Vue in Neuhausen at the Rhine Falls. Two days later was the church wedding in the Steigkirche Schaffhausen[59] followed by a dinner at the villa of the bride's parents. This permitted her father, Jean, whose health prevented him from attending a celebration elsewhere, to attend the wedding reception.

Their honeymoon of almost two months took the couple first to Paris for a week, a city that both were already very familiar with. There, at the Théâtre national de l'Odéon, they saw *Résurrection* and, at the Folies Bergères, "Die Tegernseer."[60] They subsequently spent an additional week in London before embarking in Birmingham and sailing on to Madeira, under the influence of a grueling cyclone that lasted several days. After a further fourteen days, they boarded ship for the Gran

---

59 On 1 April 1944, the Steigkirche, where Emma had been confirmed, fell victim to bombing by American planes. The church was destroyed and replaced by a new building once the war was over.

60 Postcard, Carl Jung to Emilie Jung, 21 February 1903. Concerning *Résurrection*, it must be the theatrical adaptation by Henri Bataille, based on Tolstoy's novel *Auferstehung*, which was first performed at the Théâtre national de l'Odéon in Paris on 14 November 1902. "Die Tegernseer" were a famous group of Bavarian folk musicians (named after the local Tegernsee region), touring Europe in the early 1900s.

Canaria and later Tenerife. They wrote to their parents how they were enjoying the beauty of nature, climbing mountains, walking along the coast, and being enchanted by the reflections of clouds on the sea. Leaving the Canary Islands, they headed home via Barcelona to Genoa, and then via Milan. Once home, they packed their belongings and, on 26 April 1903, moved into their own apartment at Zollikerstrasse 198 in Zurich, not far from the Burghölzli.

Now married and no longer living at home, Emma Jung moved closer to the scientific world. At their first invitation to the home of the Bleulers, Emma met Hedwig Bleuler-Waser[61] and the American physician Florence Hull Watson,[62] both of whom had studied and earned their respective doctorates. It became clear that Emma had no difficulty fitting in with the Burghölzli community, even without having studied.

In May 1903, soon after his honeymoon, Carl had to step in for Dr. von Muralt, who had fallen ill with tuberculosis. As Carl had to work a great deal, often not even coming home for lunch, Emma, if she was not visiting her parents in Schaffhausen or running errands in the city, also went to the Burghölzli, where her support was very welcome. Initially she took on clerical work, which helped her become more familiar with the subject matter.

Director Bleuler was very supportive of community life at the Burghölzli. The patients were integrated into work communities according to their abilities and prior knowledge, for example by employing them in the kitchen, in the laundry, in agriculture, or even in the office. The wives and families of the principal physicians were also integrated, which led to Emma Jung and Hedwig Bleuler collaborating on a voluntary basis, mainly in the scientific field.[63]

As Dr. von Muralt was unable to return to work because of his poor health, Carl took over his position. Carl and Emma moved to the Burghölzli—into the assistant doctor's official apartment, directly above Director Bleuler's official apartment—in the fall of 1904, shortly before the birth of their first daughter.

Although, with her work at the Burghölzli and the founding of her family, Emma's future looked bright, she was becoming increasingly concerned about her beloved father, Jean. While he had become calmer since 1901, his suffering had also increased. In contrast to earlier times, he showed no interest in his surroundings. With the help of a male nurse, Jean Rauschenbach's wife took care of him at home

---

61 Hedwig Bleuler (1869–1940): born Sophie Hedwig Waser, studied literature and history at the University of Zurich. She graduated in 1894, becoming one of the few women of the time to receive her doctorate. After completing her studies, she taught at the school for the higher education of girls in Zurich until her marriage in 1901 with Eugen Bleuler, whom she had met campaigning for the abstinence movement. Founder of the Swiss Federation of Abstinent Women in 1902.

62 Florence Hull Watson (1867–1964): wife of senior physician and deputy clinic director Ludwig von Muralt. Born in Philadelphia, Hull Watson had studied medicine in the United States and came to work under Eugen Bleuler at the Burghölzli psychiatric clinic (1899–1903), where she met her future husband.

63 See "Emma Jung and Analytical Psychology," 31.

until his last day. When he died on 2 March 1905, Emma mourned the loss of her father deeply. Through his death, Bertha and his two daughters, Emma and Marguerite, became heirs to a huge fortune—two flourishing businesses—overnight, as well as the great responsibility that came with them.

As time went on, the Rauschenbach Machine Factory was integrated into the Georg Fischer Corporation, while the watch factory continued under the new name J. Rauschenbach's Heirs. Marguerite's husband, Ernst Homberger, took over the management of the two successful companies[64] as director of the Georg Fischer Corporation, while Bertha Rauschenbach and her daughters remained co-owners.

After the death of her husband, Bertha Rauschenbach lived alone on the large Oelberg estate. She made it her life's work to manage the villa and the estate with its farm, a task she mastered with skill and a sense of duty. She retained her many interests and became involved in the psychological work of her son-in-law and daughter. She became a member of the Psychology Club Zurich and once, in 1926, invited the Club to the Oelberg. She also actively supported her two daughters in caring for their growing band of children. Until Bertha's death in 1932, the Oelberg remained a wonderful place for Emma and Marguerite, and later for their children, a place they loved and frequently visited or went to for vacations.[65]

Despite their different characters, the two sisters remained close to each other until the end of their days. Emma was more serious and reserved. In many ways, however, they shared a similar fate. They married in the same year; each had a busy and successful husband; they each had five children (some born in the same year); and they built their homes within two years of each other. They often spoke on the phone and discussed the development of their offspring and the concerns of their relatives and their respective communities. Questions about housekeeping, fashion, performing arts, or planned travel destinations also provided topics for conversation. Every now and then, the Jung and Homberger couples enjoyed trips and vacations together. From time to time, Emma lent or sent Marguerite books, which she read with interest. Marguerite also took part in Emma's development on the way to becoming an analyst. That Emma's professional work was also a part of their discussions is evidenced in Marguerite's occasional drawing on Emma's in-depth knowledge in her fields of expertise, for example, Egyptian mythology and Christianity.[66]

---

64 From 1907 onward, Ernst Homberger was the general director of the firm Georg Fischer in Schaffhausen, into which the machine factory Rauschenbach was integrated in 1921. He later became a delegated member of the Board of Directors and president of the board.

65 Memories of Helene Hoerni-Jung, as well as communications of grandchildren to the author of this essay.

66 Letters between Emma Jung and Marguerite Homberger during Ernst and Marguerite Homberger's Egyptian journey in 1928, and letters concerning Jung's *Answer to Job*, which Marguerite read in 1952.

Starting a Family and Building a House

After daughter Agathe, who was born in 1904, came daughter Margaretha, born in 1906, and then came son Franz in 1908. They were of a similar age to the children of Eugen and Hedwig Bleuler. After moving out of the Burghölzli in 1909, the births of Marianne and Helene followed in 1910 and 1914. Thanks to the large Rauschenbach inheritance of 1905, Carl and Emma were able to build a house according to their own wishes and ideas. Carl Jung, for whom a life by the water was of central importance, found a block of land in Küsnacht on the shore of Lake Zurich, next to the poorhouse and orphanage. His cousin Ernst Fiechter, a renowned architect in Munich, worked closely with them to design their new home, which included a distinctive tower on the north facade. The garden design was entrusted to the company of Mertens Erben, Emma's distant cousins.

Supported by a nanny, a cook, and a gardener, the couple raised their five children in this house. Emma Jung was a caring and liberal mother to her children. She took care of their many concerns and ensured that her husband, despite the hustle and bustle in the house, could devote himself to his work undisturbed. In their time off, the family played mah-jongg, frolicked in the garden with the dogs, or sailed on Lake Zurich. In addition to the family dogs, chickens, and goat, the children were also allowed to keep cats, two ducks, terrapins, and, at one point, even rats as pets.[67] The family's gardener worked also as their driver until Emma, by then already a grandmother, passed her driving test in 1929, at almost the same time as her husband and their son, Franz. From then on, she drove her own car—a Mercedes convertible, as her grandson Adrian Baumann fondly remembers.[68]

Emma Jung managed to do justice to her various roles. Along with her duties as wife and mother, she knew how to manage the large household on Seestrasse, receive guests from all over the world, support her husband in his work, accompany him to congresses, and, at the same time, keep track of the companies' activities in Schaffhausen. In addition, she served as president of the Psychology Club,[69] devoted herself to her personal intellectual interests, and made her own contributions to analytical psychology. To recover from their many duties and the demands made upon them, the couple took an annual vacation alone, away from the hectic pace of everyday life—always in the knowledge that their children were well cared for at the Oelberg, or at home with aunt Gertrud and grandmother Emilie Jung.

In her youth and the early years of her marriage, Emma demonstrated a character trait that was unusual in the circles she mixed in. She had little interest in a life based on convention and family background; instead, she was driven by creative

---

67   Statement of Brigitte Merk-Niehus (granddaughter), in conversation with the author of this essay, January 2018.

68   Adrian Baumann (grandson), in conversation with the author of this essay, July 2018.

69   See "Emma Jung and Analytical Psychology," 40.

curiosity and a thirst for knowledge. In a country that was not ready for women's voting rights until 1971, she defied social class expectations, which discouraged women from studying at universities and expected them to prepare exclusively for raising a family and managing a household. With the help of private tutors, Emma—by then already a mother several times over—deepened her mathematical proficiency and acquired a basic understanding of the two ancient languages, Greek and Latin, that she needed for her studies.

Emma Jung always tried to develop herself and be open to new things. From the beginning, she received support from Carl in her endeavors:

> While here, I have become completely convinced that the only right thing for you—besides fulfilling your human duties—is the development of your intellect, so that you can love me through insight, as well as your own life.[70]

Nevertheless, while Carl Jung enriched Emma's life, supported her, and steadily stimulated her growth, he also put her through painful experiences with his extra-marital relationships.[71] Most notably, the great challenge she faced was that Toni Wolff,[72] her husband's former patient and later colleague, became as of 1913 his close confidante, regularly participating in the Jungs' family life. The two women dealt with this difficult situation and found a way to treat each other respectfully. While we have few direct testimonies showing how Emma Jung personally handled this constellation, her dreams, poems, and imaginations of the period give evidence of a woman who was facing the difficulties life presented her in this respect. From the mid-1920s on, having struggled for years with her marital situation, she seems to have found her path.

---

70 Carl Jung to Emma Jung, 25 March 1913.

71 In the years 1906–11, a first relationship with Sabina Spielrein, former Burghölzli patient, then medical student and later psychoanalyst, remained by all accounts sexually unconsummated. See Lothane, "Tender Love and Transference: Unpublished Letters of C. G. Jung and Sabina Spielrein (with an addendum/discussion)," in *Sabina Spielrein: Forgotten Pioneer of Psychoanalysis*, 191–226. The contact with Toni Wolff, who first came to Carl Jung as a patient in 1910, developed after 1913 into a fully consummated and longstanding relationship, of which everyone around them was aware. See Healy, *Toni Wolff and C. G. Jung: A Collaboration*. The case of Maria Moltzer is less well-documented. She entered Jung's life around the same time as Wolff and remained close to him until Jung abruptly broke off relations in 1918, and Moltzer left his Zurich circle. The assumption that Jung had an extramarital affair with Moltzer goes back to a letter in 1912 from Sigmund Freud to his Hungarian colleague Sándor Ferenczi, in which Freud surmised that Moltzer was not only Carl Jung's analysand and analyst but also his lover. The same rumor later circulated among members of Jung's circle in Zurich. See Shamdasani, *Cult Fictions*, 57. For Freud's letter to Ferenczi of 23 December 1912, see Freud and Ferenczi, *The Correspondence of Sigmund Freud and Sándor Ferenczi*, vol. 1, 1908–1914, 446.

72 Toni Anna Wolff (1888–1953): born in Zurich as the first of three daughters of the merchant Anton Wolff and Anna Elisabeth Sutz, she became Jung's private assistant and played an important role at the time of the creation of his *Red Book*. She was a founding member of the Psychology Club Zurich and its long-term president, starting in 1928, and worked as an analyst, publishing contributions regarding the feminine psyche.

In the end, the marriage of Carl and Emma Jung withstood all these trials, and they remained close until Emma Jung passed away in 1955. By the end of his life, Carl was aware of the pain he had caused his wife by following his "inevitable life";[73] and he knew that, without Emma's support, he would not have come as far in life as he did. Even at the most critical stages he had left no doubt that she was "my center, a symbol of the human, a protection against all daimons."[74] The loss of her was so enormous that, for a whole year after her death, he could not write[75] but only work in stone, until he found some relief from the deep grief experienced since her passing away.[76]

---

73 In a late personal writing of Carl Jung, a dream record from the year 1959, he reflects that he is consumed by regret over all that he has put his wife through: "I am filled with a sad feeling of regret for all the difficult and painful experiences I have inflicted upon her through my inevitable life."

74 Carl Jung to Emma Jung, 27 July 1917; for the full quotation, see Shamdasani, "Toward a Visionary Science: Jung's Notebooks of Transformation," in Jung, *The Black Books 1913–1932*, vol. 1, 69.

75 In a diary note of 19 November 1956, Carl Jung remarks that the death of his wife Emma the previous year had been shattering, to the degree that only now was he able for the first time to write something again.

76 In a letter to his daughter Marianne Niehus-Jung, Carl Jung wrote on 17 July 1956: "Mama's death has left a gap for me that cannot be filled." He added that the void was dangerously expanding, and he could only counter it by working on the memorial stone for his wife in Bollingen (Jung, *Letters*, 2:317). For the sandstone Memorial for Emma Jung-Rauschenbach, see *The Art of C. G. Jung*, 169, cat. 78.

PLATE 1.

PLATE 2.

PLATE 1.
Bertha Rauschenbach
(1856–1932). Photog-
rapher: Atelier Carl
Koch, Schaffhausen.

PLATE 2.
Jean Rauschenbach
(1856–1905). Photog-
rapher: Photogra-
phische Anstalt Emil
Logés, Zürich.

PLATE 3.
The Rauschenbach sis-
ters, Marguerite (left)
and Emma (right),
c. 1885. Photographers:
Tronel & Koch,
Schaffhausen.

PLATE 4.
City view of
Schaffhausen, with
the parental home,
"zum Rosengarten,"
on the banks of the
river Rhine (center
left), c. 1880. Photog-
rapher: Carl Koch,
Schaffhausen.

PLATE 5.
Villa Oelberg, east
facade, c. 1899. Pho-
tographer: Carl Koch,
Schaffhausen.

PLATE 6.
Emma Rauschenbach
age seventeen, c. 1899.
Photographer: Carl
Koch, Schaffhausen.

PLATE 3.

PLATE 4.

PLATE 5.

PLATE 6.

PLATE 7.

PLATE 8.

PLATE 7.
Emma Rauschenbach
as a bride, 1903. Pho-
tographer: Carl Koch,
Schaffhausen.

PLATE 8.
Emma Rauschen-
bach and Carl Jung
holding hands, newly
engaged, in front of
Villa Oelberg, c. 1901.

PLATE 9.
Emma Rauschenbach
and Carl Jung, official
engagement, 1902.
Photographer: Atelier
C. Ruf, Zurich.

PLATE 9.

PLATE 10.

PLATE 11.

PLATE 12.

PLATE 10.
Emma Jung on Gran
Canaria, honeymoon,
1903. Photographer:
C. G. Jung.

PLATE 11.
Emma Rauschenbach
sitting in the sun,
c. 1900.

PLATE 12.
Emma and Carl Jung
in their early marriage
years, undated.

PLATE 13.
Emma and Carl Jung
on an outing on the
lake with family
friends and their
first-born daughter,
Agathe, c. 1907. Pho-
tographer: Stephanie
Ludwig.

PLATE 13.

PLATE 14.
Emma and Carl Jung
with four of their five
children at Château
d'Oex, 1917. From left:
Franz, Gret (standing
rear), Marianne, and
Agathe. Photog-
rapher: A. Lenzi,
Château d'Oex.

PLATE 14.

PLATE 15.

PLATE 16.

PLATE 17.

PLATE 18.

PLATE 15.
Driveway of the Jung
house at Seestrasse
228, Küsnacht.
Daughters Marianne
and Helene with dog,
Pascha, c. 1918.

PLATE 16.
Emma (standing oars)
and Carl Jung, on an
excursion with friends
on Lake Zurich, 1909.

PLATE 17.
Carl and Emma Jung
motorboating on the
Linth Canal, with
daughter Agathe,
1920.

PLATE 18.
Emma Jung mending
sail, camping on the
island in the Linth
River delta, upper
Lake Zurich, 1920.

PLATE 19.

PLATE 19.
Emma and Carl Jung
on the sailboat,
c. 1923.

PLATE 19.

PLATE 20.
Emma and Carl Jung
at the newly built
Bollingen Tower,
c. 1924. With Helton
Godwin (Peter)
Baynes (left) and
Toni Wolff (right).

PLATE 20.

Emma Jung and Analytical Psychology

THOMAS FISCHER AND MEDEA HOCH

WHEN EMMA RAUSCHENBACH became engaged to Carl Jung in 1901, the modern psychological and psychotherapeutic approaches with which her future husband was intensively involved at the Burghölzli psychiatric clinic in Zurich were still new to her. Therefore, when she was elected first president of the Psychology Club Zurich, founded in 1916, the question arose as to whether she owed this position to more than simply being the wife of the founder of analytical psychology, who was, by then, well-known, even on the other side of the Atlantic. Thus, Erika Schlegel,[1] a founding member of the Club, reflected in her diary: "To be sure, many things are projected onto Mrs. Jung and, as Jung's wife, it is easy for her to be given a certain importance that otherwise would not necessarily be hers."[2]

As any review of the materials Emma Jung left behind shows, through her analysis and collaboration in the early days of the psychoanalytic movement, by the middle of the second decade of the twentieth century she had already acquired

---

1 Erika Schlegel (1884–1973): born Taeuber, sister of Swiss avant-garde artist Sophie Taeuber-Arp, first came to Carl Jung for analysis through Toni Wolff. Erika Schlegel was a gifted artisan and the longtime librarian of the Psychology Club Zurich. She and her husband, Eugen Schlegel, were friends of the Jungs.

2 Diary of Erika Schlegel, 1 July 1917, Corina Fisch-Schlegel Collection.

her own independent position. Her work on the archetypes of animus and anima and the Grail legend, along with her role as a training analyst, made her one of the influential women of the founding generation of analytical psychology in the decades that followed. The portrait below profiles Emma Jung as an analytical psychologist and links her career to the texts and images presented in this volume.

Psychoanalytical Research at the Burghölzli

As Susanne Eggenberger-Jung mentions in her contribution on Emma Jung's background, the latter's independent study began with her choice of reading material during the period of her engagement. Her husband's appointment as first assistant physician at the Burghölzli psychiatric clinic after their marriage in February 1903 and his election as senior physician and deputy clinic director by the Zurich Executive Council in the fall of the same year gave her access to insights into the latest research in the field of modern psychology: "I visit the Burghölzli clinic often, so that I, too, may get some idea of the 'subject,'" Emma Jung noted in her diary.[3]

Under Auguste Forel's[4] directorship of the Burghölzli, from 1879 to 1898, Zurich had already advanced to become a center for the psychological-psychotherapeutic approach in psychiatry in the German-speaking world. Eugen Bleuler,[5] known for his work on schizophrenia, further strengthened this approach during his leadership from 1898 to 1927. He was the first European clinic director to take an interest in Sigmund Freud's concept of psychoanalysis, and he made the Burghölzli the most important research center for this method.[6] Seminal to this were the diagnostic association studies carried out by Carl Jung and Franz Riklin[7] in 1903–5. In these "word association experiments," among the so-called "healthy test material," the clinic's nurses were considered "uneducated test subjects," while the "educated test subjects" were the clinic's doctors, their wives, and other family members.[8]

---

3 Diary entry, 1904, Jung Family Archive.

4 Auguste Forel (1848–1931): Swiss neuroanatomist and psychiatrist, also an entomologist, noted for his investigations into the structure of the human brain, and his study of ants. In 1879 he was appointed professor of psychiatry at the University of Zurich and director of the Burghölzli clinic. He became an active proponent of the temperance movement. After his retirement from the clinic in 1898 he dedicated himself to the cause of social hygiene.

5 For Eugen Bleuler, see p. 8, note 22.

6 Mösli, ed., *Eugen Bleuler: Pionier der Psychiatrie*; Freud and Bleuler, *"Ich bin zuversichtlich, wir erobern bald die Psychiatrie"* (I am confident, we will soon conquer psychiatry), *Briefwechsel 1904–1937*.

7 Franz Beda Riklin (1878–1938): Swiss psychiatrist, proponent of the early psychoanalytical movement in Zurich. Worked at the Burghölzli psychiatric clinic from 1901 to 1903 and subsequently at the sanatorium Rheinau; married to a cousin of Carl Jung. In 1910, Riklin became the first secretary of the International Psychoanalytic Association. After a meeting with painter Augusto Giacometti in 1912, he established a secondary career as an artist.

8 *CW* 2, §393, 398.

In addition to Hedwig Bleuler,[9] who earned a doctorate in German studies, and her mother and sister, Carl Jung's own mother and sister are also documented as test subjects.[10] Emma Jung not only figured prominently as "Test Subject 1,"[11] but, together with the young resident physician Kurt Wehrlin,[12] she also took on the role of research assistant in this project. Their work involved recording the material obtained and processing the results for publication. When Carl Jung, together with Riklin, submitted their first paper in the series of diagnostic association studies of the Zurich clinic to the publishing house Ambrosius Barth in Leipzig in November 1904, Emma Jung had also played her part in bringing this work to fruition.[13]

After Carl and Emma Jung moved into the senior physician's apartment at the Burghölzli in 1904, where their first child, Agathe, was born on 26 December, Emma Jung followed Hedwig Bleuler's example and became part of the clinic's collective life and a member of the research team. According to the model established by Bleuler, physicians and patients formed a "therapeutic community," "which understood itself to be a microcosm of an ideally organized society."[14] Through her involvement, Emma Jung became acquainted early on with the new psychoanalytic approaches of Sigmund Freud. When, from 1904 onward, the "Zurich School" around Bleuler began to explore the psychoanalytic method of dream interpretation, not only the physicians but also their wives participated in interpreting each other's dreams and observing how their complexes operated.[15]

Meeting Sigmund Freud and First Analysis

When Carl Jung made personal contact with Sigmund Freud in 1906, Emma Jung was already familiar with Freud's ideas, and she had a self-acquired basic knowledge of modern psychology. She was present at their first visit to Vienna in the

---

9   For Hedwig Bleuler, see p. 17, note 61.

10   Bernet, *Schizophrenie*, 264ff. The participation of Emilie Jung-Preiswerk and Gertrud Jung, both of whom worked in patient care at the Burghölzli at the time, is documented in the paper "Associationsversuchen über Ablenkung" ("Association Trials on Distraction"), 1903, ETH Zurich University Archive, Hs 1055: 272.

11   Jung, "The Reaction-Time Ratio in the Experiment," *Studies in Word Association*, part 1, *CW* 2.3, §605.

12   Kurt Wehrlin (1878–1966): assistant physician at the Burghölzli clinic in 1902–4; subsequently in private practice as a general physician in Zurich. Member of the initial circle of medical doctors setting up a first Freud society in Zurich in 1907.

13   Jung and Riklin, *Experimental Researches*, *CW* 2.1, §1–497. First published in *Journal für Psychologie und Neurologie* III and IV (Verlag Johann Ambrosius Barth, Leipzig 1904 and 1905). Carl Jung gave Emma Jung an initial part to edit in February 1904; and while he was in military service in November, she was occupied with sending final corrections to the publisher.

14   Bernet, *Schizophrenie*, 274.

15   See Hilda Abraham, *Karl Abraham: Sein Leben für die Psychoanalyse*, 62; on Karl Abraham's time as assistant physician at the Burghölzli in 1904–7, see also Wieser, "Zur frühen Psychoanalyse in Zürich, 1900–1914," 27ff.

spring of 1907, as well as at Freud's reciprocated visit to Zurich in the summer of 1908. After Freud's departure, Carl Jung remarked to his wife, "It always gives me terrific pleasure that you impressed Freud so much."[16] Freud sent her several books after his visit to Zurich.[17] In the years that followed, very personal letters, hitherto unseen, from Sigmund Freud to Emma Jung document an encounter between equals.[18] She told him, for example, about how difficult she found it to realize her full potential at her husband's side.

> From time to time, I am tormented by the conflict about how I can hold my own against Carl. I find I have no friends, all the people who associate with us really only want to see Carl, except for a few boring and to me quite uninteresting persons.

> Naturally the women are all in love with him, and with the men I am instantly cordoned off as the wife of the father or friend.[19]

In his reply, Freud underscored "your aptitude and your judgment" and encouraged her to write psychoanalytical papers herself:

> On the few occasions we met, whenever you voiced your opinion, I admired your keen understanding and your good thoughts, which I believe I made no secret of. Thus, I will not be surprised if one day Frau Emma herself emerges as a writer and describes how she sees some aspect of childhood or the soul or tradition. I would vouch for it being good, and if the yearbook does not wish to accept it, then the new magazine, which perhaps might be called *Imago*, will be ready to do so.[20]

It can be concluded from her private papers that this unexpected professional recognition from the founder of psychoanalysis came at a time when Emma Jung was beginning to grapple intensively with her personal situation.[21] After the birth of her fourth child, Marianne, in 1910, the question of who she was, beyond being a wife, a mother, and an assistant to a man whom she had to share with the world,

---

16 Carl Jung to Emma Jung, 15 October 1908, Jung Family Archive.

17 Sigmund Freud and Carl Jung, *The Freud/Jung Letters*, 172ff.: Letter 110 F, 15 October 1908, and Letter 111 J, 21 October 1908.

18 There are ten letters from Sigmund Freud to Emma Jung from the period 1910–12. See Fischer and Tögel, "Der Briefwechsel zwischen Emma Jung und Sigmund Freud," *Luzifer-Amor*; Emma Jung's seven letters to Freud have previously been published in *The Freud/Jung Letters*, 301 (8 March 1910), 303 (16 March 1910), 452 (30 October 1911), 455 (6 November 1911), 462 (14 November 1911), 467 (24 November 1911), and 51 (10 September 1912).

19 Emma Jung to Sigmund Freud, 24 November 1911, *The Freud/Jung Letters*, 467.

20 Sigmund Freud to Emma Jung, 1 December 1911, Jung Family Archive.

21 Her first entries in the marbled book refer to dreams and thoughts from the year 1911.

became increasingly urgent. This came to a head when, around 1910, two women, Toni Wolff and Maria Moltzer,[22] entered her husband's life and changed her relationship to him.[23] Carl Jung's work and relationship with the Russian Burghölzli patient and later psychoanalyst, Sabina Spielrein, had already called into question the exclusivity of their marriage in the preceding years.[24]

Initially, the couple tried to discuss these challenges from a psychoanalytic perspective. After this endeavor proved impossible,[25] Emma Jung embarked upon a brief analysis with Leonhard Seif in the fall of 1911.[26] Her husband gave her his explicit encouragement to continue working on herself analytically:

> You have only to be disciplined and try to give your immortal soul the care it needs every day. The material you work on could become of the highest interest.[27]

A little later, he thanked her for her "thoroughly analytical letter, which gave me the greatest pleasure."[28]

---

22 For Toni Wolff, see p. 20, note 72. Maria Moltzer (1874–1944): born to the Dutch family that owned the liqueur company Bols, she had become a nurse in protest of alcohol abuse. She first came to Switzerland to study at the University of Lausanne before starting work at the sanatorium Lebendige Kraft of Max Bircher-Benner in Zurich in 1904, where she met Carl Jung. She trained with him in psychoanalysis and became his research assistant, until their ways parted in 1918. Moltzer thereafter remained in Zurich in private practice but was no longer part of the circle of Carl and Emma Jung.

23 On the role that Toni Wolff and Maria Moltzer played at the time when Carl Jung was experimenting with his own unconscious, see Shamdasani, "Toward a Visionary Science: Jung's Notebooks of Transformation," in Jung, *The Black Books 1913–1932*, vol. 1, 11–112, especially 26ff.

24 Sabina Spielrein (1885–1942): Russian Jewish physician and psychoanalyst. After treatment at the Burghölzli psychiatric clinic in 1904–5, she took up medical studies at the University of Zurich and became the first woman to graduate with a psychoanalytic dissertation. She left Zurich in 1912 and subsequently lived and worked as a psychoanalyst in Germany (Munich and Berlin), Switzerland (Lausanne), and the Soviet Union (Moscow). Returned to her native Rostov-on-Don in 1924, where she and her daughters were murdered by the Germans during World War II. See Covington and Wharton, eds., *Sabina Spielrein: Forgotten Pioneer of Psychoanalysis*.

25 *The Freud/Jung Letters*, 247ff. and 288ff.: Letter 155 J, 1 October 1909; Letter 175 J, 30 January 1910.

26 Leonhard Seif (1866–1949): Munich psychologist, member of the Zurich chapter of the International Psychoanalytic Association, and founder of the Munich chapter in 1911. He repeatedly stayed in Zurich at that time to work with Carl Jung, before later turning to the individual psychology of Alfred Adler. The sole documentation of Emma Jung's analysis with Seif is in the letter from Ernest Jones to Sigmund Freud of 18 September 1912: "She was analyzed by Seif last autumn (this is *strictly* private), and seems to take a fairly objective view of her husband's failings" (*The Complete Correspondence of Sigmund Freud and Ernest Jones 1908–1939*, 160). In the early days of psychoanalysis, short analyses of only a few weeks were quite common.

27 Carl Jung to Emma Jung, 2 October 1911, Jung Family Archive.

28 Carl Jung to Emma Jung, 4 October 1911, Jung Family Archive.

The Emancipation of Analytical Psychology

The fact that Emma Jung is the only "accompanying wife"[29] in the famous group photograph of the Psychoanalytic Congress held in Weimar on 21 and 22 September 1911, suggests that it was during this period that she began to establish herself as an independent voice among the representatives of the fledgling discipline. "The Weimar photograph turned out very well; it will amuse you; there is much to be seen in it. The picture says a lot," Franz Riklin told Carl Jung, "and your wife turned out to be of particular interest."[30] At this time, Carl Jung also began to introduce his wife more and more into his practical work by telling her about interesting cases and encouraging her to do her own research. She was closely involved in bringing his publication *Die Wandlungen und Symbole der Libido* (1911/12) to completion.[31] And as editor of the *Jahrbuch für psychoanalytische und psychopathologische Forschungen* (*Yearbook for Psychoanalytic and Psychopathological Research*) he entrusted her, for example, with the German translation of Ernest Jones's contribution "Some Cases of Obsessional Neurosis," which appeared in 1912 in the same edition as the second part of his work on the libido.[32]

When, as a result of the publication of *Wandlungen und Symbole der Libido*, a rift developed between her husband and Sigmund Freud over their differing views on libido theory, Emma Jung initially tried to mediate. After a further visit by Freud to Küsnacht in September 1911 and their subsequent joint participation in the congress in Weimar, she asked Freud at the end of October, without her husband's knowledge, to clarify for her his apparent differences. In his response, Freud addressed her as a member of the psychoanalytic movement and concluded by expressly thanking her for her "amicable openness."

> If we were not from the S ΨA,[33] I would simply assure you that you are, fortunately, mistaken in this; that I know of no opacity; that, as proof, the few days

---

29 Peglau, "Sigmund Freud in Weimar: A Photo from the Year 1911—and a Snapshot of the Psychoanalytic Movement," in *Weimar-Jena*, 228–38; quotation 229.

30 Franz Riklin to Carl Jung, 13 October 1911, Jung Family Archive.

31 Jung, *Wandlungen und Symbole der Libido: Beiträge zur Entwicklungsgeschichte des Denkens* (Transformations and symbols of the libido: On the history of the evolution of thought) is hereafter cited as *Wandlungen und Symbole*. Initially published in two parts in the *Jahrbuch für psychoanalytische und psychopathologische Forschungen* (part 1, 1911, III/1, 120–227; part 2, 1912, IV/1, 162–464). In 1916, this seminal work was translated into English by Beatrice Hinkle, titled *The Psychology of the Unconscious*. Hinkle's translation is the only published English edition of the original work to date. Later extensively reworked by Jung, divested of classical Freudian terminology, and retitled *Symbols of Transformation: An Analysis of the Prelude to a Case of Schizophrenia*, this work became vol. 5 in the *Collected Works* (*CW* 5).

32 Jones, "Einige Fälle von Zwangsneurose," in *Jahrbuch für psychoanalytische und psychopathologische Forschung*, vol. IV/1, 563–606. Regarding the translation by Emma Jung, see Carl Jung to Ernest Jones, 20 November 1912, ETH Zurich University Archives, Hs 1173: 10.

33 S ΨA = *Societas Psychoanalytica* (Latin), Psychoanalytic Society. Based on S. J. (*Societas Jesu*, Society of Jesus). Cf. *Freud/Jung Letters*, 452, Letter 277 J, 30 October 1911, and note.

in your house count among the highlights of my life, even though my nights were spoiled by my silly toothache; that I regret having made a wrong impression on you through some ineptitude on my part, and, for me, that would be the end of the matter. But we are, after all, psychoanalysts, which means that I have to be more expansive and be prepared to hear things about myself that I know nothing of.[34]

However, with the rift between Sigmund Freud and her husband becoming ever more manifest in the following year—1912—and the resulting split in the psychoanalytic movement, there was no further exchange between Emma Jung and Sigmund Freud. In the summer of 1914, the Local Group of the Psychoanalytic Association of Zurich, originally founded in 1910, which had evolved out of the meetings of interested physicians at the Burghölzli led by Franz Riklin, withdrew from the International Association once and for all, whereupon the majority of the psychologists and physicians who made up the group reconvened in the newly named Association for Analytical Psychology.[35] From the outset, Emma Jung was a part of this circle's core group, and she became an important female voice in the pioneering days of analytical psychology. The minutes of the meetings of the Zurich Local Group show that Emma Jung was the first woman to take the floor in the spring of 1913, when the Association still bore the name Psychoanalytic Association, at the time when part 2 of Carl Jung's libido paper was being discussed over several meetings, a topic with which she was familiar from the research she had done for her husband.[36] As a layperson, however, Emma Jung was denied formal membership until the group of physicians decided to admit laypersons as "extraordinary members"[37] in January 1914, provided that they could demonstrate their familiarity with psychoanalysis through a scientific paper.[38]

---

34 Sigmund Freud to Emma Jung, 2 November 1911, Jung Family Archive.

35 *"Verein für Analytische Psychologie"* (see Wieser, "Zur frühen Psychoanalyse in Zürich," 75ff.). The group's official name was commonly shortened to Analytischer Verein (Analytical Association). Hereafter we use the shorter name (see also Chapter I, 160, note 1).

36 Discussion held on 28 February 1913, "Protokoll der Vorträge des Vereins für Analytische Psychologie I, 1913–1916," Psychology Club Zurich Archives.

37 In addition to the Psychoanalytic Association, there was also a so-called lay association in Zurich from around 1912, whose members—mainly students—met in the restaurants Karl der Grosse or Seidenhof for lectures, discussions, and exchanges about analysis. See Emma Jung, "On the 20th Anniversary of the Club," 160.

38 At the meeting of 30 January 1914, Maria Moltzer and Toni Wolff were admitted as the first "extraordinary members" of the Analytical Association. Like Emma Jung, who was pregnant at the time, they had already participated intensively in the Association's activities throughout the previous two years. Women who had university degrees had already been admitted to the Psychoanalytic Association. The physicians Sophie Erismann-Hasse and Frida Kaiser were founding members, followed in 1911 by Mira Gincburg and Salomea Kempner, and in 1912 by Emma Fürst, Franziska Minkowski, and Eugenia Sokolnicka-Kutner.

Psychological Work with Hans Schmid-Guisan

After the birth of their fifth child, Helene, a latecomer born in 1914, Emma Jung intensified her analytical self-studies and began a lengthy analysis with Hans Schmid-Guisan,[39] her husband's colleague and friend from Basel.[40] Their talks took place at regular intervals, usually when Schmid-Guisan came to Zurich for the fortnightly meetings of the Analytical Association and stayed overnight at their home in Küsnacht. Her analysis continued at least until the beginning of 1915. Emma Jung discussed her personal situation with Schmid-Guisan, in particular the irritations that her husband's relationships with other women had caused. For his part, Schmid-Guisan showed great openness, and he confided his own problems in Emma, who then discussed the exchange with her husband.[41] Within a few weeks, the relationship between analyst and analysand turned into a friendship that lasted beyond the analysis. According to Schmid-Guisan, Emma Jung's analysis was focused on "giving the necessary importance to the personal,"[42] and, after having developed the strong personality of "Frau Dr. Jung" during her first years of marriage, consciously developing the "Emma Rauschenbach" part of herself.[43] In a letter dated 17 January 1915, he observed, "Carl has an exceptionally strong personality; I always notice just how strongly suggestive it is when I am with him for a longer period of time. Presumably, therefore, after years of living and working together, this identification has become quite strong. In the last few years, you have become conscious of this identification and, as a result, the other part of your personality has developed more and more."[44]

Emma Jung also exchanged ideas with Schmid-Guisan about her first written work on the psychological motifs in the Grimm fairy tale "The Two Brothers." In the fall of 1913, she wrote a paper which she eventually presented to the Analytical

---

39 Here it is necessary to correct the account published by Deirdre Bair, according to which, after working with Leonhard Seif and her husband, Emma Jung did her actual training analysis—an analysis in which the future analyst herself is the analysand—only in later years with Hans Trüb. In fact, her training analysis took place with Hans Schmid-Guisan from 1914 onward. The correspondence between Emma Jung and Hans Trüb shows that their conversations were no longer within the framework of an analysis but rather were an exchange within the context of the group experiments of the Psychology Club. See Bair, *Jung*, 265, and Weber, "Vom Selbst zur Welt: Zur intellektuellen Biographie von Hans Trüb," in *Hans Trüb, Welt und Selbst*, 171–206, especially 176ff.

40 Hans Schmid-Guisan (1881–1932): Swiss physician, who got to know Carl Jung and psychoanalysis during his training in psychiatry at the Asile de Cery in Prilly near Lausanne in 1910–13. Member of the Psychoanalytic Association and Analytical Association in Zurich from 1912. The two men embarked on a long bicycle tour through northern Italy in April 1914. On this occasion, Carl Jung asked his colleague if he would like to become godfather to his newborn daughter, Helene. The first written contact between Emma Jung and Hans Schmid-Guisan came about during this trip. On Carl Jung's collaboration with Hans Schmid-Guisan concerning the psychological theory of types, see Jung and Schmid-Guisan, *The Question of Psychological Types: The Correspondence of C. G. Jung and Hans Schmid-Guisan, 1915–1916*.

41 Carl Jung to Emma Jung, 20 July 1914, Jung Family Archive.

42 Hans Schmid-Guisan to Emma Jung, 10 September 1914, Jung Family Archive.

43 Hans Schmid-Guisan to Emma Jung, 17 January 1915, Jung Family Archive.

44 Ibid.

Association on 30 October and 13 November 1914, after the birth of her youngest daughter. Presumably, the two-part lecture on the theme of the brothers also served as proof of her own scientific work that was required for formal admission to the Association.[45] The psychological interpretation of fairy tales had already proved to be a fruitful field of investigation in the earlier Psychoanalytic Association. In his 1908 publication *Wunscherfüllung und Symbolik im Märchen*,[46] Franz Riklin had argued that fairy tales were spontaneous creations of the original soul, expressing its tendency toward wish-fulfillment. In *Wandlungen und Symbole der Libido*, Carl Jung describes fairy tales and myths as representations of archaic psychological pre-figurations, that is, those psychological structures of the collective unconscious that he later termed archetypes.[47]

Emma Jung's correspondence with Hans Schmid-Guisan also confirms what the texts and images reproduced in this volume show: from 1910 onward, Emma Jung worked through her psychological material not only in the conversations of her analysis and in a first lecture but also in her "black book"—which was, in fact, several notebooks—in which she recorded her dreams and fantasies.[48] At the time she was undertaking her explorations into the unconscious, she, too, like her husband with Toni Wolff, occasionally had a companion at her side in Schmid-Guisan. When, in 1932, Hans Schmid-Guisan died unexpectedly of blood poisoning after a traffic accident, Emma Jung reflected upon their collaborative analytical work, "I am also losing a good friend with whom I realized a good part of who I am in the time we shared."[49]

Texts and Images from the Unconscious

Carl Jung first described his method of active imagination, developed in *The Black Books*[50] and *The Red Book*, in an essay written in November 1916 with the title "The

---

45 We know little about the reception of Emma Jung's presentation, since there are no minutes of the discussions in the records of the Analytical Association. Presentations took place after the meetings of the Association had finished. For the lecture, "The Tale of the Two Brothers," see Chapter I, 100ff.

46 Riklin, *Wunscherfüllung und Symbolik im Märchen* (Wish-fulfillment and symbolism in fairy tales).

47 Jung, *Archetypes of the Collective Unconscious*, CW 9/1, §1–86. On the concept of archetypes, see the "Reader's Guide," volume introduction, 68ff.

48 In his letters to Emma Jung, Hans Schmid-Guisan refers to "the black book" as a generic term for records of psychological material from the unconscious in verbal or pictorial form. He himself chose the literary form of a psychological novel for the further processing of his own material, which appeared in 1931 under the title *Tag und Nacht* (Day and Night), with a foreword by Carl Jung. Shamdasani also refers to the practice of recording visions in text and image, which was initiated by Carl Jung among members of the Analytical Association; and, in addition to Schmid-Guisan, he mentions Alphonse Maeder as a further example. See Shamdasani, introduction, in Jung, *The Red Book*, 204.

49 Emma Jung to Wolfgang M. Kranefeldt, 2 June 1932, Zentralbibliothek Zurich, Manuscript Collections, Ms Z II 395.

50 Jung, *The Black Books*.

Transcendent Function."[51] In this context, transcendence means the union of consciousness and the unconscious, which is achieved by making unconscious contents conscious, for instance by giving aesthetic form to, and processing, this psychological material. Parallel to the experiments being conducted by her husband, we observe a similar concentrated focus in Emma Jung who, from 1914 to 1919, transcribed her own important dreams, fantasies, and images into a special book bound in marbled paper and leather.[52] In addition to recording inner dialogues, in the manner of Carl Jung's imaginings at that time, Emma Jung preferred to use the stylistic device of poetry to capture and shape the central themes of her work. This creative phase also led to the formulation of a personal cosmology, which Emma Jung at one point called her "System."[53] Whereas Carl Jung drafted a personal cosmology for the first time in 1916, in his *Black Books*, volume 5,[54] which he condensed into a mandala with the title *Systema Mundi Totius*,[55] Emma Jung had already found the phenomenon of the creative in an active imagination in April 1915, and later summed up her "System" in an image in her marbled book.[56] But while Carl Jung chose to proceed on the symbolic level, Emma Jung initially adopted the phenomenological approach. She documented her thoughts on creativity in abstract drawings and texts, which she then developed into a cosmology that relates the inner with the outer, the small with the large, the near with the far. Her cosmology draws on the late medieval concept of the microcosm/macrocosm, according to which the "small world," for example the earth, a state, or a living creature, repeats in miniature the structure of the universe; that is, it mirrors the "big world." And thus, in the same way, a person's self-knowledge simultaneously encompasses the knowledge of all that exists.[57]

The search for the origins of creation (*Ursprünglichkeitssuche*) saw a general revival at the beginning of the twentieth century,[58] and Emma and Carl Jung were not the only ones who were illustrating their personal cosmologies. This phenomenon is evident in contemporary European reform movements that were seeking a new wholeness in various areas of life at that time—for example, Rudolf Steiner

---

51 See *CW* 8, §131–93. The essay, however, was not published in English until over forty years later in 1957, and in German in 1958. On the related concept of active imagination, see the "Reader's Guide" below, 73.

52 That is, the so-called marbled book. The author's notebooks are described in the "Preface and Editorial Note," above, xvff.

53 The marbled book, 89. See introduction to Chapter VII, 314.

54 Jung, *The Black Books*, vol. 5, 163, 16 January 1916.

55 Jung, *The Art of C. G. Jung*, 109ff. (illustrations) and 116ff. (commentary).

56 Emma Jung, "Night Voices," 15 April 1915; also in the marbled book, 81. See introduction to Chapter VII, 315.

57 Well-known examples of comparable ideas and cosmologies can be found, for example, in the works of the Renaissance thinkers John Dee, Robert Fludd, and Michael Maier.

58 A prominent example of this endeavor was Henri Bergson's study *L'évolution créatrice*, first published in 1907, where he introduced the term *élan vitale* (life force), a concept widely discussed in the Jungs' circle in Zurich at the time. Carl Jung had first read Bergson on a voyage to the United States in March 1913, as he mentioned in a letter home to his wife. Adolf Keller gave a presentation and discussion on the subject of "Bergson and the libido theory" on the evenings of 13 and 20 March 1914 to the Analytical Association of Zurich.

(1861–1925), the founder of anthroposophy, who worked in Dornach, Switzerland, illustrated his lectures with blackboard drawings.[59] Even though the approaches by Emma Jung and Steiner differed—Steiner did not analyze the unconscious, but rather, using intuition, he tried to explore the spiritual forces in matter—both parties recognized the existence of a connection between humankind and the cosmos. They were unanimous in their view that, after the process of materialization, spiritualization sets in. Like Emma Jung, Steiner describes materialization as a process of condensation: "Everything that is combined materially with the earth-planet has been condensed out of what was previously united with it spiritually."[60]

The Swiss healer Emma Kunz (1892–1963), born in Brittnau in Canton Aargau, used the pendulum to research the laws of life. Beginning in 1938, she created large-scale geometric colored-pencil drawings on graph paper which, starting from a pendulum-divinated basic order, show "formative forces of nature."[61] Emma Jung also identified the "basic condition of all development"[62] in her abstract drawings. For both of them, the process of materialization and spiritualization was the task of life itself. According to oral tradition, Kunz illustrated humankind's evolution toward the spiritual in her crucifix-shaped picture No. 012, which depicts the horizontal, which she associated with the moral, earthly categories of good and evil, being transcended as it strives toward the vertical, the cosmic.[63] A further parallel between Emma Kunz and Emma Jung is that neither made their imaginings public.

On a personal level, in the decade of the 1910s Emma Jung was working through internal conflicts, predominantly related to her marriage, by means of analytical talks with her husband, with Seif, and with Schmid-Guisan. In parallel with these talks, she recorded and elaborated her inner material in various forms, including the creation of her personal cosmology. As yet another dimension of her psychological work, Emma Jung's cosmology not only constituted a demandingly abstract, intellectual exercise but also seems to have led the author to a personal turning point, culminating in 1919 with her painting of "an emerging world," and providing her with firmer spiritual ground for the years that followed.[64]

---

59 From around 1914 onward, black cardboard was used instead of a slate blackboard.

60 In his book *Die Geheimwissenschaft im Umriss*, 1910, Steiner discussed the evolution of humankind and the planet in seven stages, with the present fourth stage being the stage of the earth and the self-aware human being (Rudolf Steiner, "The Evolution of the World and Man" in *An Outline of Occult Science*, 107).

61 Kunz, *Neuartige Zeichnungsmethode: Gestaltung und Form als Mass, Rhythmus, Symbol und Wandlung von Zahl und Prinzip* (A New Method of Drawing: Design and form as measure, rhythm, symbol and transformation of number and principle) (self-published, 1953).

62 In her cosmology, System II, Emma Jung contrasts the "basic condition of all development" with the "basic condition of all differentiation" (Chapter VII, 352).

63 Kunz, *Emma Kunz: Leben, Werk*, in particular 30ff. Another contemporary female example is the Swedish theosophist and artist Hilma af Klint (1862–1944) with her large-scale painting project *The Ten Largest* begun in 1907, exploring the stages of life and humanity's connections to the universe in a cosmological series, in which science and spirit, mind and matter, the micro and the macro are simultaneously present. See af Klint, *Paintings for the Future*, 23ff., paintings 105–15.

64 The observation that Emma Jung's cosmological work may have marked a turning point in her life and marriage is supported by the fact that essential elements of her "emerging world" painting are also painted around the frame of an upstairs window in the Tower at Bollingen.

First President of the Psychology Club Zurich

When, on the initiative of Carl Jung, the Psychology Club Zurich was formed on 26 February 1916, in order to provide a space for analysts and their analysands to meet outside the therapeutic setting, there was also the additional intention of creating an experimental forum, to see how individuals who had been analyzed behaved as a collective.[65] At its inaugural meeting, Emma Jung was elected president of the board by its forty members, twenty-four of whom were women. In the years that followed, she was confirmed in this role until, at the Annual General Meeting on 11 April 1919, she announced that she would no longer be available for the position. Emma Jung subsequently took on other roles on the board, serving as auditor for many years, and initiating and chairing several discussion evenings in the 1940s.[66]

The role of president was a demanding one during the Club's turbulent beginning. As early as October 1916, the Club held its first discussion on the "Club problem," which, according to Emma Jung, involved the difficult attempt to "develop a collective on an analytical basis."[67] In order to motivate more active participation in Club life, she solicited the opinions of its members:[68]

> In an effort to make the Club as lively and as meaningful as possible, the Board would once like to hear the individual opinions of Club members, on what seems to them problematic, desirable, or deficient.[69]

The survey indicated a desire for a more communal form of Club life. But even the formation of an "Amusement Committee," composed of members Harold McCormick,[70]

---

65 In the statutes, the following purpose was stated: "The fostering of community life on the basis of individual and collective psychological experiences. The fostering of psychological interests and psychological science." Statutes of the Psychology Club Zurich, Psychology Club Zurich Archives. On the early history of the Club, see Emma Jung's 1936 lecture, "On the 20th Anniversary of the Club," Chapter I, 160ff.; also Muser, "Zur Geschichte des Psychologischen Clubs" (The History of the Psychology Club), a lecture delivered on 25 June 1983.

66 For example, Emma Jung's preparatory notes and her personal contribution to the central topic, discussed on 30 January 1943, "Wie wirkt sich der psychologische Tpyus in den Beziehungen zu andern Menschen aus?" (How does psychological type affect our relationships with others?), are preserved in the Jung Family Archive.

67 "Zum Clubproblem," manuscript, end of 1916 (Jung Family Archive).

68 In the debates that dealt with the organization of the Club, Emma Jung advocated democratic structures. At the General Meeting on 4 July 1936, which dealt with the relationship between the board and its members, she expounded on the Quaker model, according to which even business meetings were conducted in a respectful, consensual manner ("Protokolle," vol. 5, Psychology Club Zurich Archives).

69 Emma Jung to the members of the Psychology Club, draft of letter dated 30 October 1916, Jung Family Archive.

70 Harold McCormick (1872–1941): heir to the wealth of the McCormick family agriculture machine company (International Harvester), he was married to Edith Rockefeller (1872–1932), daughter of wealthy American Standard Oil cofounder John D. Rockefeller. They came to Jung through Harold's cousin (Joseph) Medill McCormick, who had been his patient in the Burghölzli in 1909. In 1913 Edith

Herbert Oczeret,[71] Erika Schlegel, and Hans Trüb,[72] and a "Discussion Committee," composed of members Emma Jung, Hans Schmid-Guisan, and Toni Wolff, failed to improve the low occupancy rate of the Club's boarding house at Löwenstrasse 1, with the consequence that it had to be sold. In 1918, a suitable new location was found at Gemeindestrasse 27.

Increasingly, however, deeper divisions were manifesting, which, taken together, culminated in the question being raised in November 1922 as to whether individuality or collectivity should be the Club's priority. The dispute over the direction the Club should take came to an end when a group around Carl Jung, including Emma Jung and Toni Wolff, withdrew from the Club.[73] Hans Trüb, who wanted to strengthen the shared experience, equality, and participation in the Club, became Club president.[74] At the General Meeting of 1 March 1924, those in favor of the return of Carl Jung to the Club prevailed. The then president, Hans Trüb, and his wife, Susi Trüb,[75] subsequently resigned from the Club.[76]

Despite all of its organizational challenges, the Psychology Club became an intellectual and social home for Emma Jung, and it provided her with a platform to discuss her own work in analytical psychology. Not only did she regularly attend lectures, but she also enjoyed participating in masquerade balls,[77] outings,

---

traveled to Zurich to be treated for depression by Jung, joined by Harold and the rest of the family for periods of time. The couple became staunch supporters of Jung's cause, not only funding the Zurich Psychology Club but also paying to have Jung's writings translated into English.

71 Herbert Oczeret (1884–1948): psychiatrist and analyst of Polish origin, initially came to Zurich in 1907 for his medical studies and was already an active member of the Psychoanalytic Association in Zurich in 1912. He and his wife, Irma Oczeret, were founding members of the Psychology Club Zurich.

72 Hans Trüb (1889–1949): Swiss physician and psychotherapist, studied medicine in Geneva, Zurich, Kiel, and Munich, and subsequently worked at the Burghölzli psychiatric clinic in Zurich under director Eugen Bleuler. Met Carl Jung in 1913. Married Susanna (Susi) Wolff, sister of Jung's assistant Toni Wolff, in 1915. Hans Trüb underwent a training analysis with Maria Moltzer and subsequently set up psychotherapeutic practice in Zurich in 1918.

73 Board Meeting minutes, 17 November 1922, General Meeting, 25 November 1922 ("Protokolle," Psychology Club Zurich Archives); Susi Trüb to Erna Naeff-Wolff, 26 November 1922, Felix Naeff Collection. The group included Carl and Emma Jung, Toni Wolff, Fanny Altherr, and Emma Jung's mother, Bertha Rauschenbach, although they did not officially withdraw from the Club.

74 This episode seems to have marked the end of the particularly close private relationship of the so-called "sextet," consisting of the Jungs, Toni Wolff, Emilii Medtner, Toni Wolff's sister, Susi, and her husband, Hans Trüb. In this constellation, Carl Jung was engaged in an intimate relationship with Toni Wolff, and Susi Trüb with Emilii Medtner, which led Emma Jung and Hans Trüb to discuss their personal situations analytically with each other. See Ljunggren, *The Russian Mephisto*, 136ff. See also the letters of Hans and Susi Trüb with Emma and Carl Jung, 1920–1922, in the Felix Naeff Collection and the Jung Family Archive.

75 Susi (Susanna) Trüb (1892–1979): youngest sister of Toni Wolff, married Hans Trüb in 1915. The Jung and the Trüb couples were close friends for several years, vacationing together, and being godparents to a number of each other's children. After Carl Jung and Hans Trüb parted ways in 1924, Susi Trüb and Emma Jung maintained personal contact.

76 Kiraly, "Das Clubproblem, 1920–1924."

77 At the masked ball at the Hotel Sonnenberg in 1934, for example, Emma Jung was a "veiled Indian = astrologer" and an "animal tamer." See diary of Erika Schlegel, February [1934], Corina Fisch-Schlegel Collection; and plate 24 for the costume.

---

and parties organized by the Club. On 7 May 1921, together with Erika Schlegel and Susi Trüb, she initiated the first women's evening to discuss women's issues, to present models, and to discuss topics in analytical psychology from the female perspective.[78] On 7 November 1922, precisely when Club tensions between her husband and Hans Trüb were at their peak, Emma Jung read her "Reflections on a Passage by Meister Eckhart" to a small circle of women.[79] Drawing on Eckhart's spiritual teachings, she shared her interpretation of his passage on finding God by letting him go, saying that God is able to find us when we are most fully human.[80] Erika Schlegel noted in her diary:

> Yesterday, we women were once again together and Emma Jung read a meditation on one of Eckhart's teachings, which was a true confession of faith, and it moved us all deeply. For some time, there was a profound silence.[81]

In their lectures, the female members of the Club dealt intensively with the psychology of women, but only marginally with the role of women in society.[82] "By animus, we mean a mental faculty in a woman's soul—an ability to discern which relates not to external experience but to the inner life," Linda Fierz[83] explained,

---

78 As stated in the minutes: "Approximately twelve ladies discuss seriously (one report) for several hours" ("Protokolle," vol. 2, 1919–1922, Psychology Club Zurich Archives).

79 See Chapter I, 156ff.

80 It is likely that this reflection was inspired by the chapter "The Relativity of the God-Concept in Meister Eckhart" in Jung's *Psychological Types* (*CW* 6, §407–33). At the women's evening on 7 July 1945, Emma Jung also led a discussion on the problem of the shadow.

81 Diary of Erika Schlegel, 9 November 1922, Corina Fisch-Schlegel Collection.

82 Erika Schlegel, "Rahel Varnhagen," 8 June 1922; Elisabeth von Sury, "Die psychologische Wirkung der Frau" (The psychological impact of women), 5 May 1928; Linda Fierz, "Ein Beitrag zum Animusproblem" (A contribution on the problem of the animus), 14 February 1931; Emma Jung, "Über das Wesen des Animus" (On the nature of the animus), 21 November 1931; Linda Fierz, "Mutterliebe" (Mother-love), 22 October 1932; Toni Wolff, "Einige Gedanken zum Individuationsprozess der Frau" (Some thoughts on women's individuation process), 12 May 1934; Elisabeth Heusler, "Ein kleiner Abstieg in mein Mutterland" (A small excursus into my motherland), 18 May 1935; Barbara Hannah, "On Esther Harding's Book: *Women's Mysteries: Ancient and Modern*," 29 June 1935; Esther Harding, "The Spiritual Problem of Women," 26 June 1936; Tina Keller, "Vom Animus zum Führer: Innere Erlebnisse während der Analyse" (From animus to guide: Inner experiences during analysis), 7/8 February 1938; Barbara Hannah, "The Writings of the Brontë Sisters: An Early Victorian Manifestation of the Problem of Modern Woman," 19 November 1938; Linda Fierz, "Einige Gedanken über die natürliche Einstellung der Frauen zum Leben" (Some thoughts on women's natural approach to life), 3/5 July 1941; Gertrud Lang, "Die Frau—Ausschnitte aus Sage, Geschichte und Gegenwart" (Woman—Excerpts from legend, history, and the present), 27 February 1943; Cornelia Brunner, "Auszüge aus dem Buche *Die ewige Frau* von Gertrud von Le Fort—mit anschliessendem Kommentar" (Excerpts from the book *The Eternal Woman* by Gertrud von Le Fort—with commentary), 11 December 1943. See Annual Reports, Library of the Psychology Club Zurich.

83 Linda Fierz, née David (1891–1963): German philologist, native of Basel. She had been the first woman in Basel to attend university, though she left early for marriage and motherhood. She met Carl Jung in 1920, who encouraged her to resume her academic studies and train her intellect. She subsequently trained in analytical psychology and authored books. A longstanding founding member of the Psychology Club Zurich, where she gave numerous lectures, she also taught at the

in "Ein Beitrag zum Animusproblem" (A contribution on the problem of the animus).[84]

In "Einige Gedanken zum Individuationsprozess der Frau" (Some thoughts on women's individuation process), Toni Wolff expanded the traditional types of women—the mother and the hetaera—to include the modern Amazonian and medial types, and she described individuation as the integration of a complementary type. She characterized the Amazonian as an independent, self-confident woman, who matter-of-factly realized her own talents and goals without instinct. "The teething problem of the Amazonian, however, certainly is—or hopefully, was—feminism, the so-called emancipation of women, whereby women, for the most part, emancipated themselves from their own femininity."[85] As a contrasting figure to the Amazonian, she described the medial type, discovered by Linda Fierz, which is characterized by "being affected most strongly by atmospheric influences of psychic life."[86]

> It is historically interesting that the medial type emerges at the same time as the feminists, and is, indeed, as undifferentiated as the latter. The path of the medial type runs parallel to that of the emancipated woman, as well as that of Mrs. Blavatsky, the founder of Theosophy. In the same way that feminists identify with the intellect, medial types identify with unconscious psychic content. Both took on tangible form: the former group of women became men, while the latter became spirits personified.[87]

Women characterizing both types opened up new areas of activity at the turn of the twentieth century. Both groups brought a new vision of the roles of women but with practical differences. While women's rights activists advocated an egalitarian concept of gender, that is, one that was based on the equality of all people, calling for equal rights for women and men in all areas of society, medial types generally assumed a dualistic approach, according to which men and women differ "by nature" and consequently are destined for different things. While women and men enjoyed equal rights in "medial" associations, among which the Psychology Club may certainly be counted, women in the Club generally did not challenge the traditional sociojudicial order of things.

As Tina Keller,[88] who had taken physics lessons with Emma Jung and had studied medicine as the mother of five children, recalled, Carl Jung allowed women

---

Jung Institute. She and her husband, Hans Eduard Fierz (1882–1953), a professor of chemistry at the Technical University of Zurich, were close friends with the Jungs.

84 Linda Fierz, "Ein Beitrag zum Animusproblem."

85 Wolff, "Einige Gedanken zum Individuationsprozess der Frau," 25.

86 Ibid., 30.

87 Ibid., 43ff.

88 Tina Keller-Jenny (1887–1985): wife of Rev. Adolf Keller (161, note 9), whom she married in 1912. Analyzed with Carl Jung and Toni Wolff in the years 1915–28. Obtained a medical degree in 1931 and was one of the first women in Switzerland to set up practice as a psychiatrist and

who had been analyzed to become lay analysts, but he thought it unnecessary for them to study at a tertiary level.[89] However, seen within the context of conservative Switzerland, his 1921 publication on his concept of animus and anima as the archetypal images in the unconscious of women and men, respectively, was innovative, indicating the fundamental bisexual nature of humankind.[90] Unlike in many European countries, including Germany and Austria, where voting rights for women were introduced between 1913 and 1919, Swiss women remained excluded from political participation until 1971. And it was only in 1988 that the civil rights of a married woman were no longer subordinate to those of her husband who, until then, had been able to dispose of the family resources solely as he saw fit.[91]

Even in 1927, in his publication *Die Frau in Europa* (*Women in Europe*), Carl Jung states that "neither politically, nor economically, nor spiritually" are women "a factor of visible importance"[92] and concludes, "The woman of today is faced with a tremendous cultural task—perhaps it will be the dawn of a new era."[93]

"On Guilt" and "On the Nature of the Animus"

In her lectures at the Psychology Club, Emma Jung repeatedly addressed the topic of the psychology of women. She delivered her first Club lecture on 17 June 1916, "On Guilt."[94] In it, she explored both the concept and the feeling experience of guilt, discussing the latter in relation to social change as reflected historically in superstitions, myths, and fairy tales. She also presented her own view of the Old Testament story of the Fall, and the legend of Prometheus, paying particular

---

Jungian-oriented psychotherapist. Pioneered in integrating analysis with body-based approaches such as movement and dance.

89 Tina Keller, *Wege inneren Wachstums für eingespannte Menschen: Aus meinen Erinnerungen an C. G. Jung* (Paths of inner growth for busy people: My memories of C. G. Jung), 16.

90 In the wake of World War I and the Bolshevik Revolution in Russia, a political and cultural conservatism gained strength in Switzerland where, for all its heterogeneity, a united anti-socialist and anti-feminist position in social discourse was adopted, a position that preferred to see women relegated to their role in the home. See Jost, *Die Reaktionäre Avantgarde: Die Geburt der Neuen Rechten in der Schweiz um 1900*, 100–104.

91 See Joris, "Gleichstellung," in *Historisches Lexikon der Schweiz*, online; Joris, "Geschlechtshierarchische Arbeitsteilung und Integration der Frauen," in *Etappen des Bundesstaates. Staats- und Nationsbildung der Schweiz 1848–1998*, 187–201; Hubschmied, *Frauen, Macht, Geschichte: Frauen- und gleichstellungspolitische Ereignisse in der Schweiz 1848–1998* (Women, power, history: Events surrounding politics and the establishment of gender equity in Switzerland, 1848–1998).

92 Jung, *Die Frau in Europa*, 13; first published in *Europäische Revue*, year 3, issue 7 (1927): 481–99. See *CW* 10, §240.

93 *CW* 10, §275.

94 Emma Jung's lecture was one of the first delivered after the Club's founding. On 24 June 1916, Erika Schlegel noted in her diary: "At the Club evening, Emma Jung read her major and intelligent work 'On Guilt'" (Corina Fisch-Schlegel Collection). See Chapter I, 131ff.

attention to the role that the women, Eve and Pandora, played in those stories. Her psychological conception of Pandora as an "artificially created image" in men, while identifying the phenomenon of an "imago" also existing in women—the concepts of anima and animus *avant la lettre*[95]—is remarkable. In her lecture, Emma Jung further distinguished between relative and absolute guilt: relative guilt she described as an offense against recognized laws, while absolute guilt she saw as an offense against the reality of the soul. Using the legend of Parsifal to illustrate her point, she outlined the obligation to individuation which she found to be implicit in the psychological concept of guilt.

In the discussion after the lecture, the various forms that guilt may take were considered. Carl Jung, who was working intensively on the subject himself at the time in both his *Black Books* and, scientifically, in smaller works,[96] was a very active participant in this discussion. Instead of relative and absolute guilt, he spoke of causal and final guilt: the guilt of having done something, and the guilt of not fulfilling one's obligation to one's soul, respectively. He, too, ascribed the latter to original sin.

> The guilt of having knowledge is only one side of the problem. Its indispensable counterpart is sexuality. Both forces push human beings to go beyond themselves into the fruitful error of knowing and acting. Out of this, conditions arise which burden one with further obligations—which we shun and then perceive as guilt. Consciousness and instinctuality are the two demons that push people to go beyond themselves, and further into life.[97]

Emma Jung's interpretation of Pandora as a feminine imago in a man, in her 1916 lecture "On Guilt," as well as a corresponding passage in her 1914 dream "The blue flower,"[98] suggests that she was involved in the development of the concepts of animus and anima from the very beginning. Carl Jung first mentioned the terms in his 1921 publication, *Psychological Types*, in connection with the complementarity of persona and soul,[99] but he had clearly been deliberating on the figure of the anima before this.[100] Using the images of the elusive sphinx and the ambiguous hero, he

---

95 French: before any published reference (lit., before the letter).

96 In his lecture at the Psychology Club on 26 October 1916, on the topic of "Individuation and Collectivity," Carl Jung elaborated on guilt as an element that links individuation and collectivity (*CW* 18, §1103). On Carl Jung's other discoveries and work during this period, see Shamdasani, "Toward a Visionary Science" in Jung, *The Black Books*, vol. 1, 51–55.

97 Discussion from 17 June 1916 on the lecture by Emma Jung "On Guilt" ("Protokoll der Vorträge des Vereins für Analytische Psychologie I, 1913–1916," Psychology Club Zurich Archives).

98 See Chapter I, 106, 144 *et passim*; Chapter VI, 260.

99 Jung, *Psychological Types*, CW 6, §805–7.

100 In *Wandlungen und Symbole* (1912), Jung points out for the first time the hidden aspects of the feminine in man, as well as the masculine in woman, which he later elaborates in his animus-anima theory (see *CW* 5, §324). In Jung and Jaffé, *Jung's Life and Work, as Told to Aniela Jaffé: The Original Protocols for* Memories, Dreams, Reflections (hereafter cited as *Original Protocols*), there is a statement

elucidated the many-sided nature of both anima and animus in his publication *Marriage as a Psychological Relationship* in 1924.[101] In *Die Beziehungen zwischen dem Ich und dem Unbewussten* (*Relations between the Ego and the Unconscious*), 1928,[102] he devoted a chapter to the anima and animus, in which, by way of contrast, he posited "the plurality of the animus as distinguished from what we might call the 'uni-personality' of the anima."[103]

The question of how the animus function affects one's own psychology was subsequently tackled primarily by women.[104] Emma Jung had already been pondering this topic for some time when Linda Fierz's above-mentioned lecture "Ein Beitrag zum Animusproblem" (On the problem of the animus) at the Psychology Club on 24 February 1931 prompted her to formulate her own understanding of the animus.[105] On 17 April 1931, she wrote to her German colleague Wolfgang Kranefeldt:[106]

> Apart from this, I am brooding on a little paper about the animus—whether it will hatch or not, I don't know, but I hope so; in any case, I have been brooding on it for some time. I have made several attempts and have always discarded what I have written, but I hope, as I said, that something will finally come of it. For one thing, it will be good for me to really get clear on the matter myself, and for another, I have been getting a lot of "nudging" from the Club for once to do some work on the subject.[107]

According to Emma Jung, when she presented her paper with the title "Über das Wesen des Animus" (On the nature of the animus) to the Club on 21 November 1931, it had been "exceedingly well received, which, of course, I was delighted about. It would appear that the problem is very much in the air."[108] A few days later, the

---

that makes clear that the anima, at least, was known to him in 1914, when he visited Ravenna with Hans Schmid-Guisan on their bicycle tour (*Original Protocols*, 129). *The Black Books* also show that around 1916, Carl Jung saw the anima as a counterfigure to the persona. See undated revision of "The Structure of the Unconscious," *CW* 7, second edition, §507ff., 521.

101 Jung, "Marriage as a Psychological Relationship," *CW* 17, §339–45.

102 Jung, "The Relations between the Ego and the Unconscious," *CW* 7.2.

103 Ibid., §338.

104 As an early example, Constanze Long's diaries on her participation in Carl Jung's 1920 seminar at Sennen Cove, England, contain numerous references to the analysis of the animus (see Finiello Zervas, *"Enchanting the Unconscious"*).

105 "Mrs. Fierz made a presentation on this subject in winter, and afterwards, it was thought that it would be good to have more and different contributions on this subject." Emma Jung to Wolfgang Kranefeldt, 17 April 1931, Zentralbibliothek Zürich, Manuscript Collections, Ms Z II 395.

106 Wolfgang Müller Kranefeldt (1892–1950): German psychiatrist and psychotherapist, close friend of Emma and Carl Jung. Kranefeldt was Jung's most trusted proponent of analytical psychology in Germany in the 1920s and 1930s.

107 Emma Jung to Wolfgang Kranefeldt, 17 April 1931, Zentralbibliothek Zurich, Manuscript Collections, Ms Z II 395.

108 Emma Jung to Wolfgang Kranefeldt, 29 November 1931, Zentralbibliothek Zurich, Manuscript Collections, Ms Z II 395.

C. G. Jung Society of Berlin was already planning to hold a reading of the paper, for which Emma Jung requested a female speaker.[109] In July 1932, she presented her paper in French at the Le Gros Caillou Psychology Club in Paris, and in September of the same year, she was invited to the Analytical Psychology Club of London to discuss her work.[110] Her manuscript was discussed at the Psychological Study Group in Munich in March 1934.[111] In it, Emma Jung made the many-sidedness of the animus, as outlined by her husband, more specific by distinguishing its four layers: power, deed, word, and meaning.[112]

From this lecture came Emma Jung's first publication in 1934, a chapter bearing the title "Ein Beitrag zum Problem des Animus" (On the problem of the animus) in the anthology *Wirklichkeit der Seele* (The reality of the psyche) published by C. G. Jung.[113] It was at this point that the publishing house of Rascher secured for itself the right of first refusal "for further works of the author."[114] While putting the finishing touches to the article, Emma Jung exchanged ideas with various representatives of analytical psychology in Switzerland and abroad, for example with Cary Baynes[115] and Erika Schlegel in Zurich, and with Fritz Seifert in Munich.[116] In 1941, "On the Nature of Animus," translated by Cary Baynes, appeared in the newly founded journal *Spring* of the Analytical Psychology Club of New York. The essay did not become accessible to a wider Anglo-Saxon audience, however, until 1957,

---

109 Ibid.

110 Serina, "C. G. Jung's Encounter with His French Readers: The Paris Lecture (May 1934)," *Phanês*, vol. 1, 126; Baynes Jansen, *Jung's Apprentice*, 258.

111 Emma Jung to Lucie Heyer-Grote, 15 March 1934, Universitätsbibliothek Basel, bequest 335 (Lucie Heyer-Grote): C2 45, 1.

112 Emma Jung, "Über das Wesen des Animus," typescript, Jung Family Archive (Emma Jung, *Animus und Anima*, 11ff.). Although Carl Jung originally understood the anima as singular, later, in 1946, he, too, established an order for it, made up of four personified "types of eroticism," which he identified as "Hawwah (Eve), Helen (of Troy), the Virgin Mary, and Sophia" (Jung, "The Psychology of the Transference," *CW* 16, §361).

113 Jung, *Wirklichkeit der Seele: Anwendungen und Fortschritte der neueren Psychologie, mit Beiträgen von Hugo Rosenthal, Emma Jung, W. M. Kranefeldt* (The reality of the psyche: Applications and advances in the newer psychology, with contributions by Hugo Rosenthal, Emma Jung, W. M. Kranefeldt). This volume as a whole has never been published in English. Individual chapters by Jung are found among his *Collected Works*.

114 Publishing contract between Emma Jung and the publishing house Rascher, Zurich, 17 October 1933, Foundation of the Works of C. G. Jung, Archive.

115 Cary Baynes (1883–1977): American physician, born Fink. Married first to the physician and anthropologist Jaime de Angulo, she moved to Zurich in 1921 to study with Carl Jung and became a trusted friend of Carl and Emma Jung. After separating from de Angulo, she and her second husband, Helton Goodwin Baynes (called Peter), whom she had met in Zurich, engaged in translating Jung's writings into English. For H. G. Baynes, see p. 54, note 157.

116 Fritz Seifert to Emma Jung, 1 March 1933, Jung Family Archive. Friedrich (Fritz) Seifert (1891–1963): German philosopher and psychotherapist belonging to the Psychologischer Arbeitskreis in Munich, a group of Jung followers in southern Germany, which maintained close contact with Zurich. On 17 June 1936, Seifert gave a lecture to the Psychology Club Zurich under the title, "Die Bedeutung der analytischen Psychologie in der gegenwärtigen philosophischen Situation" ("On the significance of analytical psychology in the current philosophical situation").

when it was supplemented by a contribution on the subject of the anima, which Emma Jung had written for the Festschrift she coedited for her husband's eightieth birthday,[117] and published as a small book, *Animus and Anima: Two Essays*.[118]

While Carl Jung had already partially abandoned his fundamentally dualistic concept by seeing both animus and anima as psychic complementarities of woman and man, Emma Jung circumvented gender binarity by identifying animus-figures such as the magician, the fire spirit, and the star-headed god, who, by their abstract nature, defy traditional masculinity.[119] Although the traditional distinction of nature as feminine and personal and spirit as objective and masculine can also be found in her writings, she questioned the connotation of their being inferior and superior, respectively. "Not only in Europe do we suffer from this now superannuated veneration of men, this overvaluation of the masculine,"[120] she noted in *Animus and Anima*. Despite the general adherence to there being a "natural" difference between the sexes, Emma Jung's statements in particular show how gender-specific attributions, including valorizations and devaluations, are subject to social change.

In Emma Jung's exchange with the depth psychologist Erich Neumann[121] there is evidence of a remarkable development in her conception of femininity. While she entrusted him with her work on the Grail, he, too, entrusted her with *Amor and Psyche*, his commentary on Apuleius's myth, published by Rascher in Zurich in 1951. "You have portrayed the female myth, as a process of becoming conscious, so wonderfully that it is very moving,"[122] she wrote to him in September 1949. A few months later, she presented him with her detailed and quite controversial written understanding of his text *Amor and Psyche*. She underscored an emancipatory instance in women that was not yet evident in her text on the animus:

> In my opinion, every woman has an element within herself that one could perhaps call the Artemis component: something natural, free-roaming, something that desires to be unrelated—to be sufficient unto itself, something that

---

117   Emma Jung's contribution "Die Anima als Naturwesen" ("The Anima as an Elemental Being"), which emerged out of her lecturing activities at the C. G. Jung Institute in Zurich, first appeared in *Studien zur analytischen Psychologie C. G. Jungs*, vol. 2, 78–120.

118   Emma Jung, *Animus and Anima: Two Essays* (1957). This work was first published in German by Rascher in 1967, with the title *Animus und Anima*.

119   Emma Jung, *Animus and Anima*, 27–31.

120   Ibid., 24.

121   Erich Neumann (1905–1960): German Jewish psychologist, philosopher, and medical doctor. After obtaining his medical degree in Berlin, he emigrated in 1933, first stopping to study with Carl Jung in Switzerland, then completing his move to Tel Aviv in 1934. He remained in close contact with Carl and Emma Jung thereafter. Often deemed Carl Jung's most gifted and original student, after World War II Neumann became a regular lecturer at the yearly Eranos conferences in Ascona, Switzerland, and later at the C. G. Jung Institute in Zurich.

122   Emma Jung to Erich Neumann, 28 September 1949, Foundation of the Works of C. G. Jung, Archive.

wishes to be neither daughter nor wife nor mother. Mostly, it is very hidden and unconscious, because consciously, women are most often completely tuned in to relationship; but I am convinced that, to some degree, this is somewhere present in everyone.[123]

It was also the role of women that interested Emma Jung in her ironic drama "Mystery of the Crusade," 1926, written in French in the historicizing style of seventeenth-century *vers mêlés*.[124] In it, God wants humankind to return to Paradise. He sends Archangel Gabriel to find out why it is that knights like being on the earth so much, and why women, "this hardly human creature, / who cannot think," have such power over said knights. The angel discovers that within their souls, women bear the image of the man that men wish to be. Oscar A. H. Schmitz,[125] a writer from Munich who had become acquainted with Emma Jung through the circle of Count Hermann Keyserling's[126] Darmstadt School of Wisdom, said that the play was a "vision rising up out of the very depths of our experience of our age."[127]

Work as an Analyst

Emma Jung became established in the field of analytical psychology with the publication of her paper "On the Problem of the Animus." After having taken on regular secretarial and editorial work for her husband in the 1920s,[128] from 1930 onward she began to work as an analyst with her own patients.[129] In April 1931, she wrote to Wolfgang Kranefeldt:

123 Emma Jung to Erich Neumann, 31 March 1950, Foundation of the Works of C. G. Jung, Archive.

124 French: verses in mixed meters. Emma Jung had experimented in 1921 with another extended literary form in her narrative poem "Do you see the sea?," Chapter III.

125 Oscar A. H. Schmitz (1873–1931): writer and member of the Munich bohemian society, he shared interests with Emma Jung in psychoanalysis and astro-psychology, the development of which Schmitz foresaw in his *Geist der Astrologie* (1922).

126 Hermann Keyserling (1880–1946): a Baltic German philosopher from an aristocratic family. Popular essayist, founder of the Society of Free Philosophy in Darmstadt.

127 Oscar A. H. Schmitz to Emma Jung, 20 July 1928, Jung Family Archive.

128 From 1925 to 1929, as shown by correspondence from those years, Emma Jung, partly assisted by Toni Wolff and others, took care of her husband's secretarial work (ETH Zurich University Archives). In addition, according to the editor of Jung's *Collected Works*, William McGuire, it was up to Emma Jung and Toni Wolff to check for correctness of content in the privately copied transcripts and summaries of Carl Jung's early lectures and seminars (McGuire, *Bollingen*, 17).

129 In November 1930, Emma Jung mentioned to Erika Schlegel that, for the first time, she now had four patients. See Erika Schlegel diary, 6 November 1930, Corina Fisch-Schlegel Collection. Among her first analysands was Barbara Hannah (1891–1986), an English woman who had come to Zurich in 1929 to study with Carl Jung, and who worked with Emma Jung for several months in the summer of 1930 (see Hannah, *Jung*, 201).

Did I tell you that I also have some analysands? (Cases that are too boring for other analysts!) I enjoy it and find it very interesting, and so far it has gone quite well.[130]

And in November 1931, she wrote to him:

I am also seeing an American woman who, rather than doing analysis with me, just wants to find her own theoretical orientation; she arrives each day with a list of questions whose answers often make me sweat the sweat of the righteous (pardon the variation). But it is, I believe, a very healthy exercise.[131]

Carl Jung confirmed to the Directorate of Public Health of the Canton of Zurich that Emma Jung was, indeed, working as his assistant in their house, which also establishes the official beginning of her therapeutic activity in 1931.[132] Her first documented patient, in 1929, was a former patient of her husband's, Elisabeth Heusler from Basel,[133] whom she knew well and who had suffered from a manic-depressive condition and who went into analysis with Emma Jung because of a persistent phobia.[134]

In the years that followed, Carl Jung regularly recommended cases that he could not accept for reasons of time, or for which he considered a woman analyst more suitable, to Emma Jung or Toni Wolff.[135] In 1933, Wolfgang Kranefeldt advised his wife, Hanna Kranefeldt, to travel to Zurich to discuss her personal difficulties with Emma Jung.[136] Documentation shows that the first instance of a student coming to Zurich for a training analysis with Emma Jung took place in 1937.[137] Specific requests from the Anglo-Saxon world to analyze with her followed.[138]

---

130 Emma Jung to Wolfgang Kranefeldt, 17 April 1931, Zentralbibliothek Zürich: Manuscript Collections, Ms Z II 395.

131 Emma Jung to Wolfgang Kranefeldt, 29 November 1931, Zentralbibliothek Zürich: Manuscript Collections, Ms Z II 395.

132 Directorate of Public Health of the Canton of Zurich to Carl Jung, 27 June 1931, ETH Zurich University Archives, Hs 1056: 904.

133 Elisabeth Heusler to Emma Jung, 24 September 1929, Jung Family Archive.

134 In his conversations with Aniela Jaffé, Carl Jung describes the case of Elisabeth Heusler (1876–1935) and mentions that she had been in treatment with his wife (Jung and Jaffé, *Original Protocols*, 64ff.).

135 Examples of recommendations can be found in Carl Jung's correspondence with F. Hagenbuch, 1930, G. End, 1933, Ed. Naef, 1933, ETH Zurich University Archives.

136 Wolfgang Kranefeldt applied to the Psychology Club Zurich for financial support for his wife's eleven hours of analysis with Emma Jung (Board Meeting minutes, 10 November 1933, "Protokolle Psychologischer Club," vol. 4, 1929–1935, Psychology Club Zurich Archives).

137 In her letter to Carl Jung of 9 April 1937, Ilse Heintze asked for confirmation that her stay in Zurich was for the purpose of training with Emma Jung (ETH Zurich University Archives, Hs 1056: 5553); Ilse Heintze to Emma Jung, 22 December 1937, Jung Family Archive.

138 Among the earliest Anglo-Saxon analysands was Anne Moffett, who, in a letter from Washington, D.C., in 1934, thanked Emma Jung for the important role she had played in her analysis. See Anne Moffett to Emma Jung, 13 June 1934, Jung Family Archive. For a further example; see Hazeltine

On her meetings with Emma Jung, Elisabeth B. Howes[139] recalled:

In 1955, I had the privilege of working analytically with Mrs. Jung for several months.

Many times since then I have found myself saying to groups, when speaking of my contact with the Jungs, that I found Mrs. Jung the most integrated person in Zürich. I said it quite spontaneously first, and on further reflection knew it was true.

I found myself deeply moved by a woman who had so obviously found herself and her own authenticity in the midst of so many collective pressures. She was the wife of Carl Jung, which was certainly not an easy task. And she maintained—or rather, achieved—an individuality separate from his. She became a scholar in later years which culminated in her excellent book, *The Legend of the Holy Grail*. Also she became a wise and sensitive analyst, pointing simply and directly to what needed to be looked at. She was a joy to work with.

Today, many women speak of the need for a "role model." Mrs. Jung was definitely that, in her fine balance of creative animus and feminine functioning. She seemed never to go too far in either direction.

Mrs. Jung's quiet, penetrating, active and participating attitude helped one always to know that one was working in a religious process where the unconscious was revealing—in even the slightest way—powers greater than the ego. But always I remember how she stressed the role of the ego in the development of consciousness. Mrs. Jung said to me, "There are egos and egos and egos. The problem is to find the right one." To me, as I saw her, she had found hers and had related it to the deeper archetypal powers making for wholeness.[140]

Further confirmation that Emma Jung was a gifted analyst can be seen in the fact that various members of the Psychology Club and close colleagues of her husband liked to discuss their dreams with her.[141] She was clearly a good listener and had a keen sense of the psychology of the person she was talking to. It could well be

---

Keever to Carl Jung, 28 October 1937, ETH Zurich University Archives, Hs 1056: 5635 and Jung's secretary to Hazeltine Keever, 16 November 1937, ETH Zurich University Archives, Hs 1056: 6225.

139 Elizabeth B. Howes (1907–2002): born in Maine, a pioneer of the integration of psychology and religion. Studied with New Testament scholar Henry Burton Sharman and psychologist Fritz Kunkel before attending the Jung Institute in Zurich to become an analyst. Cofounder of the Guild for Psychological Studies in San Francisco and founder of retreat centers in California.

140 Jensen and Mullen, eds., *C. G. Jung, Emma Jung and Toni Wolff*, 34.

141 After working with Linda Fierz and Hans Schmid-Guisan, Anny Stauffacher, for example, continued her analysis with Emma Jung in 1931 (see diary of Erika Schlegel, 1931, Corina Fisch-Schlegel Collection). It is known that Eugen Schlegel, Erika Schlegel's husband and a longtime member of the board of the Psychology Club Zurich, also discussed topics he was working on with Emma Jung over many years. Along with Wolfgang Kranefeldt, Gustav Schmaltz (1884–1959), another German psychologist, sent dreams and picture series on himself and female patients to Emma Jung for interpretation (Gustav Schmaltz to Emma Jung, 10 January 1930 and 12 April 1933, Jung Family Archive).

that within the context of the oftentimes exuberant environment that surrounded Carl Jung, her discreet manner was appreciated. While Erika Schlegel noted that "Emma's objective, calm manner and her integrity do me good,"[142] Susi Trüb occasionally found her to be "unfathomable and inaccessible."[143] In a written contribution to a discussion evening at the Club in 1943, Emma Jung described herself as an "introverted sensation-thinking type."[144]

It is remarkable how, from about 1930 onward, through the content of her work, Emma Jung increasingly began to stand apart from her husband. She developed her own independent standpoint on the roles of women and men in marriage, which can be seen as both a reflection of her own experiences and the outcome of discussions at the women's evenings at the Club. She summarized this in a letter to Wolfgang Kranefeldt in December 1933:

> *À propos* marriage difficulties, what I wanted to say in response to your previous letter was this: basically, it is generally the same everywhere: the impersonal is more important to the man, and the personal to the woman. But I do not quite agree that these difficulties are solved on the impersonal or supra-personal level—at least not all of them, or often this is only a pseudo-solution. My idea is rather that, at times, women must learn to put the personal behind the impersonal, while men must also learn to give the personal its due. This idea of mine did not find great favor with C. G., but I must still defend it a little, at least until really convincing experiences of the other point of view impress me sufficiently. For ultimately, the personal is also an expression of the anima function, and so often I find that men who underestimate the personal are, in that moment, assailed by their anima. In any event, in our impersonal and objective lives, this makes the air stratospherically thin, and we (one) easily burst(s) in it.[145]

In 1935, with regard to a women's group discussion at the Club that once again was focused on the nature and purpose of the Club, Erika Schlegel recorded the following energetic statement by Emma Jung in her diary: "And even if Dr. Jung has taught for the past 100 years that where the soul is concerned, nothing is absolute, *nevertheless* there is still the *need* for the absolute within the soul."[146]

---

142 Diary of Erika Schlegel, May 1921, Corina Fisch-Schlegel Collection.

143 Susi Trüb to Emma Jung, 20 March 1923, Jung Family Archive.

144 Emma Jung, "Wie wirkt sich der psychologische Typus in den Beziehungen zu andern Menschen aus?" See also 79, note 33.

145 Emma Jung to Wolfgang Kranefeldt, 17 December 1933, Zentralbibliothek Zürich: Manuscript Collections, Ms Z II 395. In the original, her final clause reads: "unsereiner (man) verplatzt darin leicht."

146 Diary of Erika Schlegel, 12 February 1935, Corina Fisch-Schlegel Collection.

Her Magnum Opus, the Legend of the Grail

Emma Jung's most comprehensive work, *Die Graalslegende in psychologischer Sicht* (*The Grail Legend*), did not become known to a wider public until after her death in 1955. At the wish of Carl Jung, and drawing on manuscripts that had been written over two decades, Marie-Louise von Franz[147] published the book in joint authorship with Emma Jung in 1960.[148] Emma Jung's preoccupation with the Grail probably dates back to 1901 or earlier. Allusions to characters and themes from the Grail legend appear in Emma and Carl Jung's engagement letters, in which the couple discussed Richard Wagner's opera *Lohengrin*.[149] While working on *Wandlungen und Symbole der Libido* in 1911–12, Carl Jung refrained from including the Grail legend, which, along with Goethe's *Faust*, had been one of his most formative early readings, "because my wife was already working on it."[150]

With analytical psychology's interest in fairy tales and myths, the Grail legend offered itself as a source for research into psychological archetypes. Other representatives of the early analytic movement in Zurich also concerned themselves with the material. Otto Mensendieck,[151] for example, gave two lectures on the Grail legend of Parzival[152] at the Psychoanalytic Association in 1913, prior to Emma Jung's lectures "The Tale of the Two Brothers," held in 1914,[153] and "On Guilt," 1916, which contain her first references to the figure of Kundry in Richard Wagner's

---

147 Marie-Louise von Franz (1915–98): daughter of a colonel in the Austrian army. In 1919, after World War I, she had moved to Switzerland with her parents and sister, where she studied classical philology and languages and ancient history at the University of Zurich. She first met Carl Jung in 1933. To pay for her analytical training with Jung, she translated works for him from Greek and Latin, which formed the basis for a long-standing collaboration in the psychological interpretation of alchemical texts. Von Franz became a prominent scholar and teacher in the field of Jungian psychology, best known for her work on fairy tales and the subject of alchemy.

148 Emma Jung and von Franz, *The Grail Legend*. The extensive lecture and manuscript material that Emma Jung left behind already contained an introduction and a psychological commentary, but it had not yet been put into book form. Marie-Louise von Franz arranged and supplemented the manuscript, adding examples from alchemy, her field of expertise, to the interpretation. The introduction and chapters 1–3 are based on a final revision of the material by Emma Jung in 1955; chapters 4–6 were compiled and supplemented from various lecture materials (1940, 1944, 1949–52); chapters 6–13 (first half) are based mainly on the 1940 lectures, while the continuation of chapters 13–23 is a reproduction of the 1944 lectures with later edits by Emma Jung and additions by von Franz. See Manuscripts Emma Jung, Jung Family Archive, and Müller, "Schlussbericht zu Emma Jungs Gralsmaterial." See also Appendix A, "Emma Jung's 'Grail' Abstracts, 1940 and 1944," 363ff.

149 Jung Family Archive.

150 Jung and Jaffé, *Original Protocols*, 114; also 113, 160ff. A brief psychological interpretation of Richard Wagner's portrayal of Parsifal can be found in Jung, *Psychological Types* (see *CW* 6, §371ff.).

151 Otto Mensendieck (b. 1871): German-born philologist and pedagogue. He was working at the time as an analyst at the Sanatorium Lebendige Kraft of Max Bircher-Benner in Zurich. He later became a student of Alfred Adler's individual psychology.

152 "Die Gral-Parzivalsage" (The Grail-Parzival saga), 16 May 1913, and "Die prospektive Tendenz des Unbewussten in Wagners erstem Worttondrama über den Parsifal" (The prospective tendency of the unconscious in Wagner's first music-drama about Parsifal), 5 December 1913.

153 The lecture was written and prepared in 1913, but its presentation was postponed until 1914 due to the author's pregnancy and the birth of Helene in March 1914.

opera *Parsifal* and Wolfram von Eschenbach's novel in verse, *Parzival*. Emma Jung made the Grail legend the subject of a public talk for the first time at Carl Jung's seminar at Sennen Cove in Cornwall in 1920.[154]

It would appear that Emma Jung postponed working on the Grail theme until her paper "On the Problem of the Animus" was published in 1934. When the well-known indologist Heinrich Zimmer from Heidelberg[155] came to Zurich to deliver a lecture in the summer of that year and stayed with the Jung family for a few days, he discussed Emma Jung's Grail research with her, and subsequently sent her some literature references on the possible Persian origins of the Parzival saga.[156] At Easter in 1939, while on a last private visit to Peter Baynes[157] in the south of England, four months before the outbreak of World War II, Carl and Emma Jung visited Glastonbury, Stonehenge, and Avebury, and viewed the hillside carvings of Cerne Abbas for her Grail studies.[158] In December 1939, in relation to her work on the Grail, Emma Jung reported that she was having "difficulty in arranging the material into a lecture,"[159] which she was to deliver at the Psychology Club on four evenings between 2 and 29 March 1940.[160] Before the final evening of her lectures, she wrote to Wolfgang Kranefeldt:

---

154 The topic of the seminar, from 20 September to 3 October 1920, was, in fact, the book *The Authentic Dreams of Peter Blobbs*. However, according to various sources, it appears that the symbolism of the Grail legend was discussed in the second part of the seminar, probably inspired by local references. Emma Jung's lecture took place on 27 September 1920 in front of a small group. The following day, her husband spoke on the symbolism of the Grail legend, after which she gave a further lecture on Celtic folklore and its references to the Grail theme. See Finiello Zervas, *"Enchanting the Unconscious."* Despite searching in the Jung Family Archive, which contains an extensive number of manuscripts and research materials on Emma Jung's later Grail works, no corresponding lecture manuscripts for the Sennen Cove presentation have yet been identified.

155 Heinrich Zimmer (1890–1943): German indologist and linguist. He became a close friend of Emma and Carl Jung, with whom he collaborated on the translation of Daisetz Teitaro Suzuki, *Die grosse Befreiung—Einführung in den Zen-Buddhismus*, Geleitwort von C. G. Jung (*An Introduction to Zen Buddhism* with foreword by C. G. Jung). In 1939 he emigrated to Oxford, England, and from there to New York City in 1940.

156 Heinrich Zimmer to Emma Jung, 1 July 1934, Jung Family Archive. When Zimmer, who gave six lectures at the Psychology Club Zurich between 1932 and 1938, announced a lecture on the Arthurian legend, Emma Jung feared that his great reputation would "take the wind completely out of the sails" of her own studies (Carl Jung to Heinrich Zimmer, 19 May 1938, in *Jung and the Indologists*, edited by Giovanni Sorge). In the end, Zimmer held a lecture on 25 June 1938 with the title "Adventures of two Arthurian Knights (Gawain and Owain) as Individuation Symbols of the Arthurian Circle."

157 Helton Godwin Baynes (called Peter) (1882–1943): English physician and army officer, who became interested in analytical psychology during World War I. He came to Zurich for analysis in 1922, where he met his future wife, the American Cary Angulo, with whom he started to collaborate in translating Jung into English. Baynes accompanied Carl Jung on his expedition to East Africa in 1925–26, and after his return to the United Kingdom became the leader of the London Psychology Club and one of the chief proponents of Jungian psychology in his home country.

158 Baynes Jansen, *Jung's Apprentice*, 284ff.

159 Diary of Erika Schlegel, 8 December 1939, Corina Fisch-Schlegel Collection.

160 The 1940 portion of Emma Jung's lecture series, "Die Graalserzählungen" (Stories of the Grail), was structured as follows: 2 March 1940: Introduction; 16 March 1940: "Synopsis of the 'Conte del Graal'"; 26 and 29 March 1940: "Psychological Commentary." In the *Jahresbericht des Psychologischen Clubs Zürich 1940/1941* (Annual Report of the Psychology Club Zurich for 1940/41), Emma Jung summarized these lectures in an abstract, here translated in Appendix A, 363ff.

You can't imagine how happy I am to have finally presented this work, after having incubated it for so long! Today is the last lecture, and if it, like the others, goes over well, I will feel greatly relieved. I must say, though, that the material has not ceased to fascinate me; it continues to do so, which is why I intend to work on other versions of the story.[161]

When the Analytical Psychology Club of New York asked for copies of her 1914 and 1916 Club lectures for its library in September 1942, and expressed their interest in publishing the Grail legend in the *Spring* journal, Emma Jung was able to reply that her Grail manuscript had already been translated into English and that an offer for a book publication was on the table:

Now with the paper on the Grail, it is so: Mrs. Mellon, who was present when I read it before our Club, asked whether she might have it translated, so as to be able to read it, and Miss Welsh made an excellent translation, which we went through together very carefully. Later Mrs. Mellon asked me whether it might be published in the "Bollingen Press." I answered her that I would rather not have it published now, as the paper, as it is, seems to me not really suitable for a book, moreover I am still continuing my studies on some other Grail versions, therefore, before publishing anything I felt I'd rather work through the whole material and perhaps then form it all into one, which of course may take a long time.[162]

The American philanthropist and proponent of analytical psychology Mary Con-over Mellon[163] had begun planning the publication of Carl Jung's *Collected Works* in English, and she also wanted to bring out Emma Jung's Grail paper with the "Bollingen Press."[164] Meanwhile, Emma Jung continued her research, this time on Robert de Boron's version of the Grail. Once again, she presented her new findings at the Psychology Club on three evenings in November 1944.[165]

---

161   Emma Jung to Wolfgang Kranefeldt, 29 March 1940, Zentralbibliothek Zürich, Manuscript Collections, Ms Z II 395.

162   Emma Jung to Victoria de Laszlo, 21 September 1942, ETH Zurich University Archives, Hs 1056: 10308. See also the letter of the same date from Emma Jung to Mary Mellon asking for a small print run of the Grail manuscript in the *Spring* journal, ETH Zurich University Archives, Hs 1056: 10328.

163   Mary Conover Mellon (1904–46): wife of Paul Mellon, heir to Andrew W. Mellon, one of the wealthiest American citizens and former finance minister of the United States. After a first analysis in New York City, the Mellons came into personal contact with Carl Jung in 1937. They traveled to Zurich in early summer 1938, where Mary attended Jung's English-language Zarathustra Seminar at the Psychology Club Zurich. In autumn 1939 they traveled to Ascona in the Ticino, in the south of Switzerland, where both she and her husband participated in the Eranos conference. Following these stays, Mary Mellon developed the idea for a broader dissemination of Jung's work in the United States. After World War II and her premature death in 1946, the project of the *Collected Works of C. G. Jung* was realized under the framework of the Bollingen Foundation, set up and financed by her widower, Paul Mellon.

164   Longtime Bollingen Series editor William McGuire confirmed that publication plans existed in 1942/43 for Emma Jung's study of the Grail (McGuire, *Bollingen*, 47).

165   "Die Geschichte vom Graal nach Robert de Boron" (The story of the Grail according to Robert de Boron), 16 November, 18 November, and 2 December 1944, in "Protokolle Psychologischer Club,"

While her manuscripts were going the rounds privately, she received other literature references on the Grail material.[166] Unlike the conventional interpretations of the Grail legend which emphasize Parzival's inability to feel compassion in the Grail castle, Emma Jung understood the search for the Grail as a path to oneself, as she explained in her 1940 lectures on the Grail at the Club:

> The search for the Grail can thus be viewed as a human developmental process, as a process of becoming conscious, and as a path of individuation. The first stage on this path is Perceval's experience at the Grail Castle, perceived as a dream or vision, that directs the hero toward his future goal. Achievement of the latter becomes his life task, which consists of connecting this world with the world beyond, that is, in a union of the unconscious with consciousness and in the integration of the personality, expressed through the fourfold symbol.[167]

Emma Jung's decades-long preoccupation with the Grail theme was also reflected in her extensive library, which eventually included more than 330 titles, some of them rare.[168]

Member of the Curatorium, Lecturer and Training Analyst at the C. G. Jung Institute

At the end of World War II, a further important step was taken in the development of analytical psychology as an institution in Zurich, in which Emma Jung was also actively involved. A growing number of voices were in favor of founding an actual teaching institution for analytical psychology in order to relieve Carl Jung and to meet the increasing number of requests for instruction in analysis and

---

vol. 7, 1943–1947, Psychology Club Zurich Archives. Emma Jung's lecture abstract in the *Jahresbericht des Psychologischen Clubs Zürich 1944/1945* (Annual Report of the Psychology Club Zurich for 1944/1945), "*Le Roman de l'estoire dou Graal* des Robert de Boron" ("*The Romance of the Story of the Grail* by Robert de Boron"), is here translated in Appendix A, 367ff.

166 Karl Kerényi (1897–1937): Hungarian scholar in classical philology and Greek mythology, gave Emma Jung references to Herbert Silberer's *Probleme der Mystik und ihrer Symbolik*, 1914. In addition to Heinrich Zimmer's references, mentioned above, she received references from Gustav Schmaltz to Leopold von Schröder's *Die Wurzeln der Sage vom heiligen Gral*, 1910, and the first volume of Konrad Burdach's *Vorspiel—Gesammelte Schriften zur Geschichte des deutschen Geistes*, 1925 (Karl Kerényi to Emma Jung, 17 August 1946, ETH Zurich University Archives, Hs 1056: 12547; and Gustav Schmaltz to Emma Jung, 29 August 1947, ETH Zurich University Archives, Hs 1056: 13996).

167 "Stories of the Grail," Appendix A, 367.

168 "Literatur zum Graal" (Literature on the Grail), *C. G. Jung Bibliothek: Katalog* (Catalog of the C. G. Jung Library) (Küsnacht-Zurich: privately printed, 1967), 109–17. Some purchases, for example, from the London booksellers J. & E. Bumpus, Ltd. and Edwards Francis, Ltd., and from the Zurich antiquarian bookshop Hellmut Schumann, are documented in the correspondence of C. G. Jung stored in the ETH Zurich University Archives.

training.[169] These discussions, which took place mainly within the scope of the Psychology Club, led to the founding of the C. G. Jung Institute Zurich in 1948 in the Clubhouse at Gemeindestrasse 27.[170] Carl Jung served the Institute for the first two years as president of the Curatorium but no longer assumed any teaching responsibilities or work as an analyst. Emma Jung, on the other hand, was involved as lecturer and training analyst from the start. In addition to her courses in English on the Grail legend, on dream interpretation, and on the psychology of animus and anima, she also lectured in German "On the Problem of the Anima" for two semesters, and these lectures became the basis of her aforementioned contribution, "The anima as an elemental being," to the Festschrift for her husband's eightieth birthday. This paper later became part of the publication *Animus and Anima*. She also conducted courses in which she read from her husband's works. As various letters and reminiscences of former students attest, her teaching activities were held in high regard.[171]

Aside from all of this, Emma Jung wished to concentrate on completing her work on the Grail. But when her husband retired from the Institute in 1950, she became, seemingly in contradiction to her earlier intent, vice president of the Curatorium.[172] From then until her death in 1955, she attended the monthly management meetings of the Institute, and she was involved in all matters concerning curriculum outline, examination regulations, and the organization of the Institute.

Along with the recurrent planning of courses to be offered and setting dates for examinations, as well as the handling of applications for admission and requests for financial aid, the Curatorium spent considerable time drafting the Institute's Rules of Procedure, as well as its initial Rules of Professional Conduct. The day-to-day running of the Institute involved organizing hours of analysis for students, purchasing books for courses, copying transcripts of Carl Jung's earlier seminars, arranging colloquia for exam preparation, and engaging external speakers. A new

---

169 The legitimization of those who wished to train as analysts had hitherto been carried out exclusively by Carl Jung. Due to health problems in 1944, however, he was no longer able to fulfill this task. At the same time, the first training centers in analytical psychology had begun to spring up abroad, especially in England and America.

170 The history of the founding of the C. G. Jung Institute in Zurich is still only fragmentary. The first initiatives by Carl Jung himself to institutionalize the various psychotherapeutic directions in Switzerland under the umbrella of a tertiary Lehrinstitut der Psychotherapiekommission der Schweizerischen Gesellschaft für Psychiatrie (Teaching Institute of the Psychotherapy Commission of the Swiss Society of Psychiatry), and to enable the psychotherapeutic training of medical doctors in Zurich, date back to the prewar period. Those involved with analytical psychology wished to be able to accept non-medical therapists for training. The Psychology Club Zurich began planning a teaching program in 1944, for which the names "Institute of Complex Psychology" and "Institute of Analytical Psychology" were also considered ("Protokolle Psychologischer Club," Psychology Club Zurich Archives; and the correspondences between Carl Jung and Linda Fierz and Jolan Jacobi, ETH Zurich University Archives).

171 Jensen and Mullen, eds., *C. G. Jung, Emma Jung and Toni Wolff*. There are also private letters of thanks from students from this period in the Jung Family Archive.

172 See Program of Lectures, Library of the C. G. Jung Institute Zurich.

series of publications of research papers from the Institute, titled Studies from the C. G. Jung Institute, was also initiated. In her role as vice president, Emma Jung carried out all these tasks with great commitment.[173]

Until the end, it was also up to her to mediate in disputed issues and, if necessary, to seek the informal opinion of her husband, whose word, as honorary president, still carried weight. This was the case, for example, when the then president Carl Alfred Meier[174] sought to implement a reform of the Institute in 1952 which did not meet with the approval of all members of the Curatorium.[175] When Emma Jung was diagnosed with a severe form of cancer in the spring of 1955, she informed her colleagues of the Curatorium the following summer that it would no longer be possible for her to fulfill her teaching obligations at the Institute.[176]

Pioneer

In early July 1955, Emma Jung was still able to take part in the large-scale celebrations for her husband's eightieth birthday. She spent her summer vacation with him in Bollingen and attended the annual Eranos meeting in Ascona. After a sharp deterioration in her health in the fall, Emma Jung died on 27 November 1955 at her home at Seestrasse 228 in Küsnacht. Her funeral service was held on 30 November 1955 at the Reformed Church in Küsnacht.

Along with Carl Jung and Toni Wolff, the Psychology Club had already appointed Emma Jung, its founding president, an honorary member in October 1952.[177] In his eulogy on 30 November 1955, in the Reformed Church in Küsnacht, Reverend Hans Schär[178] read the following words from the obituary of the Psychology Club:

---

173 Emma Jung, "Curatorium." A notebook containing meeting notes by Emma Jung from the years 1951–54, Jung Family Archive.

174 Carl Alfred Meier (1905–95): Swiss psychiatrist, Jungian psychologist, and first president of the C. G. Jung Institute in Zurich. After medical studies in Zurich, Paris, and Vienna, he worked as a resident physician for his specialization in psychiatry at the Burghölzli clinic. In the 1930s he was the secretary-general under Jung's presidency of the International General Medical Society for Psychotherapy and editor of the society's journal, *Zentralblatt für Psychotherapie*. In 1941 he became the successor to Carl Jung in the Chair of Honorary Professor of Psychology at the Swiss Federal Institute of Technology, Zurich. Following its inception in 1948, until 1957, he was president of the C. G. Jung Institute.

175 The opponents feared that Carl Alfred Meier wanted to transform the Institute into one devoted entirely to scientific research, thereby undermining the area of teaching. See Kurt Binswanger to Carl Alfred Meier, 27 June 1952, Jung Family Archive.

176 Emma Jung to the Curatorium of the C. G. Jung Institute, draft of letter, undated, ETH Zurich University Archives, Hs 1056: 18823.

177 Board Meeting minutes, 3 March and 2 September 1952, and General Meeting, 25 October 1952, in "Protokolle Psychologischer Club," vol. 10, 1951–1955, Psychology Club Zurich Archives.

178 Hans Schär (1910–68): Protestant pastor and professor of practical theology and history of religion at the University of Bern. Lecturer at the C. G. Jung Institute Zurich and a personal friend of Carl and Emma Jung.

Frau Jung was the first President of the Psychology Club Zurich. She held this office from 1916–1919—the Club's first four and most difficult years. She was a member of its founding committee, which was entrusted with the preparatory work for its inaugural meeting and with the drafting of its statutes. The challenge of these first years was particularly great, because the Club was to serve not only the scientific advancement of psychology, but also, based on the knowledge acquired through analysis, the furtherment of social and human coexistence. Under the wise and gracious leadership of Emma Jung, the stormy waters of its initial troubles were calmed, making it possible for Club life to crystallize and take concrete form. Mrs. Jung was also a member of the discussion committee, formed in the fall of 1916, to attend to the scientific side of Club life. [...]

Over the years, Frau Jung made a number of presentations at the Club. The evenings in which she spoke about the Grail were particularly well remembered for the profound meaning she assigned to the Grail legends, the abundance of her comparative material, and the simple, amiable manner of her presentation. Frau Jung also chaired a series of discussion evenings. In these psychological discussions, she repeatedly surprised her audience with how, in a very simple, natural way, and drawing on her own experience, she was able to give concrete expression to, and lay out clearly, complicated inner problems.

Amidst all the different personalities, with their contradictions and controversies, Frau Jung was the calm island, the rock upon which one could absolutely rely. And to many, in their personal psychological work, she became a second, sound, spiritual mother. The Club, and each and every one of its members, is filled with gratitude for this unforgettable, distinguished woman.[179]

Emma Jung was willing to live an unconventional life with her husband. Through her own efforts to educate herself and her psychological work, she prepared herself to become an analyst. The formative role she played in the institutional inception of analytical psychology in Zurich has long been underestimated. Her contributions to the concepts of animus and anima, as well as her posthumously published study of the Grail, continue to be reprinted in various languages to this day. Individuation proved to be a central theme in her texts and images. At the end of her seventieth birthday, in her notebook with the title "Das Buch der Tage und Nächte," Emma Jung asked herself what she had achieved, and remarked: "I know only this: that I have made every effort to become what I am."[180]

---

179 "Emma Jung-Rauschenbach (30 March 1882–27 November 1955)," eulogy by Rev. Prof. Dr. Hans Schär at the funeral service in the Reformed Church of Küsnacht, 30 November 1955, Jung Family Archive.

180 Entry on 1 April 1952 in a dream journal, "Das Buch der Tage und Nächte" (The book of days and nights), Jung Family Archive.

PLATE 21. WEIMAR PSYCHOANALYTIC CONGRESS, 1911.

Emma Jung seated fifth from right, with Carl Jung leaning over her shoulder and Sigmund Freud in the center. The partic-
ipating women in the front row, seated, left to right: Maria Moltzer, Mira Ginzburg, Lou Andreas-Salomé, Beatrice Hinkle,
Emma Jung, Maria von Stach, Toni Wolff, Martha Sigg-Böddinghaus. Other persons connected with Emma Jung, front
row: Eugen Bleuler (second from left), Franz Riklin (far right). Second row standing: Ludwig Binswanger (second from left),
Sándor Ferenczi (fourth from left, next to Freud), Ernest Jones (second from right). Third row, from left: Jan Nelken, Oskar
Pfister, Max Eitingon, Leonhard Seif (center, left of Freud), Karl Abraham (right of C. G. Jung). Fourth row: Alphonse Maeder
(third from left, behind Seif), Adolf Keller (at right). Photographer: Franz Vältl, Grossherzöglich-Sächsischer Hofphotograph.

PLATE 22.

PLATE 23.

PLATE 22.
Hans Schmid-Guisan
(1881–1932).

PLATE 23.
Carl and Emma
Jung near the stone
bench in the garden
of the Jung house on
Seestrasse, Küsnacht,
c. 1920.

PLATE 24.
Emma Jung at a
masked ball at Hotel
Sonnenberg, Zurich,
1934, with Hans
Baumann, member of
the Psychology Club
Zurich, husband of
Carol Sawyer Bau-
mann. Photographer:
Linck Erben, Zurich.

PLATE 24.

PLATE 25.

PLATE 26.

PLATE 25.
Emma and Carl Jung,
skiing in Zuoz, En-
gadine, on an outing
with the Psychology
Club Zurich, New
Year's 1920/21.

PLATE 26.
Psychology Club Zu-
rich outing to Zuoz,
New Year's 1920/21.
From right: Emma
Jung, Hans Trüb, Susi
Trüb, and further
members of the Club,
on a winter walk.

PLATE 27.
Psychology Club Zu-
rich outing to Zuoz,
New Year's 1920/21.
Sledding party,
including, from right:
Carl Jung, Emma
Jung, Emilii Medtner,
Heinrich Steiger,
Rudolf Homberger,
Hans Trüb.

PLATE 27.

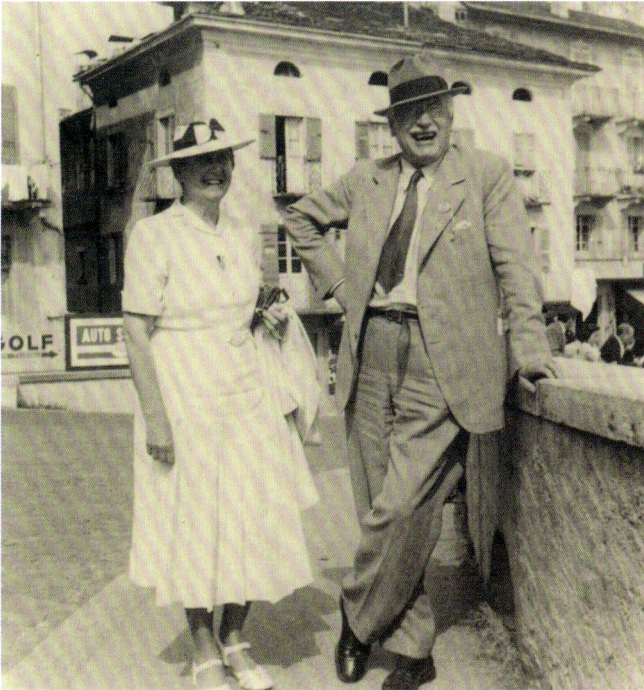

PLATE 28.
Emma and Carl Jung
arriving for the 1934
Eranos conference
at Casa Semiramis,
Ascona.

PLATE 29.
Emma and Carl Jung
vacationing in Asco-
na, 1940.

PLATE 30.
Emma and Carl Jung
with Toni Wolff at
Eranos, c. 1937.

PLATE 30.

PLATE 31.
Emma and Carl Jung
on the terrace at Casa
Eranos, c. 1940.

PLATE 31.

PLATE 32.
Emma Jung in discussion at Eranos.

PLATE 32.

PLATE 33.
Emma Jung at her desk in the Seestrasse house, Küsnacht, 1954. Photographer: Erica Anderson.

PLATE 33.

PLATE 34.

PLATE 34.
Emma and Carl Jung
at the Bollingen
Tower, 1955.

PLATE 35.
Emma Jung in the
flower garden at the
Seestrasse house,
Küsnacht, 1954.
Photographer: Erica
Anderson.

PLATE 35.

Reader's Guide

ANN CONRAD LAMMERS

Concepts and Methods in Emma Jung's Creative Work

THE FORMS OF Emma Jung's creative work appear to have been strongly influenced by her study of famous artworks and literature.[1] Framed within those forms, we find that psychological concepts and methods are integral to everything she created. Her familiarity with psychological practice and theory is seen in every facet of her work, including lectures, dream commentaries, poems, and drawings.

Given what we know of the author's education and experience, it is unsurprising to find that she was fluent in the concepts and methods of depth psychology. Most of her private discussions with her husband are naturally undocumented; but references in the available texts and their private correspondence show that they regularly collaborated, sharing in the development of ideas basic to analytical psychology. That this was a genuine dialogue, and not simply a conversation between teacher

---

1   The author's artistic education is described in "Emma Rauschenbach: Portrait of Her Childhood and Youth," volume introduction, 1ff. We know that Emma Jung began to love poetry in her early years. In a private writing, "Mother Dreams" (84, 90), she recalls reading poems and ballads at her grandmother's house, as a child. Her mature reading included poetry by Hugo von Hofmannsthal, Rainer Maria Rilke, and Alfred Grünewald, among others.

and student, is suggested by the fact that Emma Jung's dreams and fantasies were analyzed by both partners, but from separate perspectives. For example, in April 1915 Jung commented on his wife's first fantasy of the Water Nymph (266ff.). In October 1915, commenting on a related fantasy (276ff.), her interpretation of the central image is strikingly different from her husband's. The spouses' mutual discussions of their analytical work in this period are also illustrated by Carl Jung's diagram (91), sketched perhaps early in 1916, elaborating on Emma Jung's images of the negative mother.

Consistent with the spouses' close collaboration, we find evidence in Emma Jung's writings that she was familiar at an early date with many concepts that her husband only later introduced in his published work.[2] She was not only familiar with his evolving psychological theory; at times she also contributed to its development. For example, she assisted in the preparation of his groundbreaking work, *Wandlungen und Symbole der Libido* (1912), by researching many of the mythological and literary materials discussed in its chapters. Thanks to her research, she was able to refer with precision to *Wandlungen und Symbole* and its literary sources in her lecture of 1913, "The Tale of the Two Brothers" (80f., 104f.). Her close familiarity with the work is also shown in a poetic quotation that she added to a dream text in September 1915 (275).

The author's writing demonstrates her mastery of the tools of Jungian dream analysis, including the methods of amplification and circumambulation. Her dreams are often elaborated through the technique of fantasy or (as it is now called) active imagination.[3] She also addresses the distinction between objective and subjective levels of meaning, the psychological meaning of symbols, and the importance of the dream series.

The following discussion of her concepts and themes is generally limited to materials published in this volume. When necessary, however, to show the development of the author's thought or to illustrate important aspects of her work, variant drafts and unpublished writings are also cited. What follows is a brief elaboration of many of the Jungian methods and concepts seen in her work or mentioned in the editorial commentary.[4]

ARCHETYPES

In 1911 or earlier, as she assisted in research for her husband's *Wandlungen und Symbole der Libido*, Emma Jung came to understand his concept of archetypes, which he

---

2   "Emma Jung and Analytical Psychology," volume introduction, 45.

3   Carl Jung first developed the technique now known as active imagination when he began his work on *The Red Book*. He gave it various names at first: "the picture method," "active fantasy," etc. The now accepted term, "active imagination," appeared first in his 1935 Tavistock Lectures (73).

4   For reasons of length, not every Jungian concept mentioned in this volume is discussed here. For Jung's definitions of fifty-seven key terms, familiar to Emma Jung at the time of writing, see chap. 11, "Definitions," in *Psychological Types* (CW 6), originally published in 1921.

then called *Urbilder* or "primordial images."[5] The concept refers to powerful, generative patterns existing in the collective unconscious. As understood by analytical psychology, these patterns are numinous and as old as humankind. They cannot be known directly, but they have the power to produce a wide variety of representations in conscious life, all expressing the same underlying pattern.[6] Emma Jung shows her grasp of the concept when she writes in "The Tale of the Two Brothers":

> In cosmology, the pair [of brothers] became known as day and night, and soon as the evening and morning star, as sun and moon, or as heaven and earth. By mutually affecting each other while simultaneously excluding each other, they are recognized as life and death, or as a dualistic principle in general. (104)

Likewise, when she reflects on her March 1914 dream of two pictures, she finds archetypal meaning in the vision of two people walking toward the ocean—a scene that she captures in a painting, "Baptism." The title relates this scene to a sacred, ancient ritual of initiation, or psychological rebirth, which she sees, once again, in its cosmological context:

> Initiation by immersion in the sea (of the unconscious). This is also the place where two principles meet, sun and earth. (259)

Thus, in Emma Jung's earliest writings, the concept of archetypes is already present.

Carl Jung's first published use of the term "archetypes" appears in 1919.[7] A year later, Emma Jung uses the term in a private writing:

Archetypes

The primordial images are actually potential forms of energy—the human being, consisting of the same energy, also contains to some extent all these possibilities—(history of evolution). Awakening of such a potential is the coming-to-consciousness of the archetype.[8]

---

5   The concept of *Urbilder* (primordial images) first appears in part 1 of *Wandlungen und Symbole*, in a passage written in 1911. There Jung credits Jacob Burckhardt, who in 1855 had described Goethe's *Faust* as "a genuine myth, i.e., a great primordial image" (*CW* 5, §45 and note). Jung revised this work several times before it was published as volume 5 of the *Collected Works*, titled *Symbols of Transformation*. His first edition is now difficult to find; but the original text is available in reprint: Jung, *Wandlungen und Symbole der Libido* (Deutscher Taschenbuch Verlag; hereafter cited as DTV); see p. 47 and note. On sources for Jung's concept of archetypes in the writings of Schelling and Schopenhauer, see Shamdasani, *Jung and the Making of Modern Psychology*, 171ff.

6   Jung, "Approaching the Unconscious," *Man and His Symbols*, 67.

7   Jung, "The Personal and the Collective (or Transpersonal) Unconscious," *Two Essays on Analytical Psychology*, *CW* 7, §101.

8   Emma Jung, late September 1920, handwritten on letterhead of the Sennen Cove Hotel, Cornwall, UK. At this conference, led by Carl Jung, she also delivered a lecture (see "Emma Jung and Analytical Psychology," volume introduction, 54, note 154).

The concept of archetypes or primordial images is frequently present in the author's writings; and yet, as shown in this volume, in her early writings[9] she rarely uses these terms. Instead, her use of a simpler term, *Bilder* (images), carries archetypal connotations. The numinous power she attributes to images is especially clear in her poems. In "Morning in the Mountains" she writes of "that never-entered realm of images/That was forever/Home to the unstilled yearning of my soul" (243). The numinous power of images in the transpersonal realm is further discussed, below, as one of the author's major themes ("Eternal Images," 80ff.).

AMPLIFICATION

In analyzing her dreams, the author uses the technique of amplification, a central technique in analytical psychology. C. G. Jung's separation from Sigmund Freud[10] involved a major divergence in their respective understanding of dreams. Unlike the Freudian technique of free association, which seeks the source of each image in the dreamer's earlier life, Jung determined that it was necessary to look beyond the dreamer's personal associations. For him, Freud's interpretive technique was too reductive, focusing only on the personal unconscious and reducing every symbol to its causative genesis. In contrast, Jung sought the prospective value of dream images by circumambulating them (contemplating them from all sides) and comparing them with similar images, both personal and archetypal. He called this method of dream-reading "amplification."[11]

Emma Jung routinely amplifies the images in her dreams, considering them both through the lens of personal experience and through comparisons with parallel images in the collective human heritage, including folklore, religious and mythological literature, ancient and modern art, and other products of age-old human experience. In her first version of her May 1915 dream of the Grail, she amplifies one dream image (a rectangular patch of bent grasses) with reference both to her own experience and to a medieval love song (323 and note).

In commenting on her March 1917 dream of an animal enclosure, she amplifies the central image by recalling symbols from astrology:

---

9 In her mature writings, for example, her abstracts for lectures on the Grail that she presented in 1940 and 1944 (Appendix A, 363ff.), Emma Jung uses the term "archetypes" with practiced ease.

10 Jung separated himself from Freud's school of psychoanalysis in 1912–13, which roughly coincides with the beginning of Emma Jung's writings published here. The earliest entries in the marbled book are dated 1911 and 1912. Textual evidence suggests, however, that she actually began writing in this notebook after 1913. Between the entries of 1911–12 and those of 1914, she placed a succinct note: "1913: Occupied with the brother theme. Working on the tale of the two brothers. No dreams retained." Her 1913 lecture, "The Tale of the Two Brothers," is published in Chapter I, 100ff.

11 The concept is explored in Shalit and Furlotti, eds., *The Dream and Its Amplification*.

At the same time, it also makes me think about a horoscope, the *zodiac* and the twelve houses. [...] Here, the zodiac ("circle of animals"), therefore the cosmos and "compulsion by the stars." (287f.)

One of the most completely amplified dream texts among Emma Jung's writings is a long dream of her maturity, from October 1945 (301ff., also discussed below, 89f.). To begin with, she frames the dream by recalling the personal context: her day's events had involved a planned discussion of Esther Harding's *Women's Mysteries*.[12] In her commentary she circumambulates almost every image in this dream, including the figure of her sister (representing her personal shadow);[13] the search for new shoes (suggesting development in her conscious attitude); and the ornamental display of diverse vessels (understood since ancient times as symbols of the sacred feminine).

OBJECTIVE AND SUBJECTIVE LEVELS OF MEANING

Differentiation between the objective and subjective levels of meaning in dream images is an essential tool in Jungian dream analysis, with which Emma Jung seems to have been acquainted by 1912 or sooner.[14] In "The Tale of the Two Brothers," she explains that the images of a dream or story may be viewed subjectively:

> If we want to analyze a fairy tale or a dream on the subjective level, we have to begin by saying that all the figures that appear in it correspond to tendencies within the individual psyche. (105)

Human figures in dreams are liable to be misunderstood if taken only at the objective level, that is, identified entirely with corresponding individuals in the outer world. An apparently "outer" figure, such as a spouse or parent, may correspond less to the actual person, and more to a quality or process within the dreamer's

---

12   Harding, *Women's Mysteries*. Esther Harding (1888–1971): English medical doctor, psychotherapist, and writer, came to Zurich in 1922 to train with Carl Jung and in 1923 co-organized his seminar in Polzeath, Cornwall. In 1924 she moved to New York City, and from then on worked with her friends and colleagues, Kristine Mann and Eleanor Bertine. Together they were among the chief proponents of Jungian psychology in the United States.

13   Shadow: a term used frequently in analytical psychology. In its most basic usage, the shadow refers to aspects of the individual psyche which the ego does not willingly acknowledge or over which a person has little conscious control. Emma Jung's treatment of this theme is discussed below, 83f.

14   The subjective reference is clear in her comment on a dream of fall 1912. The dream text begins: "In an ugly, uncomfortable room with Carl, who tells me he must leave." Emma Jung's comment: "The identification must be resolved." Documentation from May 1913 shows that C. G. Jung had begun teaching the distinction between objective and subjective interpretation of dream imagery by that date (see Jung, *The Red Book*, 202 and note). As with all concepts of analytical psychology found in Emma Jung's early writings, it seems clear that the spouses regularly discussed such discoveries together.

psyche. Thus, in the text of her May 1914 dream, "The blue flower," Emma's first line reads: "I am walking with Carl (my masculine aspect?)" (260). With this parenthetical question, she distinguishes between her husband in outer life and her dream image of him, postulating that the dream-Carl may be understood subjectively, as a representation of her inner masculine side.[15]

When Emma Jung recorded her April 1942 dream, depicting an encounter between the figure of her husband and an eagle (300), she did not add commentary. Nevertheless, her comment on her dream of 1914, referring to her husband as "my masculine aspect," can be applied here as well. An objective reading of the male figure and the bird in this dream would involve Emma's real-life husband, pictured as intimately related to a bird of prey. If the dreamer's images of "Carl" and "eagle" are understood subjectively, they represent her inner masculine side—her animus[16]—in communion with a timeless symbol of power and far-seeing vision. By this reading, the dream may depict an archetypal dimension of the dreamer's own spirit and intellect.

THE UNCONSCIOUS

C. G. Jung described the unconscious as "a psychological borderline concept, which covers all psychic contents or processes that are not conscious, i.e., not related to the ego in any perceptible way."[17] In Emma Jung's writing, as in her husband's, the concept of "the unconscious" covers several levels. At one level, the *personal unconscious* holds contents once known by an individual but that have been forgotten or repressed. In contrast, the *collective unconscious* holds contents springing from an ancient human heritage, or "the inherited structure of the brain."[18] Such contents are not available to consciousness until they come to light through dreams, fantasies, works of art, and so forth. As they emerge, they may exercise power over the conscious psyche, such that an individual must work consciously to understand the meaning of such contents, not to be overwhelmed by them.

Emma Jung's references to "the unconscious" can generally be understood as meaning the collective unconscious. For example, she refers to the collective unconscious in her 1913 lecture:

---

15 Although she does not use the term "animus" here, her phrase "my masculine aspect" captures the concept.

16 Emma Jung's understanding of the animus, a core concept in Jungian psychology, is discussed below, 84ff.

17 Jung, *Psychological Types*, CW 6, §837 (see above, note 4). This volume of the *Collected Works* includes definitions of concepts central to Jung's work. Many terms, including "the unconscious," are also basic to Freudian theory; but as defined and used by Carl and Emma Jung, their meaning differs significantly from Freud's.

18 Ibid., §842.

We often find these secret forces that exert an influence from the unconscious in the form of animals in fairy tales. (115)

In addition to her paintings, poems, and dream texts, the writings the author calls "fantasies" or "imaginations" typically contain a wealth of images from the collective unconscious.

FANTASY (ACTIVE IMAGINATION)

"Active imagination" is the term now used in analytical psychology for a basic technique of analysis, involving conscious dialogue with the contents of the unconscious. As a practical matter, the basic approach of the technique is to focus conscious attention on a personal question or problem, addressing oneself to figures in the unconscious with the intention of entering into dialogue with whatever response emerges. The currently familiar term, "active imagination," appears first in C. G. Jung's 1935 Tavistock Lectures.[19] He began to develop the technique very early, however, between 1913 and 1915, in his *Liber Novus*. In "The Transcendent Function," a paper written in 1916,[20] Jung stressed that this technique, "the collaboration of conscious and unconscious data," differs from Freud's method of free association.[21] In 1921, in *Psychological Types*, he gave the method an extended definition under the heading "Fantasy."[22]

The collaboration of consciousness with the unconscious is an approach that Emma Jung frequently uses in relation to her inner life, varying the method to meet the needs of the moment. She refers to the practice most often with the term "fantasy" (less often, "imagination"); accordingly, the term "fantasy" is most often used in this volume's editorial commentary. In the author's writings, certain dream images provide doorways into dialogue with the unconscious. Sometimes a dream includes an encounter with a figure from the unconscious, whose identity and significance are revealed in a series of dialogues, as in her dialogues with Aranû (279ff., 284f.). At other times, she asks the unconscious for help, and it replies in various voices, as in her poem of January 1918, "A death is come upon me" (239ff.).

---

19 Jung, "Lecture V," "Tavistock Lectures," *CW* 18, §390–406.

20 Jung, "The Transcendent Function," *CW* 8, §131–93. Written in 1916, the paper was not published until 1957. In a 1958 "Prefatory Note," Jung states: "The method of 'active imagination', hereinafter described, is the most important auxiliary for the production of those contents of the unconscious which lie, as it were, immediately below the threshold of consciousness and, when intensified, are the most likely to irrupt spontaneously into the conscious mind" ("Prefatory Note," *CW* 8, p. 68). (Also see above, "Emma Jung and Analytical Psychology," 38.)

21 Jung, "The Transcendent Function," in *The Structure and Dynamics of the Psyche*, *CW* 8, §167.

22 Jung, "Fantasy," in *Psychological Types*, *CW* 6, §711–22.

FIGURE ID.I.
Christmas, 1918.
Painting by Emma
Jung, 1918.

SYMBOLIC IMAGERY

In her writings and paintings, Emma Jung used another tool of analytical psychology, the symbolic reading of images. For her, as for her husband, symbols link the ordinary world of consciousness with the archetypal or transpersonal world. The meaning of a symbol is never limited to one world or the other; it is always both-and. Because of this, symbols resist literal interpretation. Their meaning cannot be fully explained with reference to concepts or ideas. Indeed, Jung describes a symbol as "an expression of something unknown or not yet knowable."[23]

Symbolic imagery is found in most of Emma Jung's writings and paintings. Certain examples stand out, however, especially among her paintings. "Christmas, 1918," shown above, may have been inspired by a real scene near Château d'Oex, where she visited her husband during his military posting (see "Morning in the Mountains," November 1918, 243). In the painting's caption, the word "Christmas" alludes not only to a calendar event but also to the transcendent event of a sacred birth, suggested by the cone of intense light streaming from the hut. Except for a snow-covered peak on the horizon, the surrounding scene is one of darkness, in contrast to which an intense beam of light witnesses to a powerful reality, whose nature and origin can only be imagined.

---

23 Carl Jung's statement occurs in "Answer to Job," in *Psychology and Religion*, CW 11, §713.

FIGURE ID.2.
[Candelabrum tree].
Painting by Emma
Jung, January 1917.

Black-and-white renderings of three paintings by Emma Jung are included as figures 3, 6, and 20 in Jung's essay "The Philosophical Tree" (chapter 5 in *Alchemical Studies*, CW 13). The black-and-white reductions, however, fail to capture the full impact of the original paintings. Seen in color, these images reveal important details.

One of them, shown above, is a seven-armed candelabrum, rooted in the earth like an abstract tree. Radiance from the candles fills a mandorla-shaped space, its golden color clearly defined against a darker background. The whole image is mounted on a cardboard backing, giving the impression of a golden frame—a detail omitted from the previously published version. C. G. Jung summarizes the meaning of this image as "the illumination of consciousness."[24] Further symbolic meanings are suggested by its associations with a lighted Christmas tree and a Jewish menorah.

---

24 Jung, *Alchemical Studies*, CW 13, §308.

Another symbolic image, the painting of the Coral Tree, figure 6 in *CW* 13, *Alchemical Studies*, is printed in the present volume with the dream and fantasy to which it belongs (292f.). C. G. Jung's comment on this image describes the paradoxical nature of symbolic imagery in general:

> [The tree] is not reflected in the water, but grows simultaneously downwards and upwards. The four mountains in the lower half of the picture are not reflections either, for their opposites are five mountains. This suggests that the lower world is not a mere reflection of the upper world, but that each is a world in itself. (*CW* 13, §311)[25]

Another painting, on facing page, appears as figure 20 in *Alchemical Studies*.[26] The original painting, bearing no title, shows a chrysalis-like, multicolored figure embedded in the trunk of a large, fully leafed tree, its roots visible below the ground. Carl Jung treats this image as the first of a series by different patients, showing the emergence of female figures from the trunks of trees. His comment on this painting seems to echo Emma Jung's own statement. He writes:

> The painter was reminded of the harlequin motif. The fool's motley shows that she felt she was dealing with something crazy and irrational. She was conscious of having thought of Picasso, whose style was apparently suggested by the harlequin's dress.[27] (*CW 13*, §325)

If Emma Jung associated the colored patchwork with Picasso, it suggests that she and her husband shared a common fascination with the artist's emerging work.[28] Symbolic meanings of this painting are many-layered. The fully leafed tree, including roots, may symbolize the whole of creation, stretching from below the earth to the sky. The pupa-like figure within the trunk suggests gestation, which underscores the symbolic meaning of the tree as mother.[29]

---

25 In the English edition of the *Collected Works* (*CW* 13), figure 6 is printed upside-down. In the German edition of *Gesammelte Werke* (*GW* 13), it is printed correctly, consistent with Jung's description (292).

26 Emma Jung's painting of the tree enclosing a harlequin figure is discussed in *CW* 13, §325ff.

27 Emma Jung's knowledge of Picasso's harlequin drawings is known through numerous pages from art magazines that she cut and saved for her husband's pictorial research collection, now preserved in the Jung Family Archive. Carl Jung first saw Picasso's paintings during his visit to New York in 1913, when he visited a show of modern art at the Armory. In a letter to J. P. Hodin, 3 September 1955, he commented about a slightly later series of works, which Picasso had painted between 1914 and 1917: "The principle theme of the pictures was the harlequin, who dissolves in a bombed porcelain shop" (Fischer and Kaufmann, "Jung and Modern Art," *The Art of C. G. Jung*, 21ff. and 29, note 20).

28 Jung's controversial essay, "Picasso," first published in 1932, appears as the final chapter in *The Spirit in Man, Art, and Literature*, *CW* 15.

29 In Jung's comment on the next image in the series, he refers back to Emma Jung's painting: "The doll in the previous picture [i.e., figure 20] contained a sleeping human figure undergoing metamorphosis like the larva of an insect. Here as well the tree acts as a mother to the human figure

Another of the author's paintings (Figure ID.4, next page) shows even more clearly the relationship between tree symbolism and the theme of the Mother. An undated watercolor, this painting is one of Emma Jung's most representational works, and still a symbolic image. Medieval icons of the Virgin Mary are echoed in the blue semi-circle in the background, the halo, and the regal, embracing stance of the maternal figure. In the foreground, a tree's slender trunk is clearly drawn. Behind it, faintly visible, a white gown suggests the woman's form. Her head is clearly drawn, but her arms are hard to distinguish from branches, as she stretches out her cloak to embrace the world of nature. The image resembles a traditional icon of the Virgin of Mercy, except that here, in the place of human beings, the Madonna's cloak embraces birds and flowers.

---

hidden in its trunk. This accords with the traditional maternal significance of the tree" (*Alchemical Studies*, CW 13, §326).

DREAM SERIES

Jungian dream analysis observes that dreams sometimes occur in a meaningful sequence, developing a theme of importance to the dreamer. Jung found that the unconscious psyche operates progressively, continuing its work from one dream or fantasy to another, during which the psyche's response to an impasse or problem is sometimes transformed. Emma's sequences of dreams and fantasies include her dreams of a star-bird (258, 278); her fantasies of the Water Nymph (266ff., 276ff.), and those involving Aranû (279ff., 284f., 294ff.). Her important "dream and fantasy of the miraculous city," 10 April 1915 (268ff.), concludes a series of fantasies and dreams. In the marbled book, the fantasy of the Water Nymph (266) is soon followed by a related fantasy,[30] in which she travels eastward and is commanded: "Acknowledge the shadows and baptize them, that they may find rest for their souls!" The next night, continuing her inner voyage, she dreams that she is "on a new and unknown path" toward a dense forest, through which she must walk alone. Immediately

---

30 As recorded in the marbled book, this fantasy and the dream that follows, both dated March 1915, are in a series with the author's original version of "The Water Nymph." Quotations in this paragraph are from the marbled book, pp. 58–66.

READER'S GUIDE

afterward comes her "dream and fantasy of the miraculous city" (268ff.), which leads into the first draft of Emma Jung's cosmology.[31]

PSYCHOLOGICAL TYPOLOGY

In Emma Jung's writings, we find evidence that the basics of Carl Jung's typology were already a topic of their conversation at least seven years before he published his book on psychological types.[32] For example, in commenting on her May 1914 dream, "The blue flower," she notes that the dream-ego promises to pick up a gift of pears "through the *mediation* of another, who is characterized as *'intuition' i.e. as located particularly close to the unconscious*" (260). This is an indirect reference to the dreamer's own psychological type, which she describes elsewhere as introverted sensation.[33] Her comment is consistent with her husband's theory of types, which predicts that when sensation is the dominant function, the inferior function is intuition.

Three decades later, in her comments on her October 1945 dream of two churches (301ff.), the author again identifies the figure of her sister as representing her inferior function, and thus her compensatory shadow:[34]

> My sister: my other side, insofar as she is an opposite type to me, the shadow.
> [...] Sister says where I can find shoes: The shadow—i.e., probably intuition—shows me the way. (303)

---

31 In developing the first draft of her System, the author finds interwoven meanings in yet another group of dreams. See introduction to Chapter VII, 316–27.

32 An early breakthrough in Jung's psychology, his analysis of personalities according to typology, was published in 1921. In *Psychologische Typen* (*Psychological Types*, CW 6), Jung contrasts two general psychological attitudes, extraversion and introversion. In addition to these attitudes, he describes four functions, or habitual ways of relating to reality, which are thinking, feeling, sensation, and intuition. Thinking and feeling are paired, as "rational" ways of relating to the world; sensation and intuition are paired as "irrational." He theorizes that, as one develops one's most conscious function, which becomes dominant, one tends to neglect its opposite, which remains "inferior," i.e., more or less involved with the unconscious.

33 In 1934 at the Club, the author introduced a brief talk on psychological types: "Based on my own experience as an introverted sensation and thinking type, I can contribute the following to our discussion" (Emma Jung, "How does psychological type affect our relationships to others?" 1). Jung defines "intuition" as a basic psychological function, which "mediates perceptions in an unconscious way" (CW 6, §770). In contrast, he defines "sensation" as a basic psychological function, which "mediates the perception of a physical stimulus. It is therefore identical to 'perception'" (ibid., §792).

34 The personal shadow, the unconscious side of the personality, can have a positive aspect, as a compensation for the ego's one-sidedness. The inferior function, which the ego typically overlooks or rejects, is also essential for the purpose of relating fully to the world. As an introverted sensation type, Emma Jung knows that she sometimes needs the help of her inferior function, extraverted intuition, symbolized in this dream by her sister.

Emma Jung's Major Themes

ETERNAL IMAGES

As an introvert, Emma Jung naturally focuses her creative lens on the landscape of the interior life. Indeed, this feature can be observed in every chapter of the present work. As discussed above, archetypal images of the inner world are implicit in all her dreams and fantasies and in many of her paintings. In some texts, the presence and power of such images is more than an implicit feature; the author refers to sacred images, residing apart from earth. Sometimes their impersonal power is a topic on which she reflects; other times she personifies and addresses them directly.

At the end of her verse play, "Mystery of the Crusade," Gabriel's report to God on the secret power of women (223) states this theme directly. What keeps men so attached to the earth, Gabriel explains, is an Image (capitalized in the original French), an idealized masculine figure, which arises in women's dreams. "An image!" exclaims the Good Lord; who decides to descend from heaven, in order to learn what women can teach him and thereby to become complete.

This theme is also explored in the author's early poems. In "Far Off" (235) she evokes a distant, heavenly world, surpassing the material world in beauty. In "Morning in the Mountains" (243), she yearns for a realm of images, unreachable yet already known. In "Miracle," she greets an "eternal, ever-holy image" (247), which, although it cannot be seen or heard, awakens "dark words" in the poet's heart.

LIBIDO

Emma Jung's discussion of libido, consistent with her husband's, departs radically from Freud's conceptual realm, in which "libido" always has a sexual meaning. In this, she stands with C. G. Jung, who had broadened the meaning of the term in his work of 1912, *Wandlungen und Symbole der Libido*.[35] In spring 1913, as recorded in the minutes of the Psychoanalytic Association, Emma Jung gave her first public statement to that group on the subject of her husband's libido theory (35 and note).

Having worked closely with her husband on his "libido work" (114), Emma Jung not only appropriates his definition of the term but also applies it copiously in her lecture of 1913, "The Tale of the Two Brothers." There she writes:

---

35   The title of Jung's path-breaking work means, literally, "transformations and symbols of the libido." The English translation by Beatrice Hinkle, *The Psychology of the Unconscious*, appeared in 1916 (see p. 34, note 31). In *Psychological Types* Jung begins his definition of "libido" with this brief, encompassing statement: "By libido I mean *psychic energy*" (*CW* 6, §778).

Knowing as we do from *Wandlungen und Symbole der Libido* that light is a symbol of libido,[36] perhaps we may say that of the two tendencies [lighter and darker entities in a pair], one has more libido than the other, or one seems more *positive* and the other more *negative*, or one is conscious, the other unconscious. (105)

Again citing her husband's volume, she identifies gold as a libido symbol:

> Instruction on the significance of gold, the treasure or hoard, as libido, is to be found in *Wandlungen und Symbole der Libido*.[37] (106)

In the same lecture the author repeatedly brings out representations of libido in legends and fairy tales. For example, there is the enchantress who controls a child's development (108); the primitive "wild man" (109), or the adolescent's implacable urge toward growth (110). In her analysis of the hunter-figure of the ancient activity of hunting, she also identifies the universal challenge of libido as the drive or desire that each individual must learn to master:

> To pursue libido, to catch it and seize it again and again, is the skill that the human being must learn above all others. (111)

INDIVIDUATION AND SACRIFICE

Emma Jung's writings circle around the central theme of individuation, meaning the process of individual psychic development through differentiation.[38] A closely related theme, for the author, is the painful but necessary sacrifice of instinct in favor of consciousness.[39] Such a sacrifice often occurs at an early stage in the process of individuation. Sometimes, as the author's own story demonstrates, this sacrifice is not voluntary but is compelled by a process of psychological development to which the individual can only submit. Commenting on a dream dated summer 1911, one of the first texts in her marbled book, she writes:

---

36 Jung, *Wandlungen und Symbole*, chap. 3, 155ff. [*Psychology of the Unconscious*, 179.]

37 Ibid., 329, 341ff., 350 363. [*Psychology of the Unconscious*, 383f, 398ff., 409ff., 421.]

38 Individuation, as used in Jungian psychology, involves personal differentiation from the surrounding world and from powerful inner images such as the shadow, the anima or animus, and the Self. Jung's first published references to the term occurred in 1916, in "The Structure of the Unconscious" (Jung, *Two Essays on Analytical Psychology*, CW 7, §442–521; especially §462, §505). A definition added in 1928 reads: "Individuation means becoming a single, homogeneous being, and in so far as 'individuality' embraces our innermost, last, and incomparable uniqueness, it also implies becoming one's own self" (ibid., §266). An extended definition appears in chap. 11 of *Psychological Types*, CW 6, §757–62.

39 Sacrifice, as a psychological theme, was also familiar to Emma Jung from *Wandlungen und Symbole*, in which the final chapter, "Sacrifice," deals at length with the topic.

The requirement has emerged to give up the biological attitude. Despite the most violent resistance and struggle, the certainty that it's useless.[40]

Elsewhere she writes about sacrifice as a conscious choice, a deliberate turning away from instinctive life for the sake of adult rationality, culture, and the spirit. For example, in her dream of May 1914, "The blue flower" (260ff.), a red flower, standing for instinct and biology, is contrasted with a blue one, standing for intellect and spirit. Her dream-ego passes over the former and chooses the latter, a choice about which she comments:

> Foregoing the biological—life—red—in favor of the spiritual. Clear distinction of the two opposites represented by *blue and red*. (260)

This theme is also introduced in Emma Jung's lecture, "The Tale of the Two Brothers" (100ff.), where she describes the sacrifice of instinct as a necessary part of the process of transformation, calling it a constituent of individual development.[41] This transformation belongs to a universal process, she asserts, not only for humans but for every sentient being:

> Development is not a matter of simply eliminating or turning old attitudes into their opposite, but rather of creating out of them new possibilities for the future. [...] Overcoming the inner animal does not mean killing, but rather transforming it. [...] The transformation is in accordance with the enigmatic law of development, to which humanity and all creatures knowingly or unknowingly, forced or voluntarily, must submit. (114)

In her narrative poem, "Do you see the sea?" (181ff.), the dark power of the unconscious is symbolized by the wild ocean, which steals away the father and paralyzes the mother with grief, and also by the primeval forest, where two children, having grown up in nature, are driven together by a storm. The poem's plot centers on the siblings' love, innocently begun but tragic in its development. The sacrifice of instinct, symbolized by three violent deaths, concludes with the surviving brother's penitential journey toward healing and redemption, illustrating a process by which sacrifice, suffered consciously, becomes a path to transformation.

---

40 The marbled book, 2.

41 The author's first known use of the term "individuation" occurs in 1915, in her analysis of the "Dream of the Grail" (see Chapter VII, "The System: A Cosmology," 325). Earlier, in her 1913 lecture, she uses the word "development" in the same sense as C. G. Jung, when he writes that individuation is "the development of the psychological *individual*" (CW 6, §757).

Emma Jung identifies another recurrent theme by the term *Verdoppelung* (doubling). She first applies this word to a brief dream of May 1915, in which she learns that she cannot buy just one part of a stove but must buy both. Her marginal comment reads: "Doubling theme: separation of appearance from the essential."

"Doubling" also plays a major part in her fantasies about the water nymph, dated April and October 1915. In the first fantasy (266ff.),[42] the "I" of the fantasy has a fish's tail and is trapped in a well. To save her life, she must cut off her tail, which falls into the depths, while the human half escapes. Above the typed version of this text, beside which C. G. Jung hand-wrote a commentary, Emma Jung placed two titles: "Water Nymph fantasy" and "Theme of doubling."

Evidently inspired by his work on *Liber Novus*, Jung comments on this fantasy: "Izdubar ascends to heaven and becomes Abraxas. The ego winds up in hell" (267).[43] Emma Jung's later version of this fantasy differs widely, however, from the implications of her husband's commentary. She returns to the story of the water nymph in October 1915 (276ff.), with a dream that becomes a conscious fantasy, interspersing her own commentaries.

Exploring the fates of the water nymph (now called Undine), and the separated fish's tail, she imagines that they share a single shadow, waxing and waning like the moon, that travels between the two parts:

> But the shadow, which had remained whole, now always had to shift from one half to the other; for no one can exist without a shadow. (278)

As the fantasy progresses, the dreamer finds that she has a "day soul" and a "night soul," each living in its own house. Finally, she imagines that the fish's tail, far from being lost, rises into the sky and becomes a comet, or perhaps the star toward which she strives (278).

THE SHADOW

In Emma Jung's writings, the concept of the shadow is a recurring theme. It rarely arises in an abstract form, as pure evil ("Dream of the Devil," 286). More often, it is combined with other symbolic material. Human images in dreams may be

---

42 In Emma Jung's papers, two versions exist of this fantasy of April 1915. A very long first version is found in the marbled book, 42–57. A two-page typed summary, with handwritten commentary by Carl Jung, is the version published here.

43 In *The Red Book*, Jung writes about a figure he encounters in his imagination, Izdubar, who transforms into the all-good Gnostic god Phanes. Phanes then transforms into Abraxas, who is part good and part evil (Jung, *The Red Book*, 278ff.; and transformation into Phanes-Abraxas in "Scrutinies," Appendix.).

infected by shadow, as when an animus figure changes into a weird, threatening form (85), or a dragon figure represents a devouring witch or the negative mother (90ff.).[44] Natural phenomena, depicted as numinous, also have shadow aspects. In "Do you see the sea?" the ocean exerts a dangerous, seductive power, like the unconscious itself, and the "green" forest, with its nurturing goodness, coexists with the "dark" forest, with its mortal dangers (183ff.).[45]

The shadow does not always have a negative meaning. Sometimes it supplies a resource that the conscious ego lacks. Thus, Emma Jung comments that the dream figure of her sister represents her shadow, because they are typologically opposite (303), and she receives good advice from her sister's intuition.

In myths and stories, the shadow is often personified as the "inferior" counterpart of the protagonist. In her 1913 lecture (100ff.), the author discusses a classic example of this theme in the Sumerian epic *Gilgamesh*, where the king's friend is a nature figure, a wild man, whom he battles but also loves. Emma Jung's writings of 1916 also include a fairy-tale-like story, "The being who could not become his shadow."[46] In her story, a human being tries to reverse places with his enormous, heavy shadow, which does its best to help. In the end, both human and shadow choose their old relationship.

THE ANIMUS

The concept of the animus, enlarging on Carl Jung's early discovery of the anima,[47] was of particular importance to Emma Jung. Her records of early dreams, beginning before her husband discussed the concept in his published work,[48] show the meaning and function of the animus in the author's own experience. Several of Emma Jung's early dreams and poems record her personal encounters with the inner male principle. Her 1914 reference to "Carl (my masculine aspect?)" is discussed above (72). Also, in late 1915 or early 1916,[49] she ends an important prose writing, "Mother Dreams," with the following observation, containing perhaps her earliest written use of the word "animus":

---

44 The image of Urgo occurs in Emma Jung's long dream of December 1915, summarized by Jung in *CW* 9.i (§349). The symbolic meaning of this dragon figure is discussed below, 90ff.

45 This contrast is found in Emma Jung's recollection of a book she remembers reading in her youth, *Au cœur sombre de la forêt verte* (In the dark heart of the green forest) (179, 316).

46 Emma Jung's unpublished story was perhaps inspired by Adelbert von Chamisso's popular story of 1913, *Peter Schlemihls wundersame Geschichte* (Peter Schlemihl's amazing story), about a man who sold his shadow to the devil.

47 C. G. Jung published his first discussion of anima and animus in 1921, under the heading "Soul-Image [Anima/Animus]." See Jung, *Psychological Types*, CW 6, §808–11.

48 "Emma Jung and Analytical Psychology," volume introduction, 45.

49 The two pages of "Mother Dreams" are undated; but their association with the painting of "Urgo," related to the dream of December 1915, suggests a date of late 1915 or early 1916.

The feminine seldom appears alone or in its own right, but rather most often in some relationship to the animus, i.e., to a masculine being. Similarly, the feminine in its own right is only a half, not a whole in and of itself.

Using a ring binder, the author kept typed records of at least five of her dreams from 1916–17, under the heading "Animus dreams." A handwritten text in the marbled book, dated June 1916, also bears the title "Animus" in the margin. In this dream, which appears to have come one night after her first encounter with Aranû, she and "C." meet a hybrid figure, part bird and part man, which changes shape and grows to monstrous size. The bold label, "Animus," is printed sideways beside the passage where the creature appears. The "C." of the dream, who has met the creature before, assures the dreamer it will not hurt them.

Other early animus images have a hybrid character. In 1917, the "Dream and Fantasy of the Coral Tree" (292ff.) bears an additional heading: "Animus-fish theme." In it, the dreamer encounters a slender youth who is also a fish. At about the same time, Emma Jung comments on a hypnogogic vision with the title "Fish theme." Her wording shows that she was observing an inner process of coming to terms with the concept of the animus:

This image came at a time when the animus still appeared very vague and indistinct. (292, note 45).

Starting in May 1921, the women's gatherings at the Psychology Club were the setting for presentations and discussions on the animus, including a lecture by Emma Jung in 1931.[50] Her published essays show a deep understanding of the concepts of animus and anima.[51] Jung's inclusion of her 1931 paper, "Ein Beitrag zum Problem des Animus," as a chapter in his book, *Wirklichkeit der Seele* (1934), suggests that he recognized her authority on the subject.

The animus takes a more differentiated form in two of Emma Jung's poems from 1924. One of these, "The stone guest," recalls the final scene of Mozart's opera *Don Giovanni*. In it, the poet contrasts two imagined male figures. A noble, otherworldly statue, the "stone guest" of the title, has come to pass judgment on "him who dwells within my heart, who gestures there, pretending to be a king"

---

50 Emma Jung comments on these Club discussions in her 1936 lecture, "On the 20th Anniversary of the Club" (Chapter I, 160 and notes).

51 Emma Jung's 1931 Club lecture on the subject, "Über das Wesen des Animus" (On the nature of the animus), was printed in Jung's *Wirklichkeit der Seele* (1934), under the title "Ein Beitrag zum Problem des Animus" (lit., On the problem of the animus), later translated by Cary F. Baynes with the title "The Nature of the Animus" (47). In 1955, her paper "Die Anima als Naturwesen" (translated by Hildegard Nagel: "The Anima as an Elemental Being") was published in the Festschrift for Jung's eightieth birthday, *Studien zur analytischen Psychologie C. G. Jungs*. These papers were published in English in 1957 as *Animus and Anima: Two Essays*. A German edition, *Animus und Anima*, appeared a decade later.

(253). In another poem, "The stranger" (255), the same statue-like figure reappears, invisible except to the poet's spirit. The poet implores him:

> Clearly, more clearly speak,
> that I may understand
> what thou art come to tell me,
> whose messenger thou art,
> and to what thou callest me.

As described earlier, Emma Jung's 1942 dream of Carl and an eagle (300) depicts an inner male figure, appearing as her husband, in close communion with a powerful spirit symbol.

GÖTTERDÄMMERUNG

The concept of the Self, as the inner god image, central to Carl Jung's mature thinking, emerged in his published work in 1921.[52] In contrast to her husband, however, Emma Jung seems not to have applied this term. Rather, her writings frequently refer to divinity, God, or the gods.

Emma Jung's upbringing in the Swiss Reformed tradition can be detected in passages where she alludes familiarly to biblical passages (e.g., in her 1913 lecture, 122), describes church interiors in dreams (301ff.), or imagines herself singing the words of a Bach chorale (298). In many of her writings, however, conventional religious references are more or less radically reframed. When she writes of God, or the gods, her vision of deity is often deeply ambivalent. What she apparently learned as a girl, in her family or in church, she challenges vigorously and repeatedly as an adult.[53] An example of this challenge is found in her dream of March 1915, about a mouse that goes to Golgotha to gnaw through the cross. In the dream's margin Emma wrote Nietzsche's term, *Götterdämmerung* ("twilight of the gods"). Below the text, she comments:

> Like the squirrel that gnaws the world ash tree, the mouse here is probably supposed to bring down the cross, that the old gods may fall and new ones arise. (265).

---

52 Jung's concept of the Self first appeared in 1921 in *Psychologische Typen* (*Psychological Types*, CW 6, §789–91). Over the decades, his definition of the term evolved, encompassing many concepts, including the transcendent function, the governing archetype at the center of human personality, the inner god image, and the principle of ultimate wholeness, reconciling all opposites. He wrote about it again in his *Beziehungen zwischen dem Ich und dem Unbewussten* (Relations between the ego and the unconscious) (1928) (see "The Mana Personality," *Two Essays*, CW 7, §374–406). His 1948 Eranos lecture, "Über das Selbst" ("On the Self"), became the foundation for chapters 4 and 5 of *Aion*, CW 9.ii.

53 Emma Jung nevertheless remained a lifelong member of the Swiss Protestant church. Her funeral was held in the Protestant Reformed Church, Küsnacht.

This theme, the decline of the old gods and the rise of the new, is found in several of the author's poems from 1919 and 1920. A poem of January 1919 depicts the death of Aranû, her personal god image ("Journey to the Underworld," 295). In 1920 she wrote further poems on this topic, including two titled "Götterdämmerung" (March 1920) and "Götterdämmerung II" (June 1920).[54] The first laments the poet's loss of all her gods, beginning with the blazing star, Aranû. The second assures her that the old gods are still mighty and counsels her no longer to obey but still to respect them. In "Sermo ad vivos,"[55] summer 1920, a poem apparently replying to Jung's "VII Sermones ad Mortuos,"[56] she hears a prophetic voice proclaim that the dying gods must be saved by human beings (245). The poem "Expectation," 8 December 1920, tells how the gods' power has faded and expresses yearning for the dawn of a new divinity (249).

The dependence of God on human beings is a major theme in the verse drama of 1926, "Mystery of the Crusade" (197ff.). This humorously ironic play, written in pseudo-archaic French and modeled on medieval mystery plays, reframes traditional Christian assumptions. Thus, "Le Bon-Dieu" ("The Good Lord") is depicted as an old, not-very-wise male figure, who longs for the humans he banished from Eden and desires to know why life on earth is so dear to men. Finally, he learns that women possess an inner Image (capitalized in the French), an idealized, internal male figure, which may provide the answer. The Good Lord concludes that, if he wishes to become complete, he must give up his transcendence, descend to earth, live among mortals, and learn from them.

Emma Jung's personal vision of the divine, combining godlike aspects with features of the animus, is found in her active imaginations of a figure named Aranû. She first encounters him in June 1916, "stepping out of the black sky—his head a red, blazing star, and in his right hand a flaming sword" (282). A blue bird, symbolizing the dreamer's soul, is under the control of this transcendent figure, who declares:

So you know it, the blue bird? And now do you understand that I have power over you? It is your *soul* in my hand, and with it, you yourself! (282)

The theme of Götterdämmerung returns in the poem describing Aranû's fiery death (January 1919, 294). A fantasy, "Journey to the Underworld," frames this poem and depicts several of its scenes in a symbolic painting (297). During a key scene in the fantasy, an inner guide tells the "I" of the fantasy, who wishes for rescue, that she must use her own power to free herself from the divine (295). Emma Jung's

---

54 These poems appear in the handwritten booklet of her poetry that Emma Jung prepared, in August 1921, as a gift for a friend (see "Preface and Editorial Note," volume introduction, xvi and note.)

55 Latin: a word to the living.

56 Jung, *VII Sermones ad Mortuos* (Seven sermons to the dead), privately printed in 1916. Jung shared this writing with close friends and also with the Psychology Club Zurich. Wider publication occurred only at the end of Jung's life, when he allowed the work to appear as an appendix to his *Erinnerungen, Träume, Gedanken* (*Memories, Dreams, Reflections*), originally published in 1962.

self-liberation occurs first with the conflagration of Aranû, her personal image of the divine. Further elements, woven into the text of the fantasy and displayed in the paneled painting, suggest that she is in the process of liberating herself from traditional divine figures, including the image of God, "the great rogue jester," and even the image of Christ (298).

THE ARCHETYPAL FEMININE

The positive feminine image. In the author's dreams, positive god images frequently blend the feminine with the divine. Two dreams reveal that Christ's body is identical with that of the dreamer. In a dream of June 1915, the dream-ego stands before a painting of Christ and discovers that her body perfectly mirrors his (274). Again, in a dream of September 1915, a girl in a red dress has hanged herself on a stone cross;[57] "and that girl is me!" (275). The dreamer asks why the girl is hanging there; and the cryptic answer comes in the form of two lines paraphrased from a poem found in *Wandlungen und Symbole*:[58]

> Offered to the god
> I myself to myself! (275)

Emma Jung's understanding of this dream differs significantly from her husband's. As published in *CW* 9.i, the dream text concludes with a parenthetical aside: "(Suicide?)," a question that is absent in the original. The likelihood that Carl Jung added this word to the text is supported by his discussion in the following paragraph, where he remarks, "these maidens are always doomed to die." He goes on to observe, "The 'maiden' corresponds to the anima of the man" (*CW* 9.i, §355). He omits to mention his wife's last lines, where she identifies the figure of the crucified girl ("myself") with the god ("myself").

Two further dreams, also published in *CW* 9.i, present a goddess figure associated with the maternal archetype of the bear. In the first of these, "Goddess and Bear" (May 1915),[59] a dangerous bear appears on a forest path, blocking the dreamer, until it is subdued by a feminine guardian—a goddess figure—who descends from the sky. In the second, "The temple of Ursanna" (August 1918),[60] the dreamer enters the temple of a bear goddess, which is also a shrine to the Mother of God. Details

---

57 This dream was later printed anonymously by Jung (see *CW* 9.i. §354).

58 "Thus it is said of Odin (Edda, Havamal): 'I know that I hung on the wind-swept tree / Nine whole nights, / Wounded by the spear, dedicated to Odin, / I myself to myself …' " (Jung, *Wandlungen und Symbole*, 258) (*Psychology of the Unconscious*, 295).

59 Summary presented anonymously by Jung in *The Archetypes of the Collective Unconscious*, *CW* 9.i, §340ff.

60 Summary presented anonymously by Jung, ibid., §342.

in the original dream text include the fact that blood sacrifices are offered in the temple, whose shape is like an equal-armed cross. Through the temple roof one sees the Bear constellation.[61] Worshipers (including the dreamer) must be transformed into wild animals in order to enter. The oracular saying, *Vis ut sis*,[62] inscribed at the temple entrance, is also spoken to worshipers by an image of the bear goddess.

Another positive manifestation of the archetypal feminine, a woman gatekeeper, appears in the author's dreams. As the liminal guardian of a sacred enclosure, her face and body cloaked (figure 6.7), this figure has transpersonal authority. In a dream of November 1928, the dreamer is surprised to learn that she herself is to assume the role of gatekeeper (299). In her commentary on the dream of two churches, October 1945, noting that a woman guards the church, Emma Jung reflects: "It must be a 'Frauenkirche' if it has a female gatekeeper—*Frau*münster" (304).[63]

The author's dream of two churches (301ff.) offers several other positive symbols of the archetypal feminine. In her comments, she notes that wooden building materials (Latin: *materia*)[64] symbolize "the feminine principle" (303). Certain feminine images in this dream are associated with transformation, while their specificity suggests the importance of being an individual within the collective. Thus, commenting on the image of a chancel wall covered with vessels of every kind, the author writes:

> Vessels are feminine symbols *par excellence*; their diversity represents single individuals. (307).

Amplifying the image of church renovation, Emma Jung recalls a conversation that had occurred earlier that day in waking life, during a group discussion of Esther Harding's book, *Women's Mysteries* (301). In the context of her dream, she comments that feminine archetypes need to be interpreted differently in the modern era:

> The main topic of the above-mentioned women's discussion was to establish the connections between the ancient cultic forms of feminine deities and the

---

61 Bear constellation (*Ursa Major*): In an ancient Mithras liturgy described in Jung's *Wandlungen und Symbole* (104ff.) (*Psychology of the Unconscious*, 110), the constellation is described as the axis on which the heavens turn (see *CW* 5, §155).

62 Paraphrased from a passage on loving one's enemy, in Saint Augustine's Eighth Homily on 1 John. In Latin: "Non enim amas in illo quod est, sed quod vis ut sit" (In epistulam Johannis ad Parthos tractatus decem 8.10); "You love in him, not what he is, but what you would have him be" (John Burnaby, trans., *Augustine: Later Works*, Library of Christian Classics, vol. 8, 324). In Emma Jung's dream, the meaning is roughly: "Desire to be what you can be."

63 The Fraumünster (lit., women's minster) is a major cathedral in the city of Zurich, smaller than the double-towered Grossmünster (great minster) that stands several blocks from it. The author's use of the names Frauenkirche (women's church) and Fraumünster departs from their historic meaning. The Fraumünster derives its name from the cloister of Benedictine nuns to which it was originally adjoined.

64 The author relates these words in Latin: *materia* (matter) and *mater* (mother).

psychology of women today. Something ancient, then, that is looked at with new eyes. Perhaps the new shoes fit in here, too. (304)

At the objective level, the search for new shoes could be understood merely as a stereotypical feminine activity. Subjectively, and more importantly, the author identifies the image with her need, as a modern woman, for a new conscious attitude.

The dream's final image is one of openness: a passage connecting the inside of the second, more modern church with the city around it (309). Of this connection, which overcomes the opposition between sacred otherness and daily life, she writes:

> Does it also correspond to the feminine, that religion is not practiced separate from everyday life but *in* everyday life? Both churches therefore on the Bahnhofstrasse? Or does it point to a completely different religious attitude—another *stand*point (new shoes!), not turned away from the world, but connected to it. (309)

Perhaps the most fully realized image of the archetypal feminine in its positive aspect is represented in Emma Jung's painting, which we are calling "Madonna" (above, 78). The background and posture of this figure recall Christian icons of the Virgin of Mercy, while the flora and fauna reveal her association with nature in its nurturing aspect.

The negative feminine image. Emma Jung also writes about the negative or shadow aspect of the feminine archetype, personified in the witch or the evil mother. In her 1913 lecture, "The Tale of the Two Brothers," she discusses the deceptive practices of an old woman whose deadly enchantments endanger the protagonists, until her magic is turned against her and she is defeated (102, 103). A central theme in this lecture is the nature of witchcraft and the need to be psychologically defended from it. Expanding on this theme, the author also discusses "Rapunzel" and other fairy tales about maidens who are held indoors, with only a small opening for their imprisoned libido to escape (108).

Emma Jung's interest in the figure of the witch is shown in a two-page commentary, with the heading "Mother Dreams," probably written in late 1915 or early 1916. Here she gives depth to her depiction of the witch figure, while showing that the theme of the evil mother began to interest her early in life:

> The evil mother—Yve[65]—a kind of malevolent spirit, who plays a role as the wicked fairy or the stepmother in the fairy tale.
> She consumes the libido—i.e., pulls one into the unconscious, creates paralysis.

---

65 The name "Yve" may be Emma Jung's own invention, possibly a variant on Eve.

The sleep-inducing thorn of Sleeping Beauty. It disturbs or prevents relationships.

She is also a close associate, or lives in a mysteriously attractive house, where shady things are going on.

The house is simultaneously hospitable and dangerous, a sort of robbers' den.

She is skilled in magic:

"Know you not the mother's arts?"[66]

Elaborating on the family of the evil mother, the author writes:

> Yve has a son—Ym, a sort of fire spirit—without a body, only flame[67]—also a daughter, the Child of Yve—rather pushed aside—but one stage before "Girl."

A rough, undated diagram, penciled by Carl Jung on the reverse side of one of Emma Jung's paintings,[68] with words crossed out and rewritten, represents an informal commentary on his wife's symbolization of the negative feminine and hints at further connections between her symbolic figures. Some names in the diagram are written in pairs: Artemis/Apollo; Rhea/Lito (dark Isis); Ape/Female Ape; Cerydwen[69]/Ym; Firebird/Rhea. Yve's name is at the center of the diagram. Beside all of these, Emma Jung's image of the negative feminine archetype is present under the name Urgo, a figure from one of her dreams. In the diagram, this name occupies three locations. It is written once below the entire diagram, and again nearby, close to "dark Isis." The name Urgo also appears prominently, sideways in the left margin, with a line that either encloses the entire text or connects this name to the top of the diagram. From Carl Jung's point of view, then, the figure of Urgo is seen as governing and containing Yve and her whole symbol system.

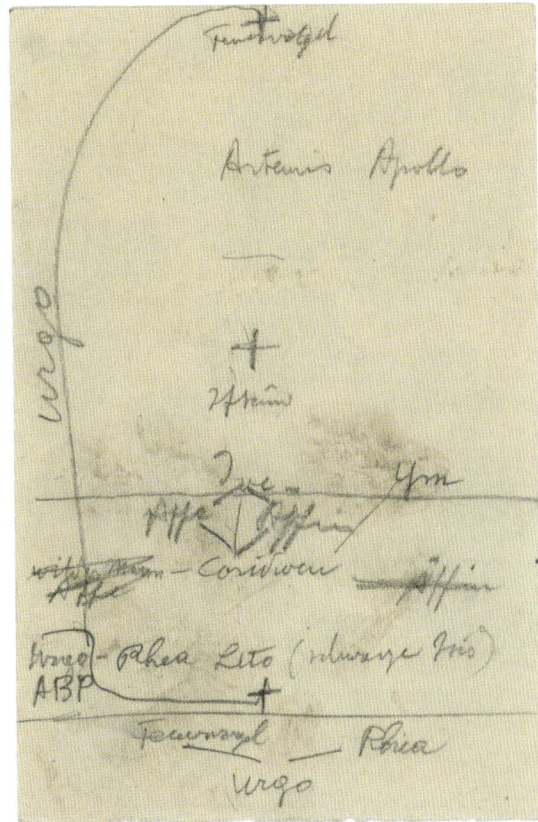

FIGURE ID.5.
[Carl Jung's diagram of Urgo and Yve], undated.

---

66 "Kennst Du der Mutter Künste nicht?": A line sung by Isolde in Act One of Richard Wagner's opera *Tristan und Isolde*, where the "mother's arts" include the skill of mixing potions for both love and death.

67 See Emma Jung's painting of "fire spirits," 310, figure 7.2.

68 This diagram was discovered among unrelated pages of the brown leather notebook. The rapid sketch, not fully legible, was apparently an experiment by Carl Jung, synthesizing his wife's ideas and suggesting further directions for her thinking. Based on the date of Emma Jung's Urgo dream (see below) the diagram can be tentatively dated to December 1915 or early 1916.

69 Here spelled "Coridwen." See reference to Cerydwen in Chapter II, "Thoughts," 173 and note.

Urgo, a shape-shifting dragon, is originally found in the author's long dream of December 1915, partly summarized in *CW* 9.i, *The Archetypes and the Collective Unconscious*.[70] In this dream, the dreamer sees a painting of a dragon holding a young woman captive. In the marbled book, where we find her original version of the dream text, Emma Jung describes the relationship between Urgo and the captive girl as follows:

> Strangely, the girl had no face, so I could not recognize her. Maybe from time to time she had to make the face the dragon dictated. She waits for deliverance. Who has the cunning to capture the dragon? And who has the power to defeat it?

The identity of the dragon is further suggested in the diamond portfolio. There we find a painting of the long-necked dragon with a captive girl, followed by a full-page title: "The Story of Urgo the Magical Dragon." At first glance, it seems that no story follows this title. But on closer reading, Urgo's story is contained in the "Mother Dreams" that follow. Urgo, the shape-shifting dragon, is an image of none other than the negative mother, the witch who lures children into captivity, the possessive parent who drains life energy from an imprisoned daughter.

YEARNING FOR ANOTHER WORLD

In March 1916, Emma Jung wrote:

> If only I could solve the great riddle: why does one yearn for things that do not exist? Where do the images in our soul come from, that do not come from reality? (175)

Her dream and fantasy of April 1915 (268ff.) tells of ruined cities in a primeval forest, built by three brothers in ancient times. A dwarflike man tells the dreamer that, in olden days, the brothers became so obsessed with building their cities that they turned away from life itself, and their cities died. The final scene shows the dreamer alone, struggling to understand who she is, as she waits to be guided out of the forest toward a miraculous city. The dream ends with an oracular poem, commanding her to throw off cloak, shoes, and her very being:

> So shadow-poor, led onward by God's grace,
> Go forth, and of thy yearning find the place! (272).

---

70 Dream summary presented anonymously by Jung in *CW* 9.i, §349.

Many of Emma Jung's poems depict a yearning for a realm beyond ordinary life. In her poem of May 1916, "The wall," outer circumstances, which may be confining no matter how dearly loved, are compared with the inner world of the imagination. This poem is associated with a painting (figure 5.5) and with a dream text. In the dream, the author's childhood city of Schaffhausen has been aggressively renovated, and the dreamer must protect the sacred structures that remain. In the poem, streams rise up to overflow the city wall. They cover "the heavy" and lift "the light," until at last the survivors receive a miracle of liberation:

To the Land Beyond is an open road. (231)

Like her yearning for "things that do not exist," Emma Jung's 1922 Club lecture focuses on a saying of Meister Eckhart (156ff.) that conveys the mystic's paradoxical relationship to an unknowable God. It concludes with the writer's embrace of a type of religious thought, apophatic (imageless) theology, which denies the knowability of the divine. This short lecture echoes the spiritual ache of not-knowing that the author had described eight years earlier in a private writing:

"I don't know." This is the only answer you give me, O my God, after I have wrestled with you for it so passionately? This, then, shall be my salvation, and I must also want this, if there is no other way: not to know. (174)

COSMOLOGY

Like the gods' death and rebirth, the theme of cosmic destruction and re-creation often arises in the author's work. An example is her series of nine paintings with poem-like captions, created in 1917 (310f.), where she pictures the world destroyed by fire and reborn from water.

Nowhere in her work is the theme of cosmology, the generation of the world, more fully developed than in the symbolic experiment that she called "the System."[71] Four notebooks, written between 1915 and 1919, contain her writings and drawings on this topic, leading to the brilliantly colored, composite image (361, figure 7.13) that coordinates many of her cosmological symbols.[72] She began to develop her System in the spring of 1915, in the process of analyzing an interwoven series of fantasies

---

71 Carl Jung called his first mandala painting "*Systema mundi totius*." Ulrich Hoerni explains that the word *systema* means "composition" or "structure" in ancient Greek (*The Art of C. G. Jung*, 16, note 7). Emma Jung's use of the German cognate, *System*, suggests that in 1915 she and her husband were both using the word for their personal cosmologies. See introduction to Chapter VII, 314 and notes.

72 This painting, attributed by Carl Jung to an "erstwhile ... woman patient," appears as a black-and-white illustration in his "Study in the Process of Individuation" (*CW* 9.i, figure 2). There it is said to depict "a world creation," symbolizing "the birth of the Self" (ibid., §550).

and dreams. From these raw materials, her cosmology evolved into an earlier and a later version, both of which are presented in Chapter VII of the present volume.

The author's thought experiment in cosmology was rooted in her dreams and dream commentaries. Personal associations quickly led to abstract questions, theoretical proposals, and symbolic drawings. Some of these drawings, such as the vortex and spiral (322, 333, 351), are actual dream images; in addition, all the drawings in Emma Jung's cosmology are interpreted as if they were communications from the unconscious.[73] Following this method, the author addresses not only the creation of the world, her ostensible subject, but also the formation of human personality through the process of individuation. To provide an entry point into this chapter, an editorial introduction (314ff.) describes the stages of the author's writing process and explores several of the images central to her cosmology.

In approaching these texts, it is helpful to keep in mind that objective and subjective meanings are interwoven in them, as are the outer and inner dimensions of cosmology. Whatever Emma Jung writes about *Weltwerdung*—the physical emergence of a world—also implicitly concerns individuation, the psychological emergence of the individual. This theme, the theory and practice of individuation, is the author's leading concern throughout her creative work.

---

73 For example, in System I the author interprets her color wheel as if this diagram, in all its specificity, had come to her in a dream and could be interpreted as such, including by the method of amplification (see Chapter VII, 340ff.).

Translators' Note

ANN CONRAD LAMMERS AND ALISON KAPPES-BATES

IN DOCUMENTS WRITTEN a century ago, we encounter terms that were accepted uncritically at the time of writing but which present-day readers find culturally insensitive or offensive. In her first lecture, for example, Emma Jung refers to "die Mythen Primitiver" (the myths of primitives, 104). In the educated European environment of 1913, the expression "primitive" was understood not as a derogatory judgment but as an objective descriptor (104, note 17). Rather than translating the term with a phrase outside of the author's thought world, we have kept such problematic expressions as written. Supported by occasional annotations, readers are asked to accept such terms, as readers contemporary with Emma Jung would have done.[1]

The policy of the translators has been to use gender-inclusive language consistent with the plain meaning of terms in German. The word *Mensch*, which in German applies to both sexes equally, is routinely rendered "human being" or

---

1   In one case we have softened an expression that cannot be read today without a strong reaction. Fritz Schultze, an early sociologist whose writings are quoted in Emma Jung's lecture "On Guilt," tells a story concerning "ein Kaffer" and "die Kaffer," words whose racist context is unavoidable today. The meaning of the story is clearly conveyed by translating these terms "a native" and "the natives" (Chapter I, 136).

"person," rather than "man." Likewise, the collective noun *Menschen* is rendered "people" or "humanity" rather than "men" or "mankind." Where the original language does not permit such variants, we follow the author, who, consistent with German grammar and the convention of her time, used the masculine pronoun to mean both male and female.

Translations of quoted passages are provided, as far as possible, in previously published English versions. For the most part, Emma Jung cited her literary sources with care. Occasional citations, however, required special research. The author's incomplete citations to passages in Hesiod (143, 144) required searching in the original Langenscheidt edition. In her lecture "On Guilt," a statement within quotation marks (134), easily mistaken for a passage from Tertullian, turns out to have no equivalent in Tertullian's writings. Instead, it is a statement that the author, apparently inspired by the Church Father, attributes to the soul.

In supplying passages from previously published English translations, we have chosen those that come as close as possible to the language quoted by the author. For example, among several translations of a passage from Nietzsche's *Also sprach Zarathustra* (130), we chose Thomas Common's version, as being most faithful to Emma Jung's interpretation of the passage.

Emma Jung's discussions of the Grail legend, as found in her lectures "The Tale of the Two Brothers" (100ff.) and "On Guilt" (131ff.) and her abstracts of Club lectures (Appendix A, 363ff.), include references to source materials in several languages.[2] Following the copyrighted English translation of *The Grail Legend*,[3] we spell characters' names according to the source in question. Thus the central figure in Chrétien de Troyes and Robert de Boron is Perceval, and in Wolfram von Eschenbach, Parzival. The knight commonly known in English as Gawain appears here primarily, from French sources, as Gauvain. The names of a few places and characters are Anglicized: for example, Uterpendragon, a British king, is given the English spelling, Uther Pendragon.

The author's personal Bible was Martin Luther's German translation. Her biblical quotations are generally from that source. Corresponding passages in English are taken from an early revision of the King James Version, published in 1901 by the American Revision Committee (New York: Thomas Nelson & Sons), whose title page declares it to be "the version set forth A.D. 1611, compared with the most ancient authorities and revised, A.D. 1881–1885." When the author paraphrases a biblical text, we translate her paraphrase faithfully, with annotation.

In translating Emma Jung's poems and "Mystery of the Crusade,"[4] we have sought to capture her use of rhyme and meter as far as possible, also paying

---

2 Medieval poets, as noted, are her major sources. In her first lecture she also refers to Richard Wagner's opera *Parsifal*, with its alternative spelling of the protagonist's name.

3 Emma Jung and von Franz, *The Grail Legend*, English translation by Andrea Dykes, 1970.

4 In this volume, Ann Conrad Lammers is the primary translator of the author's verse play (Chapter IV) and poems (Chapters III, V, VI).

attention to her diction level and her use of sound. Since it is famously difficult to do justice to poems in translation, the author's original text of each poem is published beside our effort in English or, when necessary, in a footnote.[5]

The translators have rendered both the author's meaning and her style as faithfully as possible. Emma Jung's attention to literary style is visible in every genre, with the possible exception of Chapter VII, "The System: A Cosmology." There she consciously ventures into a symbolic field, combining physics and philosophy, that, as she herself admits, stretches her abilities as a writer.

We are grateful to Thomas Fischer for his critical oversight throughout.

---

5   Where possible, the original text of each poem is printed on a facing page or pages. In Chapter VI, where poems often occur within the context of a fantasy or dream, the original texts are found in footnotes.

FIGURE 1.1.
Sapphire shield
amid the clouds of
becoming. Painting
by Emma Jung,
undated.

I

Lectures

1. The Tale of the Two Brothers

1913¹

ONCE UPON A time there were two brothers, the one rich and wicked, the other poor and good-natured. The rich brother was a goldsmith, while the poor brother was a broom-maker with twin sons who, now and again, were given some scraps to eat from the rich brother's table. One day, the poor brother went into the woods where he saw a golden bird at which he threw a stone. A golden feather fell to the ground which he took to his brother, the goldsmith, who gave him money for it. When the poor brother also brought him a golden egg, his brother said he wished to have the bird itself. Eventually, the poor brother was able to kill the bird, for which his brother gave him a lot of money. The rich brother, who was clever and crafty, knew what kind of bird it was and he ordered his wife to roast it, making sure that no part of it was lost: he wanted to eat it all by himself. The children of the poor brother, who happened to be in the kitchen, got to eat the heart and liver of the golden bird. When they awoke the next morning, they each found a gold piece under their pillow. And so it was every morning thereafter. The envious goldsmith convinced his brother that the devil had a hand in it and he should therefore send his sons away, into the woods. This came to pass. There, the brothers met a hunter, who took them in and taught them how to hunt. He kept their money safe for their future. When they were grown up, both brothers had to pass the test of shooting a particular bird from a flock of wild geese flying overhead, after which they were declared accomplished hunters. They decided to set off into the wide world. When the brothers took their leave, along with giving them guns, dogs, and their pieces of gold, their foster father gave them a bright knife. He advised them that if they were to separate from each other, they should plunge the knife into a tree at the point where their ways part. Upon returning to this place, each one would be able to see how the other brother was faring by the state of the blade: if the blade facing the direction in which the brother had gone were bright, he would still be alive, but if it were rusty, he would be dead.

The brothers soon reached a large forest where they wanted to hunt to still their hunger. A hare passed by. When one of the huntsmen wanted to kill it, it cried out,

"My dear huntsman, if you let me live,
Two of my young to thee I shall give."²

---

1   The author prepared and wrote this lecture in 1913. Its presentation was postponed until the fall of the following year, due to her pregnancy and the birth of Helene in March 1914.

2   von der Leyen, ed., *Brüder Grimm*, 15. Emma Jung's retelling of "The Tale of the Two Brothers" is based on this edition of *Brüder Grimm*, 12–32 (translated here by A. Kappes).

It brought two of its young, both of which pleased the huntsmen so well that they took pity on them and could not kill them. The same thing happened with a fox, a wolf, a bear, and a lion, from each of which they took two of their young with them. When they later separated, they shared the animals in such a way that each got one of each kind. Then they bade each other farewell and thrust the knife into a tree, whereupon one went east and the other west.

The younger huntsman soon came to a town that was draped in black, where he was told by the innkeeper that the king's daughter, the only remaining maiden in the town, was going to be given to a dragon that demanded its yearly sacrifice and that no one had yet been able to vanquish. If someone were to appear who could do so, he would win the hand of the princess. Together with his animals, the huntsman climbed the dragon's mountain. He came to a little church with an altar upon which stood three full goblets inscribed with the words, "Whosoever drinks from these goblets will become the strongest man on earth and will be able to wield the sword that lies buried at the threshold of the church."[3] The huntsman then tried to dig up the sword, but he was only able to do so after emptying the three goblets. Accompanied by her father and his courtiers, the king's daughter soon approached the foot of the mountain. When she saw the huntsman standing on the mountain top, she thought it was the dragon and was terribly afraid. But when she reached the summit, there stood the young huntsman who wanted to rescue her. Speaking words of comfort to her, he locked her inside the church. The seven-headed fire-spewing dragon now drew close, snorting as he came. After a mighty battle and with the help of the animals, the dragon was finally vanquished. The king's daughter, who had fallen into a swoon, awoke and saw that she had been saved. As a reward, she divided her coral necklace among the animals. She gave the hunter her handkerchief that bore her name, and in it he wrapped the seven tongues he had cut from the dragon. Both lay down to sleep; and, one after the other, all the animals who had been posted to watch over them also fell asleep. Then the marshal, who had watched from afar, climbed up the mountain. When he found everyone deeply asleep, he cut off the huntsman's head and carried off the king's daughter. When she awoke, he threatened to kill her if she refused to say that *he* had slain the dragon, to which she finally agreed, providing the marriage be delayed for "a year and a day."[4]

Meanwhile, the animals had woken up and were horrified to see that their master was dead. Quickly, the hare was sent to a distant mountain to gather a life-giving root that grew there. When it returned, the root was placed in the hunts-man's mouth, whereupon his head was rejoined to his body, and the huntsman came back to life. Saddened by his loss, he roamed the world with his animals, having them dance before the people. After a year had passed, he returned to the same town, which was now draped in scarlet in anticipation of the marriage of

---

3   Ibid., 17.
4   Ibid., 20.

the king's daughter to the marshal. With the help of his animals, the huntsman was able to make himself known to the king's daughter and to be invited to the castle, where, by showing the dragon's tongues, he was recognized as the rightful dragon-slayer. His marriage to the king's daughter was celebrated, and the deceitful marshal was put to death.

The two lived happily together. As he had been a hunter, one of the young king's chief enjoyments was to hunt. There was a forest nearby that was said to be enchanted. The idea of hunting there greatly appealed to the young king, and he did not rest until he had permission to do so. He rode out to the forest with a large following. Once there, he caught sight of a snow-white doe, which he pursued, telling his followers to wait for him at the edge of the forest. When evening came and the king had not returned, his people rode home to report what had happened. Meanwhile, the hunter had chased the doe without catching it, and he soon found himself so deep within the forest, there was no response when he blew his horn. Moreover, night had fallen, he was unable to find his way back. Having decided to spend the night in the forest, he sat at the foot of a tree and lit a fire to keep himself and his animals warm. While they were sitting around the fire, he thought he heard a human voice groaning. After searching for some time, he discovered an old woman sitting in the tree above him, complaining that she was freezing. The huntsman suggested she come down to warm herself, to which she replied, "No, your animals will bite me. ... I will throw you down a rod[5] from the tree. If you strike them on their backs with it, they will not harm me."[6] He did what she said, and instantly the animals were still, for they had been turned into stone. The witch then sprang down and touched him, too, with the rod. He, too, was turned into stone, whereupon she threw them all into a ditch where other similar stones lay.

It just so happened that at this time the other brother arrived in the kingdom on his travels; he had not been able to find a position and had been wandering about, having his animals dance before the people. One day, it occurred to him to go and look at the knife in the tree trunk. He found his brother's side to be half bright and half rusty, from which he concluded that his brother must be in grave danger. He quickly set off to see if he could save him.

When he reached the city, people mistook him for his brother, the young king, for they looked as similar as two drops of water. Even the young queen mistook him for her husband and was astonished when he placed a double-edged sword between them in bed every night. He thought it wise to let the people be deceived about his identity, to give himself a greater chance of rescuing his brother.

---

5   *eine Rute vom Baum:* The word *Rute* has several meanings, including "switch," "rod," "twig," "staff," "stick," "wand." Emma Jung's psychological commentary (below, 126) gives it a symbolic meaning.

6   von der Leyen, ed., *Brüder Grimm,* 28.

CHAPTER I

After making enquiries about the enchanted forest, he told the old king that he must once again go hunting there and set off with a large following. All that had happened to his brother then happened to him. But when the witch threw down the rod, he said, "I shall not strike my animals with it; come down, or I will come up after you,"[7] and he fired at her, but she was not harmed, for she was impervious to lead. He then loaded a silver button from his jacket. She could not protect herself from it and fell with a scream. He threatened to throw her on the fire if she did not tell him what she had done with his brother, and he forced her to bring all the stones back to life.

The twin brothers embraced and rejoiced greatly. After they had seized the witch and burnt her to death, the forest opened up and became bright and full of light, and the royal castle could be seen three leagues away. The brothers set off together for home, telling each other of their fates along the way. But when the older brother described how the whole town had mistaken him for his brother, and that he had had to dine and sleep beside the young queen, the younger brother grew jealous and cut off his head. He instantly regretted killing his savior, and the hare was sent to quickly gather the root that brings the dead back to life. Together with their animals, the two brothers then reached the town, and no one was able to tell them apart. The king's daughter eventually recognized her husband by seeing whom the lion with the golden clasp followed. That evening she asked him why he had placed a double-edged sword between them in the bed the previous nights. Only then did he realize how loyal his brother had been.

The theme of brothers is ageless.[8] Almost everywhere on earth one finds legends and myths of brothers and pairs of friends who are described as being either inseparable or enemies, or both simultaneously. Best known are probably the Greek Dioscuri[9] who, according to the legend, Zeus produced with Leda. Like their Indian equivalents—the Ashvins[10]—whose name means "those who are provided with horses"—the Dioscuri are also always thought of in connection with horses. According to the oldest Laconic ideas, they preside under the earth, but alive not dead, and in later versions they shift and are soon to be found both in the light and in the underworld, and, finally, they exchange places, which means they are always apart. The Palici,[11] the Molionidae[12] (see Roscher),[13] Theseus and

---

7 Ibid., 30.

8 One of Sigmund Freud's letters to C. G. Jung, dated 13 October 1911, lists several legendary pairs of brothers (Freud and Jung, *The Freud/Jung Letters*, 448ff.). Some of these pairs are discussed at length in Emma Jung's lecture.

9 Dioscuri: twin brothers in Greek and Roman mythology, named Castor and Polydeuces (Latin: Pollux). Dioscuri is derived from "sons of Zeus."

10 Ashvins: twin brothers in Hindu mythology, sons of the sun god, known as "the Horsemen."

11 Roscher, ed., *Lexikon der Mythologie*, 1281–95. In Sicilian and Roman mythology, the Palici are twin brothers, variously described as sons of Zeus, Hephaestus, or a Sicilian god, Andranus.

12 Molionidae: in Greek mythology, the conjoined twin sons of Molione and Poseidon.

13 Roscher, ed., *Lexikon der Mythologie*, 3106.

Pirithous,[14] Achilles and Patroclus,[15] as well as the Germanic Alcis,[16] etc., also belong to this category.

We also come across pairs of brothers or friends in the myths of primitives:[17] with the Cora Indians, where they are in the form of the morning and evening star; or in the myths of other American native peoples, where a pair of sun-born brothers play an important role in creation. A pair of brothers or friends can also be found in African myths, and indeed there, as in our story, we find one brother who is rich and the other who is poor, or one who is loved by the father and the other who is not. In Homer's *Iliad*,[18] the Dioscuri are characterized as "Castor, the hero on horseback[19] and the hand-to-hand combatant, Polydeuces," while in the *Upanishads* they are described in the following way:

> Two pretty-winged, closely bound friends—
> they hug one and the same tree;
> one of them eats the sweet berry,
> The other, not eating, only looks on.[20]

In cosmology, the pair became known as day and night,[21] and soon as the evening and morning star, as sun and moon, or as heaven and earth. By mutually affecting each other while simultaneously excluding each other, they are recognized as life and death, or as a dualistic principle in general. In the Atman doctrine of the Upanishads, they are posited as knowledge and ignorance—transience and eternity. There it is stated that:

---

14 Theseus and Pirithous: in Greek mythology and in Homer's *Iliad*, the hero Theseus was close friends with Pirithous, who was a demi-god and king of the Lapiths.

15 Achilles and Patroclus: heroes and close friends during the Trojan War, described in Homer's *Iliad*.

16 Alcis: in Germanic mythology, a twinned pair of young gods. Tacitus, in his *Germania* (c. 100 CE), compared them to Castor and Pollux. Like them, the Alcis were associated with horses and riders.

17 *in den Mythen Primitiver*: Emma Jung's use of the word "primitive" reflects late nineteenth- and early twentieth-century thinking. Her frame of reference includes the anthropological and ethnological works of the period. Although the term has pejorative connotations today, at the time it was considered neutral or even positive. Thanks to Robert Segal for casting light on the historical context.

18 *EJ*: *Odyssey* (XI, 300) (*Iliad* IV, 237). [The Jung family library in Küsnacht includes the Faesi edition of the *Odyssey* in ancient Greek. German translations, available when Emma Jung wrote this lecture, include *Homer, Odyssee*, translated by Rudolf Alexander Schröder (193), and *Homer, Ilias*, translated by Thassilo von Scheffer (62). Footnotes found in Emma Jung's original typescript are introduced, as here, with her initials: *EJ*. When the editors supplement the author's notes, these additions are enclosed in square brackets.]

19 *EJ*: (Literally, "the one who steers horses.") [Comment deleted by author.]

20 Here and below, Emma Jung quotes the German translation by Deussen, *Die Geheimlehre des Veda*, 176. The translation of this verse is from an English edition of the same book: Deussen, trans., *Sixty Upanishads of the Veda*, 583.

21 *EJ*: Jung, *Wandlungen und Symbole*, 269ff., under "Light quality of the horse." [Emma Jung's use of quotation marks ("Lichtqualität der Rosse") suggests a section or chapter title. The topic is discussed on the pages cited, but no equivalent title appears. See *Psychology of the Unconscious*, 308ff.]

The two are contained in a latent condition in the eternal, infinite, highest Brahman—the ignorance is *evanescent*, knowledge is *permanent*.[22]

Like every true mythical figure, the significance of the pair is found in their transformation according to the needs of the time and the place, while yet remaining always basically the same. Just how the myth of psychology in our time can be similarly understood, namely, how, in Complex Psychology,[23] it can be seen as a representation of sacrifice and rebirth, we have seen elucidated in Carl Gustav Jung's *Wandlungen und Symbole der Libido*. It is surprising to note that symbolic expressions for events that take place in the world are equally valid for events that take place within the individual, which would tempt one to conclude that there is a general parallelism, if one were not also able to think that, ultimately, it is only through the same images—through analogies within the confines of our mind—that we can understand what happens both within and outside ourselves.

I have indicated above which outer events are represented by the brother theme, and I shall not further elaborate on this, although there is much that could be said. Instead, I would like to try to shed light on the psychological states and processes they express. If we want to analyze a fairy tale or a dream on the subjective level, we have to begin by saying that all the figures that appear in it correspond to tendencies within the *individual psyche*. We may then assume that the hero of the fairy tale represents a main tendency of the dreamer, and the minor figures, minor tendencies.

If the hero appears in double form, as a pair of friends or brothers, we may expect them to represent two equally strong, complementary or opposing tendencies. The image of two brothers is particularly apt to represent something that belongs together and yet is not one, something which is the same and yet different. In myths and fairy tales, this contrast is also expressed in one of the two being light, while the other is dark. Knowing as we do from *Wandlungen und Symbole der Libido* that light is a symbol of libido,[24] perhaps we may say that of the two tendencies, one has more libido than the other, or one seems more *positive* and the other more *negative*, or one is conscious, the other unconscious. The same may be true when one is beautiful and the other ugly, when one is evil and the other good, or, as in our fairy tale, when one hero is rich and the other is poor. This is consistent with the premise that, depending upon the amount and nature of ego energy that we invest in it, something seems valuable to us, or not. As modern-day parallels, I have found the same inner division expressed in some acquaintances' dreams[25] by an

22 Deussen, trans., *Geheimlehre des Veda*, 178; *Sixty Upanishads of the Veda*, 319. (Italics added by Emma Jung.)

23 In the early years of Jung's career, his theory was called Complex Psychology. Later, the term was changed to Analytical Psychology.

24 Jung, *Wandlungen und Symbole*, chap. 3, 155ff. (*Psychology of the Unconscious*, 179).

25 At the time of writing, Emma Jung's practice as an analyst had not yet begun. (See "Emma Jung and Analytical Psychology," volume introduction, 5of. and note.)

overachieving businessman and a restrained monk, or by two female friends, one of whom was frighteningly thin.

Our two brothers are given further distinction by the one being a rich goldsmith and the other a poor broom-maker. Instruction on the significance of gold, the treasure or hoard, as libido, is to be found in *Wandlungen und Symbole der Libido*.[26] It would now be interesting to say a few words about the meaning of the smith, who is also a typical figure in myths involving gods and heroes, for example Hephaestus, Prometheus, *Wayland the Smith*,[27] and Siegfried the blacksmith.[28] The celestial smith is a figure who appears widely in Indo-Germanic mythology. He was originally a fire god, to whom the creation of the first human being, and thus of the entire human race, is attributed. Thus, at Zeus's command, Hephaestus, the celestial smith of the Greeks, fashioned Pandora, the first woman, who, as a punishment for Prometheus's theft of fire, would blight humankind. Of the Finnish celestial smith Ilmarinen, it is said that he fashioned the vault of heaven from iron on his anvil, and then went on to forge a wonderful woman out of gold.[29]

Fire is essential to the smith: it is impossible to think of a smith without thinking of fire. "To forge"[30] means to hew, to carve, to fashion; and a "smith" is someone who uses fire, the divine spark,[31] the libido,[32] to create something artful. Based on this, one could see in the rich goldsmith the *tendency toward extraversion*, where libido is directed toward the outside and creates realities. We have also learned in our studies on the libido[33] that the forest and the tree are understood to be symbols related to the mother, or more precisely, symbols of introversion.[34] So in the poor brother—although he is not, as in so many fairy tales, a wood-chopper or a charcoal-maker, but rather a broom-maker, who prefers to live in the forest—we may recognize the other tendency of the libido, namely, that of *introversion*. And just as the return to the mother or to introversion does not mean *only* regression and death, but rather should lead to rebirth, here, too, the poor brother has an advantage over his rich brother, whose focus is in the *present*; namely, he has a hope, which is also a promise for the future, in the form of his twin sons. In extraversion,

---

26 Jung, *Wandlungen und Symbole*, 329, 341ff., 350, 363 (*Psychology of the Unconscious*, 383ff., 398ff., 409ff., 421).

27 Title of Wagner's opera, *Wieland der Schmied* (Wayland the Smith). In Jung's *Wandlungen und Symbole* we find Wieland der Schmied, Siegfried, and other celestial smith-figures who are mentioned in Emma Jung's lecture. Whenever the author quotes or paraphrases her husband's work, she is conscientious in citing page references. When, as here, she gives no citation, we may infer that she is relying not on her husband's research but on her own.

28 In Wagner's opera *Siegfried*, the hero is raised by dwarfs and trained as a blacksmith.

29 Mannhardt, "Die lettischen Sonnenmythen," *Zeitschrift für Ethnologie*, 320.

30 *schmieden*: The verb in German is cognate with the noun, *der Schmied* (smith).

31 Roscher, ed., *Lexikon der Mythologie*: Hephaistos, 2035–73.

32 Jung, *Wandlungen und Symbole*, 135–65 (*Psychology of the Unconscious*, 157–90).

33 Ibid., 219ff. Emma Jung's phrase "our studies on the libido" reflects the fact that she had worked with her husband in preparing *Wandlungen und Symbole*.

34 Ibid., 239ff.

in the act, fulfillment is already present; but introversion holds the germ of the future, from which life grows and constantly renews itself.

With these twins, we encounter a doubling and rejuvenation of the theme; and, at the same time, they are the heroic pair whose fates we must now follow. The first thing we learn about them is that they receive the scraps from the table of the rich, i.e., that at least a part of the libido falls to that aspect of the personality which the two boys represent, thereby creating the possibility of the opposites becoming balanced. Here one recalls the parable of poor Lazarus, who nourishes himself with the crumbs that fall from the rich man's table and attains eternal bliss, while the rich man, who had good things on earth, must suffer the torments of hell.

One day, the father of the twins, the poor brother, sees a golden bird in the woods that he hits with a stone, whereupon a feather falls to the ground, which he then sells to his brother, the goldsmith. He later finds a golden egg, and finally he manages to kill the bird itself, which he also brings to his brother, "who knew what it was." Here, we already see a certain interaction between the two tendencies: the treasure that is found in the forest—in introversion, in the unconscious—is sold, turned into money, i.e., translated into reality.

The golden bird is a typical fairy tale figure and is one of the many magical things—for example, golden or green branches, stones, flowers, and so forth,— that bring good fortune and power to those who are somehow able to obtain them. This precious object that is difficult to obtain, and whose attainment usually involves some kind of sacrifice, is nothing other than the libido and is invariably found at a place that can be represented by a symbol of the mother—tree, woods, cave, enchanted palace, and so on. Thus it can be identified as an immersion into the darkness of the soul, in other words into the unconscious, or as a state of introversion.

To return to our fairy tale: the poor broom-maker takes the precious objects he has happened upon to his brother, who better understands how to translate things into reality. Naturally, the brother immediately wants to eat up the precious bird all by himself, that is, to devour the libido that in fact belongs to the other person. This tendency of the libido to continue blindly in any direction it has once set out upon can have a fateful outcome for the individual concerned, as we shall see from our fairy tale. Vital organs in particular have a lasting vivifying effect,[35] and in our fairy tale, too, those who eat the heart and the liver find a gold piece under their pillow each morning. From what was said earlier, this may be understood as a symbol of irrepressible libido.

Through a particularly fortunate coincidence, the poor brother's children get the scraps to eat and experience their beneficial effect. The rich brother becomes

---

35 *EJ*: One recalls Tobias, who regained his vision from the liver of a fish. [In the apocryphal book of Tobit, the healing of blindness through the gall of a fish is recounted in chapter 11, where it is Tobit, the father of Tobias, whose sight is restored.]

envious. Making his brother believe that the devil has had a hand in it, he compels him to send his children away, specifically, into the woods. Here, I have to make a small digression to look a little more closely at this motif of "sending-the-children-into-the-woods" that crops up so often, and in such a stereotypical way, that I feel I may not disregard it. That the heroes of so many legends and myths, such as Siegfried, Roland, Parzival,[36] the son of Genoveva,[37] and others, spend their early youth in the forest, then leave the forest to go out into the world, may be explained by the mother symbolism of the forest. But what does it mean if children who have already left their early childhood behind them are sent into the woods? In some fairy tales, for example in "Hansel and Gretel," in "Mary's Child" in a slightly different form, or in "The Three Little Men in the Woods," they are sent away by their parents who wish to be rid of them. In others—for example in "Little Brother and Little Sister"—the children themselves flee from their evil parents.

Particularly helpful in understanding this detail, in my view, is its presentation in the fairy tales "Rapunzel," "Allerleirauh" ("All-Kinds-of-Fur"), and "Iron John." Rapunzel's mother eats lamb's lettuce (*Rapunzel*) stolen from the garden of an enchantress, whereupon she has a child whom she calls Rapunzel. When Rapunzel is twelve years old, she comes into the power of this enchantress, to whom she actually owes her existence. The enchantress locks her inside a high tower in the woods, whose only point of entry is a single window, through which the enchantress—and later, the prince—will be drawn up by holding onto Rapunzel's long hair. Maid Maleen is similarly locked into a tower in a forest.

The enchantress to whom one owes one's existence can be nothing other than the *libido*, which begins to assert itself in a threatening way in the growing child. But the child is unable to meet these demands; indeed, it can barely understand them, and thus it falls into a state of inhibition which, in the fairy tale, is aptly portrayed as being locked inside a tower by a powerful enchantress. A striking detail is that the only connection to the outside world is through long hair.[38] In this connection, I would like to recall the introverted patient mentioned in *Wandlungen und Symbole der Libido*,[39] who, as a child, was able to busy herself for hours with boring holes and scratching at walls, and who later did the same thing to her head in her drive to create a way for her imprisoned libido to escape.

---

36 The spelling of this name depends on context. Here, the author appears to mean the hero of the epic poem *Parzival* by Wolfram von Eschenbach. Elsewhere in this lecture she refers to the hero of Wagner's opera *Parsifal*. In Emma Jung's later writings on the Grail, when she discusses medieval French sources, the name is spelled Perceval (Appendix A, 363ff.).

37 In a medieval legend, Genoveva of Brabant was a virtuous wife, falsely accused, who fled to the forest with her son and raised him there.

38 *EJ*: In "Maid Maleen," a bread knife bores a hole into the wall—a symbol drawn more from the area of nutrition. [Sentence deleted in text by author.]

39 Jung, *Wandlungen und Symbole*, "Die Verlagerung der Libido als mögliche Quelle der primitiven menschlichen Erfindungen," 135ff. (In *Psychology of the Unconscious*, this case is discussed in "The Transformation of the Libido: A Possible Source of Primitive Human Discoveries," 157ff.)

It seems to me that, in a different form, this theme is also found in the fairy tale of "All-Kinds-of-Fur" and many other similar tales. The figure called All-Kinds-of-Fur resembles her deceased mother so strongly that her father desires to marry her. The only way the girl finds to protect herself is, finally, to win *time* by requesting that a mantle be made from a thousand different types of fur. Using this ugly cover as protection, she then flees to the woods. The ghastly, repellent mantle, under which the shining hero hides—think of "The Frog Prince" or the bear in "Snow-White and Rose-Red"—may mean introversion, among other things.

I would like to go into one of these fairy tales in rather more detail, for in it this theme is particularly well presented. It is the tale of "Iron John."

While out hunting in a forest, a king comes across a wild man who is covered with hair and whose skin is brown, like rusted iron. Here, the corresponding feminine figure of Kundry[40] also comes to mind, and similarly, the companion of Gilgamesh, *Eabani*,[41] who was brought out of the woods, and to whom I shall return later. The king takes this wild man, whom he calls Iron John because of his coloring, home with him and locks him in a cage, *the key to which the queen* looks after. The primitive libido, represented by the wild man,[42] is restrained.

One day, the eight-year-old prince's ball falls into the cage of the wild man, who only gives it back to the boy on the condition that he open the cage, the key for which he must first steal, tellingly, from under the pillow of his mother. After he has freed Iron John from the cage, the boy becomes afraid and flees with the wild man back into the woods. Once there, he must take care of a crystal-clear golden spring, making sure that nothing falls into it, thereby tainting it. While he is sitting there, watching the golden fish and snakes float by in the water, his finger suddenly begins to hurt so fiercely that he involuntarily dips it into the water. When he pulls it out, it is covered in gold, which he tries in vain to wash off.[43] The next day his finger begins to hurt again. He runs it through his hair, and a hair falls into the spring. On the third day, while sitting by the stream, *he does not move his finger, no matter how much it hurts*. But time passes slowly, and he looks at his reflection mirrored in the water. As he leans further and further over the water to look into his own eyes, his hair falls from his shoulders into the water. He draws back quickly, but his entire head of hair is already golden and glistens like the sun! No matter how hard he tries to push it all under his cap, somewhere a little of it shows and can no longer be hidden. Realizing that the boy is no longer able to

---

40 A character in Wagner's opera *Parsifal*.

41 When this lecture was written, Gilgamesh's wild companion was commonly known as Eabani. After further study of the ancient cuneiform tablets, he is now known by scholars as Enkidu.

42 *EJ*: The wild man, representing the youthful life force, still plays a role in Basel, where he is ceremoniously welcomed as a symbol of spring when he comes down the Rhine. As an inviting and promising figure, his image is also popular on inn signs.

43 *EJ*: Similar to Mary's Child, who cannot wash the gold from the forbidden chamber off her finger.

take care of the spring, Iron John sends him out into the world with the promise that he will come to his aid if he is ever in need of help.

One is hard put to think of a finer and more apt description of the libido manifesting in an adolescent: after early childhood is over, at the age of eight, a considerable amount of libido that has been bound up, locked inside a cage, becomes free and detached from the mother—the key lies under her pillow. Unless it is put to some new use, this libido causes only *anxiety*, and it therefore immediately becomes introverted again—the boy goes into the forest with the wild man. Once there, he anxiously takes care of the golden spring, ensuring that nothing pollutes it. But something arises within him, like a dull search for something he does not understand. He can only experience it as a pain in his finger, which he is unconsciously driven to dip into the water. The longing and the urge within his soul become ever stronger, while the pain in his finger becomes increasingly unbearable, and it takes all of his strength for him just to be able to keep his hands still. Motionless, he stares into the spring and *catches sight of his own image* there, and all at once, he knows what he is searching for. Drawn by the irresistible force to see his own reflection, he leans further and further over until, finally, his long hair falls into the water, and when he pulls it out, it is completely covered with gold. He tries in vain to hide his head, which shines like the sun. He is completely overwhelmed by his libido, and the golden glow shines through everywhere. Only one thing can follow this powerful breakthrough of libido from the unconscious: going out into the world, into the greater outer reality. Thus, this hero, too, is sent out into the world by the wild man, with the assurance that he will always come to his aid.

From all these examples, one might perhaps conclude that these episodes equate with a period of introversion and represent some kind of protective measure for the individual. Among indigenous peoples, we also find the custom of putting youths who are about to enter manhood into isolation for a time during which they have to endure great hardships and perform all sorts of difficult tasks to test their virility. Around the same age, and precisely at this difficult phase, we celebrate confirmation, thereby channeling the libido of children into religion and away from outer reality.[44] In his novel *Der grüne Heinrich*, Gottfried Keller describes extremely well the effect of this first stormy influx of love:[45]

When I pressed her to me and kissed her so violently, and she in her bewilderment responded, we had tilted the cup of our innocent delight too far; the draught had spilt over us with a sudden coldness, and the almost inimical bodily sensation had dragged us right down out of heaven. These consequences of

---

44 *EJ*: (Christ in the temple!) [Comment deleted in text by author. Apparently referring to the three-day visit to the temple by the twelve-year-old Jesus, without his parents' knowledge (Luke 2:41–51).]

45 Keller, *Der grüne Heinrich* (Green Henry).

an emotion that had welled up in such innocence and affection between two young people, who had acted in just the same way before, as children, without any uneasiness, would appear ridiculous to many people; but it did not seem to us a joking matter, and it was with real grief that we sat beside the water that was not one whit purer than Anna's soul. I had absolutely no suspicion of the true reason of the terrible occurrence, for I did not know that at that age one's red blood is wiser than one's understanding and checks itself of its own accord whenever its waves are stirred into an excessive tumult.[46]

Thus, the libido, too, must first reach maturity, and to do so it must undergo a time of introversion or incubation, before it can be brought into reality in the right way.

To find one's libido is only the first step along the path, the goal of which is *to be its master*. Thus, our brothers, too, first have to undergo a period of apprenticeship before they can employ their riches. That is why they are sent into the woods, where they are taken in by a hunter who teaches them his skills, and who puts aside their still unneeded pieces of gold for the future. Once they are grown up and have successfully fired a trial shot, they are declared hunters and are free to leave.

Here I must say a few things about the figure of the hunter, for it cannot be without some deeper significance that it is precisely the skill of hunting that the brothers must learn. That the fate of our heroes is typical is shown by the fact that their career begins with the same activity that early humans began with—*the hunt*. In the word "hunting" lie both the idea of pursuit and capture, as well as the irresistible driving force of desire. To pursue libido, to catch it and seize it again and again, is the skill that the human being must learn above all others. Thus, Siegfried, who has been raised in the forest, learns first to hunt and then the skill of the forge. Likewise, as with so many other heroes, Tristan's and Parzival's skill at hunting is expressly emphasized. In fairy tales, too, the figure of the huntsman is tremendously common, for example, in the well-known fairy tale "Little Red Riding-Hood" in which she is swallowed by a wolf and is freed by the hunter. This fairy tale is also a particularly good example of the parallelism between the sun myth and the myth of libido. In the ancient world of legends and myths, the hunter plays a similarly significant role—Nimrod, Orion and Odin are perhaps three of the most well-known.

First and foremost is Nimrod-Gilgamesh, the Babylonian hero, whose story is the most ancient hero/hunter myth that is simultaneously a sun myth. The name and its meaning are debatable, although several Assyriologists have translated it as "shining light."[47] This is not far from the equally uncertain derivation of the name Orion from *var*, "to shine," as cited by Wilhelm Roscher, which would somehow

---

46 Ibid., 290.
47 Jeremias, *Das alte Testament im Lichte des alten Orients*, 266 (translated by A. Kappes).

fit and seems plausible, given the correlation of hero-sun-libido.[48] Orion is the Greek hunter, who, transposed to the stars, indulges his passion for hunting for all eternity. According to the legend, Orion, who assaulted Merope, the daughter of King Oinopos, was blinded as punishment for his concupiscence and, to have his eyesight restored, had to cross the sea and wander eastwards toward the rising sun. Power-hungry Nimrod-Gilgamesh, who has lost his friend and helpmate, laments, '[M]y eyes (then) want to see the sun, and I, to satiate myself with brightness. The darkness is (so) empty. [...] When shall the dead see the radiance of the sun?"[49] And he crosses over the sea, the path that otherwise only the sun-god can use, to his ancestor, Utnapishtim, the only human to survive the great flood, in order to bring back the life-giving herb for his friend.

In my view, the third of these great hunters—who are very closely related if not identical to the eternal wanderers—is *Odin*, whose myth closely parallels the Gilgamesh-Orion myth. As a wild huntsman with a fierce army he has, in accordance with his northern character and view of life, a much rougher countenance than his southern brothers. Odin lives on in German legends and, like Orion who chases the Pleione and their daughters through the forest, he preys upon the woods folk: libido personifications like brownies, thumb-sized folk, and manikins.

Odin, too, loses an eye, but not as punishment for his carnal desire, like Orion in the Greek legend, which uses more feeling-toned language. It is for a drink from Mimir's well of wisdom that this northern god sacrifices an eye. There is a verse in the *Rig-Veda* that explains very well why Odin, a wind and soul god, is also a hunter, with the typical trait of concupiscence:

The Wind (Vāyu), verily, is a snatcher-unto-itself. Verily, when a fire blows out, it just goes to the Wind. When the sun sets, it just goes to the Wind. When the moon sets, it just goes to the Wind.

When water dries up, it just goes to the Wind. For the Wind, truly, snatches all here to itself.—Thus, with reference to the divinities.

Now with reference to oneself.—

Breath (*prāna*), verily, is a snatcher-unto-itself. When one sleeps, speech just goes to breath; the eye, to breath; the ear, to breath; the mind, to breath; for the breath, truly, snatches all here to itself.

Verily, these are two snatchers-unto-themselves: the Wind among the gods, breath among the vital breaths.[50]

---

48 Roscher, ed., *Lexikon der Mythologie*, 1017ff.
49 Jensen, *Das Gilgamesch-Epos*, 27 (translated by A. Kappes).
50 *Chandogya Upanishad*, Third Khaṇḍa, 4.3.8, in *Thirteen Principal Upanishads*, 217.

It would be going too far to enumerate all the other parallels, and it would add little to the proof we have already won from our understanding of the three world huntsmen mentioned above. As the one who hunts down libido and seizes it, the huntsman signifies an initial stage of cultural as well as individual history. Whoever is in command of the art of hunting is ready to embark upon his path in the world.

Our brothers, who can no longer bear to stay in the woods, feel drawn to leave, to perform deeds and to have adventures. As huntsmen, they set off together and encounter various kinds of animals, one after the other, that they would like to shoot; but when the animals ask to be spared, they take pity on them and in their place are given two young ones each. Thus, the first deed that our hero pair performs is of a negative nature: although they are driven, by the thrill of the hunt and by hunger, to kill animals, the deed that they actually perform, out of pity, is to refrain from giving in to this urge. It is a *sacrifice*, which is not without beneficial results.

Seen purely from the outside, one could imagine that this compassion toward animals is meant to educate, and is aimed at the tendency toward cruelty in both children and primitive[51] people. But it also surely has a deeper psychological determinant, and in order to understand this, we need to first ask the question: what, in fact, is cruelty? Perhaps one might say that the strength or weakness of the expression of cruelty or its opposite, compassion, is evidence of the cultural level that has been achieved by an individual or by an entire nation. Of course, there is also cruelty among animals, but there it is actually more a matter of ruthlessness and savageness, which is how nature in general operates. What differentiates human cruelty from cruelty in nature is that the former essentially serves its own purpose and is carried out with a certain delight.

From this attribute, peculiar to human beings, we must assume that it has come about either through culture or as a result of it. Human development has been a continual, tremendous struggle between our progressive and regressive tendencies. The force of the animal drives is so great that any progress was only possible at first by completely denying and repressing them, before daring to fight them openly. One sees this process particularly well in the development of religions, where, at some stage, animal sacrifice and asceticism have almost always played a conspicuous role.

This repression, however, has not only rendered anti-cultural tendencies harmless, but has also paralyzed a number of extremely valuable forces; and this mutilation, which makes it impossible for an individual to comply with his own inner laws, must be perceived as an act of cruelty.

---

51 In context, the author may be referring to modern individuals whose psychology is at an infantile stage of development.

Thus, one could say that human cruelty is a kind of projection onto the outside,[52] a projected representation of being tortured within, which, in turn, is intimately connected to the progression of culture. The Christian faith has advocated the transformation of ancient cruelty into compassion. That compassion and cruelty are closely related is evident in the word "compassion" itself:[53] shared suffering makes the pain more bearable. The way compassion differs from cruelty is that it is no longer a projection, but a reversal. It is not the creature that has to suffer with the human being, but rather the human being who has to suffer with the creature. Compassion can only be achieved, then, if we are willing to suffer. Christianity taught us to direct our cruelty inward, against ourselves—in asceticism, for example—and to turn our compassion outward. It did this by making us aware of a feeling of which, until then, we had only had a vague sense, namely, that we are all limbs of the same body, and that we are all brothers. But now, we need to learn to direct this feeling not only outward, but also inward, and to have compassion toward every part of our own selves that deserves it. This development is not a matter of simply eliminating or turning old attitudes into their opposite, but rather of creating out of them new possibilities for the future. Overcoming the inner animal does not mean killing, but rather transforming it.

This same thought may be expressed in the custom of the sacrificial meal. When the one who is making the sacrifice consumes what is being offered in sacrifice—or a symbol of it—in a shared meal, this means one is offering something in one form and then taking it back into oneself again, so that it may be resurrected in a new, more perfect form. Whether one shares the meal with the god, or whether one believes one is ingesting the god himself, this union always results in transforming what is lower into what is higher. The transformation is in accordance with the enigmatic law of development, to which humanity and all creatures knowingly or unknowingly, forced or voluntarily, must submit.

In our fairy tale, the fecundity of the sacrifice is reflected in the gift of two young ones for each brother, given out of gratitude by the animals, who then accompany them to help them on their way, and who repay them for their lost quarry by showing them the way to a village where they are able to still their hunger. This brings us to the theme of helpful animals, which we also know from the libido-work,[54] where the animal is seen as a libido symbol.[55] In this work we also see how gods and heroes are frequently accompanied by an animal, or an animal-like being, that is occasionally even referred to as a brother or friend—Gilgamesh and Eabani, for example. About this, it is said, "the hero and his horse" appear

---

52 *EJ*: projection through collective feeling onto the body of humanity. [Phrase deleted in text by author.]

53 *Mitleid*: lit., "suffering with." The English word *compassion* is based on Latin roots having the same meaning.

54 *Libidoarbeit*: reference to Jung's *Wandlungen und Symbole der Libido*.

55 *EJ*: which contains within itself the sexual and mother symbol. [Phrase deleted in text by author.]

CHAPTER I

like an artistic formation of the idea of humanity with its repressed libido, whereby the horse acquires the significance of the animal unconscious, which appears domesticated and subjected to the will of man.[56]

Whether the animal is depicted as an animal that can be ridden or, as in so many myths, as a mother who provides nourishment, the meaning is basically the same. Both have one thing in common: *they support human beings*. Both represent that undifferentiated primal form of the libido from, or *upon*, which the human being grows. These forces that stem from the "animal unconscious" that unceasingly provides man with nourishment from the inexhaustible source of life, are, then, the helpful animals in fairy tales. These are the powers that we refer to as the divine in humankind. It is common knowledge that many peoples hold some animals to be sacred, and that they not only sacrifice but also revere their gods in animal form, as did, for example, the ancient Egyptians. It is probable that the totem animal, which was sanctified and revered as progenitor and was consumed once a year, also belongs to this category. This is also true of those myths in which the hero is created out of a human being's union with a divine animal—Leda with the swan, or Europa with the bull.

Thus, the episode with the helpful animals in our fairy tale shows, on the one hand, the forgoing of something animal-like—greed and cruelty—but also, on the other hand, it teaches: "Let the animals live"; for it is only with their help that something great can be achieved. It is this complexity that often makes it so difficult to understand and interpret both the dream and the fairy tale; they are like a fugue, the musical themes of which appear and are developed first in one voice and then in another, and it is sometimes not easy to follow the artistically interwoven lines and to tell them apart.

We often find these secret forces that exert an influence from the unconscious in the form of animals in fairy tales. In "Cinderella," for example, the birds relieve her of her heavy task, or in the fairy tale "Puss-in-Boots." It can be a fox, a snake, or some other kind of animal that helps the hero accomplish his most difficult tasks. In some fairy tales, the helpful animal proves to be a bewitched prince, for example in "The Fisherman and His Wife," or "The Frog Prince." This demonstrates both the ability of these animals to transform and just how valuable they are. Sometimes dwarves and brownies inhabit the role of the animals, and their underground or otherwise invisible activities also symbolize the unconscious source of the libido's power.

Alternatively, the animal is replaced by a friend or brother who is often equipped with animal traits. This is the case in the fairy tale "Iron John," mentioned earlier, in which the "wild man" helps the hero to overcome all of his difficulties. We find this same wild man again in the epic of Gilgamesh, which impressively address-es the problem of all of these forces interacting, and shows us that our human

---

56 Jung, *Wandlungen und Symbole*, 268 (*Psychology of the Unconscious*, 267).

conflicts today are basically the same as they were 4,000 years ago. The fragments of clay tablets upon which the epic, or at least a part of it, is preserved come from the library of Ashurbanipal, 668–626[57] BCE, who commissioned the writing down of traditional stories that had been orally handed down over centuries.

The story of this epic is roughly as follows.[58] The great hunter and powerful hero Nimrod-Gilgamesh incenses the gods by abusing his power and oppressing his people. The gods decide to send him an adversary, and they create a likeness of the sky god Ânu, called Eabani, whose long hair falls down in waves over his hair-covered body and who moves through the wilderness as a shepherd and protector of animals, grazing with the gazelle in the forest and drinking with them at the spring. A hunter seeks him out and, with the help of a temple slave, lures him into the city where he is to fight Gilgamesh. The night before Eabani arrives, Gilgamesh dreams that a star falls on his back, like an army of the sky god Ânu; and he cannot shake it off, for it is stronger than he is. Eventually, he presses himself upon the man-star, as upon a woman, and lays him at the feet of his wise mother, who makes him equal to Gilgamesh, as it literally says. After his mother has interpreted this dream as signifying his future companion, Gilgamesh greets Eabani when he arrives and, instead of fighting him, becomes his friend. Following Gilgamesh's union with the natural or wild man, a union that is portrayed in the dream as giving him equality or brotherhood with the fallen star, the two of them together successfully perform various heroic deeds. Eabani, however, is not at ease in the town and suddenly flees back to his animals, only to discover that he is no longer comfortable there either, and therefore he returns to his friend. That this union was not a complete success can be surmised from Eabani's repeated states of anxiety and his unfortunately all-too-fragmentary dreams.

This surmise is confirmed when we learn that Eabani sinks one day into a deep sleep from which he does not wake up. What Gilgamesh thereby loses is expressed in his lamentation, "Since his death, I find no 'life', wandering around like a hunter in the desert!"[59] Nothing less than life itself is lost with the loss of this animal brother. To find it again, Gilgamesh wanders through the desert and over the wide sea, until finally, in the distant west near Utnapishtim, he is able to procure the life-giving herb, which is unfortunately stolen from him by a snake on his return journey. Similarly, in the legend of the Chidr, the fish that Moses was carrying "miraculously made its way into the sea."[60] Thus, after losing the precious herb through his own

---

57 The author left a question mark after the second date. Ashurbanipal's death is dated 628 or 627 BCE.

58 The author's summary follows Jensen, *Das Gilgamesch-Epos*, 1–54.

59 Ibid., 22 (translated here by A. Kappes).

60 Jung, *Wandlungen und Symbole*, 186 (*Psychology of the Unconscious*, 218). In Hinkle's translation, this phrase is quoted from a translation of the Koran by J. M. Rodwell, whose rendering, "took its way in the sea at will," differs substantially from Jung's rendering in *Wandlungen und Symbole*. When such discrepancies arise, it is our policy to convey the meaning and tone of Emma Jung's text, while noting the conflict with the previously published English edition.

carelessness, Gilgamesh returns home, and at the end of the epic we find him the same power-hungry tyrant as he was at the outset, vainly trying again to conjure up his vanished companion. In another version, this same libido appears as a faithful servant, just as it does in the fairy tales "The Frog Prince," "Faithful John," "The Maid Maleen," and in the Faust legend, where it has a demonic character.[61]

In Faust's servant, who is "part of that force / which would do evil evermore / and yet creates the good,"[62] the dangerous nature of this elemental libido is suggested: it can develop into something evil as easily as into something good. This theme also appears in its evil aspect in the fairy tale "The Goose Girl." There the handmaid robs the princess and takes her place, only to be recognized as the false bride and punished. The theme of two brides—the true and the false—that we so often come across in fairy tales and legends, fits into this category. I shall not go into this in more detail here, but will just add that in the fairy tale of "Maid Maleen," the true bride is simultaneously the handmaid of the false bride. The latter betrays herself when she is unable to answer the questions put to her by her bridegroom, and always replies instead,

"I must go to my maid
Who keeps my thoughts for me,"[63]

which nicely captures the essence of who the handmaid is.

Kundry, the servant of the Holy Grail,[64] is also this same type of elemental being. This split that inhibits development is also vividly portrayed in the fairy tale "Ferdinand the Faithful and Ferdinand the Unfaithful." When he sets off into the world, Ferdinand the Faithful—who, by the way, is assisted by helpful animals—meets Ferdinand the Unfaithful who accompanies him, and who, through the wicked arts, knows all of his thoughts and intentions, which he tries to prevent being carried out. The fairy tale also shows that Ferdinand the Unfaithful is actually just another aspect of the helpful horse, to whom the hero owes his success. After Ferdinand the Faithful has had his head cut off by his bride and has been healed again at the end of the story, Ferdinand the Unfaithful disappears quite suddenly from the scene, and, equally surprisingly, Ferdinand the Faithful's white horse is transformed into a prince.

---

61 *EJ*: According to the latest research—unfortunately I do not know the source to be able to cite it—the name Mephistopheles—for which there is no certain etymological explanation—can be translated as "helper," "servant." [Comment deleted in text by author.]

62 Goethe, *Faust, Part One*, translated by David Luke, 42. This is Mephistopheles's self-description, in the scene "Faust's Study," ll. 1336–37.

63 von der Leyen, ed., *Brüder Grimm*, 54.

64 Kundry is a major character in Wagner's opera *Parsifal* (1882). This 1913 lecture by Emma Jung contains her earliest public references to the Grail legend, which became a central focus of her writing and teaching over the following decades. Her cited sources at this time include Wagner's opera libretto and the epic poem *Parzival* by the medieval poet Wolfram von Eschenbach (1170–1220).

The fairy tale "Faithful John" particularly emphasizes the faithful nature of the servant, who can understand the language of the animals and is therefore able to avert any threat to his master. Because of his master's mistrust, however, his efforts are only half successful, and he is turned into stone until his master realizes what he has lost and redeems him by sacrificing his children. Now that we have seen that the helpful animals mean the same thing as the brother, friend or servant, it comes as no surprise that from now on we need only pursue the fate of the one brother and his animals, while the other disappears for the moment.

Perhaps we may infer from this that a certain development has taken place, namely, that within the psyche, whose two halves were perfectly undifferentiated at first—the two brothers look as similar as two drops of water—different currents of various qualities have formed that find their symbolic representation in the animals, each with its own pronounced characteristic. As we shall soon see, the princess, whose redemption represents the pinnacle of the hero's journey, adds a further differentiation.

Before I go into this, I would like to discuss the farewell scene. At a crossroads, the brothers pledge their eternal loyalty to each other and thrust the knife given to them by their foster father into a tree. This knife serves as a common reminder, and it has the magical quality of being able to show the fate of each brother. Each side of the knife corresponds to one brother; it continues to shine as long as he lives, but rusts as soon as he dies. According to primitive beliefs, a weapon, an item of clothing or some other article of daily use is intimately connected to its owner; for these things form, as it were, a part of oneself and share one's destiny, even if they are spatially distant. This idea is behind all those magical acts that give one power over another person by getting hold of one of these used objects and doing something with it, in the belief that the same thing is happening to the person in question.[65]

The custom of thrusting in a knife or banging in a nail is used as a defense against the evil eye.[66] Sometimes, too, a knife is buried under a doorstep for the same purpose. In this context, it may mean a fixed amount of libido. Knives and weapons are well-known symbols of libido. They are *affixed* or hidden; and nails, also serving this purpose, are "a means to affix" *par excellence*.

In the British Museum in London, I saw wooden fetishes completely covered with hammered-in nails and knife blades. Whenever a certain undertaking was planned for which the deity's help was solicited, a nail was hammered into the fetish as a mutual *reminder* and to reinforce the contract.

It is probably meaningful that this [act of affixing] should serve as a protection against the evil eye. For, with some study of the material, one gets the impression

---

65 *EJ*: In his book *Magic Art*, Frazer gives many examples of this. Thrusting the knife into the tree is the equivalent of setting aside a certain amount of libido that may only be accessed under very specific circumstances. Unfortunately, I was unable to find much proof material to add here. [Sentences deleted in text by author. Cf. Frazer, *The Magic Art and the Evolution of Kings*, 52–54, 174–214.]

66 *EJ*: See Seligmann, *Der böse Blick und Verwandtes* [The evil eye and the like], 273–76.

that fear of the evil eye means nothing other than a fear of losing one's libido, a fear that it will be drained by another, stronger person. In view of how little control one has over expending or holding onto one's libido, this fear does not appear unfounded. Instead of acknowledging one's lack of power, one projects it outwards, to be confronted by it again as a dangerous, overpowering force. This also wholly agrees with primitive thinking, which equates a symbol with reality and seeks protection from this danger through sympathetic magic, a symbolic affixation.

Another instance in which the driving-in of a knife has a similar meaning is found in the legend of Iphicles,[67] which dates back to pre-Homeric times. The seer, Melampus, who understands the language of birds, promises King Phylakos to find out why his son, Iphicles, remains childless, and to discover a cure for it. He learns the origin of Iphicles's weakness from a vulture: once, when Phylakos was castrating a ram, he saw his young son Iphicles performing some obscene deed. Greatly displeased, he threatened to use his bloodied knife to do the same thing to the boy that he was doing to the ram, and when the boy fled in alarm, *he plunged the knife into a sacred oak tree standing nearby.* Bark grew over it, but Iphicles lost his potency. If the knife were removed, the rust on it scraped off and added to the wine that Iphicles were to drink for ten days, he would produce an heir. It all unfolded as the vulture said it would, and the prediction came true. Here we see how the libido of the king's young son—in this instance, his sexuality—makes its presence felt in an inappropriate moment and is used in the wrong way, and, as a result, becomes bound to a tree, or introverted, which results in the loss of his potency. He only regains it after he has re-integrated the libido, represented by the knife.[68]

The ceremony our two brothers perform upon taking their leave of each other is thus a kind of magical act that affirms their belonging together; for a shared portion of their libido is set aside, as it were, to be available in any later emergency. We now follow the younger brother and his animals, and we arrive with him in a town draped in black, in which the king's daughter is about to be sacrificed. Just as space and time flow into each other in a dream, so, too, in fairy tales one can replace the other. Thus, when setting out on his journey to reach the castle of the Holy Grail, Wagner's Parsifal says,

"I scarcely tread,
   Yet seem already to have come far."

To which Gurnemanz responds:

---

67 *EJ*: See Mannhardt, *Antike Wald- und Feldkulte aus nordeuropäischer Überlieferung* [Ancient cults of forest and field, in Northern European tradition], 30ff.

68 On introversion during puberty, see p. 110 above.

"You see, my son,
Time here becomes space."[69]

If we think of a fairy tale as a symbolic depiction of an inner development, then the episode beginning: He arrived in a town in which a sacrifice was about to take place, means something like, He reaches a place, a moment in his development, in which a sacrifice is being asked of him. While it is a repeated demand—the monster claims an annual tribute—this time it involves something particularly valuable, the king's daughter. She is the embodiment of the "treasure difficult to attain," as well as our own infantile attitude, which we love and hold so dearly that it is hard for us to imagine anything more difficult to sacrifice.

We are familiar with a monster demanding an annual sacrifice from mythology and legends: I mention only the legends of the minotaur, of St. George, and of Tristan. Just how close the animal here is to the divine is evident in those versions where the deity demands the sacrifice, as, for example, the Taurian Artemis. According to Frazer, dragons, snakes, and other animals are both royal totem animals and symbols of an elemental power.[70] Thus, for example, on Knossos, the bull was both the totem of the king and a sun symbol; the vulture had the same meaning in Egypt. In the Semitic Moloch we find the monster revered as a deity, to whom children were sacrificed. In ancient Ireland it was a gold-plated idol, and for the Kutonagua Indians of British Columbia it is the sun itself to whom first-borns are sacrificed, to bring good fortune and fertility.[71]

Almost universally, it is the child or youthful individual who is sacrificed, often the child of the king himself, though occasionally replaced by a slave, a prisoner or an animal.[72] In many cases it is the son who is killed, because the father fears being replaced by him and therefore gets rid of him. This is the case, for example, in the well-known myth of Chronos, who devours his children because an oracle has said that one of his sons will dethrone him. Frazer attributes all these legends to real events, where the father actually did kill the son who wanted to rule. A typical example of this is the ancient Swedish king Aun who, according to legend, sacrificed nine of his sons to Odin in Upsala in order to prolong his life, each time by nine years. When the Swedes did not allow him to sacrifice his tenth son, he finally had to die. Perhaps such cases did occur; but, in my view, their immortality owes much more to their innate symbolic value, which is still valid today. In some cultures, for example among the Greeks and some primitive peoples, a child of the king was sacrificed in order to avert deformity, drought or famine. Thus, we see how ancient and deeply rooted is the notion that life is renewed by sacrifice.

---

69 Wagner, *Parsifal*, 22.
70 Frazer, *The Dying God*, 82.
71 Ibid., 183ff.
72 Ibid., 160ff.

Closely related to these legends of sacrifice to the monster are legends of its conquest by the hero.[73] The myth of a battle with a dragon is to be found almost everywhere in the world; I shall only mention the Babylonian myth of Marduk's battle with the night-snake, Tiamat, out of whose body the world is later created. According to the *Rig-Veda*, after the God Indras defeats the dragon Virtra, who held the waters captive, the dammed-up rivers flow into the ocean, fertilizing the earth along the way.

Apollo kills Python, the dragon that guards the source Delphousa and watches over the ancient earth oracle, an act that fills Apollo with guilt from which he must later cleanse himself. Cadmus similarly slays the Theban dragon that guards the source Dirke. In the Persian *Hymns of Avesta*,[74] the evil demon is a black horse that guards the rain waters and must be overcome by a white horse. We know that water, by virtue of its fertile qualities, is a much-used symbol of elemental libido; and treasure in a cave, guarded by a dragon, has the same meaning. The same is true, of course, of the maiden guarded by a dragon, and of the dragon that ravages the land, whose destructive effect can only be avoided through sacrifice or conquest.

Returning now to our fairy tale: the hunter is faced with the task of vanquishing the dragon and redeeming the princess, a situation that, after all that has been said, can readily be translated into its psychological meaning. An indication that we are here dealing with an inner content, represented by various people in the story, is the fact that, from afar, the princess mistakes the huntsman, who should free her, for the dragon. This gives a similar double meaning to the princess, who is both the one sacrificed and the one redeemed. Death and liberation are so closely bound together that one easily confuses the one with the other and forgets that the willingness to sacrifice simultaneously means salvation. Almost the same thing is expressed in *Wandlungen und Symbole der Libido*:

> The hero striving toward the mother is the dragon, and when he separates from the mother he becomes the conqueror of the dragon.[75]

Let us now look more closely at the circumstances of the dragon fight. On the dragon's mountain the huntsman finds a chapel, inside which are three goblets bearing these words: "Whosoever drinks from these goblets will become the strongest man on earth and will be able to wield the sword that lies buried at the threshold of the church."[76]

---

73 Jung, *Wandlungen und Symbole*, 243ff. (*Psychology of the Unconscious*, 280ff.).

74 Ancient religious text, supposedly written by Zoroaster. In Emma Jung's typescript, the name reads *Tishtryalied* (Hymn of Tishtrya). In the *Hymns of Avesta*, Tishtrya is the benevolent deity who rules over rainfall and fertility.

75 Jung, *Wandlungen und Symbole*, 350 (*Psychology of the Unconscious*, 410).

76 von der Leyen, ed., *Brüder Grimm*, 17.

Introversion prior to performing a deed—as here, in the refuge of a church—is characteristic of the hero myth. It is represented in *Wandlungen und Symbole der Libido* by the image of union with the mother for the purpose of rebirth.[77] We find this image of *going within* or *collecting oneself*, before performing a great deed, in Christ on the Mount of Olives,[78] in Odin, who hangs in a tree for nine days and there invents the runes,[79] and in many other places, some of which have been mentioned above.

In the chapel, the huntsman finds a writing that tells him what he has to do to become the strongest man and to wield the magical sword. Not only courage and strength are necessary to overcome the dragon; rather one must first be empowered by a special consecration, the emptying of the three goblets. The magical potion that imparts superhuman strength is a very common, universally known theme. The same is true of the sacrificial potion that signifies union with the deity or the entrance of the latter into the human body. It is also interesting to note that in Mexico and Rhodes, the sacrificial victim was made drunk, thereby making them, it was thought, possessed by the spirit of the god.[80]

The significance of the goblet as a symbol of time casts a special light on our situation. To prepare for the task ahead, the hero must first empty three goblets; that is, a certain amount of time must be spent meeting the prerequisites. In other words, he must first become *ready* for the deed.

The goblets also spontaneously bring to mind the chalice of the Gospel and Christ's words: "Is it not possible for this cup to pass from me?"[81] This and the expression "cup of sorrow and pain" may indicate how this readiness is achieved. Once the hero has fulfilled this condition, he is able to dig up the sword and is ready to do battle. We spoke earlier about digging up or plunging in a knife or sword, and discussed how this is a symbol for an introverted amount of libido and, in some circumstances, for a sum of libido that needs to once again be freed. Here, however, I would like to bring to mind *the sword that Wotan thrust into the tree*, that could only be withdrawn by the one called to do so, and then only in the greatest need. The sword under the threshold means the same thing and is also dug out by the hero only in the direst of circumstances. Thus armed, he goes to confront the furious,

---

77 Jung, *Wandlungen und Symbole*, 262 (*Psychology of the Unconscious*, 302).

78 The Mount of Olives is mentioned in the three synoptic gospels: Matthew 26:30–35; Mark 14:26–31; Luke 22:39–46. The theme of introversion is illustrated better, perhaps, by the passage that follows in two of them, concerning Jesus's solitary prayers in Gethsemane: Matthew 26:36–46; Mark 14:32–42.

79 A verse depicting Odin hanging on the tree for nine days is found in *Wandlungen und Symbole*, 256; in the DTV edition, 258 (*Psychology of the Unconscious*, 295). Emma Jung quotes this verse, slightly paraphrased, as a comment on her dream showing the image of a girl on the cross (Chapter VI, 275).

80 *EJ*: A further interpretation of the goblet is given by Nork, though from a somewhat tenuous source. [Sentence in text deleted by author. Nork's *Der Mystagog* is listed in the Jung library catalog.] [Hubert and Mauss, *Mélanges d'histoire des religions*, 41.]

81 Author's paraphrase of Jesus's prayer in the Garden of Gethsemane (Matthew 26:39; Mark 14:36) and on the Mount of Olives (Luke 22:42) (translated here by A. Kappes).

snorting, devouring and fire-spitting dragon, whom he is able to overcome with the help of his animals by cutting off its seven heads, keeping its tongues as a trophy. The princess, who had been confined inside the church during the battle, where she had fallen into a swoon, wakes up liberated and, out of gratitude, shares her coral necklace with the animals, while giving her handkerchief with her name upon it to the hunter. That she is giving herself to him with her gift is evident if one knows that for primitive people one's name and the bearer of it are one and the same thing, both equally real. Some primitives cannot be persuaded to give their name to a stranger, out of fear that by doing so, they will be in their power. I would also bring to mind those magical incantations that gain their power by speaking the name of a deity or daemon. By its frequent use or intensive contact with the body of its owner, a piece of cloth can become representative of the owner; for example, the veil of Veronica that bears the face of Christ after coming into contact with his sweat and blood.

With the dragon overcome and the princess redeemed, one might think that the fairy tale is over. But this is not the case. The situation that has been attained is not an end, but rather a beginning. Failure to recognize this is extremely dangerous, a fact that even our hero cannot escape. Worn out from battle and confident that he has won and survived the danger, he lies down to rest with the maiden. One after the other, the animals who have been charged with watching over them also fall asleep; thus no one notices or prevents the approaching evil—in the form of the marshal. He is therefore able to sneak up on them, to chop off the huntsman's head, and to carry off the princess.

It is typical that the hero does not die in battle. Feeling elated by victory, the real danger is the peace and security he believes he is entitled to succumb to afterwards. This brings to mind all those myths and fairy tales in which, as the result of some small error—forgetting a word or a gesture, losing some herb or some other seemingly worthless object—the entire heroic deed is reduced to nothing; or those heroes who, after having survived the greatest dangers, are cunningly slain by some small animal, or by someone from behind who they thought was a friend. Christ's words, "*Watch* and pray, that ye fall not into temptation,"[82] address this one vulnerable spot through which the hero can be overcome by death. To recognize a danger is to have it half-defeated; more dangerous, however, are those enemies who approach from behind or while we sleep.

For this reason, being unable to sleep probably has, in some cases, a deeper meaning. Instead of trying to fight it, one should actually try to understand the warning of the unconscious: "You may not sleep right now; not at any price may you now rest; rather you must find out who is your enemy who threatens you," which, in psychological terms, means to give thought to the nature of the danger that is not allowing you to fall asleep.

---

82 Matthew 26:41, Mark 14:38. Emphasis added by Emma Jung, who slightly paraphrases Martin Luther's translation.

Unfortunately, we pay far too little attention to the advice of the unconscious, or we only understand when it is too late. Therefore, we suffer the same fate as Siegfried, who pays no attention to the voice that warns him and, in blind faith, presents his weakest spot to his enemy, thereby sealing his own death.

What the myths express, we also find among native peoples in their fear of a loss of soul. In his book, *The Perils of the Soul*,[83] Frazer has collected a great deal of material on this subject, listing the thousands of dangers that threaten the "soul," including the diverse and curious means and ceremonies that humankind believes will hold these dangers at bay. Here, we see clearly that the fear of losing one's soul—one's libido—appears to be, in fact, *the* fear of primitives. Upon closer inspection, we find that it is still *the* fear and *the* threat to modern man. I cannot elaborate here on how fear of the evil eye, the ceremonies aimed at repelling it, and the innumerable primitive taboos basically boil down to this one point—the fear of a loss of soul. I would, however, like to present a few examples that fit our case particularly well.

On the island of Celebes, according to Frazer, it would appear that a victorious hero returning home after a battle, or a bridegroom, is considered to be particularly in danger of losing his soul, for both are especially at risk of feeling sure of themselves. At the dangerous moment of moving into a new house, ceremonies should be performed to encourage the soul to remain. A loss of soul can also be suffered while hunting, which is why when a hunter leaves the woods, he must never forget to lure back his soul that might still be swirling around somewhere outside himself.[84]

In ancient times, and with indigenous people still today, there is also the belief that the soul leaves the body during sleep, and that it is dangerous to suddenly awaken a sleeping person, for the soul may not have had time to return to the body. While one sleeps, the night-demon or some other evil spirit comes, who steals one's soul—one's child—or sucks one's blood. The hero of our fairy tale is also killed while he is asleep, and is robbed of his hard-won treasure. The princess (we know what she represents) falls into the hands of the marshal, a usurper who has *stolen* the treasure and not *earned* it. This important detail is telling of the psychological situation: the hero is killed and replaced by the usurper. In other words, while he was capable of winning the treasure, he was not capable of keeping it. As soon as he thought he had the princess, he was stricken by megalomania and became a usurper. He had first to die and to rise again, before he could truly call her his own.

This resurrection is only possible because of the animals, for they are merely asleep, and the hero alone is killed. Once again, it is the elementary libido— to which we owe our ability to regenerate—in the form of the helpful animals, that creates inexhaustible vital energy and is always ready to undergo some new

---

83 Frazer, *Taboo*.
84 Ibid., 35ff.

transformation. The hare, a familiar symbol of fertility, gathered the life-giving root that was put into the dead hero's mouth, which at once brought him back to life. Belief in the existence of life-giving fruits, herbs, or roots is widespread: I need only mention the Tree of Life in the Garden of Eden, the herb of immortality in the epic of Gilgamesh, the apple of the Iduna, the magical flower in fairy tales.

These same miraculous things that bring life can also bring death, such as the apple of the Garden of Eden, the thorn tree of Odin, or the apples in the fairy tale of "Snow White." The symbolism of ingesting, in the sense of "becoming one with something," is discussed above.

After the hunter had been brought back to life, it pained him to see that the princess had disappeared, and he sorrowfully wandered off again with his animals, which he set to dancing in front of the people. Thus, he is exactly where he was before. Only after a year of wandering did he arrive in the town of the princess, now draped in scarlet to celebrate her marriage with the marshal, which was stopped at the last minute by the hunter's appearance. Through the intercession of his animals, he made himself known to the princess; and after proving himself to be the true slayer of the dragon by showing the dragon tongues, he married the princess and became king himself.

Parsifal, too, after forfeiting the Holy Grail through his ignorance, had to wander the world until he was ready to assume his role as the Grail King and guardian of the shrine.[85] That so many fairy tales reach their climax and end with the hero becoming king can be explained by the fact that it is not only the highest wish of children to become king and attain power, but that it was, is, and always will be one of humankind's highest achievements to have dominion over those reluctant subjects, the "people of his soul," as Spitteler puts it in his novel *Imago*.[86]

Now, the fairy tale continues, the young king lived happily ever after with his queen, until one day his joy in hunting prompted him to hunt in an enchanted forest. There he saw a beautiful, white doe and, leaving his companions behind, pursued it without success, until finally, as night fell, he found himself alone in the middle of the forest and unable to find his way out.

Forgetting his kingdom, he is now purely the hunter he had once been, who pursues his prey with passion and desire, losing himself in the process. Once again, he pursues the treasure that is difficult to attain, this time in the form of a white doe that constantly vanishes before his eyes.[87]

Earlier, we discussed the forest as a symbol of introversion. After previously leading our hero into the world and to people, his libido now leads him into solitude. But he loses himself so completely in this forest that he no longer finds the

---

85 This passage may be intended as a reference either to Wagner's opera *Parsifal* or to the narrative poem *Parzival* by Wolfram von Eschenbach, both of which depict the hero's lost wandering (see "On Guilt," Chapter I, 151ff.).

86 Spitteler, *Imago*, 142. Slightly paraphrased (translated here by A. Kappes).

87 *EJ*: Similar to Adonis, Siegfried, and all the other heroes who meet their death while hunting.

way out. The echoes of his cries go unheard, and he is forced to spend the night there.[88] He builds a fire, as a hero in this situation is wont to do.[89] While he had been barely able to protect himself from the fire spat at him from the seven throats of the dragon, here, in the forest of introversion, he and his animals must light a warming fire to protect themselves from the *cold* and from freezing. Nevertheless, his fate approaches in the form of a witch who also wants to warm herself, though she claims to be afraid of his animals. And he is so deeply lost that he believes her fear to be justified and allows himself to be persuaded to strike his animals with the witch's rod, a negative rod of life,[90] whereupon they are all turned to stone. Our hero suffers the same fate when the witch descends and touches him, too, with her magic rod. When he fought the dragon, his animals had stood loyally by him; but thinking that he could *sleep* under their watch cost him his life. In this scene in the forest, quite the opposite happens: when he mistrusts his animals, they are turned into stone, which also leads to his own petrifaction. In the first instance, the human being dies, and only the animals survive; in the second, everything is turned to stone.

We find both these outcomes, with their characteristic differences, in all sorts of variations. Being transformed into an animal and petrification are the dangers that correspond to the directions of the libido: external or internal, extraversion or introversion. As a mythological illustration of the former, I would mention the companions of Odysseus whom Circe turned into pigs. In the Bible, King Nebuchadnezzar eats grass like an ox.[91] In the fairy tale "Little Brother and Little Sister," the heroes are turned into animals. As illustrations of petrification, I would mention "Sleeping Beauty," who falls into a magical sleep, "Snow White" in her glass coffin, "Faithful John," who is turned into stone. And in the Bible, Lot's wife is turned into a pillar of salt because she looked back.[92] It is always a matter of not-being-able-to-resist, of boundless covetousness, that leads to ruin, irrespective of the direction it takes. The extraverted tendency leads the libido outwards, into reality, where the threat is of turning into an animal; the introverted tendency leads the libido inwards, into one's own ego, where the threat is rigidification. If we do not recognize the right moment to stop, but allow ourselves to be led, when, in fact, we should be doing the leading, we are subjected to the law of gravity and will sink to wherever our libido takes us.

---

88 Jung, *Wandlungen und Symbole*, 312, 327, on the hero in the whale's belly. (In the original typescript, Emma Jung's note cites page 317. Based on content, page 312 was probably intended.) (*Psychology of the Unconscious*, 365, 381ff.)

89 Ibid., 251ff., on the motif of fire-drilling and -lighting (*Psychology of the Unconscious*, 290ff.).

90 In the original typescript, this phrase is an exclamation *(negative Lebensrute!)*. It apparently refers to a springtime folk ritual for fertility, which involves stroking or gently hitting young females (human and animal) with a green tree-branch, in order to confer on them the vitality of new growth. The witch's rod here does the opposite; it kills. Later in the story, it brings back to life.

91 Daniel 4:25, 4:33, 5:21.

92 Genesis 19:24–26.

Overcoming the law of gravity has always been one of mankind's dearest and most meaningful dreams. Now that we have learnt to fly with the help of technology, perhaps we may hope that, despite gravity, the soul will also learn to fly, not to wherever the wind takes it, but rather to wherever it *wants* to and *can* go, because it has understood its own laws and learned to control its power.

Our fairy tale still has to tell us how our hero will be released from his petrification and return to life. We recall the moment when the brothers took their leave of each other and how they plunged the knife—understood as a symbol of a quantity of libido that they had in common—into the tree, and how the knife was to be kept as a reminder and as an aid in their hour of need. In this hour of greatest need, the brother who is still alive remembers the knife. From its rusty half, he learns of his brother's troubled situation and immediately goes to his aid. The first brother's only hope is his double, the hero himself, who, in the form of his brother, is faced with doing the same task again, and doing it better than the first time.

This twin brother is also welcomed by the townspeople as their king, eats and sleeps next to the queen, and goes hunting in the forest, where he pursues the white doe and lights a fire at the same place. But when the witch demands that he strike his animals, he refuses her request and thereby passes the test. Then he succeeds in shooting down the witch who, it turns out, is lead-proof and must be shot with a silver button. No ordinary metal will bring about the witch's capitulation: it has to be a precious metal, that is, it takes a particularly large investment of energy. Thus he forces her to bring his brother and the animals back to life by touching them again with her rod.

After their joyful reunion, the two brothers build a fire together in which they burn the witch, whereupon the forest opens up and is full of brightness and light. Together now, they set off for home. But there is still one last thing to be done for their union to be complete. While sharing what has happened to them, the first brother learns that the second brother has slept beside the queen, and out of anger and jealousy cuts off his head. He immediately regrets having killed his redeemer, and he sends the hare to gather the life-giving root, with which the dead man is brought back to life.

To illuminate this final deed—the killing and bringing back to life of the brother—I shall cite some passages from Wolfram von Eschenbach's *Parzival*. In a wizard's realm, and after having survived many adventures on his wanderings to find the Grail, Parzival encounters Gawain, who had been sent away from Arthur's round table at the same time as Parzival on a journey of expiation and adventure. Gawain, a cousin of Parzival's, is portrayed as a hero who is often tempted by the world and the senses, and who is, therefore, a particularly infantile form of Parzival. They resemble each other, and both have even brought with them a sprig from the enchanted forest that very few chosen ones are able to break off. Not knowing who the other is, and seeing in each other only an enemy, they begin to fight, a misunderstanding that is only resolved with the appearance of their true opponent. When Parzival realizes with whom he has been fighting, he throws down his sword and laments,

"If with my enmity I have done violence
to excellent Gawain,
It is *myself I have vanquished*
And heartfelt sorrow is all I have found."[93]

And Gawain says:

"Folly here has found its mark
For two hearts have shown their hate
Two hearts innocently drawn to each other,
In battle, you defeated us both.
Mourn therefore for both of us,
For here you have indeed routed yourself
If loyalty was your heart's desire."[94]

The book in which Parzival's last adventure—his fight with Feirefis—is told begins with the words:

He, whom I chose to be a hero,
Now faces his hardest battle;
Victory was his at every turn,
But he was only fighting children.[95]

In Feirefis, with his white and black patches, Parzival must once again fight his brother,[96] but this time not one who is merely infantile, but rather the heathen one, who appears endowed with immense wealth and irresistible power. Once again, these two confront each other without knowing who the other is, and a fierce fight ensues between the two evenly matched heroes. The battle is decided when, with a furious blow on the helmet, Parzival brings his opponent to his knees, breaking his own sword.

What left him in such dire need
Was the sword of Gahevies,

---

93 Wolfram, *Parzival*, 346. Italics added by Emma Jung. (Passages from *Parzival*, translated by A. Kappes.)

94 Ibid., 346ff.

95 Ibid., 363.

96 Here Emma Jung speaks of Parzival's Christian cousin, Gawain, and his heathen brother, Fierefis, as if both were his brothers. Parzival's sword-fight in each case is with a close but unrecognized relative, whose identity he learns only after they have fought each other.

That he had stolen from his corpse.
Henceforth God would no more support
That he should carry Ither's sword,
Whom he had foolishly once slain.[97]

Parzival's first deed as a knight had been to confound the "Red Knight," Ither von Gahevies, by joking and being serious in turn, and then slaying him and taking his armor for himself. The description of the general mourning that followed the death of this hero states,

His death meant that the young fool
Claimed his armor for himself.
If he once grasps his simplemindedness
His remorse will be too late.[98]

The sword that Parzival, out of infantile greed, had stolen more than earned, now fails him and breaks in this fiercest of battles. The chivalrous heathen, Feirefis, does not wish to do battle unequally matched, so they tell each other their names and discover, with indescribable joy, that they are brothers:

"Concerning fathers, yours and mine,
We thought there were three, yet they're but one.
Thus, it was with yourself you fought,
I rode to battle with myself,
Myself I gladly would have slain;
Yet without flinching, you defended
Me from myself, courageous man."[99]

Only after his fight and reconciliation with his heathen brother, and accompanied by him, is Parzival once again able to find the Holy Grail, to redeem Amfortas and, after baptizing Feirefis, to take up his office as Grail King.

Our fairy tale goes on to describe the entry of the twin brothers, finally re-united, into the town where no one is able to tell them apart. The king's daughter finally recognizes her husband by his lion, and she assures him how unfounded his mistrust of his brother was, whereupon the fairy tale ends with the words, "He then realized just how loyal his brother had been."[100]

Thus, the fairy tale provides us with a symbolic representation of a universal human problem that has remained the same throughout all ages, the solution to

---

97 Wolfram, *Parzival*, 367ff.
98 Ibid., 71.
99 Ibid., 373.
100 von der Leyen, ed., *Brüder Grimm*, 32.

which we must also work on: it is the unification of the human being with his own self, with his soul, his libido, or however one chooses to call it. The two brothers and the helpful animals are symbols of every individual's variously directed aspirations. It is always a part of one's own self that is misunderstood, loved, despised, opposed, conquered, and raised to a new, higher life until, finally, one's soul reaches that level of harmony which our fairy tale expresses in its simple, closing words: "He then realized just how loyal his brother had been." We also see how deeply ethical is the content of this fairy tale, that has often been disparaged for being immoral. In symbolic form, this fairy tale describes nothing less than the great cultural struggle of humankind, and in a decidedly progressive sense. For, despite all its peripeteia, it reveals human development toward a higher goal.

Precisely what is being fought for, the fairy tale foreshadows more than it spells out; but we have learned to understand it, and to conclude, I would like to repeat it, using the words of Friedrich Nietzsche's *Zarathustra*:

> But the worst enemy thou canst meet, wilt thou thyself always be; thou waylayest thyself in caverns and forests.
>
> Thou solitary, thou goest the way to thyself! And past thyself and thy seven devils leadeth thy way!
>
> A heretic wilt thou be to thyself, and a wizard and a soothsayer, and a fool, and a doubter, and a reprobate, and a villain.
>
> Ready must thou be to burn thyself in thy own flame; how couldst thou become new if thou hast not first become ashes!
>
> Thou solitary, thou goest the way of the creator: *a God wilt thou create for thyself out of thy seven devils!*[101]

---

101 Nietzsche, "The Way of the Creator," *Thus Spake Zarathustra*, translated by Thomas Common, 118 (italics added by Emma Jung).

2. On Guilt

1916[1]

WE ALL KNOW the poignant song from Johann Wolfgang von Goethe's *Wilhelm Meister:*[2]

Who never ate his bread with tears,
Through nights of grief who, weeping, never
Sat on his bed, midst pangs and fears,
Can, heavenly powers, not know you ever.
Ye lead us forth into this life,
Where comfort soon by guilt is banished,
Abandon us to tortures, strife;
For on this earth all guilt is punished.[3]

As fine as these words are, equally bleak is the thought that suffering humanity is but the victim of such obscure heavenly powers, doomed to suffer eternally without knowing why. The question of why has occupied people at all times and, as we can see from various myths and philosophies, the connection between suffering and guilt was made early on.

I, too, had to concern myself with this problem,[4] and, in order to make things clearer for myself, I have examined various writings and presentations on the problem of guilt.

---

1   This lecture, held on 17 June 1916 at the Psychology Club Zurich, was followed by a group discussion. According to contemporaneous Club notes, in addition to Emma Jung and C. G. Jung, attendees posing questions or comments included Adolf Keller, Th.D., Alphonse Maeder, M.D., Toni Wolff, Carl Schneiter, M.D., either Hermann or Martha Sigg (probably Martha, who was active in the Club, 163, note 16), and Jules Vodoz, Ph.D. ("Sitzung vom 17.6.1916," "Protokolle der Vorträge des Vereins für Analytische Psychologie I, 1913–1916"). These discussants were distinguished by various competencies in relation to Emma Jung's topic. Rev. Dr. Keller was a pastor as well as an analyst. Dr. Schneiter lectured at the Club on psychosexuality, on the psychology of ethnic groups, and on casuistry in the context of analytical psychology. Prof. Vodoz lectured there on the Song of Roland, the social milieux of Molière and Rousseau, and religious thought as reflected in French literature. Martha Sigg presented on poems by Ronald Fraser, as well as on the works of Friedrich Nietzsche and Jakob Burckhardt.
2   *Wilhelm Meisters Lehrjahre* was Goethe's second novel (1795–96).
3   Goethe, *Wilhelm Meister's Apprenticeship and Travels*, vol. 1, book 2, chap. 13, 126.
4   Around the time of this lecture, Emma Jung apparently devoted much thought to the suffering inflicted upon the soul by the archetypal powers. On 23 December 1916, while visiting the Rigi, she composed a poem, lamenting this experience: "Was ist anders der Mensch als ein Kampfplatz" (What is the human being but a battleground). The poem includes these lines: "If the raging of the mighty causes worlds to burst, / what do gods care for the world, or a feeling heart?"

In what follows, I shall attempt to relate what I found out.

The first question is: what do we actually know about guilt? And the answer is: we know the *word*, the *concept*, and probably most immediately, we know the *feeling* of guilt, which can be compared to a kind of fear, as, for example, when we speak of pangs of conscience. The French word *conscience*, or *Ge-wissen*[5] in German, also denotes the degree of certainty with which this feeling appears, namely, with the certainty of something that is known. The German word *Schuld* (= guilt/debt) is related to *sollen*, and shares the same root as the English word *should*.[6] It denotes a "should," a "must," the obligation to make an effort. One may perhaps see something significant in the fact that it is not formed from *shall*, but from *should*, which points toward the imperfect or the conditional. In French, the word *devoir* for *shall* is also used in its infinitive form as a noun for *duty*. As *shall* is related linguistically to *should*, so *duty* is related conceptually to *guilt*. This same sense of incompleteness, of deficiency, which resides within the word guilt, we also find in the words *error* (Fehler) or *lack* (fehlen), which mean to err, to deceive, to fall short, to miss, and are related to the Latin word *fallere*, which has the same meaning. The French word *défaut* corresponds to the German word *Fehler* (error), also in the moral sense. Thus, error, like guilt, denotes things that are not and yet should be.

Enough, then, about the word.

Moving on now to the *concept* of guilt. In its common usage,[7] *Schuld* (debt) means to owe somebody something, to be under some kind of obligation, to have something to give to someone in return for something that has been given to or done for us. But what we are mainly interested in is the psychological concept of guilt.

There are, of course, many lengthy definitions, which I will elucidate as concisely as possible here. What they all share is the view that guilt is an offence against some law, be it of a religious, a moral, or a civil nature. What those respective laws are, what they require and what they condemn, naturally depends entirely on the place and time, and are accordingly different, sometimes even directly opposite. It is impossible to go into these diversities in detail; I would like to mention only some of the aspects that have been or are decisive in the evaluation of good and evil, of

---

5 *Ge-wissen*: The German word for conscience is formed on the infinitive *wissen*, "to know." Similarly, in both French and English, "conscience" is formed on the Latin participle *sciens*, "knowing." This passage seems to have been inspired in part by Emma Jung's reading of Schopenhauer, *The World as Will and Idea*. In her reflections, she writes of "the 'conscience' that 'knows' what one actually *should* or intends [to do]" ("Night Voices," 30 July 1915). (See below, 155 and note.)

6 When writing this lecture, Emma Jung apparently contacted Emil Abegg (1885–1962), a local Swiss Sanskrit scholar and later professor of Indian philosophy and linguistics at the University of Zurich. Dr. Abegg wrote to her in May 1916, explaining that the modern High German *Schuld* probably derived from the medieval German *skal-* ("shall, should") (Emil Abegg to Emma Jung, 27 May 1916, Jung Family Archive). Abegg cited a work by Meillet, *Introduction à l'étude comparative des langues indo-européennes* (Introduction to comparative study of Indo-European languages).

7 I.e., its common usage in German. The author explains that *Schuld* may mean both "debt" and "guilt."

which laws are an expression. The most elemental is probably the view held by the natural human being,[8] that "good" is what he likes and "evil" is what he dislikes, or what seems to him or his tribe to be useful or harmful. In his work *Psychologie der Naturvölker*,[9] Fritz Schultze takes the view that because the "natural human being" lives purely instinctively[10] and unconsciously, he is unable to distinguish good from evil in our sense. He writes, "There can be no talk of innate ideas of a moral nature, or of a conscience implanted in all people in the same way, be it by God or nature."[11] It seems to me, however, that here he takes too little into account the important role played by feelings of guilt and fear and their associated atonement and purification ceremonies, particularly among natural peoples.

In these two examples, we already have two typical points of view: the first—good is what I like; bad is what I dislike—expresses the value judgment of the ego, i.e., from the standpoint of self-preservation. The second—good and bad are identical to what is useful or harmful to one's tribe—expresses a value judgment from the standpoint of the preservation of the species. The two valuations thus correspond to the two basic human drives: self-preservation and preservation of the species. Furthermore, for primitive humanity,[12] all that is foreign, alien, indeed anything unknown at all, is considered evil or dangerous, as determined by the original protective instinct. This view could, perhaps, be seen as the most primitive, since it is supremely hostile to development. For as long as there have been specific public laws of governments and religion, they have expressed what was considered good and right (both for the individual and for the species), so that "evil" was whatever did not comply with these laws.

By rightly grasping that good and evil are not labels that can be affixed once and for all, Friedrich Nietzsche proposed dropping these value judgments altogether, and instead regarding the world as being beyond good and evil. Even if he himself did not succeed in doing this—as proven by the fact that, with powerful affect, he

---

8 *des Naturmenschen*: The term is adopted from Fritz Schultze's writing, on which the author depends in this lecture. For Schultze, there is a distinction to be made between "natural" and "cultural" human beings. One definition of "natural" here, insofar as it reflects Schultze's thought, may be "pre-cultural." Schultze's views regarding categories of human being, and his corresponding terminology, arouse aversion in the light of more recent ethnological studies. A century ago, however, these views were accepted more or less uncritically by European intellectuals.

9 *EJ*: Schultze, *Psychologie der Naturvölker: Entwicklungspsychologische Charakteristik des Naturmenschen in intellektueller, ästhetischer, ethischer und religiöser Beziehung. Eine natürliche Schöpfungsgeschichte menschlichen Vorstellens, Wollens und Glaubens*, [Schultze's book is not published in English translation. In English, its title might read: The Psychology of the natural peoples: A developmental psychology of natural human beings, as related to intellect, aesthetics, ethics, and religion. The evolution of human imagination, will, and faith.]

10 In Emma Jung's writing, as in her husband's, the word "instinct" refers to behavioral impulses arising involuntarily. Carl Jung writes, "In my view, all psychic processes whose energies are not under conscious control are instinctive" (*Psychological Types*, CW 6, §765).

11 *EJ*: Schultze, *Psychologie der Naturvölker*, 146.

12 As noted above, the characterization of certain human beings as "primitive," which gives offense today, was widely accepted by educated Europeans of Emma Jung's era (104, note 17).

re-stamped some things as bad that had previously been considered good, such as Christianity—we can feel the impact of his proposal in our time, in that the present generation feel much less bound by fixed laws than the previous one.

The usual psychological definition of guilt goes something like this: Guilt is perceived as that which is contrary to the viewpoint from which it is currently being judged. Thus, from the standpoint of the urge to individuate, the collective appears as evil, and conversely, evaluated from the standpoint of collective urges, what is individual appears to be evil. This definition therefore brings together those two types of obligation that correspond to the basic drives inherent in every human being, and explains why sometimes the one and sometimes the other—its opposite—can be perceived as guilt within the same individual.

Actually, one could think that we now know what we wanted to know, for these definitions are plausible, and there is not much there to object to. But if we follow Tertullian's example and call upon the soul to testify[13]—understanding the soul here as an extraordinarily sensitive organ with highly differentiated reactions, within which thinking and feeling, conscious and unconscious, work together in a coordinated manner[14]—we hear that it is not satisfied with these explanations. "One can certainly pronounce these views to be correct," it says, "but they are not effective! Or do you really mean to say that these explanations have any influence at all on the feeling of guilt? Hasn't it more often been your experience that that feeling adheres to none of these stipulations, but appears and disappears at will, and goes its own so often inscrutable way? Precisely this unpredictability is also the most torturous thing about it. How simple it would be if it were simply a matter of following certain rules and regulations!"

I have to agree with the soul; and in what follows, I would like to try to show the pathways that the guilt-feeling follows. What has been laid down in law is what has been recognized as being in some respect appropriate. If we contravene the law, we are doing something for which the consequences are roughly predictable. In such instances, the feeling of guilt that arises stems from the fact that we are not at one with ourselves, hence one half of us feels guilty about what the other half has or wants to do. But there is also another guilt-feeling, that has no visible connection whatsoever with any known misconduct or conflict of duty, and that, through its tormenting presence, often leads us to the boldest assumptions about its cause. Evidently, in this instance, it must be a matter of something that is simply not yet known, or one would have to assume that this feeling is meaningless. This,

13 *EJ*: Kellner, ed., *Tertullians private und katechetische Schriften*, 203–14. [The pages cited contain Kellner's German translation of a brief essay by Tertullian, "De Testimonio Animae" (The Testimony of the Soul). This patristic writing inspires Emma Jung likewise to make a statement in the soul's voice.]

14 Emma Jung's description of the soul is not identical with any of her husband's definitions of "Soul" (*Psychological Types*, CW 6, §797–807). It relates more or less closely, however, to his definition, "Soul as anima" (ibid., §803–7), which includes one of Jung's early discussions of the way the soul functions in a woman as the animus (§805).

however, is very unlikely; what is more likely is that just as physical listlessness or pain draws attention to physical needs or illness, so, too, does mental pain draw attention to needs or illnesses of the soul.

The ability to feel pleasure or pain at all, and, above all, the great and deeply-rooted tendency to seek out pleasure and avoid pain, is certainly to be regarded as an extremely important factor in development, and originally may well have had its purpose in life. At any rate, if not determined to do so by nature, this peculiarity of fleeing pain and seeking pleasure was used to facilitate adaptation and differentiation by putting the forces that were awakened by those sensations to work in their service. Most of the motivational factors that led to the development of causal thinking and the formation of concepts also probably drew their strength from there. Being able to link pleasure and pain to their causes was a tremendous achievement, and the advantage this rendered was quickly recognized and gave rise in turn to further cultivation and training of causal and conceptual thinking.

From all of this, it is already clear that what is beyond good and evil is also completely beyond humankind, as it is for the world in general; for the essence of all that has come into being is differentiation and difference. Just as light and dark, loud and quiet, warm and cold are distinctions of the senses, so, too, are good and bad a distinction of inner feeling, a distinction that evolved out of the mechanism of pleasure and pain. Such an elemental and important mechanism is still not to be despised, even if the matter is much more complicated for us. Having been applied to tendencies that are hostile to development and egoistic in a negative sense, this mechanism has lost much of its initial efficacy. It might therefore also have been necessary at the outset of Christianity to reverse this natural instinct and to emphasize the *value of suffering*, even to present it explicitly as something worth striving for. "Only through suffering can one grow," it is said. But if the conclusion is drawn—and this is not uncommon—that suffering is identical with growth, then this is false. Suffering merely provides the possibility of change, precisely because of our abhorrence of pain. That we make use of it nevertheless, in the sense of development, is by no means self-evident but depends entirely upon us and upon the meaning we know how to derive from suffering. But despite all our attempts to make the reversal of this natural mechanism appear convincing, it still persists. Proof of this is our conscience, which is still effective in its way, notwithstanding all progress, insights, and the disregard we afford it. Through the pain it creates in us, it challenges us to seek the causes of this discomfort. The premise that an existing mechanism is not without meaning, but has its purpose, is also the premise of my work.

From the realm of reason and law, we have seen what constitutes the concept of guilt; but hardly anything will be gained from that realm to explain the *guilt-feeling*. Let us therefore allow the soul to take the lead once again, that she may guide us into her realm, a realm of faith and superstition, of myths and fairy tales, of images and mysterious symbols.

Even among the natural peoples, we find many things that cannot be explained by Schultze's point of view. The already-mentioned purification and protection ceremonies have no obvious, practical, reality-based background. Punishments and difficult ordeals are imposed, though the latter may also be required to train aptitude. Finally, there is the fact that the primitive human being suffers greatly from fear. All the above point to a pre-existing feeling of guilt, thereby refuting the view that there can be no talk of innate moral ideas.

Despite the fact that we like to imagine natural humans living in a paradise-like, innocent state, this feeling of guilt is quite strong even there, as may be concluded from the important role played by taboos and other prohibitions and laws that have no practical explanation. Fear is also understandable, in so far as primitive people, in accordance with their lower stage of development, and in the face of life and the forces of nature, must feel more worthless and powerless than we do, who have become better acquainted with their laws.

While it is indeed obvious to primitive people that where there is an effect, there has to be a cause, this does not make the cause a given, but rather something that has first to be found. That this is not so easy can be seen in the often quite grotesque and ridiculous causal links and explanations of primitive thinking.

Thus, Schultze, for example, recounts:

A native broke off a piece of the anchor of a stranded ship and died shortly afterwards. From then on, the natives invested the anchor with divine meaning and, to avoid its wrath, honored it by bowing as they passed by.[15]

Such unknown powers, working in unrecognized ways, embodied in primitive fetishes, can exist in any object, stone, piece of wood, rag, all of which are insignificant in themselves, but whose effect can extend to include everything. In order for this power that is represented by the fetish to remain favorably disposed, Schultze writes, the primitive human being feels obliged to perform some kind of service in return. This consists in a vow that a fetish priest imposes on the subject who needs protection. If he keeps his vow, his happiness is guaranteed. If he breaks it, he suffers the punishment of his tin god and his misfortune is sealed. Everything, then, depends on the believer sticking to the rules.

The mother must carefully oversee that even the child fulfills its vow. In accordance with the lower cultural level of tribal peoples, these vows are insignificant and morally worthless, and yet it goes without saying that the fetishist considers them to be infinitely valuable in the given context, and puts the greatest emphasis on their fulfillment. Besides petty dress codes, examples of such fetish vows are

... that one should not eat certain meats, certain birds or certain fish, also certain herbs or certain fruits and such things, or, if one does eat it, one should eat

---

15 *EJ*: Schultze, *Psychologie der Naturvölker*, 223.

it alone without any assistance and then bury the bones in the earth. Others may not cross any water, even if only small and only from the rain or some other source. Still others may not be carried across any rivers, but they may walk or ride through them. ...

Thus, everyone has a different vow; in a certain respect, everyone is a dissenter; everyone leads a somewhat different way of life; and therefore, in a certain respect, everyone is also heretical or unholy in the eyes of someone else. ... The vow which the fetish worshipper has taken upon himself forms the whole content of his religion, and its fulfillment is his whole religious practice.[16]

Summing up, Schultze states:

As crude as fetishism is, and as generally lacking in moral ideas, a certain educational element cannot be denied. To ensure his good fortune, the fetish worshipper takes a vow upon himself which he must carefully fulfill. To increase his power, he sells himself to many fetishes and submits to a myriad of rules. No matter how slight these may be, he takes upon himself the duties and obedience they demand. He commits to keeping certain laws; in a word, he erects barriers to his arbitrary self-will, barriers that are difficult to surmount and involve a loss of his happiness and power. To some degree, he learns to suppress his desires and passions and is forced to bridle himself and rein in his otherwise unlimited ruthlessness. His motivation is selfishness, but precisely this same selfishness tames his outbursts of selfishness. Thus, out of his delusional faith develops a factor that generates morality, and therein obviously lies a value that is not to be underestimated in this lowest religion.[17]

In these fetish vows, we recognize the urge toward individuation trying to assert itself, for it is otherwise given little consideration in the life of a natural human being, which is focused on caring for the tribal community. We see that it expresses itself in a religious form connected with sacrifice, and that it is no longer, or does not want to be, on that very primal level where good and evil are simply identical with a person's pleasure or pain.

What it cost the primitive spirit to free itself from the most obvious view that evil is whatever the individual or the tribe finds unpleasant, is clearly sensed in these odd vows and regulations of their own choosing, any one of which appears to make no sense. To illustrate this, I shall cite some of the sins from the sin register of the Kamchadals, according to Schultze. He writes:

---

16 *EJ*: Ibid., 233ff. [In the author's original typescript, the entire second paragraph is underlined.]
17 *EJ*: Ibid., 237.

It is a sin to bathe in hot springs or to go close to them, for the spirits of Kamuli cook there.

It is a sin to scrape snow from your shoes with knives outside your home, for this creates storm winds.

It is a sin to go out of the house with bare feet in winter, for this creates storm winds.

It is a sin to stab a piece of coal with a knife to light tobacco; you have to grasp it with your bare hands.

If a fresh sable skin is brought into the home, it is a great sin to sing.

If your shoes get wet in winter, you must not put them on a pole and dry them as long as the wagtails have not yet arrived. Once they have arrived, it is not a sin.[18] And so on.

But it is precisely in the unreasonableness of these peculiarities that their value lies, namely, in the possibility of finding a meaning that goes beyond the most obvious one, and in the challenge to seek it out. Perhaps it is the inertia or clumsiness of the primitive human being to comply with this challenge that is to blame for the fact that he remained "a primitive person." For it is by deriving new meaning and thereby new possibilities from the old and the known that all development is achieved. *And perhaps the guilt feeling can also be explained by the non-fulfillment of this demand arising from within.* For if a demand arises from within, it is a sure indication that there also exists the possibility to fulfill it. That such demands exist among primitive human beings, can, I think, be clearly seen from what has been said earlier concerning superstitious customs and views.

For us, too, superstition played and still plays an important role, differing significantly as it does from *faith* by its sterility and its power to block development, as proven throughout the ages.

And now we come to the realm of myths and fairy tales that exist on a higher level than superstition which we have just discussed. Here, in this realm, that same call that arises in all people to find meaning in both the unknown and the incomprehensible is met to a great degree and even, occasionally, in a matchless way. We will be amazed when we discover that such myths from long ago, from which we imagine ourselves to be worlds apart, can still serve as an expression of our own problems.

The power that is at work here, that has the ability both to unite what is farthermost and to give voice to what is unspeakable, we call fantasy. Fantasy and necessity may readily be called the two mothers, heavenly and earthly, of human development.

Fairy tales and myths of today's tribal peoples differ readily and essentially from those of civilized people that most often date back to earlier cultural levels.

---

18 *EJ*: Ibid., 145ff.

But in the former, the very old motif of creating fantasies—the need to find an explanation for the world and what is going on in it—becomes particularly clear.

The title of a fairy tale often indicates that it wants to explain something. Thus, in the folklore of the Bushmen[19] there are titles like:

How all the Rivers first came on Earth

Why the Sunset is sometimes Red and Stormy

How Sun and Moon went up to the Sky

How all the Stars came

How the First Rain came

How the Lame Boy brought Fire from Heaven

How the First Hippopotami came

How Black and White Men came on Earth

Why Snake has neither Hands nor Feet

Why Lizard's Head is always moving up and down

How all Stories and all History came among Men[20]

Although these fairy tales attempt to explain, inherent in them is an element that can hardly be explained by necessity and the need to understand the events of the outer world. In truth, they explain very little about the latter, and the people concerned most often have a much better and more practical understanding of natural processes than can be gained from these stories. It is possible to understand why it was important to solve the riddle of the origin of heavenly bodies and of fire, but harder to say why it was especially urgent to know why the lizard wiggles its head, or why the snake has no hands. Here it becomes clear that in addition to a drive for knowledge, born of necessity and serving the purpose of adaptation, there is a further, similar drive, whose only purpose would appear to be the desire to invent stories: that is, the drive of imagination or fantasy. The presence of such an inclination can also be observed in children who, in addition to a correct explanation, like to have or to add an imaginary one. The more comprehensive is this knowledge of reality, born of necessity, the more independently and purely the fantasy activity can develop. And so when tribal peoples, to satisfy their thirst for knowledge, have developed philosophy and natural science separate from the one original root, we see that the moment of explanation, so clear in primitive fairy tales, disappears from their fantasy products almost completely.

---

19 *Buschmänner*: The name now commonly accepted for this ethnic group is the San People.

20 The source for these story titles is evidently a book by Talbot, *In the Shadow of the Bush*, which is still found in the C. G. Jung library. In the final chapter, "Folk-Lore" (335–403), Talbot retells twenty-eight Bushman (San) stories of origin. From these, Emma Jung has selected and rearranged eleven titles.

After this digression, whose meaning will, I hope, emerge from what follows, I shall return to my actual topic: the question concerning the nature of guilt. It is, of course, impossible to enumerate all the different errors or sins that appear in fairy tales and myths, as these would be endless. We must therefore try to sort them into groups of the same kind, and distinguish those that are important from those that are less so. Some form of guilt is found almost everywhere, since the fates of heroes must have their causes. In accordance with their folkloric character, there are, however, fairy tales in which guilt is evident in a recognized vice, such as envy, hard-heartedness, pride, malice, deceit, laziness, and so on; but here the connection is quite clear and of no further interest the fantasied representation tells no more than was already known.

Such fairy tales of a decidedly moral character, where the acknowledged good is rewarded and the evil punished, I shall exclude from the outset, for they contain no new solution, even if they may otherwise be quite interesting. We shall only consider those fairy tales in which cause and effect either have no relationship to each other, or their connection is not obvious. This is where we shall perhaps find something interesting.

Two groups, above all, stand out. One sees the cause of the hero's suffering in a factor that lies outside the individual—in Goethe's words, in "heavenly powers." In myths, it is usually a benevolent or malevolent god or god-like being, or simply some form of doom, as in the Oedipus myth. In fairy tales, these roles are inhabited by wizards, witches or parents of the heroes, the latter especially in the form of the evil stepmother. In the second group, it is the hero himself who is to blame. The cause then lies within the individual. Examples of this include the biblical story of the Fall, the fairy tales of *Little Red Riding Hood*, *The Two Brothers*, and many others.

But perhaps most frequent is when both kinds occur in the same tale: being doomed and being to blame oneself, which is also probably closest to reality. Thus, in the well-known fairy tale of *Sleeping Beauty*, the fairy, insulted by the child's parents, places a curse on the infant at birth, but its fulfillment is actually only expressed through the heroine's explicit disobedience. Or in *Hansel and Gretel*, in which the parents decide to abandon their innocent children, it is the children who make the mistake of marking their path with something as unsuitable as crumbs, making it impossible for them to find their path again. *Mary's Child* is also abandoned by her parents, but she herself is later guilty of disobeying the sky queen. I must point out here that I am only looking at those aspects related to our theme, namely, *how the guilt that evokes the fate of the hero is characterized*. There is, of course, another, more final viewpoint, that would enquire after the purpose of the suffering.

I am intentionally leaving this aside and am only searching for the causal connections, for until these are uncovered, it seems pointless to me to enquire after meaning and purpose. I also believe that it is particularly important for us women to seek out and become familiar with the causal link between things. One might now object and say that there can be no talk of guilt, for everything must necessarily be as it is. Logically, it is certainly true that everything that happens is a consequence of prior causes, but the explanation that something is necessarily as it is provides no answer to the question why, which is precisely my question.

Furthermore, it seems to me that this logical point of view has not found much resonance with reality; if people were really steeped in and convinced by the viewpoint that everything must be just as it is, they would enjoy constant contentment and always be happy. But this is by no means the case, and probably least of all for those who preach such resignation.

Having said this, I am far from assuming that an event is absolutely coincidental. There is, at most, relative randomness, for as Schopenhauer says, in *On the Freedom of the Will*:

> For in the real world, where alone the contingent is to be encountered, every circumstance is *necessary, in relation to its cause*: while in relation to everything else it may coincide with in space and time it is *contingent*.[21]

This distinction is perhaps occasionally treated too loosely, by trying to see a necessary connection between things in a sequence which, although adjacent, are in fact independent, thereby confusing them with the causes and effects that follow in a causal sequence. My view that necessity and freedom could exist side by side is meant more or less in Schopenhauer's sense, who says about the constancy of character:

> The character is unalterable, motives have their effect with necessity: but they have to pass through cognition, which is the medium of motives. Yet cognition is capable of the most multifarious expansion, of perpetual correction in countless degrees: all education works toward this. The training of reason, through all kinds of knowledge and insight, is morally important because it opens the access for motives to which, without it, the human being would remain closed. As long as he was unable to understand them, they were unavailable for his will. Thus in the same external circumstances a human being's position the second time round can, after all, be really quite different from the first time: if, that is, it was only in the meantime that he became able to grasp those circumstances correctly and completely—with the result that motives to which he was inaccessible before now have an effect upon him. In this sense the scholastics rightly said, "*causa finalis movet non secundum suum esse reale, sed secundum esse cognitum*" ("the final cause (purpose, motive) moves not according to its real being, but according to its cognized being").[22]

---

21 *EJ*: Schopenhauer, "Prize Essay on the Freedom of the Will," 35ff. [Italics as in Emma Jung's typescript.]

22 *EJ*: Ibid., 71ff.

I shall now return to my topic. Having excluded from our consideration those narratives where the guilt lies in a known and acknowledged inferior trait of the hero, let us turn to those that portray something more problematic. Potent causes found here are deception, robbery, disobedience, curiosity, and lastly poor judgment, in those cases where an apparently minor cause has the most serious and surprising consequences. Peculiar to all of these is that they have not only one side, such as malice, greed, laziness, and so on, but can be either good or bad, depending on the circumstances.

We find deception in the Siegfried saga, where Brunnhilde, expecting Gunther, is deceived and overpowered by the invisible Siegfried; robbery in the saga of Prometheus, who steals fire from heaven for mankind; disobedience and curiosity with Adam and Eve; and impulsiveness and a lack of judgment with Parzival, who sometimes does too much, sometimes too little. To elucidate, I will compare the two sagas that seem to me to convey the problem most clearly. These are the legend of Prometheus and the story of the Fall in the Garden of Eden. That both are so well-known and their themes so little outdated—as testified, for example, in Spitteler's prose poem *Prometheus and Epimetheus*[23]—allows one to infer their importance and general validity.

I assume that the biblical story is familiar and shall not repeat it for the time being, but go straight to the Prometheus myth. About this myth, it is generally known that Prometheus stole fire from heaven and brought it to mankind, and as punishment for this theft, Zeus had Prometheus bound to a rock. To some extent one tends to see Prometheus, the bringer and inventor of fire, as the first man, since the art of igniting fire is a characteristic that both distinguishes the human being from beasts and raises him above them, and can be regarded as the origin of all culture.

In a figurative sense, lighting a fire is interpreted as a mental spark, which also has a bearing on the name: Prometheus means "one who thinks ahead." In this, too, the human being differs from beasts. The question, why the giver was punished so harshly for a gift so valuable to mankind, is usually answered by saying that culture, too, has evil consequences, as suggested in the myth of Pandora. This fact cannot be denied; but we need to know more about the why and the wherefore. For this, it is necessary to know the most ancient forms of the legend, beginning with the folkloric version by Hesiod and the literary version by Aeschylus.

According to Aeschylus, Prometheus is the son of Themis, goddess of justice, who, in the struggle between Kronos and Zeus, helps the latter to victory and the throne. But when Zeus later becomes a tyrant and wants to exterminate the despised human race, Prometheus alone takes the side of humanity and, through the gift of

---

23 Spitteler's narrative poem, *Prometheus und Epimetheus: Ein Gleichnis* (Prometheus and Epimetheus: A parable), is cited by Jung in *Psychological Types* to illustrate the differences between introversion and extraversion (*CW* 6, §275ff.).

fire and light, saves them by giving them the means to free themselves from their beast-like condition. As punishment, he is bound to the rocks, and each day Zeus's eagle feeds on his liver, which replenishes itself overnight. Despite having to endure unspeakable suffering, however, he does not regret his deed. Aeschylus has him call out, "Of mine own will, aye, of mine own will I erred—gainsay it I cannot,"[24] just as Goethe's Prometheus defiantly confronts the gods with his humanity.[25] This apparent lack of any sense of guilt gives the whole thing a particularly splendid touch. Prometheus consciously rebels against the gods and equally consciously bears the consequences of his actions. He is spared any tormenting feeling of guilt. His suffering is a necessary and foreseeable consequence of his act. We are all familiar with this kind of suffering and know that it is nowhere near as tormenting as the kind that is accompanied by a feeling of unfamiliar and unwanted guilt.

This is the kind of guilt we are looking for, and thus we leave Aeschylus's Prometheus, without going into the details of why his deed had such ungodly consequences, and proceed to Hesiod.[26] The latter describes the following: at Mecone, at a simple meal between gods and humans, Prometheus, a Titan and son of Iapetus, representing the human race, wants to deceive Zeus. In a skin, he wraps the meat and intestines of the slaughtered bull that was to be equally divided, placing its stomach, considered a poor piece, on top, and places it to one side, while to the other side he places the bones, covered with a deceptive layer of fat. Although he sees through the trick, Zeus selects the worse portion and decides to take revenge on the human race by taking away their fire. Prometheus, however, secretly steals it again and brings it back to the people, hidden in a pipe. This time, Zeus's pride cannot bear being truly outsmarted, and he punishes Prometheus by having him bound to a rock. He also wants to plunge the human race into ruin, again through deceit:

> "Son of Iapetus, surpassing all in cunning, you are glad that you have outwitted me and stolen fire—a great plague to you yourself and to men that shall be. But I will give men as the price for fire an evil thing in which they may all be glad of heart while they embrace their own destruction."[27]

---

24 *EJ*: "Ich kenne keine Reue. Ja! Die Tat ist mein." Aeschylos, *Der gefesselte Prometheus*, 17. [In her lecture, Emma Jung paraphrases this quotation, to read: "Gerne frevelt ich, und leugne es nie" (Willingly I did wrong, and will never deny it). The present text follows the English edition of Aeschylus, *Prometheus Bound*, trans. by Herbert Weir Smyth, 241.]

25 *EJ*: Goethe, "Prometheus," in Werke: Vollständige Ausgabe letzter Hand, vol. 2, 76–78. [Goethe's poem "Prometheus" appears in the section "Vermischte Gedichte" (Assorted Poems).]

26 *EJ*: Hesiod, "Theogonie" and "Hauslehren, oder Werke und Tage," in *Hesiod's Werke verdeutscht im Versmasse der Urschrift* (Hesiod's works, translated into German in the original meter), translated by Eyth, 2nd ed. [The author cites her complete source as the Langenscheidtsche Bibliothek sämtlicher griechischen und römischen Klassiker, in neueren deutschen Muster-Übersetzungen (The Langenscheidt Library of complete Greek and Roman classics, newly translated into German), vol. 2. The second volume contains Aesop's fables, Hesiod's works, and Quintus's continuation of the *Iliad*.]

27 *EJ*: "Hauslehren, oder Werke und Tage," *Hesiod's Werke*, 67ff. [English text from Hesiod, *The Homeric Hymns, and Homerica*, translated by Evelyn-White, 7.]

And through Hephaestus, he has a woman formed out of water and earth, who, endowed by the gods and goddesses with all seductive gifts, is brought to earth by Hermes to Epimetheus. Unmindful of the warning of his brother Prometheus, he accepts the deceptive gift and, true to his name "Hindsight" ("The One Who Knows in Hindsight"), realizes too late its nature. Pandora, the All-Gifted, brings with her a closed box. When she opens it, out flow all the evils and diseases that were kept in it and now populate the world, which had previously been so happy. Pandora, horrified herself, quickly slams down the lid, so that hope alone is left inside.[28]

In the writings of Hesiod, Prometheus is not depicted as a benefactor, as Aeschylus portrays him, but as an evildoer. This is the version I am choosing, to address the problem of guilt. Here, too, we find those two causes, lying outside and inside the individual. Where the personal fate of Prometheus is concerned, the cause—the deception of Zeus—also lies within himself as an individual. But where the fate of mankind is concerned, the figure of Pandora is to blame, for whom Prometheus, the Titan, is responsible. Humanity is a defenseless victim in the face of this otherworldly power. In the figure of Pandora are found the explanation and consolation for all the sufferings whose causes lie completely outside the realm of human power, and for what is called the decree of fate, from which no one can escape.

Examples of cases that are completely dependent on higher powers are natural catastrophes, earthquakes, volcanic eruptions, floods, failed crops and so on. Then there are the collective catastrophes for which mankind as a whole is to blame, but not the individual, like war and mental and physical epidemics. Further, there are the special circumstances of birth that make one person's life so much more difficult than another's. And finally, which is also one of the most important, there is one's innate character, which determines one's fate so strongly, and with which everyone has to come to terms as best they can.

The idea of a state of guilt imposed upon humanity is found in many religious and philosophical systems. The Christian doctrine of original sin is one example. Another is the Indian teaching that our fate in this life is the result of our behavior in a previous life.[29]

Orphic-Pythagorean teaching tells of a Fall of the World Soul, which, despite its divine origins and through its own fault, had to leave behind its heavenly home

---

28 *EJ*: Ibid., 68ff. [Here the author departs slightly from her source. Hesiod attributes to Zeus, not to Pandora, the decision to keep Hope inside the box. In Eyth's German edition, these lines read: "Hoffnung blieb da noch einzig im unzerbrechlichen Hause / Unter'm Rande der Büchse darin ... / ... denn flink schloss Jene den Deckel der Büchse, / Nach Zeus' göttlichem Rathe, des donnernden Aegisträgers" (*Hesiod's Werke*, 69). In Evelyn-White's translation: "Only Hope ... did not fly out the door; for ere that, the lid of the jar stopped her, by the will of Aegis-holding Zeus who gathers the clouds" (Hesiod, *The Homeric Hymns, and Homerica*, 9).]

29 *EJ*: Another Indian doctrine (according to Deussen) sees the cause of the suffering of existence in the fact that the Purusha and Pakrisi, subject and object, are or seem to be eternally entangled in each other. [Sentence in text deleted by author.]

for the impurity of life on earth within the prison of a body, from which it can be redeemed through atonement and purification while undergoing the cycle of births. Very similar thoughts can be found among the Gnostics, to which I will return later. Plato speaks of originally round, probably meaning perfect, primordial beings who were cut in two by the gods as punishment for their evildoings and to prevent them from becoming too powerful, thereby causing each half to suffer throughout their lives from both their feeling of imperfection and their longing for their other half. And finally, Schopenhauer sees Original Guilt, or guilt as such, in the will that objectifies itself, by which he means that the original One enters into definite, limited forms.[30] This is the same thing that the Orphics and Gnostics meant by the Fall of the World Soul into its earthly existence.

In fact, this other, cosmic aspect, this superhuman aspect of world suffering plays a part in the biblical story of the Fall, that seems concerned with humanity's own self-inflicted guilt. Indications of this can be found in extra-biblical traditions, for example in the Jewish-Gnostic tradition, and particularly in Jewish legends. Just as for the Greeks the reign of Zeus was preceded by that of Kronos or the Titans, so, too, for the Gnostics the creation of the world was preceded by an age in which some of the angels fell away from the perfect primeval God, called Man.[31] It was one of these fallen angels who created the world and made in the human being a failed copy of that primeval God.

In a Jewish legend, the angels are jealous of the human being, created and favored by God, and therefore decide to destroy him using snakes.[32] Of course, these versions had to be avoided by the Bible and Christianity, for they could awaken doubts about God's omnipotence and benevolent disposition. They can raise questions such as whether the evil angels were stronger than God, or why God created humans so imperfect that they had to fall victim to temptation.

The Christian view, that God himself tempts human beings in order to test them, is not readily acceptable to the natural spirit, as demonstrated by an experience I had with my own nine-year-old child. When saying the "Our Father," my child categorically refused to make the request, "Lead us not into temptation," since such a request was simply unworthy of a god. If, then, the world has come into being, as it were, through the transgression of a divine being, then it follows that any atonement can only be through this divine being. Therefore Christ, the sacrificed Son of God, becomes the redeemer of the world.

---

30   Apparently a reference to Schopenhauer's work *Die Welt als Wille und Vorstellung* (The World as Will and Idea), on which Emma Jung wrote reflections when she was resting at Klosters in the summer of 1915. In her private notebook she reflected, among other things, on Schopenhauer's concept of the Fall (*Die Welt als Wille und Vorstellung*, 207–19). Schopenhauer depicts the will as the sun, whose rays are obstructed and split up by an obstacle (the earth). Emma Jung relates this image to the concept of original sin ("Night Voices," 30 July 1915).

31   Similarly in the Lurianic Kabbalah, *Adam Kadmon* (the primeval human being) is said to be the microcosm of the entire creation.

32   *EJ*: bin Gorion, ed., *Von der Urzeit*, 92–97.

Schopenhauer sees the redemption of this world, which in truth has no right to exist and is the worst of all possible worlds, as happening when the Will—God—is mirrored back by the Intellect—the Son—who thereupon negates himself and returns to himself.

Enough, then, about supra-individual guilt, or guilt that is greater than the individual. Now we come to guilt within the individual, which I shall seek to elucidate by comparing the myth of Prometheus with the biblical story of the Fall. At the sacrifice of the bull in Mecone, Prometheus, wanting to take advantage of the gods for the benefit of humankind, becomes guilty of deceiving the gods and also of robbing them, when he secretly steals their fire. One could perhaps say that robbery and deception belong to those obvious vices that we declared earlier to be of little interest to us. But this is not so. At any rate, it seems impermissible to me to interpret the Promethean myth as one of those moralizing fairy tales that glorify or condemn a commonly held view.

This is already evident from the worldwide significance of this saga, for which parallels can be found everywhere, and from the fact that there are poets who, time and again, feel the need to revisit the material anew. According to the Bible, the guilt of the first human beings in the Garden of Eden consists in breaking God's commandment and eating the fruit of the forbidden tree. Through this act of disobedience and their lack of willpower, they bring down the curse of God upon themselves and all who come after them.

One often encounters the view that the fruit of the forbidden tree means sexuality, thereby making this the root of all evil. It is true that sexuality distinguishes the adult from the child, as expressed in the story of the Garden of Eden by the fact that the blissful, childlike state comes to an end as a result of eating the forbidden fruit. As punishment, as it were, people have to take upon themselves the pains and troubles of toil and birth—in other words, adulthood.

But there is no indication of this interpretation in the biblical tradition. There, on the contrary, God commands his creatures to be fruitful and multiply, which cannot readily be taken as a sexual prohibition. Rather than being associated with the Tree of Knowledge, sexuality could be associated with the Tree of Life. Rather than through sexuality, the human being differs from animals through knowledge, and the handling of fire. The erroneous view arguably arose from the fact that Eve tempted Adam to sin, as Pandora is the bringer of all evil in the myth of Prometheus. What may have particularly supported this view is the fact that there were or are times in the life of mankind, as well as of the individual, where a certain repression and restriction of sexuality is required in the interest of development. Being in conflict with this demand, sexuality must be regarded as sin. It harbors—*as, incidentally, knowledge does, too*—enormous dangers for the human person.

The Tree of Knowledge equates to fire in the Promethean myth, for, in contrast to all other creatures, it designates something unique to humanity. Both fire and knowledge are fundamental conditions of culture. According to the Bible, *agriculture* also emerges as a consequence of eating from the Tree of Knowledge. One can now understand the guilt of Adam and Eve in the Garden of Eden, or of Prometheus, as a necessary precondition of culture and therefore emphasize its usefulness and its meaningfulness. In that case, the gods that man defies are to be equated with nature. Insofar as it goes against nature, cultural development can be expressed as a disobedience, as in the story of the Fall, and, insofar as it comes about at the expense of only a part of nature, it can be expressed as a robbery, like that of Prometheus. Guilt in this sense, however, is necessary; it is a form of guilt that is *relative*, since it is judged as such from the standpoint of nature, which is not the only possible standpoint. One can also understand the god in the biblical story and the figure of Zeus in the Prometheus myth differently, namely not as one half of a pair of opposites, but as a superordinate principle that unites the opposites, which, as such, is entitled to unconditional obedience.

Disobedience to this principle is then no longer a relative, but an absolute guilt.

Furthermore, Adam and Eve lack what makes Prometheus seem so splendid: the consciousness and deliberateness with which he performs the deed intended to save humanity. Adam and Eve, in contrast, allow themselves be tempted by the serpent who promises them, "Ye shall be as God."[33] Thus, Adam's motivation for the act is, at bottom, his drive for unlimited power, to which he spinelessly gives in, and not any desire for knowledge, or out of distress. Through this compelling greed, the knowledge that is gained is again instantly put to the service of this drive. There is also a Jewish legend that seems to point toward just such an abuse of spirit or of the ability to understand. It tells how, when the angels wanted to corrupt humanity, they chose the serpent, the beast whose cleverness is most often aimed at evil.[34] Perhaps one may also see an instance of guilt in the manner in which Adam and Eve attained knowledge, namely, not through toil, but by *magical means*—by consuming the apple. One can then understand the guilt in the story of Adam and Eve as an abuse of mental powers, a specifically human trait. In a similarly wrongful way like Adam and Eve, human beings, through Prometheus, whose name also means knowledge, came into possession of the divine fire or spiritual spark. The fact that they must have previously been in possession of fire is not important, for it is said: Zeus took fire from them and Prometheus brought it down again from heaven.

Only through this theft did it become the cause of all misery. One may per-haps interpret this as follows. The fact that Prometheus, whom one may regard as undifferentiated human mental power, should deceive the gods for the benefit of humankind, signifies an abuse of humanity's higher abilities. It is also a failure to recognize the superordinate principle, corresponding to the disobedience of Adam

---

33 Genesis 3:5.
34 *EJ*: bin Gorion, ed., *Von der Urzeit*, 92–97.

and Eve. The consequence is the loss of the divine fire that people had previously possessed. When the same cunning Prometheus robs it back from the gods and returns it to humankind, it is weighed down with the curse of the gods, which, in the form of Pandora, brings all misfortune into the world. Similarly, the consequence of the Fall in the biblical story is also the end of the blissful, paradisal state of being. If higher human capacities are obtained in an improper way, perhaps through robbery or curiosity, or are likewise employed, perhaps to cheat a higher principle, divine healing is forfeited, and those same abilities become the source of all evil and suffering. For, like fire, the mind is a dangerous gift, with which it is not advisable to play. A parallel story of being deprived of fire by an angry God can be found in a Jewish legend with the title *What Was Taken from Adam*:

> Before committing sin, Adam was able to hear the voice of the Lord and to remain standing on his feet; but after committing sin, whenever he heard the voice of the Lord, he quickly had to hide himself. Six things were taken from Adam after he had sinned, and these are: his brilliance, his growth, eternal life, the fruits of the earth, the fruit of the tree, *the great light of the sun*.[35]

If he forfeited his brilliance and the great light of the sun, this surely refers to that luminous, divine aspect of the spirit, which he lost through misuse.

One may assume that of all mental capacities, cunning was among the first to be developed and cultivated, for the undeniable advantages it offered humans were surely recognized very early on. There was a time when, instead of courage and strength, cunning was the main characteristic of the hero. I need only bring Ulysses to mind, or the often sly Nordic gods. And in the biblical story of Esau and Jacob, the latter knows how to use a trick to win his father's blessing for himself. If there are higher or lower forms of mental activity, one may view cunning as being somewhere in the middle. While it may have significance as a mental achievement, its merit will vary, depending on how it is used. For the same reason, fraud and robbery are also not to be counted among the clear offences mentioned above, for it depends on who is being deceived, and what or from whom something is being robbed. There are instances in which they make good sense, can even be justified, and instances in which they must be assessed as being purely, or predominantly, negative. Deceiving a god would appear to belong to the latter category. The superordinate principle, at any rate, always seeks revenge. That the eagle of Zeus eats a piece of Prometheus's liver every day indicates that this higher power knows how to extract the tribute it is owed, and indeed does so in some form, whether humans like it or not. Even Odysseus, the much-vaunted schemer, was only finally redeemed by relinquishing his own craftiness and obediently meeting divine commands.

---

35 *EJ*: Ibid., 110. [Italics by Emma Jung.]

I see Adam and Eve's guilt, then, in their irresponsibility and instinctual driven-ness, and in their cleverness directed at evil. To my mind, this is a misuse of the higher human qualities, one that consists of using the ability to distinguish good from evil, through thought or feeling, purely for the enhancement of one's own personal well-being in the strictest sense of the word, and possibly even at the expense of others. This is precisely how the originally useful mechanism of pleasure/pain, which I mentioned earlier, forfeited its value. This may be, then, that piece of nature which mankind lost through the Fall, and which, to its own detriment, it gave up in exchange for the corresponding piece of culture.

I would now like to discuss another important element that is in both our legends, namely the role of women.

In the story of the Garden of Eden, Eve is depicted as the main culprit, since she allowed herself to be persuaded by the serpent and then tempted Adam. This is probably why women are thought to behave more instinctively than men, and are more readily tempted, although Adam's behavior does not exactly lend any conviction to this assumption. There is, however, some truth to it, which may be related to the fact that, because of her biological role, a woman's mental spark probably remains undeveloped longer. Men experience a thirst for objective knowledge early in life, while for women this thirst long remains simply curiosity.

In what follows, I shall venture a different interpretation, which to my mind is suggested in the Promethean myth, specifically in the figure of *Pandora*:

For from her is the race of women and female kind: of her is the deadly race and tribe of women who live amongst mortal men to their great trouble, no helpmeets in hateful poverty, but only in wealth. And as in thatched hives bees feed the drones whose nature is to do mischief—by day and throughout the day until the sun goes down the bees are busy and lay the white combs, while the drones stay at home in the covered skeps and reap the toil of others into their own bellies—even so Zeus who thunders on high made women to be an evil to mortal men, with a nature to do evil. And he gave them a second evil to be the price for the good they had: whoever avoids marriage and the sorrows that women cause, and will not wed, reaches deadly old age without anyone to tend his years, and although he at least has no lack of livelihood while he lives, yet, when he is dead, his kinsfolk divide his possessions amongst them. And as for the man who chooses the lot of marriage and takes a good wife suited to his mind, evil continually contends with good; for whoever happens to have mischievous children, lives always with unceasing grief in his spirit and heart within him; and this evil cannot be healed.[36]

---

36 *EJ*: "Theogonie," in *Hesiod's Werke*, Langenscheidtsche Bibliothek, vol. 2, 28. [English translation taken from Hesiod, "Theogony," *The Homeric Hymns and Homerica*, translated by Evelyn-White, 123.]

With this lament of the good Hesiod and all that has since been heard in the same key, one must ask why, then, men, who cope with everything, should not also cope with women, and why women are perceived as a power which can only be countered with resignation or violence. The answer to this seems to me to be contained in the myth of Pandora. It is from her that this evil and feared race is said to stem.

This is probably not supposed to mean that no women had existed beforehand, but rather that with Pandora, and indirectly as a result of the theft of fire, a new kind of woman appeared, or, as we would say psychologically, a *new attitude toward women*. I think of Pandora not as a real woman, but as an artificially created *image*, an *imago*. For part of the mental activity symbolically expressed by fire is also the power of imagination, that is, the possibility of creating images. Since the development of this ability, a man no longer sees simply this or that real female being, but also the image he makes of her, which does not always correspond to external reality. Naturally, the same phenomenon is found in women.[37] If such an *imago* is confused with reality, it gets much too much power, in view of which the complaints of a Hesiod may seem more readily justified. This same phenomenon, albeit in a different light, is behind the popular contempt for women. Added to which, the meaning of the word "image" becomes clear: *idol*. People are inclined to worship the images, or *imagines*, that are created in the imagination, even to make idols of them. Just how great is this inclination toward image-worship and idolatry, we can see clearly in the Old Testament where warnings against idolatry are given repeatedly, under threat of the most severe punishment. Tertullian, too, warns the early Christians:

> Idolatry is the chief crime of mankind, the supreme guilt of the world, the entire case put before judgement.[38]

More than all the other religions of antiquity, Judaism has the merit of having recognized the sin inherent in idolatry, and of having laid it down in its law:

> Thou shalt not make unto thee a graven image, nor any likeness of any thing that is in heaven above or that is in the earth beneath, or that is in the water under the earth: *thou shalt not bow down thyself nor serve them*.[39]

This commandment has a deep psychological meaning, which comes to light even more clearly in the teachings of Christianity.

---

37 At the time of this lecture, Emma Jung had already begun to identify the animus as an important presence in her dreams ("Reader's Guide," volume introduction, 84ff.).

38 *EJ*: Kellner, ed., *Tertullians private und katechetische Schriften*, 138. [English translation as found in Tertullianus, *De Idololatria*, *Critical Text*, 23.]

39 Exodus 20:4–5a. Italics by Emma Jung.

Perhaps Tertullian's well-known words that the soul is Christian by nature[40] is referring to the pronounced monotheism of the soul that, in its innermost being, despises all veneration of idols and images. For, despite all theories to the contrary, we experience again and again that for the soul *just one is always best*, that there is *just one path* for it, and that every deviation from this path is relentlessly avenged.

It is difficult to say where the proclivity to venerate images comes from, which is so pronounced in both feeling and intellect. Perhaps it comes from the same instinct a mother has to love her child above all else. It is probably partially based on the fact that the *imago*, like the symbol, has a certain power to promote development which should not be underestimated. The dominion of such *imagines* or symbols is always temporary—they are gods that are betrayed, and *must be* betrayed.

If asked what idols we then worship, we can say, as Schultze says of the fetishists: there is nothing that cannot somehow become a fetish.[41] Sometimes it is an *imago*, sometimes a real object, sometimes a feeling, and sometimes a theory that we idolize. In psychological development, too, as soon as one of Hydra's heads is cut off, another appears. Once we have learned to distinguish the *imago* from reality, new idols appear, either as a symbol, a fantasy, or the unconscious in general, which one fervently believes must be worshipped. Meanwhile, I see in them only servants of that one supreme principle that tolerates no gods other than itself.

To conclude, I would like to mention another cause of guilt, namely the non-use or misuse of emotional or intellectual power of judgment, which can also be called a kind of stupidity. By this I do not mean mental incapacity, for, where that is concerned, it would be difficult to find a sense of guilt. Rather, I am thinking of a certain artificial stupidity, which, in order not to be misunderstood, I would like to explain in more detail below.

In the two examples discussed above, this element of lack of judgment is only hinted at. In the biblical story, it is present when Adam and Eve immediately believe what the serpent says. In the myth of Prometheus, it is seen in the figure of Epimetheus, who does not listen to the warning of his brother—his other side—but blindly embraces destruction.

To make things even clearer, I am selecting another example, namely Wolfram von Eschenbach's *Parzival*. Parzival forfeited the Grail, which was within his grasp, in a very stupid way, by omitting to ask what ailed King Anfortas.

We two must let happiness slide
And together fasten on grief!
The five senses that God gave you

---

40 *EJ*: Esser, ed., *Tertullians apologetische, dogmatische und montanistische Schriften*, translated by Kellner, 88. [The reference is to Tertullian's "Apology for the Christians" (Apol. 17.6). In one English translation, the famous phrase "anima naturaliter christiana" is rendered: "the testimonies of the soul thus far by nature Christian" (*The Apology of Tertullian*, translated by Reeve, 53)].

41 *EJ*: Schultze: *Psychologie der Naturvölker*, 223ff.

Shut off their aid from you—
How they betrayed your compassion then,
When faced with Anfortas's wound![42]

One may object that folly belongs to the nature of the hero, for without it he could not achieve what he achieves. But I am saying that the hero does not need to be without *judgment*, but rather without *prejudice*, and that is something quite different.

Knowledge is not required to be a hero or to find the Grail; what is required is a childlike disposition, i.e. a lack of prejudice and the willingness to learn. Parzival does not forfeit the Grail by his natural naivety, but rather by his unnatural behavior. It would have been more natural, more in tune with the heart, to ask about the strange things surrounding him. Nor does he neglect to ask because the question did not occur to him, but rather because he is following the age-old advice that he should not ask too many questions when out and about in the world. This is immediately generalized to the point that he wishes to ask no questions at all. Because he takes a quite useful rule literally, completely excluding his own judgment and feeling, it becomes harmful to himself. He does something similar with his mother's instructions: she warns him of murky fords, so he rides for a whole day beside a stream darkened only by flowers that "a cock would have crossed with ease,"[43] until, the following morning, he finds the place where he dares to cross.

His mother tells him:

"Wherever you can win a lady's ring and greeting,
Take it—it will rid you of the dumps.
Waste no time, but kiss and embrace her.
It will bring you good fortune
and raise your spirits."[44]

And he obeys by doing the following: Once, while walking, he finds a sleeping woman in a tent wearing a ring on her finger and a clasp on her robe. Remembering this advice, he lunges at the lady, who is scared to death, kisses her, removes her jewelry and, after he has eaten everything he can find, finally says goodbye with the words:

"… God be with you!—
That's what my mother told me."[45]

---

42 *EJ*: Wolfram, *Parzival*. [English from the translation by Hatto, 248.]
43 *EJ*: Ibid., 76.
44 *EJ*: Ibid., 75.
45 *EJ*: Ibid., 77.

Here again he does not act of his own accord, nor naively, but according to an instruction that comes from outside, which is so thoughtlessly applied, it becomes unnatural. This not only results in his being pursued by the offended knight, but also brings down misfortune upon the lady, as she is rejected by her husband, who has become suspicious and angry at the false appearance of things. Parzival is unable to reach the Grail until he has made amends for the misfortune he has wrought.

Revenge for such folly is taken not only upon the person responsible, but effects a wider circle. Thus, the sufferings of Anfortas will also be prolonged through folly. This attribute, then, is not the one that makes Parzival what he is. One could say that Parzival attained the Grail precisely through his errors, making error, as it were, *necessary*, indeed almost inevitable. But if we say this, we cannot help but err, over and over again. Parzival found the Grail not because he *erred*, but because he *learned*!

As far as error is concerned, every human is a Parzival. Not everyone, however, finds the Grail; so error cannot be responsible for that! What allowed Parzival to attain the Grail was not that error, self-evident and inevitable, happened to him, but rather that he *did* something not at all self-evident or inevitable: he acknowledged his guilt and did not let himself be deterred from starting all over again.

Just as it is not a lack of judgment that the hero needs, but rather a lack of pre-judgment, so, too, it is not error that redeems him, but rather the circumstance that he learns through his experiences and errors. That is, he is invested with that childlike quality of being willing to learn and to be taught. But every "stupidity," every unwillingness to be taught, in so far as it is unnatural, implies guilt.

This may sound strange, if one was so sure of oneself that one could not help it. But here, the objection "we can't help it" is no longer valid. The feeling of guilt drowns out this objection and says we *can* and *must*, because we feel the obligation. This feeling of obligation would be absurd, if there were not a necessity and a possibility to fulfill it. The possibility lies within our power, and the necessity lies within the ever-changing and ever-renewing hardships and sufferings of life.

We would like to assume that we are no longer in great danger of sinning through stupidity. But if we once take a close look, we discover that it is only up to a point that we are any different to fetishists with their offensive rag bundle and their feelings of great anxiety. We find it improbable that anyone who reaches into the fire ten times, burning his fingers each time, will not notice the result of his actions; but we can suffer the same effect many times over without realizing its cause. This is particularly so where the connections are not found in the external effect. The laws of causality of the outer world are relatively well known to us, and we are used to working with them. But now, thanks to analytical psychology, we know that there is also an inner reality whose laws we have to deal with. Analytical psychology has only recently taught us to explore and understand the inner world, just as we have long done with the outer. First, we had to discover its laws and thoroughly understand them. Just as it cost people a great deal of time and effort to learn anything much about the external forces, we must not be put off if it takes us some time to understand and master the internal causal connections, which previously were dark to us, as well as we do those of the outer world.

To get to this point, we must first acquire the childlike naivety and impartiality of which I spoke above. If in analysis we are required to accept our "other side," that is, everything that is considered stupid, ugly, or worthless, this does not mean that we must strive *to be this way*, just as the hero must also not deliberately strive to be stupid. It is simply a matter of seeing these things, bearing in mind that in the inner world neither the conscious judgment of our mind nor that of our feelings is valid. We do not have to accept what is evil and ugly because they are of intrinsic value, but because of the possibility that they might reveal a value, or might not. In order to get to know these inner values, however, we must let go of all judgment, and surrender to the agony of doubt and uncertainty. It is no mean achievement to move into a realm in which our best and most helpful powers, thinking and feeling, can no longer be of any use to us, indeed, may even betray us. But this is precisely what is being asked of us. I mentioned earlier[46] the words of Christ:

> "If thou knowest what thou doest, thou art blessed, but if thou knowest not, thou art accursed."[47]

The first thing analysis teaches us is to shift out of that quite irresponsible, primitive state to a point where we know what we are doing. But then it teaches us yet another thing, namely not to know what we do, and with the conscious awareness that we do not know, to do it nevertheless. We must learn what Parzival knew how to do: to wander with hope, but without any certainty of finding the Grail.

As difficult as uncertainty may seem to us, we must learn to bear it, for, after discovering the inner world, we do not yet have an organ with which to grasp it, in the same way that our mental and sensory functions grasp outer reality. That is to say, we probably do have an organ, but as yet, it has been too little considered and developed. It is in our *guilt-feelings*, as well as in many other phenomena, that this organ, *our soul*, can be recognized. By exploring guilt and its connections in my work, I have reached the following conclusion. Besides supra-individual forces that bring about the fate of mankind, there is also guilt of the individual human being. This latter form of guilt can either consist in some violation of recognized laws, in which case it is relative, or it is independent of such laws, and shows up through guilt-feelings. Through the course of our work, we have met with sins that may be termed absolute, such as:

---

46 Author's reference is unclear.

47 A statement attributed to Jesus in one of the noncanonical gospels. In *CW* II, §29, the corresponding footnote reads: James, *The Apocryphal New Testament*, 33.

1. Misuse of the cognitive and mental faculty for inferior personal purposes.
2. Idolatry, or the misuse of imagination.
3. Non-use or wrong application of intellectual or feeling-related judgment, and the associated irresponsibility and stupidity.

In every case, we are dealing with a misuse of specific *human characteristics*. Misuse can only be spoken of, however, on the assumption that there is a certain right use. We deduce the necessity for the latter from our sense of guilt. To some degree we can understand this unfulfilled obligation if, with Schopenhauer, we begin with the assumption that, like every part of nature, the human being is an objectivation of a great will that underlies everything.[48] And just as every such objectivation is based on its own idea, in the Platonic sense, the same is true of the human being, who in his inmost self must perceive as guilt all that does not correspond to this idea or serve its best embodiment. In general, human beings are probably worse than animals or plants at embodying the objectivation we represent, precisely because we abuse our abilities. But thanks to the human cognitive capacity, it is precisely we who have the possibility and the duty to represent our idea more perfectly than any other creature; and it is out of this contradiction that the feeling of guilt arises.[49] For all the suffering thus engendered, however, we ourselves are responsible, and from it we alone must redeem ourselves.

---

48 This final paragraph reflects the author's recent study of Schopenhauer's *Die Welt als Wille und Vorstellung* (145, note 30).

49 One passage that Emma Jung copied out in "Night Voices," on 30 July 1915, compares the innocence of plants with the moral responsibility of human beings. There Schopenhauer states: "Guilt does not lie in willing, but in willing with knowledge" (*The World as Will and Idea*, translated by Haldane and Kemp, 204).

3. Reflections on a Passage by Meister Eckhart

1922

IN ONE OF Meister Eckhart's[1] so-called "Talks of Instruction" I read the following passage:

> You should know that the pure will cannot lose God. It is true that the sensibility of one's temperament sometimes misses him and often succumbs to the belief that God has gone away. What, then, should you do? The very same as you would do if you were experiencing the utmost consolation: learn to do the same when you are suffering most, and behave as you did then. There is no better counsel for finding God than to leave him.[2]

There is no better counsel for finding God than to "leave God."[3] What does that mean? How can that be? When the very feeling of having lost God is what goads us on most to seek him?

How far from self-evident this advice sounds.

The state in which we feel abandoned by God, or that we have lost him, is a terrible thing.

A deep night surrounds us—life and all that otherwise had meaning and value for us seems poor and senseless. All strength is gone from us—we are all weakness, all emptiness, without any comfort.

---

1 Eckhart von Hochheim, O.P. (c. 1260–c. 1328): German theologian, philosopher, mystic, and Dominican friar. Revered for his mystical teaching and beloved for preaching in the vernacular, he was examined by the Inquisition on suspicion of heresy. One of Eckhart's best-known works is the tractate "Reden der Unterweisung" (Talks of Instruction). He is also mentioned in several of Jung's published works (see *CW* 6, 7, 9ii, 10, 11).

2 *EJ*: Pfeiffer, ed., *Meister Eckhart*, 554. [Emma Jung may have translated this passage independently, or she may have been inspired by the work of Josef Bernhart, whose slim translated volume, *Meister Eckhart: Reden der Unterweisung*, was published in 1922. Emma Jung delivered this lecture at the Club in November 1922. Bernhart's reading of the final sentence in this passage supports her interpretation. This English translation by A. Kappes.]

3 "Es ist kein Rat so gut, Gott zu finden, wie, dass man 'Gott lässt.'" [The final sentence of the Eckhart passage, as Emma Jung quotes it in her lecture, reads: "Ez enist dehein rât alse guot, got ze vinden, denne wâ man got lât." Her paradoxical understanding of this line, which forms the starting point for her reflections, differs from the commonly accepted reading; but both interpretations are possible, based on alternate interpretations of the word "*wâ*." The more common reading runs, in English: "One's best chance of finding God is to look in the place where one left him." Emma Jung's reading, like Bernhart's, is a viable alternative. Linguistic advice kindly offered by Niklaus Largier.]

And not only that: there is also fear, for in this weakness and helplessness of ours, are we not exposed to all the dark forces? Have not all the devils and demons been waiting for just this moment, to burst in upon our emptiness and make us their playground?

With our soul in such distress, it is only natural that we want to find what we have lost at all costs, that we set out to seek God, whom we miss so painfully at all depths, on all heights, in the foggy past, in the distant future, on all the paths we can think of, and by any means. With weeping and prayer, with repentance and penance and good resolutions, in any manner possible, we want to compel him to appear.

And isn't it necessary to try everything? Is not our fear more than justified? Is not everything in peril in times like these? And then we are told not to be bothered by it: I am to act as if I were "in the greatest comfort"—precisely what seems to me the least enlightening, the least promising, and the most difficult thing of all for me.

And why should I leave God? Why shouldn't I seek Him? Here I find only one answer:

I really do not know what God is. Suddenly it is clear to me that I do not know God at all; how, then, am I supposed to search for him; how am I supposed to find him?

Or is it not like this?

If my feeling tells me that God is far away, is it necessarily so? Does my feeling know what or where God is?

The thought that feeling can give me no certainty about this, that it could even lead me astray, dismays me. Upon what, then, should I depend? I have already seen that what I thought about God are simply my own—or someone else's—thoughts. I had to learn that what I sensed as God turned out to be the devil. I found the image offered to me to be only one of a thousand images by which we believe we know God. And now even feeling, that seemed to provide me with the greatest and most immediate certitude, shall that also fail? Everything, then, that I am used to relying upon as my compass, must now be called into question, and the only certainty I am left with is the insight that I cannot know God. Yes, for my powers can only serve me in this world for which they were created; they are no use to me in another.

Therefore, no advice on how to find God will perhaps be as good as the advice to leave God.

For when I want to seek him, I seek either my idea of him or my feeling, the image that I created of him, or my sense of what *I* called God. But all this is not God; all this is, at bottom, just me again. So, instead of God, I always find only myself, and—of this I am certain—God is definitely *not me*. Or has it not everywhere and at all times been the case that for humans, the unknown was always the most divine aspect of their gods? Did not the gods' vitality, their divinity, steadily diminish in equal measure to the definite and clear form people gave them, in the belief that their essence could be understood? Some powers were, of course, left to us, powers that we were even able to put to use; but where is the Divine?

The might of the Christian God is also on the wane, and the affliction of our time is that it is "missing God." Knowledge has killed faith; for faith lives only where there is no knowledge, where there can be none. But God can never be attained through knowledge; his essence is mystery. But if I am convinced of this, then I give up seeking God; I "leave" him.

But suddenly I also see that it is not at all a question of my finding God, but rather of *my being found*; and I can only be found when I am standing in place— each of us in our own place. That is why Meister Eckhart says,

> (Do) exactly the same as you would do if you were in the greatest comfort. Learn not to vary in the depths of woe but to behave in every way the same.[4]

And this is not because, through patient suffering, I shall secure a place for myself in heaven, or—according to the Indian view—escape more quickly from the cycle of death and rebirth. Rather it is because I do not know if this, now, here—perhaps precisely this strange, frightening thing is God.

And because I must be aware that God is seeking me, at this hour, here and now, I must therefore be in my place at this hour, at every hour.

For all of us, our place is the earth. Here we live, and here God must find us. And we must be ready to be found today, this hour, this minute.

By shifting all the weight from the here and now onto eternity, away from this earth and this life, Christianity has shown us the way to the next world. By doing so, however, we have not found God, but rather we have lost both him and ourselves.

The troublesome thing for us now is to be ourselves, now and here on this earth, just as we are, today and here, not as we want to be or should be. But that is not all that I have to learn: I also have to face everyone else as they are, now and here—not as they were yesterday or may be tomorrow—as the person *I* am, right now and here. And the same is true for life in general. This is particularly difficult for us, for we want anything but what is now and here, just as it is. We are always looking for possibilities, past or future, that could invalidate the here and now. This tendency within us still has to die, along with the dying God[5] who taught us to disdain this life for the sake of another, far-off one.

---

4   *EJ*: Pfeiffer, ed., *Meister Eckhart*, 554.

5   *mit dem untergehenden Gotte*: lit., with the setting God. In some of Emma Jung's dream texts and active imaginations, we find the image of a God (or god) who sinks like the setting sun. In one dream text (Chapter VI, 265), she names the theme of *Götterdämmerung*, an allusion to Nietzsche's "twilight of the gods." Elsewhere, in an active imagination, she writes about the death of a godlike figure, Aranû, who burns out like a star (Chapter VI, 295).

Now that I see that I do not know what, or where, God is, that I have fallen into a complete nothingness, into a frightening darkness, I also see that my only choice is to hold on to what is given to me:

The closest Here,
The shortest Now,
And the firmest Earth.

For if today my truth is that I know nothing about God, then this is to be accepted as my present reality, not as something to flee or to overcome, but rather as something that exists and rightly persists.

Only in this way am I completely human; and only when I am completely human can God be completely God. And thus, it is up to us to prepare a place for him, by "leaving God."

4. On the 20th Anniversary of the Club

29 February 1936

I WOULD LIKE to tell you a little about the pre-history and early history of our Club, to give those members who did not experience its early years some idea of what it was like.

By 1912 or 1913, along with the psychoanalytical association to which only analysts belonged,[1] there already existed a so-called "lay-persons' association," whose members were either analyzed persons or those currently in analysis, students for the most part. We got together in the Carl der Grosse[2] (for a while also in the Seidenhof)[3] for lectures and discussions. I particularly recall some discussions on Ibsen's plays, especially *Nora*, *The Lady from the Sea*, and also, I believe, *The Wild Duck*, to which we applied the new psychological discoveries.

What gave rise to our sense of togetherness, however, was not only our common interest in psychology, but also the experience of analysis, the more so as this made us feel different from the rest of the world. At that time, analysis and those who engaged in it were considered highly suspect. In 1912, i.e., after the publication of *Wandlungen und Symbole der Libido* and the resulting separation from Freud, the so-called "Zurich School" took shape, i.e., a group of analysts who likewise distanced themselves from Freud. Aside from Dr. Jung, members of this society included Dr. Schmid,[4] Dr. Maeder,[5] Dr. Riklin,[6] Dr. Schneiter,[7] Dr.

---

1 The International Psychoanalytical Association was founded in March 1910, under the patronage of Freud, on the initiative of Sándor Ferenczi, with Carl Jung as its first president and Franz Riklin as secretary (1910–14). In the same year a local Zurich group was formed under the auspices of Eugen Bleuler, director of the Zurich psychiatric clinic Burghölzli, with Alphonse Maeder as president and Johan van Ophuijsen as secretary. The group separated from the Burghölzli and the University of Zurich in early 1912 and officially became the Zurich Psychoanalytical Association, according to its statutes dated February 1912.

2 The building of the restaurant "Charlemagne" in the old town of Zurich dates back to the eighth century. By the time of the lay association's gatherings, it was run by the Zurich Women's Association for Temperance and Public Health (Frauenverein für Mässigkeit und Volkswohl), which had turned it into a non-alcoholic restaurant and coffee house.

3 At the time, another non-alcoholic hotel and restaurant run by the Zurich Women's Association, off the exclusive shopping street Bahnhofstrasse in the city center of Zurich.

4 For Hans Schmid-Guisan, see 36, note 40.

5 Alphonse Maeder (1882–1971): Swiss physician who specialized in psychiatry, psychotherapy, and psychoanalysis. Worked as an assistant physician to Eugen Bleuler and Carl Jung at the Burghölzli psychiatric clinic from 1906 to 1910.

6 For Franz Riklin, see 30, note 7.

7 Carl Schneiter practiced as a general physician before taking up psychiatry at the Burghölzli clinic in 1911. See also 131, note 1.

Lang,[8] Rev. Keller,[9] among others, who later formed the so-called "Analytical Convent."[10]

In Freudian analysis, the main focus was on discovering and resolving infantile complexes, and for Adler,[11] adaptation to the collective signified both the goal and the healing; whereas for us, increasingly, the central experience of analysis became individuation. In the foreground of this process was the conflict between individuality and collectivity; indeed, this conflict was considered a symptom, as it were, of the onset of the individuation process. At the time, almost everyone who was a part of our circle found themselves to be somehow in conflict with the ruling forms of the collective or with their family, and their protest often found expression in a demonstrative individualism which nowadays, when traditional forms and values have largely changed, appears grotesque (black sheep). But at that time, the old values had begun to crumble, their forms too narrow, too artificial and too wooden. More and more, one felt the need to have one's own life.

And then the war broke out, which was to become a watershed between two epochs. Because of it, much that was old got buried forever, and what was new surged ahead. At the time, however, one was not able to assess it as we can now; instead, one was simply caught up in it as it unfolded. We were in the grip of something, the significance and scope of which could neither be gauged at the time nor integrated into already existing forms. Arguably, this state of possession also created the wish for amalgamation, which was reflected in the plans and fantasies that appeared in various quarters. We dreamed of a place where, together with like-minded people, one could devote oneself to one's soul in peace, far from the world and its chaos, or of a new kind of communal life, in which people would encounter each other not only in a conventional manner as *personae*,[12] but rather

---

8 Josef Bernhard Lang (1881–1945): Swiss physician and psychotherapist, close friend and analyst of writer Hermann Hesse (Hesse, *"Die dunkle und wilde Seite der Seele": Briefwechsel mit seinem Psychoanalytiker Josef Bernhard Lang, 1916–1944*).

9 Adolf Keller (1872–1963): Swiss Protestant theologian and professor, active in the ecumenical movement. One of the first pastors interested in psychoanalysis. Family friend of Carl and Emma Jung. See 131 and note.

10 *den sogenannten "Analytischen Convent"*: "Convent" means literally (from Latin) "coming together." The name "Analytischer Convent" occurs only rarely in Jungian writings of the period. It was used in 1912–13 by members of the Zurich school, being quickly replaced by the name "Verein für Analytische Psychologie" (formally, the Association for Analytical Psychology; commonly called the Analytical Association). Such changes in terminology marked a period of rapid organizational adjustment, after the publication of Jung's *Wandlungen und Symbole* made it necessary for Jung's followers to separate from Freud's. For more on these developments, see "Emma Jung and Analytical Psychology," volume introduction, 34f. and notes.

11 Alfred Adler (1870–1937): Austrian medical doctor and psychotherapist, who belonged initially to Freud's Wednesday evening circle, the nucleus of the psychoanalytic movement. In 1910 he became chairman of the Vienna Psycho-Analytic Society but resigned in 1911 because of his increasing divergence from Freud's theories. Together with a number of supporters, he subsequently formed the school of individual psychology, emphasizing the social context of neuroses.

12 Latin, plural of *persona*: a technical term in Jungian psychology, referring to the public face, or "mask," that individuals adopt, consciously or unconsciously, in order to match social expectations.

as individuals. And we asked ourselves whether and how these dreams could be realized. Mrs. McCormick[13] favored the idea of a kind of monastery, where each person would have their own little dwelling (as in a Carthusian hermitage), either to live there long-term, or simply to retreat there for shorter or longer periods of introversion or study. For her, Zurich and analysis were very much a refuge (which had been quite true during the war). This led her to have small brooches made for herself and for some of us, marked with the letters "R Z,"[14] that we were to wear as a badge.

Along with this fantasy of a refuge, another one had arisen and had become outlined especially clearly in the mind of Miss Teucher,[15] who was later charged with looking after the Club house. Her idea was to establish a cooperative community where one could try to live a new kind of communal life, based on the new psychological insights. It was to be a kind of settlement, with a shared budget, common rooms and social events, and a common library. Members would contribute to the operating costs according to their pecuniary circumstances; and those who could not afford to do so, or could only pay a little, would have the opportunity to work for the whole—in the office, kitchen, house, or garden—or to contribute in some other way. The spirit should be an analytical one, which meant above all showing mutual respect for the individuality of the other, and what was called analytical openness.

After further discussion, these fantasies became more and more delineated, especially because the analysts also thought it desirable for there to be a place that could serve as a kind of home for the new psychology, and where analysands, too, could live in a suitable environment.

Mrs. McCormick, who was very much attached to the realization of this idea, wished to finance the project as an expression of gratitude for her analysis. This made the plan a tangible possibility that soon became a fact. With Miss Teucher's help, she avidly set about inspecting building sites, and she came very close to buying a huge block of land for the proposed settlement high up on the hills between Küsnacht and Zollikon. She presented her plans to us. After an in-depth

---

13   Edith Rockefeller (1872–1932): daughter of wealthy American Standard Oil cofounder John D. Rockefeller. She married Harold McCormick (1872–1941), himself the heir to the wealth of the McCormick family agriculture machine company (International Harvester). They came to Jung through Harold's cousin (Joseph) Medill McCormick, who had been his patient in the Burghölzli in 1909. In 1913 Edith traveled to Zurich to be treated by Jung for depression, where she was joined by Harold and the rest of the family for periods of time. The couple became staunch supporters of Jung's cause, not only funding the Psychology Club Zurich but also paying to have Jung's writings translated into English. After extended analysis, Edith left Zurich in 1922 and became a successful Jungian psychoanalyst herself.

14   "R Z": These initials, unexplained in the text, may stand for *Refugium Zürich* ("Zurich Refuge").

15   Ida Teucher (1892–1993): At twenty-three, she had already had several years of analysis with Jung, and it was he who asked her, despite her young age, to become involved with the planning for the new Club.

consultation, we, the so-called founding committee,[16] found it too risky to begin with such a large project, since we had no clear picture of what the level of future participation might be. Furthermore, the number of those who, at the time, would consider living there was too small to justify the building of such a settlement. There was also some uncertainty about whether and how such a plan for an analytic communal life would work in practice.

We therefore decided to try it on a smaller scale, in the form of a club that would be connected, in the American style and at the express wish of Mrs. McCormick, to a guest house. The idea of creating a situation in which foreigners,[17] for example, would be able to live in a congenial environment, where they could feel at home, was very dear to Mrs. McCormick's heart. To this end she rented the large and magnificently furnished house on Löwenstrasse,[18] initially for two and a half years. She purchased additional furniture—mostly to furnish the bedrooms—and engaged what I believe was a staff of five to service the facility, including a waiter who, incidentally, later caused us great vexation.

With the matter having progressed thus far, the friends of the analytic-psychological movement were invited to attend a meeting at the Club house, at which the Psychological Club was officially founded. How things then developed externally, you have heard from the excerpt of the minutes that Mrs. Fierz[19] read to us. If you are interested, I would like to add a little about the inner history of the Club.

At the beginning, it seemed to me to be rather like how Christmas used to be, when we were allowed to enter the beautiful living room to play with our new presents, and a whole new year filled with undreamed-of possibilities lay ahead. But this festive, expectant atmosphere did not last long. All sorts of unforeseen difficulties soon arose, and the board, of which I was a member,[20] had a great deal of work to do, not only to address practical questions, but also to clarify and discuss issues in principle, and even to handle and smooth over personal difficulties and conflicts. Very soon, various members began to show a certain disgruntlement, primarily about the fact that a small founding committee had planned and prepared

---

16 Members of the Founding Committee were Harold and Edith McCormick-Rockefeller, Carl and Emma Jung, Hermann Sigg, Toni Wolff, and Ida Teucher. Hermann Sigg (1875–1927): Swiss businessman, specializing in olive oil imports. A Küsnacht neighbor and close friend of Carl Jung, he often accompanied him on cycling, sailing, and mountain-climbing trips. His wife, Martha Sigg-Boeddinghaus of Munich, had come to Zurich in 1910 to study with Jung and become an analyst. In 1911 she attended the International Psychoanalytic Congress in Weimar. Other committee members are identified in notes above.

17 The "foreigners" in question would have been people who had traveled to Zurich for analysis and lacked either daytime work or a social network.

18 Located in the Zurich business and shopping district, a short walk from the city's main train station.

19 Linda Fierz-David: see 42, note 83.

20 The founding board of the Psychology Club Zurich consisted of Emma Jung (president), Hermann Sigg (treasurer), Irma Oczeret (secretary), Edith McCormick (board member), and Ida Teucher (overseer of the Club house).

the whole thing and had presented it to a larger number of potential members only after the house had been rented and business was underway.[21] Secondly, there was criticism that the Club had not been worked for and grown in and of itself, but rather had been presented to us as a gift, a done deal, which gave it an air of unreality. One often had to wonder, as well as feeling annoyed, at the stubborn inability on the part of so many to graciously accept Mrs. McCormick's generous gift, which was not merely a "done deal" but was rather something in process, that brought with it responsibilities and the need to prove oneself worthy of it.[22] It did not, as some seemed to think, provide an opportunity or give license to crawl under mother's skirts again. Such surliness can only be put down to the unsettled state of the individuals concerned, and perhaps to the new psychology in general. I am certain there would be no such reactions in our circle today.

A further difficulty that arose out of the prevailing developmental phases at that time was the practice of analysts and patients mingling, outside of analysis, in the social setting of the Club. It was customary to meet in the Club on Saturdays to dine together, followed by a lecture or a social evening. At the time, of course, an analyst was much more of a god for his patients than he is today; and this was true not only from the standpoint of the patient. Many thought this was how it had to be and constantly emphasized the need for unquestioning obedience or complete submission to the analyst.

In our Analytical Convent,[23] which embodied the psychological-scientific side of the Club, we had an entire guild of gods, and there were often great disappointments and resistances when the latter showed their more human side in Club life, particularly when analysands discovered that what they had believed to be their unique transference relationship proved to be not so unique after all. One even asked oneself not only whether it was advisable for analysts and analysands to intermingle socially, but also whether it was even possible.

Among Club members themselves, it was also natural that the typological opposites stood out strongly; and these enjoyed special attention, and prominence, as the book on types had just been published at that time.[24] These oppositions,

---

21 Added to the original typescript, in unidentified handwriting: "which made one feel blind-sided by it."

22 Much of Emma Jung's time as president of the Club in 1916–1919 was consumed by these discussions. Following a decision by the board, she first addressed the "Club problem" in a presidential circular letter on 26 October 1916, with a questionnaire on how to structurally improve Club life (Muser, "Zur Geschichte des Psychologischen Clubs von den Anfängen bis 1928" [History of the Psychology Club from its beginnings to 1928], 15–17).

23 The author's language is slightly anachronistic. In 1916, when the Club was founded, the name "Analytical Convent" had already been out of use for two years, replaced by "Analytical Association."

24 The analysis of different psychological types was a focus of discussion and a topic for presentations in the early years of the Club. Carl Jung gave seminars on the topic and read chapters from his forthcoming book on the subject. As early as February 1915, Alphonse Maeder presented in two meetings of the Analytical Association on "Hodler und die Typenfrage in der Kunst" (Hodler and the type question in art), which led to lively discussions. Carl Jung first presented to the Club

too, caused the board a great deal of work. Indeed, it soon became obvious that realizing an analytical collective would not be as easy as we had imagined. While frictions, ill humor and the like among the Club members who met daily could not, of course, be avoided, recognition of the other person's individuality and the postulated analytical openness proved to be in very short supply, even though there was no lack of effort and good intentions in that direction. The bar had been set too high. It became clear that the attitude and behavior that were necessary between doctor and analysand could not simply be applied *tel quel*[25] to a collective. That would require a society of already whole personalities who no longer had any shadow.[26] In every other society a persona is essential, i.e., certain forms are necessary and may not be infringed upon. It took a long while for this to be realized; for the persona seemed to belong to old, discarded conventions, and to nevertheless put them to use was almost a betrayal of the new science, and of the real purpose of the Club. We dealt with this problem for years. After we moved to Gemeindestrasse,[27] giving up management of the guest house was the first concession we made toward the insight that it was not possible—or at least not yet—to realize the community we envisaged, or at least not in this form. This problem of a community, however, remained a matter of great importance to us, and we were greatly preoccupied with it for several years until finally it led to the great crisis which, in 1921, threatened to destroy the Club.[28]

Since then, we have become much more levelheaded and have learnt to be more modest. Now and again the reproach is voiced that we have dropped our main goal, or that the Club has not fulfilled its main purpose and has become a merely intellectual society. I find this reproach to be unjustified. To my mind,

---

on the subject on 3 June 1916, with a lecture titled "Historische Beiträge zur Typenfrage" (Historical contributions to the question of psychological types). As early as 1914, Emma Jung discussed the topic of psychological typology with Hans Schmid-Guisan, who later engaged in a programmatic letter exchange with her husband on the subject (Jung and Schmid-Guisan, *The Question of Psychological Types: The Correspondence of C. G. Jung and Hans Schmid-Guisan, 1915–1916*). Jung's book *Psychological Types* was published in 1921.

25 French: as is.

26 Shadow: a key term in Jungian thought and a central theme in Emma Jung's writings. The shadow theme is discussed in the "Reader's Guide," volume introduction, 17 note 13; 83f.

27 After the lease for the house at Löwenstrasse had been given up, in 1918 the Club bought a new house at Gemeindestrasse 25/27. They had to move into a temporary location until the previous tenants vacated the place in 1919, when the Club found its permanent home.

28 The looming conflict, about whether to give priority to the individual or the collective, had broken out after Hans Trüb, as the new president, initiated an open discussion on 10 August 1920 with his circular "Clubblatt Nr. 1" (Club sheet no. 1), containing his personal view favoring the latter over the former. This put him and a group of followers at odds with Carl and Emma Jung, Toni Wolff, and others who maintained the opposing view. In 1922 Carl and Emma Jung, together with Toni Wolff, temporarily left the Club, to return only in 1924 after Trüb resigned from the presidency and the following year, together with his wife, Susi Trüb (née Wolff, sister of Toni), gave up membership. See Weber, "Vom Selbst zur Welt: Zur intellektuellen Biographie von Hans Trüb" (From the Self to the World: An Intellectual Biography of Hans Trüb), in *Hans Trüb, Welt und Selbst*, 171–206, especially 176–79; also Kiraly, "Das Clubproblem, 1920–1924."

when one recognizes and accepts one's limitations, it is an expression of psychological understanding; and to restrict oneself to what is possible, while remaining a person who "strives on and lives to strive,"[29] ultimately gets one somewhat closer to the longed-for goal.

Furthermore, in spiritual terms, the Club offers us so much that is lively and valuable that it is quite misplaced to speak of it as being "merely" anything. I hope you will agree with my taking this opportunity to thank the board for all the pleasant, interesting, and stimulating evenings that are provided for us at the Club, thanks to its efforts.

In fact, with our evening lectures, we are fulfilling the original meaning of the Club; for, along with our aspiration to establish a community, it was a declared aim of the Club from the outset to foster psychological science and interests. The science aspect was taken care of more by the "Association," which held regular meetings in the Club house at which theoretical questions were discussed. There was, for example, a discussion of the libido theory for which every member was asked to contribute his thoughts on the theory in writing.[30] The relationship of the Zurich School and the Club was also the subject of one of these discussions, and entire essays were written on it.[31] Lectures were given at the Club by analysts and members. I recall, for example, a lecture by Mrs. McCormick on the evolution of women, if I remember correctly.[32] Dr. Hans Schmid's lecture on Tristan[33] led to lively discussions, dealing as it did with a problem that was very much in the foreground, namely, the path of the individual versus that of the collective. Dr. Jung read aloud—I believe his was the first such reading—Barlach's *Der tote Tag*,[34] which a Club Cassandra interpreted as an evil omen. Later, we also heard chapters from the book on typology,[35] which was being written at the time. We had communal reading evenings during which we read and discussed *The Golem*[36]

---

29 "He who strives on and lives to strive / Can earn redemption still." From the scene "Mountain Gorges," ll. 11936–37 (Goethe, *Faust, Part Two*, translated by David Luke, 234).

30 Jung's libido theory, as developed in *Wandlungen und Symbole der Libido*, was discussed by members of the Analytical Association (then still called Analytical Convent) over a series of four meetings in early 1913, between 31 January and 14 March. See "Protokoll der Vorträge des Vereins für Analytische Psychologie I, 1913–1916," Psychology Club Zurich Archives.

31 Maria Moltzer read a paper, "The Relation between the Zurich School and the Club," on 1 September 1917. On 21 January 1918 Eugen Schlegel presented a request that members of the Club should also be allowed to attend the lectures of the Analytical Association (the "Zurich School" of analysts).

32 No such talk has been identified in the materials of the Club archive. It is possible that Edith McCormick gave her presentation in the framework of one of the women's evenings at the Club, which took place regularly as of early 1921, but for which no detailed protocols exist.

33 Hans Schmid presented his lecture "Tristan" in two parts on 6 and 19 May 1916.

34 Jung's reading of Barlach's *Der tote Tag* took place in the Club on 26 February 1916. See Fischer and Kaufmann, "C. G. Jung and Modern Art," *The Art of C. G. Jung*, 19–31, in particular 27.

35 Jung, *Psychological Types* (CW 6). On 8 and 21 April 1918 Jung had presented another draft chapter on "Das Typenproblem bei Schiller" (The type problem in Schiller), before giving a full seminar on the finished book at the Club, 10 March 1921.

36 Meyrinck, *Der Golem*, was first published as a book in 1915, after the fantastic novel had been published in 1913–14 as a series in a journal. The reading and discussion mentioned by Emma Jung

and other works. And later on, when we were already on the Gemeindestrasse, there were, for a time, women's meetings during which we spoke of and shared personal inner and outer experiences,[37] and where we even tackled the animus problem,[38] only to then get bogged down in it.

This brings us almost up to the present time; and it was my intention, if you recall, to tell you only about the Club's early history.

All that now remains for me is to ask you all to raise your glasses to toast the further flourishing of the Club, although we must postpone this until the second act.

---

had possibly been stimulated by a Club presentation by Dutch analyst Johan van der Hoop on "Die Bedeutung des Golem" (the meaning of the Golem) on 1 January 1917.

37 The separate women's gatherings at the Club commenced on the initiative of Emma Jung, Susi Trüb, and Erika Schlegel, with a first meeting on 7 May 1921. In the first year, seven women's meetings were held, followed by another ten the following year, and continuing from there. It was to the women's group that Emma Jung gave her presentation "Reflections on a Passage by Meister Eckhart," 7 November 1922 (Chapter I, 156ff.). On the women's meetings in the Club, see "Emma Jung and Analytical Psychology," volume introduction, 42f., 52).

38 Fierz, "Ein Beitrag zum Animusproblem" (On the animus problem), 14 February 1931; Emma Jung, "Über das Wesen des Animus" (The nature of the animus), 21 November 1931. (See also "Reader's Guide," volume introduction, 46 and notes.)

FIGURE 2.1.
[A gathering]. Paint-
ing by Emma Jung,
undated.

II

Thoughts

Thoughts, 1914–1916

February 1914

IDEAS

God is not, nor was; *God is becoming.*

"Death is for free." Yes, but one pays with one's life!

The devil is most dangerous when he starts to be ashamed of himself.

One thing seems certain: there is no suffering without guilt; but guilt not in our narrow sense, as transgression against human laws, conventions, etc., but rather as transgression against a higher power or purpose. Mental suffering, like physical pain, is how nature drives us away from a dangerous direction that runs contrary to a higher will or fate.

The worst suffering is suffering that is not understood, i.e., that we ourselves do not understand. This is the suffering we call "blameless" or tragic—when we simply do not see the connections. It may not be blameless, but it is tragic, for it misses its purpose. And if we are great at not understanding, we are almost even greater at misunderstanding. We always see, say, do, feel, leave undone what we should not.[1]

Are human beings really so stupid? Here you are, wondering why you feel bad. You should be wondering instead that you are doing so well. It is pointless to rebel against the fact that the large can devour the small—that is simply rebelling against nature, which is presumptuous—and inasmuch as you are a part of this same nature, you would be rebelling against yourself, which is stupid and futile. But if you feel at one with nature and are subject to its will, you can be indifferent to how big or how small you are. If there are strong and dangerous predators, then others have wings or fast legs, and still others protect themselves with poisonous stings or with mimicry, and the really clever ones—I'll let you in on the secret—allow themselves to be eaten to be safe from danger.

Indeed, if only you humans also understood how to make a virtue of necessity: but you have distanced yourselves so far from nature and have, though it defies belief, forgotten your mother tongue. Forgotten—at the tree of knowledge! (And one has to be hung from the Tree of Life to learn these runes[2] again.) To forget

---

1   An earlier version of this thought continues: "Numb, deaf, and blind we stagger from one anguish to another—when we should be silent, we speak, and when we should speak, we are silent (Parsifal and Lohengrin)."

2   A verse depicting Odin hanging on a tree until he learns the runes is found in Jung, *Wandlungen und Symbole*, 258 (*Psychology of the Unconscious*, 295). Emma Jung paraphrases or alludes to this verse several times in her writings.

one's mother tongue means to lose paradise and to burden mankind with the curse of original sin. And why did this have to happen to Adam and Eve? What do you think? Probably because, once they possessed the gift of knowledge, they knew nothing better to do with it than to abuse it. Certainly, they soon "knew" how best to dodge the demands of life, and with that, misfortune arrived. And because they no longer *wanted* to do what they *had* to do, and therefore did it reluctantly,[3] childbirth and work became torture to humankind. Coercion is torture, and the ultimate joy of freedom is to be willing to do what you must do. For you to learn this again, Christ pointed to the lilies of the field and the sparrows on the house-top. But you cannot become lilies and sparrows. Humans are what you have to become, *humans!* I say become, because you are, in fact, hardly human yet. You are no longer plants or animals; you have lost their beauty and not yet found that of human beings.

Beauty is a rare guest: it comes late and disappears early!

The task, then, is to become human. What you now know by that term is actually only a part of it. If you look closely, you will discover that the world is full of heads, hearts, arms, hands, eyes, ears, mouths and legs, some of which act on their own and occasionally also want to join together. But how has this worked out until now? Here, too much head and too little heart, there, too little head and too much mouth, or too much belly and too little hand, and someone always wants to be king, not to govern the others but to oppress them. That is why the whole thing is found to be useless and has to fall apart, again and again. It has to be torn to pieces and reassembled until the right One, the Whole, has come together, in which no piece is too big or too small, too much or too little.

You can love devils as well as angels; you even should, because, as you know, the former often help more than the latter. But on no account should you confuse them with each other, for that is sin.

It is also sin to confuse concrete with abstract, symbol with reality.

What man already achieved thousands of years ago, namely establishing his right to exist beyond biology, woman has yet to do. And let her not attempt to achieve something in a few years that first requires nature to be overcome. Only in the struggle will she come to understand what it means to have nature as one's opponent.

---

3   In a marginal note, the author comments: "Discord of the will is the root of all evil."

"As a creative person, one is simply infantile; nothing can be done about it."

I would like to reverse the statement. Put this way, it sounds to me too much like an excuse.

It is not that, as a creative person, one must or even may be infantile, but rather that, as an infantile person, one must create. To be infantile means to have the inner potential for development and, at the same time, the *duty* to make something out of this potential, in whatever field.

Only one in whom no such potential exists anymore is no longer infantile and is discharged of this duty, for he has reached his limits.

The opinion that intellectual or artistic creation is more valuable than other creative forms of expression seems to me too great an overestimation, probably stemming from a time when it was only thanks to this overestimation that the libido could be directed into such elevated forms.

But it appears that we must gradually overcome this standpoint and accord the same respect to creativity, to development, *to becoming*, even in the humblest forms. The capacity for intellectual creation brings with it primarily not a privilege, but rather a duty.

Does the eagle deserve credit for being able to fly? At most, it would be a sin if it did not use its wings—but only a fool would ask the same of a mouse.

Be fair, then!

Can we move beyond marriage yet? May we do so? Yes, beyond marriage as it has been up to now: a compulsory or protective measure for the husband, which is abused by the wife in order to lead a parasitic existence. This, we should move beyond, not by leaping beyond it, but by growing. Only when marriage is a free act for the husband, and the wife no longer allows herself to be hampered by it in her development, only then will we no longer *need* it. And then this *useful* institution can also become a *beautiful* one.

CHAPTER II

[Spring 1914]⁴

Love—yes, whoever might have you!

Where are you? For now, it lives only in our dreams; but humanity has been dreaming about it for so long, perhaps the time is not too far off when it will really begin to live. But for now, we still cannot behold it. What we know is torment: the torment of the deceived deceiver, who abuses the holiest name and gives and receives, in the name of love, something that isn't.

[Spring 1914]

I think I now understand the ancient myth of Cerydwen and Gwyon,[5] which always impressed me greatly.

Yes, that is something one has to be able to do, to transform oneself and take on a different form according to the needs of the moment. So, this must be learned.

[Spring 1914]

We are already familiar with the meaning of words; now we need to convince ourselves of their meaninglessness.

---

4   Brackets indicate that Emma Jung did not specify a date. Information in surrounding pages of the notebook suggests when the entry was written.

5   In Emma Jung's handwritten original, the name Cerydwen appears first. Above it, apparently as an afterthought, is the name Gwyon. A medieval Welsh myth tells of an enchantress, Cerydwen, who brewed a magical potion for her son. A different youth, Gwyon, drank the potion by mistake and fled from the angry Cerydwen, changing shape many times. Changing shape as he did, Cerydwen finally became a hen and ate Gwyon, in the form of a grain of corn. Later, she gave birth to a beautiful child, whom she recognized as Gwyon reborn. The myth tells that this child grew up to be the bard Taliesin.

[Spring 1914]

You want to understand people? First learn to understand what they want you to understand.

[Spring 1914]

"I don't know." This is the only answer you give me, O my God, after I have wrestled with you for it so passionately? This, then, shall be my salvation, and I must also want this, if there is no other way: not to know.

January 1916

It speaks to me:

The point where you all get stuck and many generally fail is in bringing inner knowledge to life. The task is by no means complete with the most beautiful and profound insight. What is needed, rather, is *doing* and *living*.

This happens of its own accord, you think? But how, and when? Think of that dream where you had to go through the same birth twice, once in spirit and again in reality. All births are like that.

And even if giving birth in spirit is as painful as giving birth in reality, it is not the same thing, and is no substitute for it; for spirit, too, only comes to life by being born twice. Otherwise, it is only image and shadow, and as unreal and ineffective as image and shadow are. You must not be content with that, or the dead will come and claim their right. For there are not only the dead who died long ago, but also those—and these particularly make themselves felt—who could have come to life long ago.

Those who want to come to life and to whom you have to give life, if you yourself want to live.

How can this happen?

It is not easy, a long, long task, not a great deed. It means thinking about the dead every day and every hour, thinking about them with love, until you feel that they are alive.

How does one feel that?

Only by feeling that there are no dead any longer. Then you will say: now they are at peace; now they are fully dead, and you do not know that now they have come alive.

But first, you have to recognize the dead. How are you to think of them with love if you do not recognize them?

[Spring 1916]

What does love actually mean?

A question that can hardly be answered.

Really just a striving from one to another, or from two toward each other. One wants the other, yearns toward the other—wants to merge with the other.

Why should one turn this around and want nothing, especially from the being one loves, and leave them in peace? This is not in the nature of love, which, as I said, is a striving toward the other. Why do people twist it like that?

People like to say that higher love wants only what is best for the other, only their well-being. But it takes a certain amount of self-assurance to trust that one knows what is best for the other person. Tend to your own well-being first, then, and learn to recognize here what is true and what is false.

Love that wants nothing does not exist, just as there is no striving without direction. Therefore, do not struggle to figure out how love is supposed to be *self-less*—on the contrary, it must be *self-full*; just see that it is filled with the right self.

[March 1916]

If only I could solve the great riddle: why does one yearn for things that do not exist? Where do the images in our soul come from, that do not come from reality?

Why do we believe in them, and why can this belief, or at least this hope, not be eradicated, even by the most compelling arguments of experience?

Or might there be people with nothing in their souls that could not be learned from reason and experience, people who do not know the baffled torment that afflicts us when we confront the power and force of things or images in our souls to which no outer reality has ever corresponded, things with which no arguments, knowledge, or experience can ever come to terms? What kind of tremendous, compelling powers are these, at once so dreadful and so beautiful?

FIGURE 3.1.
[Cross and scorpion].
Painting by Emma
Jung, undated.

III

Narrative Poem

THIS NARRATIVE POEM is open to a host of mythical and literary interpretations.[1] In composing "Do you see the sea?" Emma Jung apparently drew on her lifelong fascination with the primeval forest. In commenting on the first version of her dream and fantasy of April 1915, "The miraculous city" (273ff.), she wrote:

> The pine forest is dark and uncanny. No color penetrates it—no light—no warming ray from the sun. Spooky, yet inviting—how the Black Forest always lured me![2]

In the same commentary, she discusses a favorite book of her youth, whose depiction of the primal forest included an idealized vision of children unconsciously discovering their sexuality:

> *Au coeur sombre de la forêt verte*[3] was the name of a book that made a strong impression on me at one time, because it depicted love in the primal forest; no, to put it better: *deux enfants, corps et âmes vierges, vivent ensemble dans une forêt vierge et de toute cette virginité naît un amour de pureté adorable.*[4] I had always wished I could be so completely in and with nature, could grow in and with it, and in and through it could find myself and my love.

In contrast with this youthful fantasy, Emma's mature poem confronts the shadows of instinctive nature, the reality of loss, and the painful process leading at last to wholeness.

---

1   One literary association, the medieval epic poem *Gregorius* by Hartmann von Aue, tells the legend of a baby, born of sibling incest, who through suffering and penance grows into sainthood and finally becomes pope. The theme is also prominent in *Die Walküre*, the second opera of Richard Wagner's Ring cycle, and in ancient Nordic ballads, whose literary form is echoed in Emma Jung's narrative poem (Böldl and Yngborn, eds., *Ritter und Elfen, Liebe und Tod* (Knights and elves, love and death), 26ff., 130ff.).

2   Emma Jung's commentary on her dream and fantasy of 10 April 1915, in her notebook "Night Voices," is discussed in the introduction to Chapter VII, "The System: A Cosmology," 316ff.

3   French: In the dark heart of the green forest.

4   French: two children, virgin in body and soul, live together in a virgin forest, and from all this virginity is born a love of adorable purity.

Siehst du das Meer?

c. 1921

Siehst Du das Meer?
Weit liegt es da—von grauem Himmel überwölbt.
Ein wilder Strand:
Nur schroffe Felsenklippen, dunkles Buschwerk.—
Mit rauem Schreien fliegen Möwen auf und nieder.
Und siehst du dort am Strand das alte Mauerwerk?
Es ist ein Schloss, das teils dem Meere, teils dem Fels entstiegen
die grauen Türme in den Himmel reckt.
Wild und trotzig wie der Fels auf dem's gebaut,
so steht es dort;
und düster, wie das Land dem spärlich nur
die Sonne Licht und Wärme spendet.
Der Meerwind streicht darüber hin,
die Wellen netzen seinen Fuss.
O Winde, nehmet mit euch, traget fort den Fluch,
der auf dem Turme liegt seit alter Zeit!
O Wellen, waschet, waschet rein
die Steine von der Schuld, die sie befleckt!
Wohl mancher Stein, benagt von Wind und Wasser
ward morsch, zerfiel, entschwand in Luft und Wasser,
doch Schuld und Leid der Menschen
bleibt immerdar bestehn.

Vor Zeiten lebten dort ein Mann und eine Frau
in jenem Schloss am Meere, das nun lange öd:
des Wassers Sohn der Mann
und wie die Welle stets bewegt
hin übers Meer zu fliegen wie ein Vogel,
die braunen Segel vom Wind gebläht,
der weit in fernste Lande ihn entführt,
War seine höchste Lust.
Doch sein Weib ein Kind der Erde,
der grünen Hügel und der weiten Felder,
der Waldesbäume und der Blumen Schwester.
Ein Knabe und ein Mädchen ward dem Paar geboren,

Do you see the sea?

c. 1921

Do you see the sea?
There it lies, vast, under the grey vault of heaven.
A wild shore:
Only rugged rocky cliffs, dark thickets.
With raucous screeches seagulls rise and fall.
And do you see the old wall there, upon the shore?
It is a castle that rose from the sea and from the rock,
its gray towers straining toward the heavens.
Wild and defiant as the crag on which it's built,
there it stands;
and gloomy, like the land to which the sun
grants only sparingly its light and warmth.
Sea winds brush the tower,
waves lap at its feet.
O winds, bear forth the curse, carry it away,
that rests upon the tower since ancient times!
O waves, wash the stones, wash them clean
of the guilt that stains them still!
Many a stone, gnawed by wind and wave,
has softened, crumbled, vanished in air and water;
but human guilt and suffering
endure forever.

There long ago a man and woman lived
in that castle by the sea, now long deserted.
The man, the water's son,
was always moved as waves are moved.
To fly like a bird across the sea,
his brown sails billowed by the wind
carrying him off to farthest lands,
was all his heart's desire.
His wife, though, was a child of earth,
of green hills and the spreading fields,
a sister to the forest trees and flowers.
Unto this couple a boy and girl were born.

jedoch des Vaters wildes Seemannswesen,
im Mädchen trat es wiederum zu Tag,
derweil der Bruder schwer und schweigsam war geartet
wie die Erde
und auch wohl zart und weich, wie ihrer Blumenwies.
Den Vater, der zu Kampf und fernen Fahrten stets auf Meereswogen zog
sahn kaum die Kinder.
Und ob gleich nah, war ferne auch die Mutter,
denn sie, dem Meere grollend, weil es süss und mächtig
lockend ihr den Liebsten untreu machte,
sass tagelang am Fenster ihres Turms,
weit über alles Nahe weg den Blick gerichtet,
dem Fernen nach, den ihr der Wind entführte
sehnsuchtsvoll sinnend, ob er ihr wohl wiederkehrte;
oder auch der grünen Wälder ihrer Heimat denkend,
die sie dereinst verlassen um den Mann
in sein einsames Schloss am Meere zu begleiten.

Wie die wilden Vögel der See
und die würzigen Blumen der Heide,
so wuchsen die Kinder heran,
der Welt der Menschen ferne und allein.
Eines dem andern Mutter, Vater
Gespiel und Freund und Alles.
So zogen Jahre hin
die Kleinen wurden gross—vom Vater keine Botschaft,
der Mutter Geist in Sehnsucht mehr und mehr verzehrt.

Als eines Tages, wie so oft die Beiden
im Walde stundenlang selbander schweiften,
dem Jagdwild nach, und unter einem Baume sich zur Rast gesetzt,
verdunkelte mit einem Male sich die Sonne,
voll schwarzer Wolken war der Himmel
und schwül und schwer und still die Luft.
Schon manch Gewitter hatten wohl erlebt die Beiden,
doch nie noch däuchte sie die Welt so bang—
und was sie nie gekannt,
die Angst, der grause Wurm,
kroch über ihre Herzen, schnürt sie ein,
und zwingt die Hände fester sich zu fassen.
So sitzen regungslos sie unterm Baume, Hand in Hand.
Entfesselt ist der Sturm,

Now, the sailor father's untamed nature
came to light again within the girl,
while her brother, grave and silent as the earth,
was tender, even soft, like a flowering meadow.
Their father, always drawn across the waves for battle and distant
    journeys,
the children rarely saw.
And although close, their mother too was distant,
for she, glowering at the sea, whose sweet and mighty
luring made her dearest one unfaithful,
sat all day at the window of her tower,
her gaze directed outward, over all that lay nearby,
toward the far-off one the wind had taken from her,
wistfully wondering if he would return to her;
or pondering the green woods of her homeland,
that she had left one day to follow him
to this, his lonely castle by the sea.

Like wild birds of the sea
and fragrant meadow flowers,
the children grew,
far from the world of people, and alone.
Each to the other was mother, father,
playmate and friend and all.
And so the years went by;
the little ones grew big.
No tidings from their father,
their mother's spirit with longing ever more consumed.

There came a day when, as so often,
the two spent hours roaming through the forest
in search of game, and, as they rested underneath a tree,
the sun began to darken all at once,
black clouds filled the sky,
sultry, heavy, and still the air.
The two had lived through many a thunderstorm,
but never before had the world seemed so fraught.
And what they'd never known,
fear, the gruesome worm,
crawled over their hearts, squeezing them tight,
and forcing them to grip each other's hands.
Hand in hand, as still as stone, they sit beneath the tree.

es zucken Blitze
gefolgt von fürchterlichen Donnerschlägen,
ein Strom von Regen flutet auf die Erde.
Da, ein blendend heller Schein,
ein Schlag, der Mark und Bein erzittern macht—
in Flammen steht der Baum, wo die Geschwister Schutz gesucht.
Vor Schrecken zitternd stürzen sie davon,
die Hände krampfhaft immer noch verschlungen,
als ob sie nimmermehr sich lösen könnten.—
—die hohe Eiche nicht allein
ward von des Blitzes Flammenstrahl entzündet
der wahllos treffende, er fiel auch in zwei Herzen,
und fachte dort ein wildes Feuer an.—
Anders kehrten die Geschwister heim als sie gegangen,
und anders däuchte sie von diesem Tage an die Welt.
Sie sahen alles nur noch in dem Scheine
des Feuers das ihr Inneres durchglüht,
und was sie dieser Flamme feindlich glaubten,
ward ihnen selbst verhasst.
Selbst ihre Mutter wards, ob diese schon
in ihren Träumen immer tief verloren
nicht Aug noch Ohr für ihrer Kinder Tun besass.

Eines Abends, als die zwei heimlich beisammen waren
hörten sie der Mutter Schritte draussen auf der Treppe;
die stieg zum Turm empor, um dort zu sehen,
ob nicht ein fernes Licht im Meere draussen
ihr kündete die Heimkehr des Vermissten.
Doch anders deuteten die Schritte ihre Kinder:
"Man will zu uns!—uns trennen wohl sogar!"
Und wild wie eine Löwin stürzt zum Schaft die Schwester
nimmt dort den spitzen Dolch und eilt hinaus.
Dunkel ist der Flur und ohne viel Besinnen
tritt sie der leise Wandelnden entgegen
und stösst den Stahl tief in der Mutter Brust.
Inzwischen kommt der Bruder, zu sehen was geschah, ihr nachgeeilt.
Sie holen Licht und sehen mit Entsetzen
die Mutter tot zu ihren Füssen da.
Was tun? dem Bruder grauts—er zittert.
Allein die Schwester mit dem wilden Seemannsherzen
weiss wieder Rat.
Und was sie riet geschah:

Unleashed, the storm begins
with lightning flashes,
followed by fearsome claps of thunder;
a torrent of rain floods the earth.
Here, a bright light blinding,
a strike that sets marrow and knees to shaking.
The tree where the pair had sheltered stands in flames.
Trembling with fear they bolt from the place,
their hands still frantically entwined,
as if they could never again break free.—
Not only the lofty oak was kindled
by lightning's flash. The fire,
striking randomly, fell also on two hearts,
fanning in them the flames of a wild blaze.—
Different from when they left, the two came home;
and different, too, the world seemed from that day.
Now they saw everything only in the light
of the fire within them;
and whatever seemed hostile to this flame
became their enemy as well.
Their mother, too, became thus, even though,
being deeply in her dreams forever lost,
she had no eye nor ear for what her children did.

One evening, when the two were secretly together,
they heard upon the stairs the footsteps of their mother.
Up the tower she climbed, to search from there
for any distant light across the sea
announcing the return of him she longed for.
But her children gave her steps a different meaning:
"They are coming for us!—perhaps to tear us apart!"
Wild as a lioness the girl dashes to the closet,
Seizes there the pointed dagger, and hurries out.
Dark is the hall, and without further thought,
she closes on the quiet wanderer
and plunges the blade deep in her mother's breast.
Meanwhile her brother hurries to see what's happened.
They fetch a light and see with horror
their mother dead and lying at their feet.
What should they do? The brother shudders in fear.
Once again the sister, with her wild sailor's heart,
has the answer; and what she said was done.

Von dem Turme warfen sie die Leiche
ins tiefe Meer hinab.
Das Gesinde, das am nächsten Tag die Herrin misste
glaubte die Verschwundne
von ihrer Sehnsucht in die Flut getrieben,
um dort zu suchen, was sie lang verlor.

Nur ihrer Liebe lebten nun der Bruder und die Schwester,
nachdem sie eins ums andre, Knecht und Magd hinweg geschickt,
bald ganz allein.
Noch flammt und glüht das Feuer wie am ersten Tag,
allein sein Rauch verwandelt sich in grause Spukgestalten
welche—drohende Daemonen
die liebenden Geschwister immerfort umschwebten.
So kam der Tag an dem ihr Kind geboren wurde,
doch in der Nacht darauf trat zu den Schlafenden
der Geist der toten Mutter,
und er sprach den Fluch:

   "Was einmal geschah,
    geschehe nicht zum zweiten Mal.
    Nie soll es dir, du Kind,
    noch keinem eueres Geschlechts
    bis in die fernste Zukunft je gelingen
    die Mutter zu ertöten;
    nie, zu überwinden
    der Liebe Leidenschaft,
    Für Bruder oder Schwester."

Voll Schreck und Trauer hörten sie das Wort,
ob dunkel auch sein Sinn, Verzweiflung packt sie an.
So fluchbeladen, ihrer Liebe schönes Kind!
Entsetzlicher Gedanke,
der ihnen keine Rast mehr gönnt bei Tag und Nacht
"Der Tod bring einzig Ruhe",
denkt das unglückselge junge Weib
und stürzt mit seinem Kinde
sich in die tiefe Flut.

   "Du Mutter, nimm den Fluch zurück
    und nimm uns selbst zur Sühne!"

From high in the tower they threw the body
into the sea below.
The following day, missing their mistress, the servants
believed the vanished one
had been driven by her longing into the flood,
to seek there what she lost so long ago.

Now brother and sister lived only for their love.
Sending away the man-servant, then the maid,
soon completely alone.
The fire still blazes and glows as on the first day,
only now its smoke transforms to gruesome, ghostly figures,
threatening demons, which float
perpetually around the loving pair,
until the day on which their child was born.
But to the sleeping pair that night
appeared the ghost of their dead mother,
and pronounced this curse:

> "What once took place,
>   shall not take place again.
>   Never shalt thou, O child,
>   nor yet one of your race,
>   unto the last generation,
>   succeed in murdering a mother;
>   never, to overcome
>   the passion of a love
>   for sister or for brother."

Filled with shock and grief they hear this saying,
if shrouded in its meaning, and are seized by despair.
Burdened with a curse, their love's beautiful child!
The horrifying thought
gives them no rest, neither by day nor night.
"Only death will bring us peace,"
so thinks the doomed young woman,
and plummets with her child
into the deep flood-tide.

> "O mother, take back thy curse,
>   and take us, too, for our atonement!"

Allein blieb nun der Mann zurück
im Schloss am Meer,
und elend grenzenlos.
Was war geschehn?
Was hatte solches Unglück über sie gebracht?
Es war ein Licht gewesen,
Draus ein Feuer bald geworden
und diese Flamme hatte alles nun verzehrt.
Ihn litt es nicht mehr in dem öden fluchbeladnen Hause.
Hinaus und fort,
nur weit, und immer weiter,
um doch dem Grauen endlich zu entrinnen!

Und Tag um Tag gewandert,
nicht gefragt, wohin,
doch stets das Grauen auf dem Fusse mit.

Endlich traf im Wald er eine Hütte
auch einen Mann der dem erschöpften Wandrer
Speis und Obdach gern gewährte
und ihm erzählt von einem neuen Gotte
der durch seinen Tod von allem Übel hab erlöst die Welt.
Und gierig, wie wer am Verschmachten
nach dem Wasser greift,
nahm das versengte Herz die Hoffnungsbotschaft auf.

"Sprecht mir mehr von diesem Gott!
    Gibt es Erlösung auch für meine Qual?"

Sein Leben und sein unglückselges Schicksal
erzählt er drauf dem guten Mann.
Der hörte stumm ihm zu und sprach am Ende:

"Auch für dich, mein Sohn, kann es Erlösung geben,
    Doch ohne Sühne nicht!
    Dies sei das Zeichen dir, dass Gnade dir zu schenken
    unser Gott gewillt ist,
    dass er im Traum dir zeiget
    was deine Sühne sei.
    Nun bet' und faste in gedul'gem Harren,
    auf dass du wissest welches dein Geschick."

The man alone was left now,
in the castle by the sea,
in boundless wretchedness.
What had happened?
What had brought down such misery upon them?
There had been a light,
which soon became a fire,
and the flame had now consumed all that there was.
In this house, deserted and accursed, he could not stay.
Out and away,
far, and always farther,
until at last he might escape the horror!

And so he wandered, day after day,
not asking where he went,
but always with the horror at his heels.

In time he came upon a forest hut,
and there a man who gladly gave
the exhausted wanderer food and shelter
and also spoke to him of a new god,
who by his death redeemed the world from evil.
And greedily, like someone who is parched
reaching for water,
the wanderer's seared heart drank in this hopeful message.

   "Tell me more about this god!
    Is there also redemption for my agony?"

His life and wretched fate
he then related to the good man,
who listened silently, and said at last:

   "For you, too, my son, there can be redemption,
    but not without atonement!
    Let this be the sign that our god is willing
    to grant you his grace:
    that he shows you in your dreams
    what shall be your atonement.
    Now pray and fast in patient expectation,
    that you may come to know your destiny."

Gehorsam tat er nach des Alten Rat
und in der neunten Nacht
sah er im Traume dieses Bild:
am Ufer eines grünen Stroms
ein wilder finstrer Wald;
und rings der Boden war mit Blut befleckt.
Drauf hört er eine Stimme, welche sprach:

"Dorthin, gen Süden wandere
  und reinige jene Statt,
  so wirst du selber rein!"

Dem heilgen Mann erzählt er das Gesicht
und also deutet's dieser ihm:

"Zieh über's Meer, gen Süden hin,
  dort steig ans Land und wandre durch die Wälder.
  und keines Herdes Feuer wärme dich
  bis du die Stätte fandst, die dir der Traum gezeigt.
  Den neuen Gott sollst du mit in die Ferne tragen
  und dort an jener blutbefleckten Stelle
  errichte seinem Ruhm und Dienst ein Heiligtum."

Also geschah's.
Weit über's Meer hin zog der Büsser, südwärts
dann wandert er durch wilde Wälder.
und als der Mond zum zwölften Male neu geworden
da fand er endlich jene blutgetränkte Statt,
im Wald, an Stromesufer,
wie er sie im Traum geschaut.

Als erstes richtet er an diesem langgesuchten Orte
das Zeichen seines neuen Gottes auf, ein Kreuz;
drauf baut' er sich aus Zweigen eine Hütte
und lebte ganz dem heilgen Dienst geweiht.

Jedoch nicht ferne von des Büssers Klause
führt eine Strasse hin,
auf der des Weges zog viel Volks.
Bald war der fremde Siedler hier entdeckt
und Kunde rings ins Land gebracht.
Von dem weit her gewanderten,

Obediently he followed the old man's counsel
and in the ninth night
saw this image in his dream:
Upon the bank of a green river
a wild dark forest;
and all around the ground was stained with blood.
And then he hears a voice proclaiming:

   "Wander southward
    and cleanse that place,
    then you too will be cleansed!"

To the holy man he tells his vision,
who in turn explains it thus:

   "Go across the sea, toward the south,
    there go ashore and set off through the woods,
    unwarmed by the fire of any hearth,
    until you find the place shown in your dream.
    You shall take this new god with you on your journey,
    and there, where the ground was stained with blood,
    build a shrine to his glory and his service."

And so it came to pass.
Far o'er the sea the penitent traveled southwards,
and on he wandered through wild forests.
And when for the twelfth time the moon was new,
he finally found that blood-soaked place
in the forest, on a river bank,
as he'd seen it in his dream.

Upon this long-sought place he first erects
the sign of his new god, a cross;
then out of branches built himself a hut
and lived his life devoted to holy service.

Not far however from the penitent's retreat
a roadway passes, where many people travel.
Here the foreigner was soon discovered,
and word spread deep within the country
of one who'd journeyed from afar,
and who had crossed the sea.

der übers Meer gekommen
und einen neuen Gott verehre,
der nicht nur stark, wie es die Alten waren,
sondern auch gut sei und von aller
Angst erlösen könne, die gläubig ihm sich nahn.
Wie geheimer Zauber gings von dem Fremden aus,
Es kam zu ihm von Fern und Nah
wer sich in seinen Nöten keinen Rat mehr wusste,
und allen kündet er die frohe Botschaft
vom neuen Gott, der von der Angst die Welt befreit.
So lebt er ratend, helfend, lehrend manches Jahr;
es mehrten sich die Gläubigen,
die ihre wilden, alten Götter
vertauschten mit dem Einen, neuen, guten Gott.

Ein Gotteshaus ward später an der Stelle,
wo einst der Wanderer sein Kreuz errichtet hatte,
erbaut,
und ward dem Schutze aller Heiligen empfohlen,
weil es an einem unheiligen Ort
von einem Unheiligen war gegründet worden.

He worships a new god,
who's said to be not only strong, like the old gods,
but also good, and able to set free
from fear all who come to him in faith.
It spread from the stranger like a mysterious magic,
and people began to come from near and far,
those who could find no counsel in their troubles.
To all who come he proclaims good news
of the new god who frees the world from fear.
For years he lives like this, advising, helping, teaching;
and the devoted grow in number,
replacing their old, savage gods
with the One new God of goodness.

A house of God was later built upon that site
where once the wanderer had set his cross.
It was commended for protection to the saints,
because it had been founded
in an unholy place, by an unholy man.

4.1.

4.2.

4.3.

4.4.

FIGURES 4.1–4.4.
Many-colored sphere.
Series of paintings by
Emma Jung, 1917–1918.

FIGURE 4.2.
Painting by Emma
Jung, 17 September
1917.

FIGURE 4.1.
Painting by Emma
Jung, undated.

FIGURE 4.3.
Painting by Emma
Jung, undated.

FIGURE 4.4.
Painting by Emma
Jung, 16 January 1918.

IV

Verse Play

Mystère de la Croisade

1926

Dem verständnisvollen Freunde Hr. S.

E. J.
24. VIII. 1926.

Première Partie

PREMIÈRE SCÈNE

La scène est un endroit céleste. Au milieu se trouve le trône du Bon-Dieu, qui consiste en un rayonnement lumineux. Le chœur des anges est rassemblé autour de lui.

LE CHŒUR CHANTE: Louange à Toi, ô Dieu!

LA VOIX DU BON-DIEU: Assez, assez! vos éternelles louanges
me font mal aux oreilles;
cessez, les anges, cessez!

LES ANGES: Comme Tu le veux, céleste Majesté,
nous obéissons à Ta sainte volonté.
Ordonne ce que nous devons faire,
dis-nous comment Te plaire, ô Seigneur.

LE BON-DIEU: Vous donner des ordres? Non, jamais plus!

LES ANGES: Un mal Te tourmente, Toi, notre Dieu?
nous ne croyions pas qu'il pût en être ainsi dans les cieux!
Indique-nous, alors, comment Te soulager,
nous sommes tous prêts à faire Ta sainte volonté!

LE BON-DIEU: Laissez-moi!
D'adoucir ma peine, vous tous êtes incapables,
vous ne faites que l'accentuer.

(en s'éloignant) Peut-être trouverais-je un remède en méditant.

Mystery of the Crusade

1926

To my understanding friend, Herr S.

E. J.
24 August 1926

Part One

FIRST SCENE

Somewhere in heaven. In the middle stands the throne of the Good Lord, composed of luminous radiance. The angelic choir is arranged in ranks around it.

THE CHOIR SINGS:	Praise to Thee, oh God!
VOICE OF THE GOOD LORD:	Enough, enough! Your eternal praises
	are painful to my ears;
	cease, angels, cease!
THE ANGELS:	As you wish, celestial Majesty,
	we obey Thy sacred will.
	Only command us what we ought to do,
	tell us how to please Thee now, oh Lord.
THE GOOD LORD:	Command you? No, never again!
THE ANGELS:	Something distresses Thee, oh God?
	We did not think such things could be in heaven!
	Command us, then, how we should console Thee,
	for all of us await Thy sacred will!
THE GOOD LORD:	Leave me alone, all of you;
	unable to assuage my pain,
	you only make it ache more keenly.
(moving away)	By meditating I may find a remedy.

DEUXIÈME SCÈNE

Le jardin du Paradis, une partie du ciel un peu plus rapprochée de la terre. Le Bon-Dieu se promène sous les arbres au bord d'un étang. Il revêt une forme visible et ressemble à un homme assez âgé.

LE BON-DIEU: Je commence déjà à me sentir mieux,
car cela repose de se trouver dans un endroit créé.
L'infini des cieux m'oppresse,
et l'adoration éternelle des anges m'indispose.
Ici, au moins, je me sens vivant,
tandis que, là-bas, je ne fais qu'exister.

Il passe devant l'arbre de Vie.

Ah, maintenant je me souviens:
il y avait trop longtemps que je n'avais plus goûté
aux fruits de l'arbre que ici,
c'est l'arbre de Vie
et son grand secret: il faut au Maître Suprême s'en nourrir
de temps à temps pour récupérer sa jeunesse.

Il prend un fruit et, le mangeant, s'assied au pied de l'arbre. Après une pause:

Une vie nouvelle commence déjà à m'envahir,
je sens en moi surgir des pensées nettes et claires.
De l'heure propice, je veux donc profiter
en pensant au remède qui pourrait bien m'aider.
Mais d'abord faut-il connâitre la juste cause du mal,
quand et comment a-t-il commencé?
Ah, j'ai trouvé: l'homme, voilà la cause!
Adam et Eve, pourquoi vous ai-je chassés?
Je me languis de vous! comment vous regagner?
Que je maudis le jour qui vous à éloignés!
Quelle idée m'a piqué de mettre à l'épreuve,
mes chèrs enfants, des créatures toutes neuves comme vous,
ne sachant pas moi-même qu'attendre de vous!
Oh! Pourrais-je donc découvrir le moyen de vous retrouver!
Sans vous le Paradis n'est plus si beau,
il manque des êtres humains—et tous les animaux
si parfaits soient-ils, ne peuvent vous remplacer,
ni me donner cette joie que vous m'avez procurée

SECOND SCENE

The Garden of Paradise, a part of heaven located closer to the earth. The Good Lord walks under the trees, beside a pond. He now has a visible form, resembling an aging man.

THE GOOD LORD: Already I begin to feel consoled;
in a created place, I find, there is relief.
The infinite skies weigh on me heavily;
and how faint I feel, with the angels' endless adoration.
Here, at least, I feel alive,
even if there I exist supernally.

He passes by the Tree of Life.

Ah, I remember now:
for too long I have failed to taste
fruit from this tree I now see here before me,
which is the Tree of Life,
with its great secret: that, from time to time,
to restore his youth, the Supreme Master
must take this nourishment!

He takes a fruit and eats it, seating himself below the tree. After a time:

Already a new life sweeps over me;
clear, well-formed thoughts are rising in my mind.
So let me profit from this happy hour
by thinking of a useful remedy.
But first, what is the nature of my malady,
when did it originate, and how?
I know: it all began with human beings!
Adam and Eve, why did I banish you?
I long for you! How can I regain you?
How I abhor the day I sent you forth!
What spurred me, then, to put you to the test,
entirely new creatures as you were, beloved children,
when even I knew not what to expect?
Oh, if I knew the means to bring you back!
Without you, Paradise is not so lovely,
lacking men and women. The animals,
perfect though they be, cannot fill the lack,
nor fill me with that joy you used to give,

avec vos rires et vos idées à vous!
Les anges ne savent que chanter et obéir,
vous, chers enfants perdus, vous saviez devenir!
Je dois vous retrouver, il le faut absolument,
sinon, je ne puis être Dieu plus longtemps.

Il se promène près de l'étang et voit son portrait sur la surface de l'eau.

Est-ce bien là mon image? Ai-je donc tant diminué?
Et, ce que je vois ici, n'est qu'une moitié de moi-même.
C'est fort inquiétant,
l'image me trompe-t-elle,
ou suis-je ainsi vraiment?
Si seulement quelqu'un pouvait me dire
comme je lui apparais—mmm—comment donc faire?
Au ciel, je suis toute lumière,
pour apparaître, il faudrait la terre
ou tout au moins, le Paradis.
C'est là qu'on acquiert forme et vie,
mais le clair miroir d'eau qui reflète mon image
ne me suffit pas:
pour me reconnaître, il faut davantage,
car je ne suis pas satisfait de causer à moi seul.
Que faire?
J'appellerai mon ange Gabriel.
L'air de cet endroit,—c'est bien étrange—
donne forme aux choses vagues d'ordinaire,
et donnera peut-être aussi à mon ange
des idées claires.

Il ferme les yeux et se replie sur lui-même, c'est la manière dont il appelle les êtres célestes.
Bientôt l'ange Gabriel paraît.

GABRIEL: Tu m'as appelé, Seigneur, quelle est Ta volonté?
Je viens obéir, veuille donc nous ordonner!
LE BON-DIEU: Je veux te parler, mon Gabriel,
ici dans ce jardin, ce merveilleux endroit,
où des pensées se détachent et des mots se forment
et où l'on trouve que tous les cieux dorment.
Mais, avant tout, goûte de ce fruit luisant
et tu vas tôt sentir son effet vivifiant.

with your laughter and your ideas of your own!
Angels know only how to sing and to obey;
but you, dear lost ones, knew how to become!
I must find you again, there is no other way;
or else, and soon, my Godhead will be done.

He walks beside the pond and sees his reflection on the water's surface.

Is that my image? Have I shrunk so much?
What I see here is no more than half.
It is disquieting:
does the image deceive me,
or am I really thus?
If someone could but tell me truthfully
how I appear to him—mmm—what shall I do?
In heaven I am only light;
to be visible would require earth,
or Paradise, at least:
for there one may acquire form and life.
But my reflection in the water's mirror
is insufficient for me
to recognize myself. More is needed;
nor am I satisfied, hearing my voice alone.
What can be done?
I'll call my angel Gabriel.
The air here, strange to say, bestows a shape
on things that ordinarily are vague;
perhaps it will endow my angel, too,
with clarity of mind.

He closes his eyes and turns his attention inward; this is his manner of calling to celestial beings. Soon the angel Gabriel appears.

GABRIEL: Lord, Thou hast summoned me. What is Thy will?
I hasten to obey, do but command!
THE GOOD LORD: I wish, my Gabriel, to speak with thee
here, in this garden, this most wondrous place,
where thoughts take shape and words are formed,
and where, it seems, the heavens are all asleep.
But first, taste of this radiant fruit;
e'er long thou'lt feel its vivifying power.

Il offre à Gabriel un fruit de l'arbre de Vie. Celui-ci mange et commence à devenir plus concret. Puis il prend Gabriel par le bras et le conduit à l'étang, lui faisant signe d'y regarder.

LE BON-DIEU: Regarde cette surface
et dis ce que tu y vois.

GABRIEL: Ô Seigneur, serait-ce Ta face
que réfléchit cette eau?

LE BON-DIEU: Tu le devines, dis, me connais-tu?
Te suis-je toujours apparu ainsi?

GABRIEL: Non, c'est la première fois,
mais je me dis: cela doit être Toi.
Au ciel, on ne Te vois point de forme,
là, Tu es toute splendeur,
tandis qu'ici, Tu prends des contours distincts.

LE BON-DIEU: Et dis-moi aussi comment tu les trouves,
ces formes dont tu parles!

GABRIEL: Je les trouves belles, cependant, c'est à peine si j'ose
le dire: c'est comme s'il manquait quelque chose.

LE BON-DIEU: Dis-le sans gêne,
à moi aussi il semble de même,
et je t'ai appelé pour t'entendre dire
si je me suis trompé ou si c'est bien moi.
C'est moi, sans doute, mais moi incomplet,
aide-moi à trouver comment y remédier.

GABRIEL: Je veux faire de mon mieux.

LE BON-DIEU: Écoute donc: la peine dont je souffre
est d'avoir perdu les hommes, mes chers enfants,
les hommes que j'ai crées, les hommes que j'aime tant
que leur absence me rend tout malheureux.
Combien de fois ai-je essayé de les rappeler,
hélas, en vain, car je sais ce que c'est
la terre leur semble tellement chère
qu'à tous les délices du ciel, ils la préfèrent.
Et croyant punir leur désobéissance,
je me suis puni moi-même, plus qu'on ne pense,
parce qu'ils se plaisent tant là-bas
qu'ils ne veulent plus revenir vers moi.

GABRIEL: Quels moyens as-Tu choisis, Seigneur,
pour ramener les hommes dans cette demeure?

LE BON-DIEU: D'abord, je leur ai rendu la vie dure:
je leur fais éprouver
malheurs et difficultés innombrables,

He offers Gabriel a fruit from the Tree of Life. Gabriel eats it and becomes more concrete.
Then he takes Gabriel by the arm and leads him to the pond, gesturing to look at it.

THE GOOD LORD: Look at this surface,
tell me what thou see'st.

GABRIEL: Oh Lord, can it be Thy face
reflected in this water?

THE GOOD LORD: Thy guess is right. But tell me, dost thou know me?
Have I appeared always thus to thee?

GABRIEL: Nay, never before;
but I thought it must be Thee.
In heaven we cannot see Thy form,
Thou art all splendor there;
but here Thy forms are clear.

THE GOOD LORD: And tell me also what thou thinkest of them,
these forms thou speakest of!

GABRIEL: I find them beautiful; and yet—I hardly dare
to say this—something may be lacking.

THE GOOD LORD: Speak without fear;
the same occurs to me.
I summoned thee to ask thee what thou see'st.
Am I mistaken, or is this truly I?
'Tis I, no doubt, but yet not all of me.
Help me to find a means of remedy.

GABRIEL: I shall do my best.

THE GOOD LORD: Hear me then. My present suffering
is that I've lost them, my dear, human children,
whom I created, whom I love so much,
whose absence now is causing all my pain.
How often have I tried, but tried in vain,
to call them back; for—I know not why—
earth seems so dear to them, they seem to love it
over heaven's delights, and will not leave it.
I meant to punish them for disobeying,
and punished myself, more than I could know.
For they will nevermore return to me,
so well-contented are they, there below.

GABRIEL: What methods hast Thou chosen, Lord,
to gather them into this high abode?

THE GOOD LORD: At first, I made life difficult for them,
forcing them to endure
uncounted hardships and misfortunes,

espérant que leur joie de vivre, leur courage
serait réduit ou brisé et que leur seul désir
deviendrait enfin: vers moi revenir.
Mais loin de là: ils aiment, ils adorent la lutte,
ils ont trouvé, au lieu d'être brisés,
maintes façons d'alléger leur sort,
et comme cela, ils ont appris qu'ils sont forts.
Nul obstacle à leur esprit n'est de trop,
et si, pour un instant la lutte fait défaut,
ils vont en inventer pour leur plaisir!
Ainsi, ce moyen n'a pas pu réussir.

GABRIEL: Et qu'as-tu essayé encore?

LE BON-DIEU: Ensuite, je voulus
les attirer d'une autre manière,
et, tu le sais:
j'ai envoyé mon fils vers cette terre.
Il devait leur rappeler le Paradis perdu,
leur peindre l'éternelle béatitude,
les persuader, leur faire envie,
en promettant une nouvelle vie.
Mais tout en vain—
les hommes ne voulaient pas entendre,
et mon envoyé, ils l'ont fait pendre.
Et ce qui m'a troublé le plus,
c'est que lui aussi, mon saint fils,
fut gagné par cet amour de la vie,
crois-tu? Il ne voulut pas revenir!
Il préférait vivre pauvre et peiné,
alors qu'il pouvait au ciel, auprès de moi régner.
Cela semble être ainsi: qui vit là-bas
doit être ramené par force
ou ne me revient pas.
Enfin, je veux savoir
ce qui là-bas les fait ainsi tenir
et pourquoi les délices des cieux
ne peuvent les séduire.
Quelle est la force qui rend douteuse ma puissance?
C'est là mon chagrin et peut-être là la cause,
qu'à mon image il manque quelque chose:
À vrai dire, je le dois confesser,
depuis le temps d'Adam je ne me sens plus entier.

GABRIEL: Seigneur, je suis bien étonné
de T'ouïr de la sorte parler.

hoping their joy in life, their courage
would be reduced or broken, and at last
their whole desire would be to come to me.
But far from that! Such struggles they adore.
Instead of breaking, they grew ever more
adept at lightening their destiny,
and by this means they learned how strong they are.
No obstacle is too great for their spirit,
and if their struggles briefly are suspended,
they will invent new challenges for pleasure!
This method having failed, the trial was ended.

GABRIEL: What didst Thou then essay?

THE GOOD LORD: Next, I wanted
to bring them to me by another path.
So, as thou knowest,
I sent my son to earth. His duty there
was to remind them of lost Paradise,
depict for them eternal blessedness,
persuade them, make them yearn to share
the new life that he promised.
But all in vain—
the people did not want to hear,
and they sent my envoy to be hanged.
This, though, concerns me most of all:
my son, my blessed son, he, too,
was conquered by this love of life,
canst thou credit this? and wished not to return!
He would have lived there, poor and suffering,
rather than join me in my heavenly reign.
So this appears to be the rule: All who live
on earth must be gathered in by force,
else they do not return to me.
Finally, I would know
what binds the people there below,
and why the delights of heaven
fail to attract them?
What is the force that casts my power in doubt?
There's my distress. And mayhap it explains
why my image here lacks something.
In truth, I must confess:
since Adam's time I have not felt complete.

GABRIEL: Lord, my astonishment is great,
hearing Thee speak this way.

Les hommes qui sont là-bas, Tu dis,
aiment tant leur misérable vie
qu'en vain Tu les appelles!
Est-elle donc tellement belle
qu'elle l'emporte sur le ciel?

———————

Tu demandes mon conseil,
mais tout ce que je sais dire,
est: descends Toi-Même
pour enfin parvenir
à connaître la force égale à Toi, ô Suprême!

LE BON-DIEU: Descendre moi-même?
Penses-tu ce que tu me dis?
Jamais jusque-là au delà du Paradis,
dedans la création je ne me suis porté!
Pourtant elle m'émeut, ton idée!
Mais, m'approchant autant de la matière
ne vais-je pas perdre ma divinité?

———————

Non, je ne puis, c'est vraiment trop risqué!
vas-toi, à ma place, mon Gabriel,
dès maintenant descends sur la terre
et tâche de découvrir mon adversaire
et de ramener les hommes au ciel.

Ils disparaissent.

TROISIÈME SCÈNE

Une forêt sur la terre. Sous un arbre, un chevalier endormi. Son cheval est attaché à un arbre voisin. Le chevalier rêve: un ange lui apparaît et lui adresse la parole.

L'ANGE QUI EST GABRIEL: Salut à toi, chevalier,
où te conduit ton chemin?
LE CHEVALIER: Quel est cet être merveilleux qui me salue?
(tout en dormant) Comme une étoile il brille,
du ciel sûrement, il vient ici!
À l'Ange: Mon haut Seigneur, soyez béni,
vous demandez où je vais,
si seulement je le savais,
car j'erre par le pays
cherchant un roi que je puisse servir

Thou sayest that the people down below
so dearly love their miserable lives
that, when Thou callest, they do not attend!
What then? Is life on earth so fair
that life in heaven cannot compare?

———————

Thou seekst my counsel,
all I can say is this:
if Thou wouldst understand the power
that equals Thine, Most High,
Thou must Thyself descend to earth!

THE GOOD LORD: Myself descend?
Hast measured what thou sayest?
Never have I ventured out so far,
outside of Paradise, into Creation!
And yet it stirreth me, thy notion!
But, coming close to matter in that way,
will I not lose my own divinity?

———————

No, I cannot, the risk would be too great!
I'll send thee in my place, my Gabriel.
This very hour, thou shalt descend to earth.
There to seek out the secret hiding place
of my great foe, and gather men to heaven.

They vanish.

THIRD SCENE

A forest on earth. Under a tree a knight is sleeping, his horse tied to a nearby tree. While the knight dreams, an angel approaches and speaks to him.

THE ANGEL (GABRIEL): Hail to thee, fair knight,
                    where does thy journey lead?
      THE KNIGHT: What marvelous being greets me?
      (still sleeping) Like a star he shines;
                    from heaven he comes, 'tis sure!
      To the angel: Blessing upon thee, most high lord!
                    Thou askest where I'm bound.
                    If only I could say!
                    I wander through the countryside
                    seeking a king whom I may serve,

	et que je puise aider à gagner ses batailles
	et vaincre l'ennemi,
	car le combat, sachez,
	j'adore plus que la vie!
GABRIEL:	Voilà qui se trouve bien!
	Tu cherches un roi et tu cherches bataille,
	je t'offre tous les deux, si avec moi tu viens.
	Écoute ce que je te dis:
	un roi grand, plus grand que tous les maîtres,
	va livrer combat à son mortel ennemi
	qui menace son pouvoir.
	Il ne le connaît guère
	ni ne sait en quel lieu
	celui-ci est caché,
	cependant, il doit être sur la terre,
	et moi, je fus mandé pour le trouver.
	Pour vaincre, il nous faut des preux, comme toi,
	qui sont prêts à servir mon roi,
	ce roi, qui est Dieu!
	Veux-tu lutter pour lui?
LE CHEVALIER:	Je veux et je te suis.
	Mais dis, où est l'armée?
GABRIEL:	En peu de temps, j'escompte, elle sera sur pied.
	Par ordre de mon roi, je cherche des combattants,
	et toi, tu m'aideras.
	Ensuite, il faut trouver les ennemis de Dieu.
	Sais-tu où ils demeurent?
	Sinon, il faut chercher, et fût-ce par toute la terre,
	afin de leur livrer bataille.
LE CHEVALIER:	Pour sûr que je le sais où l'ennemi de Dieu habite,
	Loin d'ici, outre mer, vers l'est il a son gîte,
	ainsi j'ai ouï dire.
	Allons là-bas, haut Sire,
	et je le jure, nous trouverons en peu de temps
	maints chevaliers pour la lutte au pays distant.
GABRIEL:	Alors allons, cheminons par le pays,
	acquérons compagnons pour notre entreprise,
	pour que la force de l'ennemi se brise.
	Enflammons tous les cœurs pour cette sainte guerre
	que les prêtres prêcheront du haut de toutes les chaires.
	Et notre roi suprême avec son pouvoir
	veuille nous assister et nous donner victoire!

	beside whom I may fight, and battles win
	against the enemy.
	For know this: combat I adore,
	e'en above my own life!
GABRIEL:	Well met, indeed!
	Thou seek'st a king, thou seekest battle,
	I offer both, if thou wilt come with me.
	Listen to what I say:
	a great king, greater than all masters,
	goes forth to fight the mortal enemy
	who threatens his domain.
	He does not know this enemy,
	nor does he know the place
	where his force is hidden;
	yet here on earth his enemy must be,
	whom to discover, I myself was bidden.
	To win this fight, I now seek valiant knights,
	such as thyself, ready to serve my king,
	this king, who is God!
	Wilt thou fight for Him?
THE KNIGHT:	I will, I'll follow thee.
	But tell me, where is the army?
GABRIEL:	Soon, no doubt, the army will assemble.
	By order of my king, I seek for warriors,
	and thou shalt help me.
	Later, we shall find God's enemies.
	Dost thou know where they live?
	At need, we'll seek them all across the earth,
	and bring the battle to them.
THE KNIGHT:	Surely, I know. The enemy of God
	lives far from here, eastward, across the sea,
	or so the tale is told.
	Let us go there, noble lord,
	I vow, in little time we'll find
	many a knight to join this distant war.
GABRIEL:	Then let us make our way across the land,
	acquiring fellows for our enterprise.
	If we would break the enemy's power,
	all hearts must be kindled for this holy war,
	which shall be preached by clerics from on high.
	And may our supreme ruler, with his power,
	be pleased to help and give us victory!

LE CHEVALIER: Quel sera le signe de camp des combattants de Dieu?
Et quel leur cri de guerre?

GABRIEL: Les hommes de Dieu, en signe de leur roi,
à l'épaule porteront une croix
rouge de couleur.
Et pour leur cri de guerre,
"Pour Dieu sans peur!"
il sonnera par terres et par mers.
En avant maintenant,
cherchons des partisans,
qui veulent nous rejoindre au signe de la croix,
et lutter avec nous pour le céleste roi!

Avec un geste invitant le public:

Venez tous, jeunes et vieux,
avec nous, sans peur, pour Dieu!
Fin

Seconde Partie

PREMIÈRE SCÈNE

La croisade est terminée. Gabriel retourne au ciel. Le Bon-Dieu se trouve à l'entrée du ciel proprement dit, dans une sorte de portique d'où il voit le jardin du Paradis où un nombre de chevaliers se trouvent.

GABRIEL: Seigneur, Dieu, Salut! Me voilà de retour,
la guerre est terminée et conquise la terre
où semblaient se tenir les ennemis de Dieu.
Vers Toi sont venus maints preux et chevaliers
qui ont quitté la terre pour toi volontiers.
La preuve que tu demandais, la voilà donnée:
saisis d'amour pour Toi, sans hésiter,
ils se jetaient dans la plus rude mêlée,
ne craignant ni douleur ni mort,
oubliant tout, la vie, la terre et ses attraits,

THE KNIGHT: What standard shall we bear, who fight for God?
What will be our battle cry?

GABRIEL: As witness to their king, upon their shoulder,
the men of God shall wear this sign:
a cross in red.
And for their watchword,
"Fearless for God!"
shall sound on land and sea.
Let us at once set forth,
seeking for partisans who agree
to bear the standard of the cross,
and battle with us for the king of heaven!

To the public, with a gesture of invitation:

Come one and all, young and old!
Come with us, "Fearless for God!"
    Finis

Part Two

FIRST SCENE

The crusade is finished. Gabriel returns to heaven. The Good Lord is seated at the very entrance to heaven, in a sort of portico. From there he can see the garden of Paradise, where a number of knights are standing.

GABRIEL: Hail to Thee, Lord God! I have returned.
The war is ended, and the land is conquered
where once the enemies of God held sway.
Many a gallant knight has come to Thee;
who for Thy sake left earth most willingly.
Here is the proof that Thou didst ask me for:
seized by love of Thee, without delay,
they threw themselves into the rude mêlée,
untouched by fears of pain or death,
forgetting all—life, earth and its delights,

pour Toi, qui ainsi Te trouves plus fort
que l'adversaire là-bas.
Es-Tu content?

LE BON-DIEU: Content?—non.

Gabriel le regarde très surpris.

LE BON-DIEU: Pourquoi? Je vais te l'apprendre:
Tu disais vrai, des milliers sont venus à moi
par cette guerre,
et je les accueillis au Paradis
comme accueillit un père ses enfants,
afin de leur donner l'éternel bonheur.
Mais sais-tu ce qui arriva?

Gabriel secoue la tête.

LE BON-DIEU: Tu verras à l'instant.

Un ange arrive devant le siège du Bon-Dieu et s'incline, muet.

LE BON-DIEU: Qu'est-ce que tu viens me dire?
L'ANGE: Un de ces chevaliers, venus tout récemment,
Te demande la faveur de pouvoir Te parler.
LE BON-DIEU: Qu'il vienne.

L'ange va chercher le chevalier et celui-ci se met à genoux devant le Bon-Dieu.

LE BON-DIEU: Qu'est-ce que tu veux, mon fils?
LE CHEVALIER: Seigneur Dieu, permets-moi une demande
au nom de tes chevaliers:
depuis que nous sommes là,
fervents à ton service,
et attendant tes ordres,
jamais Tu ne nous appelles.
Pourquoi es-Tu comme cela?
N'as-Tu pas besoin de nous
et dans Ton royaume, n'y a-t-il pas de combats?
LE BON-DIEU: Combats? Mais non, mon fils,
ici règne la paix éternelle,
vous pouvez en jouir,
ayant fait votre devoir.

	and all for Thee. Thus Thou art proven stronger
	than the earthly adversary.
	Art Thou content?
THE GOOD LORD:	Content?—Nay, Gabriel.

Gabriel looks at him, deeply surprised.

THE GOOD LORD:	Why not? I will explain:
	In truth thou sayest, thousands came to me
	through this war,
	and I received them into Paradise
	as a father receives his children,
	meaning to give them endless happiness.
	But dost thou know what happened?

Gabriel shakes his head.

THE GOOD LORD:	Thou shalt see forthwith.

An angel approaches the seat of the Good Lord and bows silently.

THE GOOD LORD:	What comest thou to say?
THE ANGEL:	One of those knights who recently arrived
	has asked to be allowed to speak with Thee.
THE GOOD LORD:	Let him approach.

The angel goes in search of the knight, who comes and kneels before the Good Lord.

THE GOOD LORD:	What wishest thou, my son?
THE KNIGHT:	Lord God, allow me a request
	in the name of all Thy knights:
	Since we arrived here,
	fervent to serve Thee,
	awaiting Thy commands,
	Thou hast not called upon us.
	Why is this, Lord?
	Dost Thou not need us?
	Are there no battles in Thy realm?
THE GOOD LORD:	Battles? No, my son,
	here reigns peace eternal.
	You may take joy in it,
	Your duty being done.

LE CHEVALIER: Pas de combat, Seigneur,
oh, comme c'est dommage,
en combattant, seulement, nous sommes heureux,
mais si cela ne se peut,
donne-nous au moins des femmes!

LE BON-DIEU: Des femmes, au Paradis,
mon beau garçon, qu'est-ce que tu penses?
Dans cet heureux pays, nous n'avons que des anges!

LE CHEVALIER: Mon Seigneur, je Vous demande pardon,
ni combat et ni femme, c'est pour un homme trop peu.
Ton Paradis est beau, mais qu'est-ce que nous y ferons?
Laisse-nous retourner!
Nous aimons mieux là-bas la vie pleine de dureté
que de la splendeur du ciel, étant ainsi privés.

LE BON-DIEU: Ah! que je me trompais!
Ce n'est point l'amour de moi
qui vous a amenés ici,
mais l'amour du combat!
Et mon ciel pour vous est sans attrait,
puisqu'il n'y a pas de guerre!
Je ne vous retiens pas, retournez sur la terre,
une nouvelle vie vous soit donnée,
car nul au Paradis de rester n'est forcé.

LE CHEVALIER: Merci, merci Seigneur, Tu es bon
de nous laisser aller.
Revivant sur la terre, nous te louerons
et tuerons tes ennemis, autant que nous pourrons.

Le chevalier se retire. Le Bon-Dieu reste seul avec Gabriel.

LE BON-DIEU: Et l'as-tu entendu?
Ce n'est pas Dieu qu'aiment les hommes,
c'est le combat et, ce qui est encore pire,
la femme!
Faut-il pleurer ou rire?
Que n'ai-je ouï se plaindre
des hommes que la femme faisait souffrir,
maintenant, ils veulent les rejoindre,
pour elle le Paradis fuir!

GABRIEL: Seigneur, une chose reste à faire
si Tu veux conquérir l'humanité,

THE KNIGHT:	No battles, Lord?
	Oh, how unfortunate!
	In fighting alone we are truly happy.
	But if we may not fight,
	at least allow us women!
THE GOOD LORD:	Women, in Paradise?
	Dear lad, what art thou thinking?
	In this happy land, we have none but angels!
THE KNIGHT:	My Lord, I beg Thy pardon,
	no battles, and no women? A man needs more.
	Paradise is lovely, but what shall we do here?
	Permit us to return!
	We would choose earth, with all its hardship,
	over heaven's splendor, being so deprived.
THE GOOD LORD:	Ah, how great was my mistake!
	What drew you here
	was not your love of me
	but your love of battle!
	For you, my heaven holds no attraction,
	because no war is here!
	I will not keep you here, return to earth,
	a new life will be given you.
	None are compelled to stay in Paradise.
THE KNIGHT:	Thanks, thanks, oh Lord!
	Thou'rt kind to let us go.
	In our new lives on earth we'll give Thee praise,
	and slay thine enemies, as far as in us lies.

The knight withdraws. The Good Lord remains alone with Gabriel.

THE GOOD LORD:	Didst thou hear him?
	Men do not love God, after all,
	they love combat, and worst of all,
	Woman!
	Shall I cry or laugh?
	How often have I heard men moan
	that Woman caused them misery.
	Now, they want so much to reunite with her,
	they even flee from Paradise.
GABRIEL:	Lord, one thing remains to do,
	if Thou wouldst conquer humankind:

c'est: conquérir la femme, qui est dessus la terre
ton adversaire le plus dangereux.

LE BON-DIEU: Tu as peut-être raison, dans le temps
j'ai cru que gagner l'homme serait assez,
et que la femme que j'ai créée esclave
suivrait où il la mènerait, sans entrave,
son maître, même jusque dans les cieux.

GABRIEL: Je l'ai pensé aussi, mais il ne semble ainsi se faire,
mais cette énigme, vraiment, commence à me plaire.

LE BON-DIEU: Comment se peut-il donc: la femme,
(pensif) cette créature à peine humaine
qui ne sait pas penser,
à qui je n'ai donné qu'une minuscule âme,
à qui je n'ai pas même soufflé mon haleine
peut-elle me résister?
De retenir les hommes loin de nous
aurait-elle le pouvoir?
Et si elle le possède, d'où?
Cela, je veux savoir!

À Gabriel: Mon fidèle serviteur,
va donc trouver la femme et chercher son secret!

GABRIEL: Je ferai ce que je pourrai,
dès maintenant je m'y mets, sans plus attendre,
tout d'abord, voyons comment il faut s'y prendre.

À soi-même: Le secret de la femme, cela semble peu de chose,
et pourtant, dès la création du monde on ne l'aurait trouvé!
Serait-il que personne n'ose?
ou est-il trop caché?

Après avoir réfléchi un temps

Je m'en vais vers Marie, la mère de Jésus,
que je me rappelle obéissante et douce au temps jadis
où je lui annonçais la naissance de son fils.
Elle saura me dire quel est ce grand secret.

DEUXIÈME SCÈNE

Il s'avance vers le trône de la Sainte Vierge:

Marie, Sainte Mère, prête-moi ton oreille,
toi qui, nulle part, n'as de pareille,

	Thou must now conquer Woman, who on earth
	remains Thy most dangerous adversary.
THE GOOD LORD:	Thou'rt in the right. At one time I believed,
	to conquer Man would be enough;
	and Woman, whom I made to be his slave,
	would follow him, her master, without fetter,
	where he might lead, even to the skies.
GABRIEL:	I thought so, too; but things are otherwise.
	Yet truly, this enigma pleases me.
THE GOOD LORD:	How is it possible that Woman,
(pondering)	this hardly human creature,
	who cannot think,
	to whom I gave only a tiny soul,
	and never even filled her with my breath,
	how does she have the power to resist me,
	to hold men far away from us?
	Does she have such power? And if so,
	where does she get it from?
	That I would like to know!
To Gabriel:	Go then, find Woman and her secret,
	my faithful servant.
GABRIEL:	I shall do what I can,
	setting forth at once, without delay.
	First, though, I need to think about the task.
To himself:	The secret of Woman—it seems no great matter;
	yet none has found it since the earth's creation.
	Could it be that no one dares?
	or is it too well hidden?

After reflecting for a time:

> I'll go to Mary, Jesus' mother. Long ago,
> she was obedient and sweet, as I recall,
> when I announced her son's nativity.
> To me, now, this great secret she will tell.

SECOND SCENE

He approaches the throne of the Blessed Virgin:

> Holy Mother, Mary, bend thine ear,
> thou who art unequaled anywhere.

veuille m'aider à servir notre Dieu
qui m'a mandé en quête d'une chose mystérieuse,
que tu sais peut-être, ô Vierge bienheureuse.
Je cherche le secret de la femme, ni plus ni moins,
parce que sur la terre elle retient
les hommes et semble ne pas croire
au Dieu Tout-Puissant, à notre suprême maître.
Peux-tu me dire, Marie, quel est cet être
contraire à nous et quelle est sa force noire?

LA VIERGE: Mon ange, tu demandes beaucoup, mais tu me plais,
et je te répondrai autant que je pourrai:
sache donc, que moi-même, j'éprouvais
quelque chose de la sorte, quand j'étais encore femme.
Car, quand je consentais à donner naissance au Fils-Dieu,
je ne me doutais point que le père
ne fît naître le fils que pour le faire mourir.
Cela semble mauvais jeu et un cœur maternel
jamais n'y pourra voir aucun sens.

GABRIEL: Comment donc, aucun sens?
Mais comprenez, le sens de cette mort
a été de sauver l'humanité!

MARIE: Pourquoi ne l'a-t-il pu faire sauver par la vie
au lieu de par la mort?
Est-ce là tout son pouvoir?

GABRIEL: Mais, pour sauver l'humanité il le fallait!

MARIE: Sauver l'humanité, vous répétez toujours,
mais est-elle donc sauvée?
Regarde donc là-bas, regarde le ciel et l'enfer et dis,
est-elle sauvée?

GABRIEL: Et bien, si tu veux, non, pas encore,
mais voilà justement ce que nous voulons faire.

MARIE: Et ne vous trompez pas une seconde fois,
car sachez que jamais
la femme n'est conquise par la mort,
mais seulement par la vie!
La mort peut vaincre, mais la vie convainc,
et la femme toujours veut être convaincue!

GABRIEL: Est-ce là le secret?

MARIE: Pas tout, il y a un autre point,
écoute:
Ce père de mon fils, ce Dieu,
il n'était point amoureux,

I beg thy help in service to our God,
who bids me seek a thing of mystery,
a thing thou know'st, perchance, oh blessed Virgin.
'Tis Woman's secret, neither more nor less.
On earth below, she restrains the men,
while she herself, it seems, does not confess
faith in the Almighty, our master high.
Canst tell me, Mary, the nature of this being
who works against us? What is her dark power?

THE VIRGIN: My angel, you ask much. But your arrival
pleases me, and I'll try to reply.
Know this: when I was a woman, I also
observed a thing resembling what you say.
When I agreed to bear the Son of God,
I never thought the Father of this Son
would have him born, only to have him die.
This seemed to me a villain's trick, whose sense
a mother's heart will never learn to see.

GABRIEL: What's this? Not see the sense?
But understand, the meaning of this death
was to save all of humanity!

MARY: Then why could it not be saved by his life,
instead of by his death?
Is that all His power?

GABRIEL: To save humanity, there was no other way!

MARY: To save humanity, you keep repeating.
But truly, is it saved?
Look at the earth, at heaven and hell, and say,
is mankind saved?

GABRIEL: Well, if you insist, no, not yet,
but that is just what we intend to do.

MARY: Then don't make the same mistake a second time;
for you must know that death can never
bring about Woman's conquest,
but only life!
For death may vanquish her, but life convinces,
and Woman ever wants to be convinced!

GABRIEL: Is that the secret?

MARY: Not all of it; there is another point.
Now listen:
This father of my son, this God,
he was never in love.

il s'est servi de moi, il m'a fait obéir,
mais sans me faire aimer.
Et comment veux-tu donc qu'une femme au profond de
son âme
soit convaincue, si ce n'est par l'amour?

GABRIEL: Oh! qu'est-ce que vous me dites!
La Reine du Ciel, vous, la Sainte Mère, Marie,
pas convaincue de Dieu!
Vous-même une déesse entourée de splendeur
et louée jour et nuit!

MARIE: Oui, il m'a donné grande gloire,
mais que je ne demandais pas.
Mille fois, j'aurais préféré l'amour
et la vie de mon fils.
A présent le seul attrait de ce lieu,
est d'être près de lui.
Pour lui je suis venue, pour lui je veux rester.

GABRIEL: Et tous ces anges autour, qui jadis furent des femmes
comment sont-elles venues ici?

MARIE: Elles furent attirées par l'amour de mon fils
jadis et le suivirent.

GABRIEL: Ne vois-tu donc pas que le dessein du Père était bon?

MARIE: Peut-être le fut-il un temps,
mais c'est fini, elles ne viennent plus.

GABRIEL: Pourquoi, alors?

MARIE: Le fils est devenu trop un avec le père
et il n'est plus le même qu'il a été naguère.

GABRIEL: Mais ont-elles quelque chose là-bas
qui saurait les tenir,
qui égalerait ton fils,
qu'elles aiment plus que lui?
Les hommes de la terre, sont-ce eux qui se font tant aimer?

MARIE: C'est difficile à dire, oui et non.

GABRIEL: Ou sont-ce les enfants qui, réclamant leur mère,
les empêchent de venir vers Dieu?

MARIE: Peut-être, parfois, mais aux enfants
quand ils deviennent grands
la mère n'est plus besoin
et souvent même de trop.
Ainsi, ils ne la retiennent pas.

GABRIEL: Mais enfin, qu'est-ce alors?
Dieu le veut savoir.

He made use of me, made me obedient,
without making me love him.
How do you think a woman, in her deepest soul,
can be convinced, unless it be through love?

GABRIEL: Oh! what are you saying!
The Queen of Heaven, Mary, Blessed Mother,
is not convinced by God?
Thyself a goddess, with splendor all around,
and praised both day and night!
MARY: Yes, he has given me great glory,
a glory that I never wanted.
A thousand times I'd have preferred
the love and life of my son.
The sole attraction of this place for me
is to be close to him.
For him I came here, for him I remain.
GABRIEL: And all these angels, these who once were women,
how did they come to be here?
MARY: They were drawn by love for my son,
and in time past they followed him.
GABRIEL: Do you not see, then, that the Father's plan was good?
MARY: Perhaps at one time, yes;
but now it's done; they come no longer.
GABRIEL: And why is that?
MARY: The son is too united with the father;
he is no longer as he used to be.
GABRIEL: But is there something down below
that holds them back,
something equal to your son,
that they love more than him?
The men on earth, do they inspire such love?
MARY: The answer is not easy. Yes and no.
GABRIEL: Or do the children, in their neediness,
prevent their mothers' coming to God?
MARY: Sometimes, perhaps; but children grow.
When they're no longer small,
a mother is no longer needed,
often, not even wanted.
So, no, they do not hold her back.
GABRIEL: Finally, then, what is it?
God wishes to know.

MARIE: Je ne puis te dire davantage,
va chercher toi-même,
descends encore une fois sur la terre,
regarde bien dans l'âme des femmes que tu vois
et surtout tâche de connaître leurs rêves.
C'est là que sera trouvée
la réponse de l'énigme.

TROISIÈME SCÈNE

Gabriel est redescendu sur la terre. Sa qualité d'ange lui permet de pénétrer dans l'âme et les rêves des femmes. Après un temps, il retourne auprès du Bon-Dieu qui l'attend impatiemment.

LE BON-DIEU: As-tu enfin trouvé, mon ange, dis,
et quoi?
GABRIEL: Et bien oui, Seigneur, enfin, enfin je sais.
C'est la sainte Mère Marie qui m'a prêté son aide.
Elle m'a dit où chercher et cela était juste:
dans l'âme de la femme, j'ai trouvé la raison.
Et sais-tu ce que c'est, ce quelque chose de si puissant?
Ce ne sont ni les hommes, ni l'enfant.
À peine est-ce à croire:
Seigneur, c'est une Image!
LE BON-DIEU: Une Image, rien que cela?
Cela semble peu, mais cependant je le crois
en voyant l'effet et le grand pouvoir qu'elle a.
Mais quelle Image, alors? Raconte-moi, Gabriel.
GABRIEL: Écoute donc, Seigneur,
j'ai parcouru là-bas la terre de long en large,
partout où sont des femmes,
et voilà ce que j'ai vu:
chacune a dans son âme un sanctuaire secret,
et dans ce sanctuaire est l'image d'un homme,
cachée à tel degré qu'elle connait à peine elle-même
et souvent pas du tout.
LE BON-DIEU: Cet homme, comment est-il?
GABRIEL: Un homme pas ordinaire et comme on n'en trouve guère
dans toute Ta création.
Il semble tout pareil aux hommes de la terre
et, cependant, ne l'est pas, car

MARY: Beyond this, I can tell you nothing more.
Go yourself and search.
Descend again to earth
and gaze into the souls of women there.
Above all, try to discern their dreams.
There, if anywhere, you will find
the answer to this enigma.

THIRD SCENE

Gabriel has descended again to earth. His angelic nature permits him to penetrate into women's souls and their dreams. After a time he returns to the Good Lord, who waits impatiently.

THE GOOD LORD: My angel! Didst thou find something at last,
and what?
GABRIEL: Yea, Lord, at last, at last I know.
The holy Mother Mary aided me,
by saying where to seek with certainty.
In Woman's soul I found the source of all.
And dost Thou know wherein this unnamed power
consists? Neither men nor children are the cause,
but something almost unbelievable.
My Lord, it is an Image!
THE GOOD LORD: An image, nothing more?
It seems a little thing; yet I believe
from its effect, this image has great power.
But now, what image? Tell me, Gabriel.
GABRIEL: Hear then, oh Lord.
Upon the earth I wandered far and wide,
above all where the women are,
and this is what I saw:
within each woman's soul she has a secret sanctuary,
and in this sanctuary, the image of a man
is hidden so deeply, she herself may know it
scarcely, or not at all.
THE GOOD LORD: This man, what is he like?
GABRIEL: A man so far from ordinary, one would hardly find
his like in all creation.
He seems no different from the men of earth,
yet he is quite unlike them, for

il est fort, comme eux, si fort
qu'il sait même être faible et doux sans avoir honte
et il est brave, si brave
qu'il peut même avoir peur sans perdre courage.
Et il est juste, si juste
qu'il ne veut point être infaillible.
Il peut pécher, sachant que c'est péché,
sans chercher vaines excuses
et porte sans hésiter
le poids du repentir!
Aussi est-il fier,
si fier qu'il s'incline
devant tout ce qu'il sent plus grand que lui.
Enfin, il a le grand amour, celui qui contient
le mépris et la haine
et reste amour quand même!
Mais ce qui le distingue entre tous
les habitants des terres et des cieux
c'est cela:
il peut reculer aussi bien qu'avancer,
et il peut s'arrêter sans y voir de dommage.
Les hommes par Toi créés,
nous-mêmes, Tes Anges, Seigneur,
nous ne savons pas cela:
dans une seule direction, nous continuons toujours,
tournant sans cesse dans un cercle éternel,
comme les astres sans âme,
sans âme et sans liberté.
Arrêter, reculer, pour nous veut dire: choir,
tandis que pour cet autre, pour l'homme de l'Image
cela veut dire: *choisir*.
Voilà Seigneur, ce que j'ai vu,
l'Image que crée la femme
retient les hommes loin de Toi:
dans chaque homme qu'elle aime,
la femme croit l'entrevoir,
et cent fois déçue, cent fois reprend l'espoir
de la trouver vivante et même incorporée.
Ainsi, l'homme est atteint
par la force merveilleuse
qui le fait T'oublier.
À l'Image créée par la femme,

he is as strong as they are, and so strong
that, without shame, he can be weak and kind.
And he is brave, so brave,
he can feel fear, yet never loses courage.
And he is just, so just,
he does not wish to be infallible.
He can sin, acknowledging the sin,
seeking no vain excuses,
and bears without reluctance
the burden of repentance!
Beyond all this, he's proud,
so proud, he bows his head
to everything he feels surpasses him.
Finally, he possesses the great love, love that contains
scorn and hatred,
yet love it still remains!
But what divides him from all others
on earth or in the heavens
is this:
He can withdraw as easily as he advances;
and, equally unharmed, he can stand still.
The men by Thee created,
even ourselves, oh Lord, Thine angels,
cannot do so much.
In one direction we keep turning, always,
in an eternal circle without cease,
like stars without a soul,
without a soul, and without liberty.
To halt or withdraw for us means: to fall,
whereas for this other, the man of the Image,
these mean: *to choose*.
There, my Lord, there is my news:
the Image that by Woman is created
is holding men away from Thee.
In every man she loves,
she thinks she glimpses it; and though she be
disappointed a hundred times, still she hopes
to find the image, living and embodied.
Thus Man is stricken
by the marvelous force
that makes him forget Thee.
Of the Image made by Woman

il voudrait ressembler.
Moi-même, je Te confesse, je commence à subir
ce magique pouvoir,
j'hésite à le dire,
des états jamais connus m'envahissent,
des pensées inouïes, des élans me remplissent.
Elle semble toute changée, Seigneur, Ta création,
et je Te demande, mon maître:
Es-Tu vraiment Bon?

LE BON-DIEU: Oh! étranges nouvelles que je reçois:
Marie, Mère de mon Fils, pas convaincue de Moi!
Mon Ange Gabriel, fasciné par une image,
faite par la femme, là-bas,
à tel point troublé, mon fidèle messager,
que de mes œuvres et de moi il veut douter!
Mais plus étrange encore:
au profond de mon être, quel émoi curieux?
Par cette puissance, serais-je aussi touché?
Hélas, je le crains, mais aussi le désire,
et je sens qu'irrésistiblement l'Image m'attire.
Dois-je suivre? dois-Je résister?
Quelle situation pour un Dieu!

Il réfléchit et combat avec lui-même pendant un temps.

Enfin, je vois clair:
il n'y a qu'un moyen de me guérir,
qu'un seul, je suis certain,
c'est d'abolir
le Ciel et l'Enfer,
les Anges, les Saints et Dieu!
Descendons vers la terre,
mélangeons-nous aux hommes et femmes,
ensemble avec eux faisons vivre l'Image,
pour qu'enfin par Elle
un nouveau monde soit créé,
où, quoique différent,
je me trouverai entier!
Fiat.

he would fain the likeness be.
Lord, I confess, I, too, begin to yield
to that magic power.
Although I'm loath to tell Thee,
I'm overrun by states I've never known,
filled by unexpected thoughts and energies.
Thy whole creation seems transformed, oh Lord.
And, Master, I must ask Thee:
Art Thou truly Good?

THE GOOD LORD: Oh, what strange tidings I receive:
Mary, the Mother of my Son, unconvinced by Me!
My Angel Gabriel, fascinated by an image
made by the woman, there below,
to such degree, my faithful messenger
claims to be doubtful of my works, and me!
But stranger still,
deep within my being, what curious emotion?
Can I, too, be affected by this power?
Alas, I fear, but I desire it, too,
and feel the Image draw me irresistibly.
Must I follow it? Must I resist?
What a situation for a God!

For a time he reflects and struggles with himself.

Now at last, I see it clearly:
one way exists to heal myself,
and one way only, surely,
which is to abolish
Heaven and Hell,
Angels, the Saints, and God!
Let us descend to earth,
to mingle with the men and women there.
Together with them, we'll make the Image live,
so that through It, at last,
a new world may be created,
in which, though changed,
I'll find myself complete.
  Fiat.

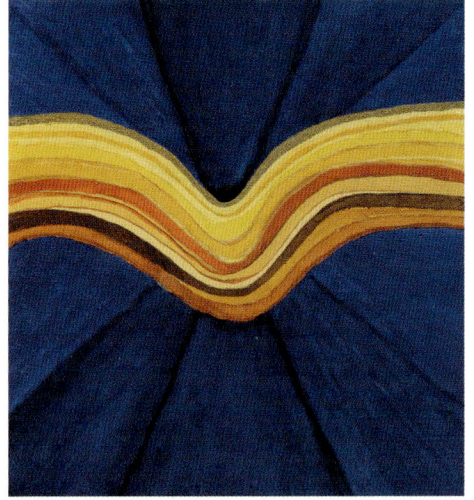

FIGURES 5.1–5.4.
Emergence of the
star-bird. Series of
paintings by Emma
Jung, April 1917.

Poems

DIE MAUER

Mächtig und hoch erhebt sich die Mauer,
riesenhaft sie, doch Mensch der Erbauer.
Stein an Stein gefügt mit Fleiss,—
was sie birgt, Niemand weiss,
nur die am stillen Mittag lauschen
hören drüben Ströme rauschen.

Doch mag es sein, es kommt ein Tag,
wo der See die Wasser nicht fassen mag,
dann brechen sie über die Mauer ins Tal,
erfüllen das Land, die Welt zumal,
bedecken was schwer, das Leichte sie heben,
jenes im Tode, dieses zum Leben,
tragen es höher und höher empor,
und was sich nicht in der Tiefe verlor
sieht welch Wunder die Flut getan:
Ins Jenseitsland ist freie Bahn!

Mai 1916

FIGURE 5.5.
The wall. Painting by
Emma Jung, c. 1916.

I.   THE WALL

Mighty and high the wall arises,
Gigantic, yes, but human its builder.
Mortared with zeal, stone upon stone,
what it's holding, no one knows;
only those who heed, in the noonday hush,
will hear beyond it the currents' rush.

But a day may come, as the days unfold,
when the lake its waters cannot hold.
Breaking through, into the valley they pour,
filling the land, and the world even more.
Shrouding the heavy, they lift up the light,
the former to death, the latter to life,
borne ever higher and higher aloft,
till all below, in the deep not lost,
will see what a miracle the flood bestowed:
to the Land Beyond is an open road!

May 1916[1]

---

1   This untitled poem and painting are found in the marbled book, together with a dream text,
dated "III 1916." The dream takes place in the city of Schaffhausen, Switzerland, where Emma Jung
was born and grew up. The dreamer is struck by changes in the city's architecture. She stays close to
the medieval structures, which have not changed. A later, handwritten copy of the poem is found in
the 1921 poem booklet, bearing the title and date shown here.

In Nebel, in Wolken, meine Seele in Dir,
lass hören o Seele, was sagst du mir?
Wolken reden nicht du Kind,
Wolken lassen sich tragen vom Wind,
fliegen über die Welt dahin,
lieben es hoch am Himmel zu ziehn,
haben nicht Form noch Festigkeit,
wogten gestern und wandeln sich heut.
Von der Erde zum Himmel, vom Himmel zur Erden,
das ist der Wolken ewiges Werden.
    Du meinest sie zu greifen,
    und sie ist himmelsweit,
    bald hüllet sie dich wieder
    ein ringsum als ein Kleid.
    Du kannst sie niemals fassen,
    verloren ist die Müh,
    und flögst du auch zum Himmel
    so hoch empor wie sie.
    Denn Mensch und Wolke, wisse,
    sie sind ungleicher Art:
    er kann sie nur erkennen
    wenn sie zu Wasser ward!

Rigi, Juni 1916

2. THE SOUL—A CLOUD

In fog, in clouds, my soul in Thee.
O soul, wilt Thou not speak to me?
Ah, my child, clouds have no words.
To and fro above the world,
carried by the wind they fly
across the heavens, in lofty joy,
having no shape nor lasting form,
daily they billow and transform.
From earth to heaven, from heaven to earth,
eternally, clouds come to birth.
  The cloud you think to touch
  is distant as the sky,
  and then it wraps around you
  and veils you on all sides.
  Never will you catch it;
  no point for you to try,
  even if to heaven
  aloft you were to fly.
  Remember, mortal, truly,
  the cloud and you are twain:
  you cannot know it fully
  until it turns to rain!

Rigi,[2] June 1916

---

2   The Rigi, a low peak in the Schwyzer Alps, is a popular day trip from Zurich. Its top is sometimes thickly clouded.

WEITE

Wohl ist er schön, der wilde Tanz des Lebens,
und die bunte Schar der Tänzer, die nie rastend
in immer neuen Lichtern und Gestalten
unserm Blick vorüber zieht!
Doch schöner ist es, über all das wandel-wechselvolle Treiben
hinweg den Blick zu lenken
weit—
dorthin wo in blauen Fernen
der hohe Himmel unserer Erde Rand berührt,
und andachtsvoll die heil'gen Toren grüssen,
durch welche göttlich strahlend unsre Sonne
uns Tag um Tag erscheint und wiederum entschwindet.

Januar 1917

3. FAR OFF

Yes, beautiful it is, the wild dance of life,
and the colorful troupe of dancers, never resting,
in ever-changing lights and new formations
passing before our eyes!
More beautiful is it yet, beyond the shifting, changing bustle,
to steer our gaze
far off
to where in boundless blue
the towering sky touches our earthly rim,
and solemnly to bow before the holy gates
through which our sun, divinely radiant,
day after day appears and vanishes again.

January 1917

TRAUER

Liebe, warum entflohst du mir?
Kein Wort, keine Stimme, die Antwort mir gäbe.
Ein kalter Hauch nur weht mir ins Gesicht
und tot ist alles, was einst lebensvoll gegrüsst.

November 1917

4. GRIEF

Love, why did you flee from me?
No word, no voice would give me a reply.
Only a cold breath blows into my face,
and everything that once was full of life is dead.

November 1917

Es ist ein Tod gekommen über mich:
Die Welt, sie ward mir stumm.
Nicht höre ich mehr die Stimme der Erde
Wie einst, wo Felsen, Blumen, Bäume
Und Wasser zu mir sprachen.
Der Himmel auch mit Sonne Mond und Sternen
Schweigt meinem Ohr.
Allein bin ich, von Allem abgeschieden–
Zerrissen sind die Bande, die ganze weite Welt
Verknüpft mit meiner Seele.
    Wie geschah dies nur?
    Wo liegt die Schuld?

(Eine Stimme):
"Die Antwort höre:
Was die Welt dir sprach, das log sie dir!
Keine Mutter ist die Erde, an deren Herzen
In seligen Träumen du ruhest als Kind!
Der Himmel ist nicht schön,
Nicht freundlich glänzen Mond und Sterne!
Nein, alles dies ist Trug!—
Ein endlos dunkler Raum nur,
Erfüllt von Eis- und Steingebilden,
Die ewig sinnlos kreisend ihn durchziehn,
    Das ist das All;
Und deine 'liebe goldne Sonne' gar,
Ein schrecklich wütend und verzehrend Feuer!
Doch Du, du bist ein Mensch,
Und nicht ziehmt es Menschen
    Lügen zu glauben.
Was du erleidest ist die Strafe, welche
Der Wahrheit Gott verhänget über Alle,
Die schuldge Ehre ihm nicht zollen."

(Andere Stimme):
"'Der Gott der Wahrheit' sagst du?
Was ist Wahrheit?
Heute so und morgen anders

5. A DEATH IS COME UPON ME

A death is come upon me.
The world has fallen mute.
The voice of earth no more I hear—
the rocks and flowers, trees and water
no longer speak to me.
The heavens, too, sun, moon, and stars
are silent to my ear.
I am alone, cut off from all.
Torn are the bonds that link my soul
with the whole, wide world.
    How did this happen?
    Where lies the blame?

(A voice):
"Now hear the answer:
What the world promised you, it promised falsely!
The earth is not a mother, on whose heart
you rest, a child, in blissful dreams!
Heaven is not lovely,
nor do the moon and stars in kindness shine!
No, all these things are lies.
The All is only space, an endless dark,
Filled with ice and stony forms
that endlessly, forlornly, circle round.
    This is the universe;
and even your 'dear, golden sun'—
a terrifying fire that rages and devours!
But you, you are a human being;
and human beings should not
    believe in lies.
Your suffering is the punishment
the God of Truth inflicts on everyone
who does not pay him proper reverence."

(Another voice):
" 'The God of Truth', you say?
And what is truth?
Today it's this, tomorrow something else,

Und Wahnsinn je sie wirklich zu entdecken.
Schönheit aber ist ewig
Und allein verehrungswürdig,
Und die Welt ist schön!"

(Dritte Stimme):
"Trug, alles Trug!
Wahrheit ist wahrer Schein
Und Schönheit schöner Schein,
Doch Schein bleibt alles;
Und ohne Menschen
Auch nicht einmal Schein.
Also:
Wirklich und wichtig ist allein
    Der Mensch und seine Seele."

Januar 1918

and madness ever to discover it.
But beauty is eternal;
it alone deserves your reverence,
and the world is beautiful!"

(Third voice):
"Illusion, all illusion!
Truth is a true illusion,
beauty a beautiful illusion,
yet illusion it all remains;
and without human beings, not even that.
Therefore:
Real and of meaning is only
    the human being and the human soul."

January 1918[3]

---

3   Written two months after "Grief," this poem resembles a fantasy or active imagination in its depiction of the poet's conversation with inner voices.

Über hohe Berge dringt herein das Licht.
Aus nächt'gen Schatten heben sich die weissen Gipfel,
Die braunen Hänge und die dunkeln Wälder;
   Der Tiefe Nebel fliehen,
   Helle wird das Tal,
Aus Nacht ersteht dem Auge eine Welt.

Nun nennt mir keine Namen,
   Freunde, keine Stunde!
Sagt nicht: "Hier geht die Sonne auf,
   Dort ging sie unter"!
Lasst mich sie schauen namenlos und ohne Zeit, die Dinge,
So wähn' ich mich entrückt von diesem Ort des Wandels und des Scheines
Nach jenem nie betretnen Reich der ew'gen Bilder
Dem von jeher
Die ungestillte Sehnsucht meiner Seele galt.

November 1918, Château-d'Oex

6. MORNING IN THE MOUNTAINS[4]

Over high mountains the light is breaking through.
Out of night's shadows the white peaks emerge,
The brown inclines and the somber forests;
    Mists flee from the deep,
    The valley brightens,
From night, a world arises to the eye.

Name me no names now,
    Friends, tell me no hours!
Don't say: "Here the sun rises,
    There it went down"!
Let me behold these things, unnamed and timeless,
So I can think myself out of this place of change and seeming,
Transported to that never-entered realm of images
That was forever
Home to the unstilled yearning of my soul.

Château-d'Oex,[5] November 1918

---

4   In the 1921 poem booklet, this poem is titled simply "Morgen" (Morning). The full title appears over an earlier version in the manila poem folder.

5   In November 1918, Emma Jung evidently visited Carl Jung in Château d'Oex, Switzerland, where he was stationed as commander of the camp for British wartime internees for almost the whole month (information from C. G. Jung's calendars and private letters, Jung Family Archive). The year before, during a military service from June to September 1917 at the same internment camp, Carl Jung drew his mandala sketch series. Despite being on military duty, it seems that he could often have visitors. A well-known photograph of C. G. and Emma with the children—except for their youngest, Helene (Lill)—was taken in Château d'Oex in 1917 (26, plate 14).

Ich hörte eine Stimme rufen durch die Nacht:
"Hört, ihr Lebenden, höret!
Öffnet euer Ohr meinem Wort, und durch eure Träume dringe es zu den
Herzen:
Siehe ich wanderte nach fernen Welten und kam in das Land der Götter,
das war aber dunkel und trübe und eingehüllt in graue Nebel.
Und die Götter sah ich in ihrem Lande,
aber es waren nicht lebendige Götter, die in Herrlichkeit wohnen,
es waren traurige, wesenlose Schatten.
Und ich sah, dass sie hungern und dürsten nach Leben,
dass sie sich verzehren in Sehnsucht nach euch, Menschen,
und dass sie machtlos sind,
gewährt ihr nicht ihnen Leben von euerm Leben
und Blut von euerm Blut.
Da erbarmte mich der Götter.
Die der Erlösung bedürfen sollen erlöst werden.
Darum rufe ich euch, in der Nacht,
ihr Lebendigen!
Frühe beginnet das Werk!
Die Pforten der Zukunft sind aufgetan,
wohlauf, beschreitet den Weg:
Gotterlöser sollt ihr sein!"

1920

7. SERMO AD VIVOS[6]

I heard a voice crying through the night:
"Hear me, hear me, ye who are alive!
Open your ears to my word, and in dreams let it move your hearts:
Behold! I traveled to distant worlds and came to the land of gods,
only it was dark and dingy, wrapped in grey fog.
And I saw the gods in their land;
only not living gods, dwelling in glory,
they were shadows, sad and insubstantial.
And I saw that they hunger and thirst after life,
consumed by their yearning, humankind, for you.
Indeed, they are powerless,
unless you grant them life from your life,
blood from your blood.
Then I had mercy on the gods.
Those who need redemption should be redeemed.
Therefore I cry to you by night,
living ones!
Begin your work, even now!
The future's gates are open;
arise, stride forth upon your way:
ye shall be redeemers of the gods!"

1920[7]

---

6   Latin: "A word to the living." The title is probably a reference to C. G. Jung's "VII Sermones ad Mortuos" (Seven sermons to the dead), printed for private circulation in 1916.

7   In the August 1921 poem booklet, "Sermo ad vivos" (undated by author) follows a poem dated July 1920, and precedes "Miracle," dated August 1920. We conclude that this poem was written in the summer of 1920.

Du kamst zu mir!
Aus fernen Himmeln weit dahergezogen
Stiegst Du zu mir herab!
Ewig urheiliges Bild
Du wardest mir lebendig,
Dich Langersehntes[8] fühl ich endlich nah.
Dem Auge nicht erkennbar,
Nicht dem Ohre,
Kein Licht bist Du, kein Ton
Dennoch ein Sein,
Und mir zum Gruss
Erweckest Du in meinem Herzen
Die dunkeln Worte:
"Sternengleich und Erdentreu!"

August 1920

---

8   An earlier version of this poem, found in the brown leather notebook, shows that the author corrected *Langersehntes* (long-yearned-for)—a neuter-gendered noun, consistent with the antecedent *Bild* (image)—changing it to the feminine form, *Langersehnte*. In her 1921 poem booklet, however, the author reverts to the original form.

Thou cam'st to me!
Out of the distant sky, drawn from afar,
On me hast thou descended!
Eternal, ever-holy image,
Thou cam'st to life for me.
Long-yearned-for one, I feel thee near at last.
Unseen by eye art thou,
Unheard by ear;
No light, no sound art thou,
Yet still a being.
And at thy greeting, in my heart
Dark words awaken:
"Like to a star and faithful to the earth!"[9]

August 1920

---

9   *Sternengleich und Erdentreu!*": These terms are probably borrowed from Nietzsche. "Und dem Sterne gleich, der erlischt, ist jedes Werk eurer Tugend; immer ist sein Licht noch unterwegs und wandert" (Nietzsche, *Also sprach Zarathustra*, 13); and "Ich beschwöre euch, meine Brüder, *bleibt der Erde treu* und glaubt Denen nicht, welche euch von überirdischen Hoffnungen reden!" (ibid., 9). In Thomas Common's translation: "And like the star that goeth out, so is every work of your virtue: ever is its light on its way and travelling" (Nietzsche, *Thus Spake Zarathustra*, 146); "I conjure you, my brethren, *remain true to the earth*, and believe not those who speak to you of hopes beyond the compass of the earth!" (ibid., 68).

Götter waret ihr einst
Und herrschtet
In hohen Himmeln
Über die Welt.
Aber ihr stieget herab—
Zog euch der Sterblichen Sehnsucht?—
Und ihr wohntet bei uns.
Im Wandel der Zeiten
Wuchsen die Menschen heran;
Nicht mehr wie früher
Ehrfurchtsvoll, verhüllten Haupts
Knieeten sie vor euch.
Ihr standet im lichten Tag,
Da schwand euch Macht und Gewalt,
Es schwand die Gottheit dahin.
Zu nahe kamet ihr uns,
Da ergriff euch des Lebens Rad,
Nun müsst auch ihr vergehen,
Uns, den Irdischen gleich.

Doch wir wenden den Blick
Suchend in ferne Nacht;
Wann wohl steiget uns dort
Neue Gottheit herauf?

8. Dezember 1920

9. EXPECTATION

Once you were gods
And ruled
In heavens high
Above the world.
But you descended—
Did mortals' longing draw you?—
And lived among us.
As times changed,
The human race grew up;
They knelt to you no more
With covered heads, in awe,
As once they did.
In broad daylight you stood,
Drained of your power and might,
Drained of divinity.
Too near to us you came, and now,
Seized by the wheel of life,
Like us, the earth-born,
Even you must perish.

Yet still we bend our gaze,
Searching the distant night;
When, if ever, in that sky,
Will new divinity arise?

8 December 1920

Wir stehen an den Pforten eines fremden Landes,
    den Blick verhüllt,
    die Herzen bang,
Unsicher tastend sucht der Fuss den Weg.
O leuchte, Licht, den Pfad uns zu erhellen,
O heilig Feuer in den Herzen
    wolle nie verglühn!
    Und Nacht, du tiefe
Sende du aus deinem Schosse
    ein Bild als Führer uns
    zum fern geahnten Ziel!

Neujahr 1921, Zuoz

10. WE STAND AT THE GATEWAY

We stand at the gateway to a foreign land,
    our view shrouded,
    our hearts afraid.
Unsteady, groping, our feet seek the way.
Shine out, O light, illuminate our path,
O holy fire in our hearts,
    may you never die!
    And night, deep night,
Send forth from within thy womb
    An image to be our guide
    to the dim, foreshadowed goal!

New Year's Day 1921, Zuoz[10]

---

10 Zuoz is a mountain village in the Engadine region of the Canton of Graubünden, where members of the Psychology Club Zurich held their 1921 New Year's celebration (62, plates 25, 26, 27).

Du bist es, mit der Flammenkrone,
steinerner Gast!
Dein Leib, du ganz von Stein,
jedoch dein Haupt umlodert
von einem Feuerblumenkranz!

Daran erkenn ich dich,
du bist es, Unvergleichlicher,
ich grüsse dich.

Wen suchst du hier, bei mir?
Mich selbst? Ich will dir dienen,
gebiete über mich.

Oder suchst du ihn, der mir im Herzen wohnt
und sich als König dort gebärden will?
Ein falscher Herrscher ist er,
du, mit der lebend'gen Krone, bist allein der Wahre,
und du kommst zu richten den Falschen, der dich äfft.
Nimm ihn in deine starke Hand
und zeig ihm, was sein Dienst, und wo sein Weg,
so wird er recht gerichtet,
der ohne Willen, wahllos sich bewegt
und nur zum Knechte tauget, nicht zum König.

April 1924

Thou art the one, with crown of flames,
stone guest!
All made of stone thy body,
and yet around thy head
a blazing wreath of flowers!

By this I recognize thee,
Incomparable One,
I greet thee.

Whom dost thou seek here?
Me, myself? I will serve thee,
give me thy command.

Or seek'st thou him who dwells within my heart,
who gestures there, pretending to be a king?
A false ruler is he;
true ruler art thou alone, with thy living crown,
and com'st to judge the impostor aping thee.
Take him in thy mighty hand,
show him his duty, point him on his way;
then he will have what he deserves,
whose aimless movement, without will or choice,
befits a servant only, not a king.

April 1924

Stehst du noch draussen, vor meiner Tür?
Wartest du noch, dass ich komme?
Aber die Türe find ich nicht mehr,
die ich gestern durchschritt,
und der Garten, wo ist er,
in dem ich Dich sah?
Alles ist anders, ich erkenn es nicht mehr
und weiss nicht, wo Du zu finden.
Nur im Geiste seh ich dich stehen
wie dort, hoch und still,
und du siehest mich an mit mächtigem Blick, unverwandt—
deutlicher, deutlicher sprich,
So kann ich vernehmen,
was Du zu sagen mir kamst,
wessen Bote du bist
und was Du mich heissest!

19. Juni 1924

Dost thou yet stand outside my door?
Waitest thou yet upon my coming?
But the door is lost to me
that yesterday I stepped through—
and the garden where I saw thee,
where is it now?
All is changed, unrecognizable,
I know not where to find thee.
In spirit alone I see thee standing
there as before, silent and tall,
and thou regardest me
with mighty gaze, unwavering.
Clearly, more clearly speak,
that I may understand
what thou art come to tell me,
whose messenger thou art,
and to what thou callest me.

19 June 1924

FIGURE 6.1.
[Night sea journey].
Painting by Emma
Jung, undated.

VI

Dreams and Fantasies

I. [DREAM OF SWAN AND STAR]

January 1914

I dreamed I am flying through the heavens on a swan, straight toward a shining star.[1] As I climb higher and higher, the swan that is carrying me gradually transforms into the star that I am heading for.

---

1   Emma Jung refers to this image in relation to her fantasy of seeking Undine, 18 October 1915 (Chapter VI, 278, note 30).

FIGURE 6.2.
Baptism. Painting by
Emma Jung, March
1914.

2. DREAM. [TWO PICTURES]

March 1914 (after the birth of Helene)[2]

I see two pictures by an unknown painter: one is called *Engadine*, and depicts a mountain road across which three small fir trees are laid, like those that are used in winter to mark the way along the side of the road.[a]

The second picture, with the title *Baptism*, depicted a sparse grove of tall conifers (pines) on the verge of the sea.[b] Through the middle is a path that leads to the sea, visible in the background, upon which two white figures are strolling toward the coast.

Emma Jung's commentary:

[a] As associations, mainly the words: the signposts have fallen, no more signposts—so a new way, for which there is no longer any signpost: one's own way. And the story of Joseph's dream in the Bible, where the eleven sheaves of wheat bowed before the one.[3]

[b] Initiation by immersion in the sea (of the unconscious). This is also the place where two principles meet, sun and earth.

---

2   The youngest child in the family, Helene (nicknamed Lill) was born on 18 March 1914. Her astrological sign, Pisces, has a symbolic meaning in Emma Jung's commentary on a dream of May 1915 (Chapter VII, 320f.).

3   Genesis 37:5–8.

3. DREAM. THE BLUE FLOWER

May 1914

I am walking with Carl (my masculine aspect?) along a sunny road in a rural area, through wide green meadows, where single houses stand among fruit trees. We pass by a cornfield, and among the golden ears of corn I catch sight of a bright *blue flower*[a] that I hurry to pick, for I have been searching for it for a long time. I thought I would find it *in the most impenetrable, deepest forest*, and it never occurred to me that *it would be so close to the path, and in a cornfield*. As I pick it, I notice that there are also some red flowers—glowing poppies. For a moment I hesitate, wondering if I should take them, too, for they are beautiful. But I refrain from doing so and take only the blue one that I have been seeking for so long.[b]

I return to the road, and there stands a pretty farmhouse with a trellis full of splendid pears. A woman steps outside, greets me in a friendly manner, and asks whether I would like to take some of the pears, adding that I had already had some. I say I cannot take them right now, but I will send another woman to fetch them later. (A dancer with oriental charms.)[c]

The area seems suddenly so familiar to me, and I realize that I'm behind the insane asylum[4] in Schaffhausen.[d]

Emma Jung's commentary:

[a] "The blue flower," the long-sought-after gem of the "spiritual," is not found in wild nature,[5] but in *culture*, in the cornfield—i.e. also in or through work.

[b] Foregoing the biological—life—red—in favor of the spiritual. Clear distinction of the two opposites represented by *blue and red*.

[c] Possibly temptation by the mother—("the tree was beautiful to look at")[6] but I resist—point out that I will fetch the *fruit later* and, even then, through the *mediation* of another, who is characterized as *"intuition" i.e. as located particularly close to the unconscious*.[7]

[d] Again,[8] reference to the proximity of the insane, and fruit, and blue flower!

---

4 *Irrenanstalt*: insane asylum. An accepted term at this time (8, note 23). At the time of writing, Kantonale Irrenanstalt was the official name of the Schaffhausen psychiatric hospital.

5 In the writings of some German Romantics, the blue flower (*die blaue Blume*) is described as an exquisite flower that does not occur in nature, thus symbolizing a deeply desired but unattainable goal.

6 Allusion to the temptation of Eve in the Garden of Eden (Genesis 3:6).

7 A reference to C. G. Jung's theory of psychological types. Because Emma Jung's most conscious function was sensation, her least conscious was intuition, represented in this dream by "a dancer with oriental charms." (See "Reader's Guide," volume introduction, 79 and notes; also author's commentary on dream of two churches, Chapter VI, 303f.)

8 A dream dated February 1914, recorded by Emma Jung in the marbled book, contains similar

May 1914

The magician

I find myself in a crowd of people, watching a magician. He has shown us a cage with a hen, and then covered it with a black cloth. Now, he rolls up his sleeves, empties out his pockets and explains in a torrent of words what will and will not happen next. "When I now lift this cloth, ladies and gentlemen," he says, "The hen will have disappeared and in its place … well, you shall see; I am counting: one, two …" But before he could say "three," the magician disappeared, and no one knew what should have appeared in the place of the hen.

The camel

But as I look around me, I find I am on a broad plain—all around me nothing but sand, yellow sand. Far off to the left, I see a group of palm trees sharply silhouetted against the golden evening sky. To my right, nothing but sand, swept into small heaps by the wind. No living creature anywhere. But then, striding along is a camel, lonely and majestic, that I address, for lack of other company: "Do you live all alone in this desert?" "Yes, for a camel is at home in the desert, though people aren't." "But how did you come to be so alone?" "Oh, I thought it would be nice to live in freedom, and I secretly made off, but since then, I have been miserable, and my dearest wish is to return to my master and my companions. Do me a favor and take me with you. I will gladly carry you on my back."

The dancer

Then we are back with our magician, who is about to lift up the cloth. I watch with bated breath—what will appear? A beautiful brown girl with black hair. She is dressed in colored veils, her upper body and feet are naked. Looking at her more closely, I see that she must come from the farthest corner of the East, from some Indian or Australian island. Correct! It seems that we are in India, at least according to the appearance and costume of the magician. And more precisely, we are in a beautiful garden, a fairy tale of lush, exotic plants and sweet perfumes. To the right is a white house, the palace of the prince, who is sitting on a lounge on a veranda extending out into the garden, calmly watching the magician perform his tricks. The latter now takes the brown girl by the hand and leads her before the prince. She throws herself to her knees before him and touches the ground

images. In April 1914, in relation to another dream, she mentions that divine madness is associated with initiation.

with her forehead. She remains in this position, motionless, while the magician says to the prince, "Oh Master, you so graciously deigned to watch my art; my final and most difficult act was to use my magic to summon this girl who is lying at your feet. I am retiring now, and she shall show you what she can do—she shall dance for you." Soft music is heard. At a cue from the magician, the girl gets up and slowly walks down the steps of the verandah onto the lawn encircled with trees. She keeps her eyes half closed and, as if dreaming, moves back and forth to the beat of the music. Slowly she loosens the veil from her hair, swings it through the air, and then she dances more and more lightly, her feet hardly touching the ground. It is as if she had been given wings. I see only the floating veil, and the music—the music is only a soft, gentle humming. The sound, this humming, is now coming from all sides.

I look around and see now—no longer a floating veil, but a swarm of bees—all blossoms, all trees are filled with the busy humming, the whole garden is filled with their fine song. They must have their dwelling over there in that tree, for it is particularly lively there right now. One bee, larger than the others—it must be the queen—comes out. She flies back and forth but does not stop at any particular flower. A whole band of others fly after her—they seem to be chasing her—but the big one is always in the lead. Her strength never flagging, she flies higher and higher. High and ever higher, the swarm follows her until they completely disappear into the blue, and one hears only their soft, gentle buzzing.

It makes you sleepy, this buzzing, and it is hot—or haven't I already slept? A moment ago wasn't there a dancer here? Oh, there she is again, still swaying on the lawn with her brownish veil. It is getting unbearably hot, the sun is stinging, the dancer is also looking for shade. Very quietly she walks between the trees of the small wood that borders the lawn. The sun casts peculiar lights on her—she is dappled all over by the shadows of the leaves. Quietly, quietly she walks, strangely, like a cat. Appalled, the music falls silent. That is not the dancer, it is an animal, a spotted animal, a leopard, that is creeping closer over there with inaudible steps. There, it pauses, perhaps alerted by the sudden cessation of the music, and with a single leap, it is on the next tree, where it stretches out along one of its boughs and now seems to be waiting, almost hidden by leaves. You can't make it out clearly, only occasionally you see a pair of eyes glinting out of the dark greenery. Just then, a servant with a shotgun steps out of the house and cautiously starts to approach the grove.

A cloud moves in front of the sun; it stops flickering and shimmering before your eyes and now we no longer see the leopard, but instead the brown dancer, who steps out between the tree trunks. Everyone breathes a sigh of relief. The prince beckons her—she falls down before him, and he throws her a pearl necklace, which she places around her neck, bowing her thanks in silence. Once more, she steps down into the garden. The music has started to play again, and she dances between the trees, sometimes slowly, sometimes with quicker movements. A colorful butterfly then flutters up. She wants to catch it and follows it from bush to bush across the whole meadow to the fountain, which throws silver jets of water into the air, and they fall back into the marble basin with a quiet splash. The butterfly seems to be dancing in a race with the water: you see it, then you see only the silver jet of water, finally it blurs, and I see only green-silver water.

But what is this? Am I asleep again? I see nothing but water around me— am I in the sea? There, a reef; that must be corals—strange plants and animals of wonderful colors. But what do I see there? A hideous polyp has attached itself to the rock and stretches its long tentacles in all directions. It doesn't have to wait long for prey: already something large, brownish is coming along through the green twilight. It is a human being, a boy who wanted to dive for pearl oysters but, oh dear, one of the polyp arms has already grabbed him. He wants to free himself, but the gruesome arms are already wrapping themselves around him from all sides, tighter and tighter, and all effort is in vain. Horrible. I want to scream, or I do scream, then I'm already back at the fountain and hear its soft splashing.

The dancer has seated herself on the edge of the basin to rest. What an enchanted place this is! Is it the heat, the music, or the dancer? Now she comes toward us again—but I still seem to be bewitched: that's not her at all, but a donkey with her colt. On her back, she carries two baskets with wonderful fruit. She steps closer and holds still before the prince, as if she wanted to offer him her fruit.—Her foal jumps up, nuzzles up to her and begins to drink. We all look at each other in amazement, but the dancer is already standing there again, completely wrapped in different colored veils. She looks at the prince and smiles at him questioningly. He nods and throws her a flower, which she kisses and fastens in her hair.

Then she begins to dance again. Slowly, she lifts one of the veils. Is it the evening sun that makes it appear so blue and green-golden? No, it is a peacock that struts across the meadow, allowing its magnificent plumage to play in the sun. But no, no longer a peacock. It is again the dancer. She has thrown off the blue veil and once more dances past the prince, who now, completely captivated by her beauty, no longer takes his eyes off her. Evening draws closer. A peculiar light lies over the garden. The flowers exude sweet and heavy fragrances. She still has to dance—one veil after the other she drops—her dark eyes directed questioningly at the prince, who nods at her with a smile. And as she dances ever faster and wilder, so, too, does the music play more and more ravishingly. Already the last veil falls. The delighted prince beckons her to him. But she no longer pays him any heed, no matter how anxious she had been to please him beforehand. She seems completely out of herself. Dancing more and more wildly, she has cast off the last veil—naked, she dances on.

But heavens, what is this? Now she even tears off her skin and casts it aside. Ghastly sight. And still she dances on. At last, she starts to stagger, falls and her body lies there, lifeless. I want to avert my eyes from the horrible sight, but I cannot. Like withered leaves from a tree, even her flesh now falls away, and in front of me lies a naked skeleton.

I shudder. I look around. The prince has disappeared and it is almost night. Over there is another servant, whom I summon. He must help me dig a grave and put the sad remains to rest. Then I, too, lie down to rest and dream of the wonders and horrors of this day, until a cold morning wind awakens me. Around me, all is damp with dew. The sun has not yet risen. There is the dancer's grave. Am I seeing right? There stands a lily; it has grown overnight. Its blossom is still closed. I go to look at the miracle, as the first ray of sunlight falls between the trees, right on the lily. And as it falls on it—a new miracle—the calyx opens and a wonderful white woman emerges radiantly. She approaches me, seems to float, beckons me to follow her, and slowly floats higher and higher.

Then a ray falls on me, too. I wake up, this time for real, and high in the blue wafts a white, shimmering cloud.

March 1915

I see a small, winding path leading through green meadows to a hill. A mouse is going up the hill. With this comes the saying:

> To Golgotha a mouse did go,
> "What did it there?" you'll want to know.
> The labor is long and far the climb,
> The cross won't fall before its time.[9]

Emma Jung's commentary:

Like the squirrel that gnaws the world ash tree, the mouse here is probably supposed to bring down the cross, that the old gods may fall and new ones arise.

(By associations via image from the Life of Mary, the mouse = the servant of Mary, thus servant of the divine or the holy—similar to Mephisto!)

Theme: Twilight of the gods.[10]

---

9 Es geht eine Maus nach Golgatha. / Nun fragst du wohl: "Was tut sie da?" / Die Arbeit ist gar lang und weit / das Kreuz fällt nicht vor seiner Zeit.

10 *Götterdämmerung*: Nietzsche's term was also familiar to the author as the title of the final opera in Richard Wagner's cycle, "The Ring of the Nibelungen."

Early 1915[11]

I am on a walk in an enchanted forest and there I chance upon a small, round temple[a] in which I suddenly find myself confined. Nowhere is there an opening above.[12] In the middle is a well[13] that draws me to it. But as I step in, I am given a fish tail and am now completely trapped. Perplexity. Finally, a golden bird[b] (bird of paradise) appears and makes a proposal to help me out—I should let him lay his eggs under my fish scales. He pecks holes in them with his beak, into which he then lays an egg every few days (horrible feeling!). The eggs develop into shiny bubbles that gradually lift me out of the water, just enough so that I can see over the roof—no further. The bird has disappeared. Unbearable situation.

Because of the bubbles, I can no longer go down into the water, and they are not able to lift me all the way up and out. I am standing on my fish tail, and it becomes more and more unbearable.

Now I see a shepherd outside and ask him for a knife. With it, I begin to cut off my fish tail[c] to at least put an end to this ghastly state of being "neither fish nor fowl." That is my only thought—I couldn't care less about what will happen. And what happens is what had to happen, namely, as soon as the heaviness of my upper body is removed from it, my fish tail with the air bubbles rises into the air, and my human part, being only heavy, falls infinitely far down into an impenetrable darkness.

So: completely torn apart, without connection.[d]

Emma Jung's comment:
Theme of doubling[14]

C. G. Jung's commentary:
[a] Temple = uterus, baptismal font, new church (expressed in the ancient manner), analysis. Through growth and separation from the collective, escape is possible.

---

11   This version of Emma Jung's Water Nymph fantasy was probably written sometime after March 1915. An original, longer version of the text, found in the marbled book, is undated but bracketed by writings bearing that date.

12   In the original version, the roof of the temple is open to the sky, "and in the center, the blue, open sky looks down upon the well."

13   In the original version, the well is described: "It is a deep well, dark and unfathomable, and from its center bubbles the unquenchable spring."

14   *Verdoppelung.* Six months later, Emma Jung's fantasy of the Water Nymph (here titled "Seeking Undine," Chapter VI, 276ff.) expands on the theme of doubling. Imagery and commentary in the author's later vision contrast with the interpretations offered by Carl Jung.

^b Anticipation of Phanes, who, however, begins as Abraxas in the collective unconscious (impersonal unconscious). (Parallel to the transformation of Izdubar.)[15]

^c Separation of the *ego* (individual) from the impersonal collective unconscious.

^d Izdubar ascends to heaven and becomes Abraxas. The ego winds up in hell. Before, we were completely carried by the power of the unconscious. Afterwards, therefore, the ego must fall into the vacuum, into hell. The libido goes completely with the new god. What remains to the ego is infinitely little, only the negative, the evil, so to speak.

---

15 Phanes, Abraxas, Izdubar: see Jung, *The Red Book*. Regarding the transformation of Izdubar, see "Liber Secundus," ibid., 278ff.

April 1915

After I had wandered like this for a time,[16] my path led me up a mountain, always in deep forest. At the top, fully hidden and overgrown, I found three old towns (Anglo-Saxon or Breton settlements) that had remained unnoticed and untouched all this time. But the ground was so soft and loamy that I couldn't get close to them. What to do? It occurred to me that the best thing would be to build a proper road to the towns, and so I set about making a road with logs, of which I could find sufficient in the forest, a kind of log causeway upon which one could reach the towns without sinking. A tedious and long job, especially having to do it on my own! But it seemed necessary.

It is a dark, dense forest,[17] mostly firs, here and there a beech or oak tree, but it has the character of a dark pine forest, the Black Forest. This brings to mind the little verse, "Keeper of dark woods of pine,[18] all its lands are only thine." The story of *The Cold Heart*[19] takes place in such a dark forest. It is dark and eerie here, no light, no warming ray of sunshine penetrates.—Full of spectres, and yet also enticing and compelling.—And in the midst of this forest, there lie my cities—the "cold heart" of this enchanted forest. It is, indeed, enchanted and eerie here: no living creature—even the birds don't like it here. The dark trunks are tinged green by the eternal damp, and black—black the dense limbs hang down. It comes as no surprise that the city lies here as forsaken as it was 1,000 years ago. Was the forest already here when they were built, or did it grow around them over time? The ancient Celts who lived here, they, too, had such gloomy hearts, rigid and dark and wild—but cold?

I am still not completely finished with my road, which means that I can always only see the city from a distance. So I keep on working.

---

16   In the marbled book, the author introduces her dream with a phrase linking it to the preceding dream, dated March 1915. At the end of the earlier dream, the dreamer seeks a guide to lead her through a dark forest. An old woman advises her: "No one can accompany you on this path, which is only *your path*. So farewell, remember my words, and have courage!"

17   From this paragraph onward, the text records a fantasy or active imagination. The transition from dream to fantasy is less clear in the revised text (in the marbled book) than in the first draft (in the notebook "Night Voices"). In her first draft, the author dates the dream to "10th/11th April 1915," adding that she dreamed it at the Oelberg (see below, 289 and note), where she and the children were visiting while Agathe, her eldest, recovered from a severe bout of scarlet fever.

18   In quoting, the author changes the word "green" to "dark."

19   A story published in 1827 by a poet, Wilhelm Hauff, *"Das kalte Herz"* (The Cold Heart, best known in English as "Heart of Stone"). In it the lines "Schatzhauser im grünen Tannenwald,/ Bist schon viel' hundert Jahre alt" (lit., Treasure-keeper in the green pine woods/thou'rt many hundred years of age) are an incantation to conjure the Little Glass Man, a friendly, magical spirit governing the Black Forest (Hauff, "The Marble Heart," in *Tales of the Caravan, Inn and Palace*, 158, 275).

Suddenly, I hear voices nearby. Have people come here after losing their way? I don't want them to see the cities and my work, so I go to find them. They are lost and ask me the way, which I show them by accompanying them a short distance downhill, steeply steeply downward, almost like a mountain gully, on which I sometimes slip. After showing them the way, I turn back and want to continue building my road. But I feel a little tired and sit down beneath a pine tree to rest.

Suddenly, standing between the roots of a neighboring tree, I see a little man with a pointed hat and a long beard. It must be old Schatzhauser![20] Suppose I call out to him, "Hey, old man, can't you tell me what's going on in this place?"

Little Man: "Who is calling me? Oh, a human being! What brings you here?"

I: "I wandered a long way here, and I would like to know what kind of place this is. Won't you be good enough to tell me about it? I am in the process of building a bridge to that strange triangle of human dwellings—it seems to me that I must go there. The place seems entirely deserted and abandoned."

"So it is," said the Little Man, "and I will tell you the story of that place:

Long ago there lived three brothers who decided to make this place their home, and each one built a house here. With some distance between them, each house was surrounded by garden and field, and together, they formed a large triangle.

You can still see there are three small hillocks with a group of houses upon each one.

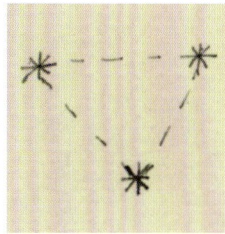

Their land was richly fertile and blessed; they married, had children, and enjoyed all that was good and beautiful. The son of the youngest brother once went on a long journey, and when he returned, he could not stop talking about the magnificent houses, castles and temples he had seen out there in the world where other people lived. And he began to build such a stone house for his father, which became so beautiful and pleased the others so well, that they, too, wanted to have similar ones. And because everyone wanted his own to be even more beautiful than his neighbor's, they were constantly dreaming up new and more beautiful things, and the master builder was not the only one who was infected by this great love for beautiful houses, but all the others were as well.

And their skills evolved with their desire: they created true marvels from the stone, which, divested of all its heaviness, obeyed the artist's every whim. They could not stop dreaming up more and more artistic ideas. They neglected their gardens and fields, no longer sowed and planted, but thought only of building. See for yourself what marvels they created in stone; look at that delicate, airy gable; how boldly and almost improbably it soars, and you feel that whoever made it must have put his whole life, his whole heart, into the stone.

---

20 In Hauff's tale, the forest spirit called Schatzhauser wears "a peaked hat with a wide brim, as well as a jacket and knee breeches and red stockings" (ibid., 152ff.), and has "a beard as fine as a spider's web" (ibid., 159).

One day, a girl from a distant land came to the area. No one knew from where exactly; she asked people for work and they gave her work. She took care of the gardens and fields, and everything prospered under her care. But she herself seemed not to be content, for she soon changed her position and went to the second brother, but there, too, it was the same, and she came to the youngest of the brothers. With her tireless diligence, her beauty and her exotic nature, she had caught the eye of his son, the master builder, who wanted to marry her, to which she gladly agreed.

It seemed that everything really did blossom under her care, but the longer it went on, the paler and thinner she became. For a long time, she didn't know what the matter was, but finally it occurred to her that the stone houses, so big and magnificent, were to blame; she was a child of the earth, only comfortable out in the open air, and the stones oppressed her and robbed her of her breath. And little by little, she discovered, too, that the people up here all had something strangely cold and rigid about them, that pressed down on her like a hundredweight. Her husband had just begun the construction of a church that would surpass anything that had ever been built, and he thought and spoke of nothing but his work and the stones from which he would build it. And oh, what emerged from beneath his artistic hands: flowers, trees, animals, people—a whole world in stone!

And as the construction grew, so did the pressure on her. She felt very unwell. Then, one night, a shining figure stood at her bedside and said to her, 'I know what is wrong with you and what weighs you down: the people here have put their hearts into the stone, and because of this, their hearts have turned to stone.[21] If you do not wish to perish, you must flee this place, for no living heart can bear it here.' The next morning, she was gone. From then on, however, no one tended the fields and everything lay fallow and rotted away.

The master builder went on building his temple for many years and hardly noticed when his parents died, and many of his relatives, and because of his work he completely forgot that his wife had disappeared.

Thus, the years went by, and little by little the families died out because they were unable to feel any kind of love with their stony hearts. Instead of gardens, a thicket of trees and bushes gradually grew around the houses, and for centuries no one has found their way to this place. You are the first, and you astound me."

I: "Thank you for the story, and now I shall go back to building
my road with double the zeal, for I must see this miraculous city
that turned people's hearts to stone."

"I would like to help you," said the Little Man. "Every day, from twelve to one o'clock,[22] I can come and help you with the timber."

---

21 Several characters in the tale allow their hearts to be magically replaced by stones. Having gained his stone heart, the central figure in the story becomes cruel and grasping, caring only for wealth, to the point of starving his mother and killing his wife.

22 In Hauff's tale, the only people who can see the Little Glass-Man are those born on a Sunday between noon and one.

"Thank you, and I gladly accept your suggestion. But for now, farewell until tomorrow. It's almost one."

Once the Little Man had gone, I was again overcome by a strange tiredness, and shortly after, a deep sleep. I don't know if I slept for a short or long time; in any case, I recall lying half-awake for some time, and thinking about the enchanted city. Suddenly, I was gripped by a powerful desire to see it, and I opened my eyes. But what was this? In the place where I had seen the houses shining from afar, there was nothing to be seen; just black, dense, pine forest all around, allowing only a triangular piece of dark blue sky to be seen, directly above the place where I had previously seen the houses shimmering. Did they turn into blue air or am I looking from the wrong direction? But wherever I look, I see nothing but trees. Only far off to the left do I see something bright: a small light that darts back and forth two or three times and then disappears between the trunks.

Well, here I am in a completely enchanted forest, but my longing for the miraculous city is stronger than my fear of spectres, so I decide to stay in the forest and to wait and see if luck will nevertheless smile on me and lead me to the place of my longing. But I wonder if the Little Man was also just a spectre and won't keep his promise?

So I sat for a long time and thought about all sorts of things—how I had actually got to this forest, what I wanted here, where I came from, and above all, who I really was. In truth, I had no idea who I really was. What kind of being was sitting here under the pine tree? Well, let's see. I had believed that this being was "I," that

FIGURE 6.3.
Far to the left I see something bright. Painting by Emma Jung, April 1915.

this "I" was a person, a woman. "I" spoke about "I" and "me" and had a certain notion about this being.—And now, how strange! "I" no longer means anything, no longer says anything to me.

What is that actually, "I"? Was it ever anything at all, and what lies at the root of it? What kind of a sound is that, "I"? It seems so familiar, and yet I haven't the faintest idea what it means. What agony, not to find it!

Cast off, cast off
Thy robe and shoes;
Thy very being
Dare to lose.
So shadow-poor, led onward by God's grace,
Go forth, and of thy yearning find the place![23]

---

23 "Wirf ab, wirf ab / Gewand und Schuh'; / dein eigen Wesen / noch dazu. / So schattenarm, geführt von Gottes Rat, / geh hin zu finden deiner Sehnsucht Statt!" This verse concludes Emma Jung's second version of the dream and fantasy, as found in the marbled book. The text of her first version, found in the notebook "Night Voices," is identical up to the end. But instead of ending with a verse, in "Night Voices" the author reflects at length on the final scene of this fantasy, together with a series of interrelated dreams. Her commentary, full of hand-drawn illustrations, becomes the raw material for the System (see introduction to Chapter VII, 314ff.).

May 1915

I am on a mountain heath that is completely overgrown with heather. In one spot I see the shrubbery all crushed, as if something had been deposited there.[24] A beautiful bird with black and bright red feathers is perched there, but then flies away. I go there and find one of the red feathers.

I want to call the others to show them my find—then the scene changes: everything is covered with heavy snow and I am standing on a steep, almost vertical incline. Above me, I hear my mother and the children calling out to me that they are about to sled down. Because the slope is so steep, I am very afraid that they might plunge down and carry me away. The rock face seems steeper and steeper to me, until it is almost overhanging. I try to gain as firm a foothold as possible, but I am quite prepared to be dragged down with them. The sled comes hurtling toward me—but to my astonishment, it is now only an ordinary slope with no excessive incline, and the sled comes to a halt quite gently and smoothly.

Then, in some inexplicable way, I come to a large, magnificent house. Walking through a long, wide corridor, I reach a door via a white marble staircase, above which is written: "To the Grail."

I walk past it, but I soon regret doing so and turn back in order to see the Grail. It is no longer a door through which I enter, but an opening, high up in the wall.

All is bathed in a radiant glow.

Many people, actually only children in bright colored robes, are sitting there. It is a kind of divine service.

Without hesitating, I walk through the room.—Then the service is over. The children get up and swarm higgledy-piggledy toward the door with joyful laughter and noise. They go out and stream through the wide corridors—with me in their midst. The "bustle" does not frighten me, but gives me a pleasant feeling of being at ease.

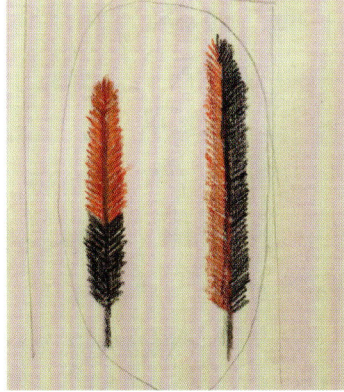

---

24 In the author's analysis of her Grail dream, she relates this image of crushed grasses to the first lines of a medieval love-poem (Chapter VII, 323 and note).

9. DREAM. [FIGURE OF CHRIST]

June 1915

I am in a church that is ancient and very plain. Besides me, there are two other women or girls present, and a priest in a red, shirt-like vestment. Painted on one wall is a large god image—so large that it takes up almost the entire wall. It resembles a figure of Christ, with outstretched arms, wearing a red robe and surrounded by red rays of light. The whole thing is painted in an early medieval style, quite simple and somewhat primitive. On the ground, I notice a strange drawing, a system of linked squares, one after the other, like what children draw when they play "hopscotch."

I am in a side corridor separated from the main room by a low wall, and from there, I see how the priest is evidently instructing the girls in the divine service, by taking one after the other by the hand and moving to and fro with them in curious dance steps, paying careful attention to the squares on the floor. I am afraid that it will be my turn, too, and I do not want to dance with this priest, who seems to me so unpleasantly prophet-like. It also pains me to dance barefooted, as my feet are not pretty enough. Besides, I do not have the right faith, and the god will not want to be worshipped by unbelievers, so I am sure I will remain undisturbed.

But then the priest suddenly calls my name, and I feel very clearly that declining is not an option. I approach, and the priest, without saying a word, takes me by the hand and walks to and fro with me in a peculiar rhythm through the figures drawn on the floor and finally up to the god image. There he tells me to spread out my arms in such a way that my hands and arms match those of the god.

But suddenly, the priest has disappeared, and the girls, too. I am standing on my own in front of the image, my arms reaching toward those of the god. Then I slowly move them from my forehead to his forehead, from my eyes to His,[25] from my chest, my body, my legs to those of the god, as if I were creating a connection between me and him. Everything fits exactly together and matches. It's like a child looking in the mirror for the first time and realizing that everything matches, forehead to forehead, mouth to mouth, body to body. Thus I recognize the god, and myself as a small likeness of the great one.

---

[25] The author is inconsistent in her pronouns for the divine. Sometimes, as here, she shifts from lowercase (*zu seiner Stirn*) to uppercase (*zu den Seinen*) within a single sentence. Since the editors do not know how she would have chosen to resolve the ambiguity, we have let this slight inconsistency stand.

19 September 1915[26]

Once again, I am in a church with many other people.

The building is made of gray sandstone and has a raised apse. There, in the holy of holies, a girl in a red dress has hung herself from the window crosspiece—and that girl is me!

Why does she hang there, this girl that is me? In response, these words spring to mind:

Offered to the god
I myself to myself![27]

---

26 A summary of this dream appears anonymously in *CW* 9.i, §354. There the dream text omits the author's closing comment and is followed instead by C. G. Jung's speculative question: "Suicide?" Emma Jung's records offer no support, however, for this association.

27 Adapted from a verse about the god Odin, cited in Jung's *Wandlungen und Symbole*, 256 (DTV edition, 258): "I know that I hung on the windswept tree / Nine nights through, / Wounded by a spear, dedicated to Odin / I myself to myself" (*Psychology of the Unconscious*, 295). Emma Jung's 1913 lecture, "The Tale of the Two Brothers," refers obliquely to this passage (Chapter I, 122 and note).

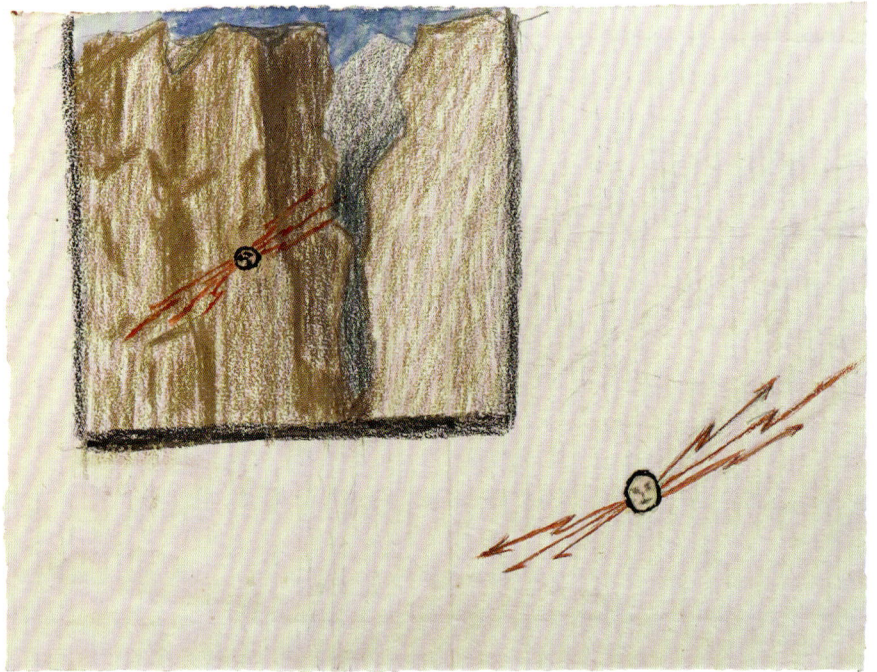

II. DREAM AND IMAGINATION. [SEEKING UNDINE]

18 October 1915

Then I search again for the old town on the mountain and find a settlement of small huts—as if made of woven cane—on a plateau halfway up. They seem to have been standing here since the beginning of time; perhaps they were covered or overgrown and have now become uncovered again.

They look like ghost houses.

And walking on, later, I find an old, long-forgotten spring. It seems to be called the Aïda Spring.

My journey continues: I pass over a high bridge, and then along a peculiar stretch of water, sometimes flowing, sometimes still, as if it were divided into two halves of different colors that flow alongside each other.

And then I come to a rugged high mountain valley and there I see a horrible apparition: a strange creature—like a human face—flew along the steep rock face, carried not by wings but by red arrows or rays. This face looked at me eerily and floated slowly upwards past me. I stood, filled with trepidation, as if spellbound.

Then I seemed to hear a voice urgently whispering something in my ear. I strain to understand what it is saying. I hear more and more clearly how it is calling me, and I respond:

"Come away, come away,
 Risk riding with me!
 Come quickly and gently,
 Leave your body asleep."
"But where am I going?"
"With me, far away,
 Through the night, through the air,
 The Other is calling!
 Come outside,
 Leave this house!"
"I can't find the door!"
"Just follow me."
 I dare it, striding,
 Floating and gliding,
 My feet no longer touching the ground,
 But still I hear: "Come along, come along!"
 I'm horrified, dizzy,
 My senses are fading—
 It moves far, far away—
 Going where? Going where?[28]

Where have I gone?

Well, to a beautiful house, glittering in the sunshine, on the shore of a blue lake or sea. And it was my house; I lived in it. My very own house that I would never sell, but I would like to show it to other people, as I told the people who came to me.

This house is my home, it seems to me—but there is also something strange about it. Why so strange? So strangely familiar, yet foreign as well. Now it no longer seems so brightly lit, but closely surrounded by trees that stretch their branches almost through the windows.

But am I at home here? Don't I also have some other home? Perhaps this is the home of my night soul, and my day soul is at home elsewhere. My nighttime ride must have brought me here to this home of my other "I" that I had completely forgotten in my daytime life. But I must have been here often before, without ever being able to remember it afterwards.

Like Undine, who returns to her well at night, because no one may know about her.[29]

---

28 "Komm mit, komm mit, / so wag doch den Ritt! / Komm schnell und sacht, / dass der Leib nicht erwacht." / "Wo soll ich denn hin?" / "Weit mit mir ziehn, / durch die Nacht, durch die Luft / das Andere ruft! / So komm doch hinaus, / verlasse dies Haus!" / "Wo find' ich die Tür?" / "Folge nur mir." / Ich wag es und schreite, / schwebe und gleite, / ich spür keinen Boden mehr unter dem Tritt / nur immer dasselbe: komm mit, komm mit! / Mir graut, mir schwindelt, / mir vergehen die Sinn'—/ fort geht es, weit fort.—/ Wohin? wohin?

29 Reference to the first fantasy of the Water Nymph, April 1915 (Chapter VI, 266).

Yes, that's right: this is the place where one half of me always disappeared to when I did not know where it was, and people asked me, "Where are you?"

Here is this other "I," here in its house, its home. How astonishing that I've finally discovered it! And that I was able to follow it here.

But what is it doing there?

A deep, mysterious darkness still covers it. Will I be able to fathom it?

What does Undine do in her well?

Indeed, what became of the water spirit? I have to think about that again: the last thing that happened was that she cut off her fish tail to put an end to the unbearable floating. Then a fall—and darkness—and nothing more for a long time.

Now it seems I'm about to find out what has happened since then:

After a long, long night, one half woke up on earth. This human half, that had so often wished to become human, and for whose sake it had separated itself from its other, non-human half, now saw its wish fulfilled. It lived among people as a person, even though it was really not one. But no one noticed. This being—as I will call it—hardly knew this either. It tried hard to be like other people, prompted by the dark feeling that it lacked something, and that no one should notice. Indeed, there was nothing special about it, but for these two things: a human hunger for love (as if that could help it somehow) and a peculiar shadow. For the shadow could not be harmed by the knife, and so it had remained whole. In this way, the human being always had behind it the shadow of the being that it had previously been.

But the shadow, which had remained whole, now always had to shift from one half to the other; for no one can exist without a shadow. And just as the moon waxes and wanes, so, too, does the shadow. Sometimes it is small, then it grows and grows, until finally it devours almost the whole human being.

And at these times, when the shadow grows and the human being becomes the shadow, it takes the human with it on its journey to its other half. Then people find this being strange and incomprehensible. But when the being returns, and the shadow disappears, it has forgotten everything. Only sometimes, some coincidence awakens a memory of the shadow-side, and with it a puzzled wondering and searching and the longing for unifying love.

But where has the other half gone? When I ponder this, my eyes are drawn again and again to the dark night sky, as if that were where I must search. And it occurs to me that the bubbles on the fish's tail carried it away. Once the weight of its upper body had been detached, they must have carried it upwards, who knows how high. Again, I have to look at the sky. What kind of star do I see up there?

It has a long, bright tail—it is a comet. This, then, is what has become of the fish's tail! And now I recall an earlier dream,[30] in which I flew through space toward a star and became a star myself. Was this the comet that I wanted to encounter? This former half of myself, now circling the sky in uncharted orbits, can I, will I ever come to know its orbit? Do I have to search for it?

---

30 Reference to the dream of swan and star, January 1914 (Chapter VI, 258).

16 June 1916

I am walking through open country, a beautiful green valley dotted with trees, and I have taken a path branching off to the left and leading upward. Singing dreamily, I walk on, leaving the green valley behind me, following the steep path. It is almost noon. The sun is burning hot and it is both still, as it can only be still at noon on a hot summer's day, and at the same time full of sounds. My path runs along a wooded slope. On my right is a steep drop, where there are bushes and all kinds of saplings, and on my left are widely spaced pine trees. The trail itself is white and stony, tedious to walk and bordered by densely intertwined bushes and vines. It all has a southern character and is quite different from the valley I left behind. It gets hotter and hotter as I walk. Suddenly my singing is cut short—by what? By the fact that I become aware of the silence all around me which seems to put a spell on my voice. The great solitude makes me feel almost anxious and I try to get clear about what I actually want or am supposed to be doing here. Nevertheless, I go on walking.

Now, some 20 steps in front of me, I see a child who is also walking uphill, and I am relieved that I am not the only person here. We continue walking, always keeping the same distance. The child disappears around a bend, and it seems to me I hear a voice asking me, "Where are you going?"

ı: Upward, as you can see.

voice: What is it you seek above?

ı: What I'm seeking, I don't even know myself. I just wanted to be up high.

voice: Probably because you think there's something special about getting up high! Why do you humans have this idea?

ı: Actually, I don't quite know, but probably because when you are up high, you have a broad view and the wonderful feeling of being on top of the world.

voice: Aha, because you want to feel like God and get above the earth?

ı: Yes, that has certainly been our dream since the dawn of time.

voice: But who tells you that the way to this goal leads upward?

ı: It has always been said that God dwells in heaven.

voice: Oh, so you still believe in that old chestnut? Perhaps it was an important insight once, thousands of years ago, but now it's only fit for the nursery.

ı: Do you have something better to say? I am willing to be taught, but first tell me who you are, so I may know if I can believe what you say, or if you're just some foolish spectre.

voice: Oh, no, so naive! The child thinks that if she knew my name, she would also know whether I could be trusted. As if the most beautiful name could not hide the most wicked deceiver, and as if such a person, who makes a joke of tricking people, would write it on his business card. Just see if what I say makes sense to you, that's what matters!

But I will tell you who I am; then you can make your own decision about my character: I am the Lord of the Forest.

I: Can't you show yourself to me?

HE: That is impossible. I am invisible to the human eye.

I: Are you formless, then, or what form do you have?

HE: Yes, I have one, but not a corporeal one—the form of a tree, and I am as big as the whole forest put together, so that I am in every part of the forest at once.

I: And that's why you think you know more and better than we humans. Then let me hear something of what you have to say, for I am also convinced of our ignorance.

HE: You see, I am much older than the human race, as old as the trees, and in my long life I have learned a lot.

For like you, we trees have the fantasy that goodness dwells above, or, as they say, in the drive upward, for height and the sun. The tallest of us, do you know what they do? They go down the deepest. Those that do not can be felled by the slightest gust of wind.

It was now very quiet again and I felt as if I were waking from a dream. Only now did I really see how stony the path was, and how the higher I got, the sparser the trees became, the more meager the bushes and grass. I wondered why we always believe that fertility is to be found at high altitudes, when everywhere, the higher one climbs, the more barren and inhospitable it becomes.

Suddenly, the child appears in front of me again. There is something strange about it; although it is actually not far from me, I cannot tell whether it is a boy or a girl. All of a sudden, it turns around and starts to go back the way it came. As if I were connected to the child by invisible threads, I also turn around after it has passed me, and now I follow it back to the green valley that I had previously left.

I see everything now with different eyes: it seems enchanted, lit by a strangely soft yet intense light. It is dusk; all is a beautiful green-gold, a wide, wide valley, gently sloping toward its center, like a funnel.

Now I see a building standing there; a castle made of red brick with round corner towers. I did not see it earlier. We are far from it, but with every glimpse between the trees, it appears again, as if it were always intruding of its own accord into the center of my field of vision, and again as if it were being drawn very closely past my eyes. Compelling me to really take note of it, my attention is directed toward it again and again, unable to escape it. This probably indicates a destination. So I shall try to get close to it.

Through forest and green meadows, along the side of streams, I finally come close to the castle. The valley is really a picture of fertility, watery and green; all the water from the heights has flowed together there.

I no longer see anything of the child, but it seems as if I were being led by an invisible guide. Finally, I am standing in front of the castle, which is elongated and low. At both corners of the facade are bulky, round towers. From the middle part of the building, large doors lead into the open air.

Now I hear a voice that says, "This is where you live, it's your house—look, your husband is already standing there."

I enter and, through a cool hallway with a stone floor, I reach a large room. The shutters are closed, and the room is bathed in green twilight; it is pleasantly cool, with the characteristic feel of a dark, cool room in summer. But it is also as if the room had not been aired for a long time and had only now woken from a long sleep. It brings to mind the dream house that always captivated me so much, with its sleepy seclusion behind the green trees—like Sleeping Beauty's castle. Now I also hear someone saying that this castle once belonged to French kings.

I suddenly sense all the magic of the past, which is also so present in the countryside. I can only describe this feeling as a feeling of timelessness; my "I" is lost to the present moment and, from the surroundings, absorbs instead all that the past has contributed. It's as if all that is past were simultaneously present, as if, in certain circumstances, this "I" had detached itself from its way of looking at time and, free of this fetter, could perceive everything that has been and that is, all at the same time.

I now go to a window with white muslin curtains, and open it. The curtains flutter so strangely in the breeze, as if startled birds were fleeing them. It becomes brighter, and I see a large, urn-like, earthenware vessel, similar to the funerary urns of ancient peoples. On its inner surface are black characters that I try to decipher. But I am not familiar with them. Is there no one here who could help me? Is no one else here? Earlier, it seemed to me that I was not alone.

Where did my invisible guide go? "Is anyone here?" I call out again, startled at the sound of my voice in the empty house.

"Yes," I hear from above, from the curtain rod. A round head, like an apple, peers down, its body and limbs indicated only by lines. The head nods toward the table, which stands in the middle of the hall, and toward the pot standing close by. From its base, it is as high as the table itself, and sufficiently wide for a crouched person to fit inside, and it is of a reddish-brown color, like terracotta. The castle itself is the same color, by the way. So I turn my attention to the pot. There are bones in it. From whom, I wonder involuntarily aloud. "From a woman," comes the answer from the curtain rod. And the head goes on to say, "Whoever can read the writing can assemble the bones."

The signs look something like this: but I cannot read them.

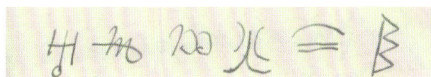

I wonder what kind of woman she was? She must have belonged to one of the kings who lived here? Perhaps they also built the castle, which in a certain sense resembles the urn. The one, the dwelling place of the living; the other, of the dead, the decomposed. Now it seems like my house, my bones, and I have to think of that dancer who danced until her body fell to pieces.[31] Now, here await the parts to be fitted together. But will I be able to understand the runes?

> Where shall I find the land I've sought so long?
> the city long vanished, long forgotten;
> I lived there once, a thousand years ago.
> The old house; the old country.
> So far away, yet still so nigh.
> How deeply art thou hidden?
> where can I find thee now?[32]

VOICE: Over the white-flowered meadow, by the shady river.
  You too must become a shadow!
  Go downward, down!

ARANÛ

This name irresistibly forces itself upon me, as if it were the name of the "mighty one" who demands the sacrifices. I want to cry out to him:
  Aranû, Mighty One, are you he for whom I shall sacrifice myself?
  Let me see you!
  Who are you, from where does your power come, and for what purpose?
  "Let the curtain of night be torn!"
  Now I see him stepping out of the black sky—his head a red, blazing star, and in his right hand a flaming sword.
  In his left hand, what is he holding?
  I can't quite see it.
  I dare to address him:

I: How do you have such power over me, Fiery One?
ARANÛ: How do I? Look what I'm holding here in my hand.
I: A bird? The blue bird?
ARANÛ: So you know it, the blue bird? And now do you understand that I have
  power over you? It is your *soul* in my hand, and with it, you yourself!

---

31 Reference to the author's fantasy of the dancer, May 1914 (263).
32 Wo find ich doch das längstgesuchte Land?/die lang entschwundene vergessene Stadt;/einst lebt ich dort, vor tausend Jahren wohl./Das alte Haus; das alte Land./So fern und doch so nah verwandt./In welcher Tiefe bist Du?/wo kann ich dich finden?

ɪ: But how did you get it? How did it escape from me in the first place?

Xaver intervenes: Why does he need to say right away that this is your soul? It's not necessary to know everything right away.

ɪ: (Thanks for your critique, but it would be better, Xaver, if you'd back off a bit; you're bothering me.) Aranû, listen, how did you get the bird? Did you find it? Did it seek you out?

ARANÛ: From heaven through the world to hell,[33] and back through the world again.

XAVER: You seem to know *Faust* up there, too, or perhaps Goethe even lives nearby, for you to express yourselves in such classical terms!)

ɪ: Shut your cheeky mouth for once, Xaver. This is not the place for you to ruin things.

VOICE (to me): Aranû speaks with the words he finds in you.—He himself has no language that you could understand; so he takes what is suitable from inside your head.

ɪ: Aranû himself doesn't speak?

VOICE: He breathes life into the words within you.

ɪ: Very well, and who are you, who is telling me this?

VOICE: Aranû. He has brought these words to life, so that they rise up and reach your ear.

ɪ: Aranû, will you give me back the blue bird?

ARANÛ: Blue bird? To have? Come and take it!

ɪ: How can I get up there? So far and high?

ARANÛ: Only *one* way: the way of the bird.

ɪ: The way of the bird, so you mean through hell! There's something floating toward me, isn't there? A veil—a golden veil. What for?

ARANÛ: To wrap around your head—for your journey to hell.

ɪ: And there? A wild animal, a panther? Does he want to pounce on me? No, he lays himself at my feet, invites me to mount. Shall I ride? On the panther?

How strange it now becomes. Aranû has disappeared.

I see a strange sign, this:
and over there something moves: round things flying through the air, into an open maw. Thrown toward this target, or sucked into it, as if by a whirlpool? Now a white shadow with a black line through his head. He makes a sign that I should not speak to him. Then again something white, like a shadowy fish or a snake.

Then everything is blurred.

---

33 The figure of Aranû borrows language from the opening prologue of Goethe's *Faust*: "Thus on these narrow boards you'll seem/To explore the entire creation's scheme—/And with swift steps, yet wise and slow/From heaven, through the world, right down to hell you'll go!" (Goethe, *Faust, Part One*, "Prelude on the Stage," ll. 239–43, translated by David Luke, 9).

13. [FANTASY]. CONVERSATION WITH ARANÛ

c. 1916

I: Aranû, will you listen to me?

ARANÛ: Speak.

I: I must know, finally, who you are. Are you God, or a spirit?

ARANÛ: I am not God, and yet a god—*your* god, or your angel, if you prefer.

I: My god, you say? Are there many gods? Or do you mean my idea or concept of God?

ARANÛ: Not that, no. Your god *is* one god; another is the God of All. Every creature has its god; the All has its own,—that is the greatest. But people have no access to him; they can only turn to their own god, who represents them to the All-God.

I: So you are a mediator for human beings? What are you to the All-God?

ARANÛ: Guardian of his laws. To *humans*, a guide, a star, a shepherd, a keeper. To the *All-God*, a servant, a hand. He gives me power with which to do his work.

I: Do human beings also give you something?

ARANÛ: They give me life, for they are the cause of my movement; they always draw me after them.

I: Are humans so powerful that they can draw you after?

ARANÛ: No more than I do them, but we are bound to each other—so the one pulls the other along.

I: You say that humans give you life? Do you also give it to them?

ARANÛ: Not I, the All-God gives it to them.

I: And to you? Not the All-God, but the human being?

ARANÛ: Just as I am the human being's mediator to the All-God, so, too, is the human being the mediator of life to me.

I: Who came first? You or me?

ARANÛ: When you came into being, I came into being; when I came into being, you came into being, grown together by inseparable bonds.

I: And every creature has such an inseparable shadow-brother beside it?

ARANÛ: Each has its own, but not all are equally close, and not always. You must already have felt that?

I: I'm not sure. Sometimes I clearly sense your closeness; sometimes you seem to move away; and often, it's as if you had completely abandoned me. Why is that?

ARANÛ: I, too, am still in the dark about that.

I: But I would like to know more about you. How did you end up with me? Where did you come from?

ARANÛ: You ask me difficult questions; I know only dimly myself. But if you understand what I am saying, perhaps you can find out:

I, Aranû, have only existed since you exist. What became Aranû existed as Not-I before.

I: Where were you and I previously?

ARANÛ: A part of the All-God—a finger of His hand, a tooth from His mouth? I don't know exactly. A cut, a blow, the limb fell off, and blood dripped from the wound. Whether the All-God wanted it thus, or whether it was the pain that made Him realize what was happening, I cannot say, but I do know this:

When the blood flowed, *you* came into being, and when the All-God saw where it was flowing from, *I* came into being. Thus, stemming from the same cause, we are inseparably linked.

I: What is the bond that binds us? What makes it so strong?

Can't twins, born of the same mother, separate and each live their own life?

ARANÛ: We are not siblings, only comparable to such. Each of us does not have our own life to live; we have only one life together, because what each of us can have of our own life, only comes to be through the other.

I: And our goal?

ARANÛ: That the future alone will teach; for today, it is for you to be humble.

14. DREAM OF THE DEVIL

15/16 February 1917

I am standing in a rather large, oblong room with doors at both ends. I am roughly in the middle of the room and seem rooted to the spot, aware that something terrible is happening behind me, or rather, is coming in through the door behind me: namely, the devil. There is a tremendous din, and I know: Now he is coming.

I can't move, and I look desperately straight ahead at the other door in front of me, which is the "Gate of God." I stretch my arms out horizontally and whisper, "God, God," but I am still unable to move. At last, the din subsides and I have the feeling: It is over now—and I'm still alive.

Now I am able to turn around and look behind me, and I see an *actual lead ball*, as if that were the devil, or would have been, but now it's just a pile of lead.

(Violent affect in the dream and awoke with anxiety.)

March 1917

I am at a place in the forest; it is a sort of round clearing encircled by a fence made of tree trunks and branches. Within it, radial divisions are arranged in a similar fashion. There are cattle in them, including bulls, which we can see from afar. I and my unspecified companions think the animals probably came in here to spend the night; I find it a bit eerie and want to get out. Now, it is as if the fence were a wall, and right where I am is a small, very low door of brown wood, through which we go, or crawl, and pull it closed behind us. I think, hopefully the animals won't push it open somehow and follow us.

It now appears that the place is enclosed by a double wall, of which the inner one is higher, while the outer one is much lower and forms something like a passageway. From there, steps lead down to the earth. For the time being, however, we are still standing before this passageway wall when the dream ends.

Emma Jung's commentary:

This dream was immensely impressive; I had the feeling of being transported to some primeval time, to a time of nomadic life, for example, when the herds were driven into such pens in order to separate them, perhaps, or to mark them.

At the same time, it also makes me think of a *horoscope*, of the zodiac[34] and its twelve houses.

And of Indra, who leads his cattle, the stars, up and down the sky—the cattle herds of the gods.

The wall that leads all the way around brings to mind the "firmament of heaven,"[35] and also those round, primitive houses in England and Sardinia, the Nuraghe, buildings of an ancient civilization. The wall, which replaces the earlier fence made of trees, forms a more solid and defined partition between inside and outside—a separation of a domain. Here, a separation of the "zodiac," that is, of the cosmos and of the "compulsion by the stars."[36] The small door through which we get out is like a birth—the birth of the individual out of cosmic participation and identity.

---

34 *Tierkreis* (zodiac): lit., "circle of animals."

35 *"Feste des Himmels"*: In the biblical story of creation, as translated by Luther: "Und Gott sprach, Es gebe eine Feste zwischen den Wassern." / "And God said, Let there be a firmament in the midst of the waters" (Genesis 1:6).

36 *des "Gestirnzwanges"*: The term is found in C. G. Jung's early writings, including *Wandlungen und Symbole*. For example: "The Stoics called this condition Heimarmene, compulsion by the stars, to which every 'unredeemed' soul is subject" (*CW* 5, §644; also §102, notes 51, 52).

But, on the other hand, the association of the round house means a first, initial expression of the human being as an individual. It is said that the principle behind the most ancient walled settlement was "to achieve in the smallest space the most secure and largest perimeter."[37]

It is also a temenos—a demarcated, sacred domain—and seems like the suggestion or prefiguration of a mandala. What is strange, however, is that, here, the animals are encircled and the people are outside.

Of course, this could also point to the domestication of the animal. From the feeling in the dream, it seemed as if fencing animals in like this was a wholly new invention. But on the other hand, it may indicate that the instincts, i.e. the archetypes, most resemble the celestial bodies and their "eternally fixed paths," which would make being caught in the "zodiac" a danger to the individual. The same symbol also reveals, however, that what is most innate and most individual is created according to the same pattern.

---

37 The author's quotation marks suggest that she referred to a published work on the subject. The exact work is unknown.

March 1917

I'm with Mama at the Oelberg[38] in the brown living room. It's morning, and we're about to have breakfast.

Suddenly the sky darkens strangely from above, until eventually only a bright streak can be seen along the horizon. Finally, it is completely dark, which leads me to think the shutters are closed, and I ask someone to open them.

An eerie, indefinable roaring and droning fills the air. We seem to be petrified with astonishment and horror. I suggest going to the upper floor, for perhaps from there it is possible to see better what is actually happening; but we remain standing, as though rooted to the spot.

At last, it is once again possible to discern things outside, and we see, in fact, a starry sky. Directly above the trees to the west is a constellation that is completely new to me, clearly resembling a snake. I exclaim, "Look at the snake—it's Carl's white snake."[39] It makes a tremendous impression on me. Then I notice other constellations that I'm not familiar with, one of which looks like a crab or a spider. The thought occurs to me that the only explanation is that the earth has turned upside down, so that above us is the southern sky, whose stars have always been invisible to us until now. The earth must now be in a completely different position in relation to the sun.

Emma Jung's commentary:

I was extraordinarily impressed by this dream: there must be a fundamental reversal going on, so that what was below is now above, and an entirely new orientation is taking place. The unfamiliar constellations are probably contents of the unconscious now becoming visible. The white snake refers to the one that Carl painted. It is a primordial animal, as are the spider and crab, which bring to mind the vortex and spiral of the earlier dream, in which they appeared as symbols of

---

38 The Oelberg (Mount of Olives) was the Rauschenbach family property in Schaffhausen. The original Oelberg house included an old chapel, which had been converted into part of the residence. Until 1896, when Emma Rauschenbach was fourteen, her family spent summers at the old house. Then her father purchased the property and ordered the old house torn down and a new one built. In 1898 the new "Oelberg Villa" became the permanent family residence. (See "Emma Rauschenbach: Portrait of Her Childhood and Youth," volume introduction, 7 and note. See also Stiftung C. G. Jung Küsnacht, ed., *The House of C. G. Jung*, 19ff.)

39 Here and below, the reference may be to Jung's painting of a white snake with black markings (Jung, *The Red Book*, 109, 111).

something primordial, a first becoming, a movement just beginning.[40] What has been lying until now in the darkness below—that is, the unconscious—is now coming up.

It is also reminiscent of an earlier dream of a "magnetic mountain"[41] that was in the north, and at the same time was like a crater, in which a white worm (snake) was lying.

Perhaps the "enchanted house" that plays a role in many dreams also belongs to this other world that is now becoming visible. In the night after the dream of the world turned upside-down, it makes another appearance: I am with a group of unspecified people in a strangely remote house—there, we dance. I notice someone peeking through the low-set window to see what's going on. This is probably the conscious personality wanting to see what is going on in the unconscious.

This dream has something magical and fairy-tale-like about it, but it is also eerie. Here, it seems as if I had found my way into a completely different life to the one I lived consciously, which I nevertheless feel to be my life, or at least a part of it, but one that is miles away from my consciousness, separated from it by thick walls, and into which I have only a momentary insight every now and again through a dream, or when this house suddenly appears to me in reality, as it did that time in Klosters.[42]

There, while walking alone, I came to a house with trees in front of it, whose branches were so close to it that they were almost looking into the room, spreading a greenish semi-darkness inside. The sight resonated deeply in me, as if I were recognizing something that had been familiar to me from my earliest youth and then been forgotten. Later, when I wanted to show the house to the others, I could not find it.

The old Oelberg also comes to mind, which seemed to me just as sleepy and enchanted and full of unfathomable life. I still remember very well my first visit there with my father, on a hot, beautiful summer's day, and the still, warm air. Everything seemed to be asleep: the tall grass, the overgrown garden, the house with its closed shutters; it all made an ineffable impression on me. The house itself I found eerie. The people who lived there, a brother and sister, were supposed to be dreadful eccentrics, who slept during the day and were awake at night, or so I was told. I could barely believe that this completely enchanted place was so close to our mundane city and its life. It seemed like a strange, eerie and, at the same time, wondrously beautiful and fairy-tale-like world. On a later visit—I was about six years old—the old lady, who I thought looked like a witch, wanted to give me a bun, but I didn't dare eat it, out of fear that it was poisoned![43]

---

40 See introduction to Chapter VII, "The System," 324f.

41 "*Magnetberg*": the author's earlier dream has not been identified.

42 Klosters: a mountain village in the Prättigau, in the Canton of Graubünden, where Emma Jung had spent time in late July 1915 (Chapter I, 145 note 30). The house, that "appear[ed] to me in reality" there, is unidentified.

43 In reflecting on her dream image of "the dragon and the maiden" (see *CW* 9.i, §349, §351),

The house, the dream house, also has something haunted about it, giving it an eerie feel. It is as if meetings of ghosts with living people were taking place there, with sinister things going on. And stories also come to mind of elves luring mortals to dances and festivities, and of their being lost to the world.

This house is like that—a dwelling place of elves, that you come across unexpectedly, and from which it is difficult to find your way home again. It is like the Mountain of Venus in the Tannhäuser legend.[44] Only those who enter consciously can leave unscathed—and then with benefit.

Emma Jung wrote about women who had struck her, in childhood, as being witches ("Reader's Guide," volume introduction, 9off.).

44 Tannhäuser legend: In Wagner's opera *Tannhäuser*, the "Mountain of Venus" is a crucial scene.

FIGURE 6.5.
The Coral Tree.
Painting by Emma
Jung, undated.

17. DREAM AND FANTASY OF THE CORAL TREE[45]

1917

I had to dive to the bottom of a deep lake (or sea?), where a luminous red coral tree is growing.

A voice tells me to break off a flower; it is meant for me. I break off the flower and hold it in my hand. Then I meet a very slim young man who is actually a fish, standing on the end of his fish tail, with a kind of human face. When I ask who he is, he says, "I am the great fish who is lord of these waters. This is Lake Memi; in it grows the coral tree whose guardian I am. You have stolen the flower; explain yourself!"

---

45   *EJ*: Animus-fish theme. [At about the same date the author recorded a hypnogogic vision with the title "Fish theme," on which she commented: "This image came at a time when the animus still appeared very vague and indistinct."]

I say that I did it on the command of a god, and I offer the fish my services if he would allow me to keep the flower.

He agrees, on condition that I decipher the runic signs inscribed on his body, which I prepare to do.

Emma Jung's commentary:

The signs are partly intersecting, partly converging or diverging lines, with a round intersection where the lines meet—an ellipsis with a center that is said to mean the "circle of images" (zodiac?), that I also have within me. The whole thing is supposed to be a kind of cosmic view. The motifs resemble those in my wall-hanging.[46]

Compare to the Babylonian Oannes, the fish-human, who brought writing, art and science to the people.

Compare to the legend that Jonah saw images in the whale's belly.

---

46 The wall-hanging is unidentified.

18. [FANTASY]. JOURNEY TO THE UNDERWORLD

January 1919[47]

EDITORIAL COMMENT

"Journey to the Underworld" begins with a dialogue between *Ich* (I) and *Stimme* (Voice). The "I" of the fantasy learns that she has offended the Ka, a mighty spirit. In order to mend the offense, she must descend into the realm of shadows, carrying a lyre and singing, to seek for Dionysos. While walking in darkness, calling out the name of the god, she comes to a body of water. There she sees a head floating on the waves, which she recognizes as the severed head of Orpheus. Traveling on by boat, she arrives at a dark island on whose shore is the beautiful stone figure of a queen with blue-green crystals for eyes. The queen had been the bride of the island's lord, who, in dying, stabbed her to take her with him. Now they rule together in this realm of darkness. At this point, the "I" of the fantasy connects herself with the figure of the queen.

Am I the bride?
And my beloved, too, dwells in the shadows?
What kind of enchantment is veiling my sight?
What narrow house is engulfing my limbs?
Are my eyes also petrified?
Has my whole body turned to stone?
Again I hear that voice, which says,
No, crystals are not thine eyes;
thou see'st only through those of the dark queen.
So I am inside the statue now.
How did this happen?
And how do I escape this coffin
enveloping me like a stony sculpture?

How should a savior ever find his way into this underground cave? And if he found it, how would he ever know that someone was lost inside the image of stone?

---

47 Excerpt from a long fantasy, much of it written in free verse. The author's handwritten text fills the second half of the green linen notebook, following the first draft of her narrative poem, "Do you see the sea?" (Chapter III, 177ff.). Editorial comment (above) summarizes the pages leading to the excerpt printed here.

Once more the voice speaks softly in my ear:

Thou must be born,
break through the carapace unaided,
burst the shell,
the power that lives in thee.
Then of divinity thou art free.

Darkness still surrounds me—only a very faint glimmer that penetrates through the stone eyes makes it seem like the first light of dawn. I notice that the room I am in is not narrow, and soon I feel I can distinguish something like pictures on the walls; but only very shadowy in this shadowy place.

I look more keenly, trying to recognize—then I become wonderfully sleepy. It seems the shadows are moving; but heavily, ever more heavily, sleep descends upon me. Yet now all is bright, and I find myself in unfamiliar territory, a wide, flat field, on the horizon far away two large trees—between them, glowing red, the ball of the sinking star.[48]

An invisible guide speaks to me: Behold—those are the sacred oaks. Once they were gods!

I ask: And the star, what is it called?

The guide replies: Its name is Aranû. It is sinking, and a new sun is rising.

I: Aranû, you say!

The evening of the red star now draws near,[49]
Yet mightily, in sinking, he unfolds
once more his splendor,
bathing the world in flames.
Never before has earth been stained so red
As by the autumn of this god.

Bend thy knee, mortal,
Thy head uncover,
A god is dying.
Aranû sinks down, the blazing one,
  His day is spent.

48 This scene, and many that follow, are illustrated in the paneled painting (figure 6.6, 297). Many of the panels include internal captions in which Greek characters spell German words.

49 In February 1919 the author slightly revised this poem, making it independent of the fantasy text. A major revision is found in the final lines, addressing the poet's blue bird. The revised poem ends: "Doch nein, Du lebst, Du lebst!/Ein zart Gefieder fühlt ich meine Wange streifen/Und es ist mir, als hört ich Flügelrauschen durch die Lüfte./Das bist Du, lang Gefangener, ich weiss,/Der durch des Gottes Untergang befreit." (But no, thou livest still!/I feel a feather softly brushing past my cheek,/and whirring in the air I seem to hear, as if from wings./Thou art the one, I know, the long-held captive;/the setting of the god has set thee free.)

But my blue bird, the one
    he once protected,
Where might it be?
Seek, eyes, O seek!
Tell me what you see?
 "We see naught but fire!
 But wait—a lance approaches;
 it pierces Aranû's heart,
 where thy blue bird is locked away."
Speak further! What more do you see?
"Nothing, the red blaze
 pains us too fiercely;
 We can look no more."
Then art thou, even thou, my blue bird, snatched away
by the god's death?
Woe to me, woe to the world!

Yet, through the air, is that a sound of whirring wings?
Something like feathers brushes past my cheek,
and far off, overhead, I see them streaming,
a very flock of the blue-feathered ones.[50]

They have passed from view—the red fades, and twilight's glow surrounds me in its faint light.

Where the star, like a sun, went down, I now see close by, almost tangible, a great, alien, dead world—yellow rock, wild crags and crevices, and mounds of slag, charred stone, ash—the waste of a scorched, spent world.

This too disappears, and in the sky I see another image:

Like a bowl upturned
hanging in the ether—
pointing toward it, from below, a peculiar structure, divided into three—
And with these, the words:

---

50 Des roten Sternes Abend naht heran, / Mächtig entfaltet er seinen Glanz / Im Sinken noch einmal / Und taucht in Glut die Welt. / Nichts färbte je sie also rot / Als dieses Gottes Herbst. / Neig deine Knie, o Mensch, / Dein Haupt entblösse, / Es stirbt ein Gott! / Aranû sinkt dahin, der rötlich glühende / Sein Tag ist um. / Mein blauer Vogel, den er einst in seine Hut genommen, / Wo ist er? / Augen, sucht, o, sucht. / Was seht ihr, sagt? "Wir sehen nichts als Glut — / Da, halt, es fährt heran / gleich einem Speer, — / Es trifft Aranûs Herz, / Darin dein blauer Vogel eingeschlossen." / Und weiter, sagt, was seht ihr mehr? "Nichts, allzu heftig / schmerzt uns der rote Schein / Wir können nicht mehr schauen." / So rafft auch dich des Gottes Tod dahin, / Mein blauer Vogel? / Weh mir, weh der Welt! / Doch tönt es nicht wie Flügelrauschen durch die Lüfte? / Wie Federn streift es meine Wange sacht / Und ferne hoch am Himmel seh ich's ziehen / Der blaugefiederten ein ganzer Zug.

FIGURE 6.6. *The great eye has opened. Painting by Emma Jung, January 1919.*[51] The great eye has opened[52]—and instantly, it draws to itself all the peoples of its world. First are the snakes, crawling on their bellies, then the wild wolves of the forest with glowing red eyes. Then the gray herons, whose home is on the water. Then comes the tribe of the white-headed, who like to dance. And also the triangular people, where girls are paired with girls, and boys with boys. And what are those kneeling figures? They are the human mothers, and behind them come the spirits. Following the power of the gaze as if spellbound, they fly in like clouds and flames of fire.

Urania the heavenly
finds the one she yearned for.
Yet heavenly remain the Two.[53]

A further image:
One substantial eye.

---

51   In two panels of the painting, Greek characters are used to spell words in German. At the far right in the top panel, the caption reads: *Ourania findet den ersehnten / doch himmlisch bleiben die Zoei* ("Urania [the Heavenly] finds the one [she] longed for / Yet the Two remain divine"). Far to the left in the middle panel, next to the triangle with open eye, the caption reads: *Das Auge Gottes des grossen Schalksnarren* (The eye of God the great rogue jester).

52   This description of the painting, written by the author, was found on a loose sheet of paper.

53   *Urania die Himmlische / sie findet den Ersehnten / Doch himmlisch bleiben die Beiden*: In Emma Jung's paneled painting (above), she spells out these lines in Greek characters. Her "Greek" spelling of the last words is ambiguous: "die Zoei." Based on the Greek language, the word suggests "living creatures"; but it more likely represents "die Zwei" (the Two), parallel to "die Beiden."

In front, a motley, seething mass
of appalling snakes
wild wolves
beasts and birds of all kinds,
who worship it—
and the words:
> the eye of God
> the great rogue jester!

Behind the animals now also appeared human figures, something like dolls,
paired two and two, although not
boy and girl,
but two girls coupled here, and two boys there.
And then a wild bevy of beings,
neither animal nor man,
and yet resembling both.
Monsters and witches of all kinds—
Mere outlines, they stand in the background,
As if emerging from the wall, like pictures on it,
unable to detach themselves.
Astonished and musing, I see all this,
When of a sudden there is music in me;
I sing the song aloud:
> O sacred head, sore wounded,
> defiled and put to scorn;
> O kingly head, surrounded
> with mocking crown of thorn:
> What sorrow mars thy grandeur?
> Can death thy bloom deflower?
> O countenance whose splendor
> the hosts of heaven adore![54]

But it is not Christ's head to whom these tones apply:

Far off I see the waves of a surging sea, and floating upon them a human head,
perhaps divine, but not the head of Christ.

And sleep once again descends upon my eyelids—or am I waking from the
previous dream?

---

54 "O Haupt voll Blut und Wunden, / Voll Schmerz und voller Hohn, / O Haupt zum Spott um-
wunden / Mit einer Dornenkron; / O Haupt sonst schön gekrönet / Mit höchster Ehr und Zier / Jetzt
aber gar verhöhnet —/ Gegrüsset seist Du mir." The "I" of the fantasy sings words by Paul Gerhardt,
set to music by Johann Sebastian Bach in the "Passion Chorale." This English translation, by Robert
Seymour Bridges, is found in *The Hymnal 1982, according to the use of the Episcopal Church*, #168, #169.

FIGURE 6.7.
[The gatekeeper].
Painting by Emma
Jung, undated.

19. DREAM. [THE GATEKEEPER]

November 1928

I enter a vaulted stone hall underground. There, someone puts a dark brown cloak around me, because I am supposed to fill the role of "gatekeeper" for another woman, who has held this position up to now. Astonished, I agree, and it seems as if the other person—a girl with a beautiful face—who wants to leave for some purpose, smiled at me gratefully.[55] The girl has disappeared through the archway into the light; I remain in the dark, underground room. I then see myself standing upright against a pillar in the gray vault, with a kind of hood or cowl on my head and a staff in my hand.

---

55   *EJ*: While I am putting on the coat, I hear or say something like the words: [Line crossed out by author.]

End of April 1942

(Carl is in Bollingen.) I dream:

Carl and I are on a dirt road that leads between fields. On the one side is a freshly ploughed field with deep furrows. A group of people are walking across it, like audience members at a lecture, with their teacher or professor leading the way. They are walking across the field, treading only on the raised earth, as if from one wave crest to the other, which looks strange, almost comical. It is meant to represent or demonstrate a ritual act belonging to the Brahma cult. The teacher (resembling Abegg or Zimmer)[56] points to a tree standing at the end of the field, a poplar, and says: "A bird was sitting there earlier—where is it now?" Everyone, including Carl and me, looks up in the air to search for the bird. Finally, I catch sight of it at a great height. It is an eagle, circling majestically, occasionally descending as if to seek its target, then flying up again. Finally it swoops down directly to Carl, as if he were the target it was seeking. Carl opens his arms and the eagle flies straight into them. When it starts to peck at Carl's cheek with its beak, I become anxious and tell Carl to be careful; but he assures me the eagle won't hurt him; it just wants to say something in his ear. It was extraordinarily clear and deeply impressive.

---

56 Emil Abegg and Heinrich Zimmer, both indologists, were personal friends of Carl and Emma Jung. She sometimes exchanged letters with each of them about her lectures, asking their expert advice on the subject matter. (See "Emma Jung and Analytical Psychology," volume introduction, 54 and notes; also author's lecture "On Guilt," Chapter I, 132 and note.)

17/18 October 1945

(The previous day, conversation about upcoming women's meeting to discuss Dr. Harding's book, *Women's Mysteries*).[57]

I'm in Zurich with my sister, and I look around for a store where I might buy shoes. We see some on display in a kiosk, but only about three pairs, made of black patent leather, which are out of the question for me, since they would not fit and are also no longer fashionable. We continue walking and are somewhere on the Stadthausquai[58] (the place where the Fraumünster Abbey[59] used to stand), when my sister says she knows of a store nearby, on "Bauhof- or Bauholzweg,"[60] which is supposed to be in the vicinity of Bahnhofstrasse-Börsenstrasse.[61] I imagine that this road must run somewhere behind or between the houses and be quite hidden, since I have never seen it. I am to go ahead, while my sister first takes care of something in Enge.[62]

So I set off, and—in what seems like the upper part of the Bahnhofstrasse—I come to a church. At the entrance is a woman who invites me to have a look at the church, which is quite newly renovated. She says it's a Carthusian church.[63] Its portal is made of gray sandstone with sculptures decorating it on both sides, as is the case with Gothic churches. The woman—obviously the gatekeeper—picks up one of these sculptures, a bishop's crosier, also made of sandstone. Like the other figures, it was fitted into the wall, and I am surprised that it can be taken out like that. The woman shows it to me, as if it had some special meaning for this church,

---

57 Harding, *Women's Mysteries*. Emma Jung created three copies of this dream, two handwritten and one typed, and two handwritten copies of her commentary. In the first handwritten dream text, her introduction includes this statement about Harding's book: "It seems as if its content doesn't speak to me that much—I can't really relate to it. I think the woman problem is apparently not very pertinent to me, as the material leaves me rather cold."

58 Stadthausquai: a street in downtown Zurich, across the River Limmat from the Old City.

59 *Fraumünsterkloster*: lit., women's minster cloister, a Benedictine abbey founded in 853, site of the present-day Fraumünster. The Fraumünster is one of four great Zurich churches that today belong to the Evangelical Reformed Church, the other three being the Grossmünster, the Predigerkirche ("preacher's church," mentioned below, note 66), and St. Peter's.

60 *Bauhof-*, *Bauholzweg*: lit., Building Court Way, Building Timber Way (names arising in the dream).

61 Bahnhofstrasse-Börsenstrasse: intersection at the center of the city's business district.

62 Enge: a quarter of the city lying slightly further south, adjacent to Lake Zurich.

63 The Carthusian Order of the Roman Catholic Church, founded in the eleventh century, is an enclosed order, allowing either monastic (communal) or cenobitic (solitary) life. Its members include both monks and nuns. See author's commentary, 304.

or as if she were performing some kind of *"rite d'entrée"*[64] with it, and then she puts it back in its place.

I then enter the church and find myself in a not too large, square room whose walls taper at the top like a tent. The inside of the roof is visible. It seems made of shingles of a yellowish and dark brown color, that form a pretty pattern reminiscent of fish scales or honeycombs, or a primitive ornamentation.

After taking in this room, I enter the nave, which is like a room unto itself, and I walk forward down the left side aisle. In the center aisle, the ceiling is quite low, similar to a crypt, and with painted figures, but I cannot quite make them out.

I am approached by a very tall man who reminds me of Dr. Baynes,[65] except for being significantly taller and much slimmer. He walks past me, seemingly without noticing me, but then turns back and greets me by silently shaking my hand, whereupon he continues walking. There seem to be other people in the church, whom I hear speaking English, though I'm unable to see these visitors.

Rather than having a choir, the front end of this church which I am now approaching ends with a straight wall—I'm thinking of the iconostasis in the Greek church, which divides the chancel from the nave. But here, there are neither doors nor images of saints, but something else instead. At the top, where the vault of the nave curves down to meet the wall, a strange sort of sculpture has been installed. All kinds of vessels—jars, bowls, dishes, etc., of various sizes, shapes, and colors—are embedded in the ceiling and arranged in such a way that they form a mosaic-like ornament, which also resembles a constellation. I am impressed by this peculiar structure: it is very beautiful and obviously important, since it occupies such a central place, where there would otherwise be the altar and an image of Christ or the Madonna.

Now I leave the church and continue walking along the "Bahnhofstrasse." After a few steps, once again I come to a church, which, like the other one, stands directly facing the street. It reminds me somewhat of the Predigerkirche.[66] With its stuccoed walls and lack of ornamentation, it has a sober Zurich look, as I realize in my dream. Here, too, I enter and am met with a big surprise, for instead of a roof, a vine-covered pergola stretches high above the room. The columns on the left and right are also covered with grapevines, and beyond, a wonderfully blue sky peeks through, and the leaves glow in the sunlight like precious stones.

Unlike the other church, this one does not have a sanctuary; rather the front end of the nave is formed by the transept, which also consists of an open pergola that

---

64 French: rite of entry.

65 H. G. (Peter) Baynes: see "Emma Jung and Analytical Psychology," volume introduction, 54, note 157.

66 Predigerkirche (the Preachers' Church): One of four main, historic churches in downtown Zurich. A Romanesque and Gothic building, it was built in the Middle Ages by the Dominican Order (Order of Preachers). In the 1500s, at the time of Zwingli, it became a Protestant church and was stripped of much of its ornamentation.

tapers on both sides, as if it turned into pathways. I now recall reading or hearing somewhere that this church had been converted into a *passage*. There, where the center aisle and the transept meet, a kind of crossroad[67] has been created. I wonder where the various paths may lead, whose ends I cannot see.

Here I wake up.

Commentary:[68]

My sister:	my other side, insofar as she is an opposite type to me, the shadow.
I want to buy shoes:	shoes = standpoint, attitude.
Patent leather shoes:	old-fashioned, worn in company, so an outdated, conventional point of view, ill-suited to me or to the present time.
Stadthausquai:	Near the Fraumünster church and area where the affiliated abbey once stood.[69]
Sister says where I can find shoes:	The shadow—i.e., probably intuition—shows me the way.
namely at the Bauhof- or Bauholzweg:	Where the present-day Bürkliplatz[70] is, there used to be the so-called Bauhof,[71] where municipal building materials were stored. The name Bauschänzli[72] still harks back to this. Bauholzweg[73] also suggests the idea of construction, and precisely with *wood*, lat. *materia* = building with wood = feminine principle. If the shoes are to be found there, that means that the new, sought-after attitude has to do with building, with building material and the feminine principle.

---

67 *Kreuzweg*: an alternate translation, "stations of the Cross," is possible; but in context, the ordinary meaning of the word seems more likely. (See author's commentary, below, 308.)

68 *Commentar*: Emma Jung's interpretive notes for this dream, which exist in two handwritten versions, are titled by the author. Her earlier version of the commentary, being more fully developed, is published here.

69 *EJ*: Earlier a store had been there, where we bought women's handicrafts. [Sentence deleted in text by author.]

70 Bürkliplatz: a town square, located at the north end of Lake Zurich.

71 *Bauhof*: lit., Builder's Yard.

72 Bauschänzli: an artificial island in the river Limmat, downtown Zurich, now used as a public square and recreation area. The name, diminutive for "construction entrenchment," refers to the Baroque fortifications that originally stood there,

73 *Bauholzweg*: lit., Building Timber Way.

I go ahead and sister must first go to Enge:[74]	I = conscious personality
	Sister—intuition knows where to find what is being sought and tells me—but she does not accompany me, for she must first go to Enge, i.e. perhaps the inferior function or shadow personality is not yet ready to adopt the new standpoint, even though it is she who intuits it.
	Concerning Enge—narrow pass[75]—one thinks of a difficult passage, perhaps the passage of what is still unconscious into consciousness? Or a kind of birth?[76]
I come to a church on the upper part of the Bahnhofstrasse:	In reality, only commercial buildings are found there; the church, then, stands in the bustle of everyday life. Coupling of religion and daily work, or even worldly concerns.
Carthusian Church:	Unlike other monastic communities, it is characteristic of the Carthusians to take individuality into account, insofar as everyone has their own small dwelling. It is therefore a church in which community is combined with individuality.
Woman at the entrance who invites me in:	It must be a "Frauenkirche" if there's a female gatekeeper—*Frau*münster.[77]
Church newly renovated:	Something old that was renewed. —The main topic of the above-mentioned women's discussion was to establish the connections between the ancient cultic forms of feminine deities and the psychology of women today. Something ancient, then, that is looked at with new eyes. Perhaps the new shoes fit in here, too.

---

74 The literal meaning of *Enge* is "narrowness, tightness, constriction."

75 *Engpass*: in the mountains, "defile, narrow pass"; in a roadway, "bottleneck"; figuratively, "tight spot, difficulty."

76 *EJ*: "Dream in Locarno" *[illegible words]* "… a word that also might be 'Enge.'" [Partially illegible sentence, deleted by author.]

77 The Fraumünster (lit., women's minster) is a major cathedral in the city of Zurich, smaller than the double-towered Grossmünster (great minster) that stands several blocks from it. Emma Jung's use of the names *Frauenkirche* (women's church) and *Fraumünster* departs from their historical meaning. (See also "Reader's Guide," volume introduction, 89 and note 63.)

Bishop's crosier at the entrance:	Shepherd's staff. Bishop = spiritual shepherd—masculine spirit who leads—convents also have priests—*leading* idea is something masculine. Being touched by this staff is like a *rite d'entrée* or initiation. The masculine spirit, the leading idea, is necessary to understand what is seen.

But the staff is placed out of sight, behind the other sculptures—i.e., this masculine leadership only steps forward by way of exception and otherwise remains out of sight—so it's not the animus! |
| Square space, tent-like: | Narthex—intersection of the nave. Base of a tower, primitive construction style. Perhaps the upward tapering form of the tent led to the building of towers? Primitive precursor of a tower. |
| Inside of the roof with the decorative pattern: | It, too, has a primitive character; brown and yellow are natural colors, not crass opposites like black and white; the latter would correspond to the Christian viewpoint. Here they are softened opposites, as they are in nature.

This "softened" also corresponds to the feminine, in that feminine consciousness is not as bright as the masculine, and the unconscious is not as dark. The functions, too, are less sharply differentiated, but more balanced, closer to a natural state. There the functions are more well-rounded than in a culture of extreme differentiation on the one hand, and complete unconsciousness or lack of differentiation on the other. |
| Pattern reminiscent of fish scales or honeycomb: | Pre-human levels of "collectivity"; among fish, it is simply a swarm of similar individual creatures (fish also bring to mind mermaids—Harding's mermaid as a precursor of woman—a semi-natural being)—among bees, the swarm is more organized; it is a colony—indeed, it is a *matriarchy*—it has a queen. This again leads to the women's church. |

The nave:	low, like a crypt—unlike the narthex, which leads upwards, the *terre à terre*[78] seems emphasized here; possibly even the subterranean (crypt)—unconscious church?
	Here, too, what is worth seeing is above, as was the ceiling previously.
	Thus, the viewer is *below* and must look up. Indian myth[79] of people drawn by the light, coming out of the depths, up to the surface and into the light. Actually, what is emphasized here would be the opposite of the soul's descent into matter.
	The figures on the ceiling are indeed much more differentiated than the ornament on the ceiling of the narthex, but I cannot recognize them clearly. Perhaps my eye is too little differentiated for it—or it is too dark in the space—since this is, in fact, in the unconscious.
A man comes toward me and greets me silently:	He reminds me of Baynes, who has died—the man in the dream also has something ghostlike or shadowy about him. Particularly the way he passes me by and comes back to silently shake my hand has this effect.
	Baynes was an analyst who had a good understanding of feminine psychology—as a feeling and intuitive type, he had a kind of feminine spirit. Is he the spirit who haunts this women's church? He seems somehow to belong to the church or to be at home in it. Perhaps the crosier is his: just as the latter is inconspicuously there, this "spirit" is inaudibly present.
Englishman:	Baynes is an Englishman—I hear English being spoken somewhere in the church.

---

78 French: down-to-earth, mundane.
79 *Indianermythos*: Native American myth.

Baynes really had the special kind of closeness to nature that one finds so often in England, the mentality that still knows a world of elves and nature spirits—an irrational-feminine nature-mentality.

Perhaps such a mentality is characteristic of a women's church—that is, of a feminine religion.

Our silent encounter has something similar to the *rite d'entrée* with the crosier. Does this contact with the "spirit" bring about understanding?

Mosaic of vessels on the ceiling:

The way the vault connects to the wall, curving down to meet it, is striking, like the sky meeting the earth at the horizon: it emphasizes the place where lower and upper merge into each other. No choir—nothing striving *upward*, but rather a vault curving downward.

The mosaic on the ceiling brings to mind a constellation—the front wall of the church would be the east side, so the image = an ascending sign? It is not an image in the Christian style, rather it is one from nature—ornament = decoration = cosmos.

Vessels are feminine symbols *par excellence*; their diversity represents single individuals. The *varying* individual vessels are arranged into a *whole*—not randomly thrown together like a swarm (bees or fish, cf. ceiling pattern in the narthex) but an *ornament*, something *aesthetic*—not *practical*.

It is a whole, in which each individual has their place, and the special nature of the whole is expressed precisely through this, namely that it forms an image, an ornament.—The vessels embedded in the ceiling give the impression of a constellation.

Ornament—cosmos.—Is it the image of a community that is not a working team?

	The arrangement of complex individualities probably has something to do with the fact that it is a Carthusian church.
The second church:	like Zurich on the outside—sober—inconspicuous—conforming to the common style—also a part of the business of everyday life (Bahnhofstrasse)—reformed—puritanical—Zwingli-style.[80]
Interior with pergola:	Italian—southern—pagan—nature is included—indeed, living nature, not carved in stone like the Gothic. This inclusion of nature once again corresponds to the feminine.
Grapevine:	Dionysian—also a cult particularly cultivated by women.
Transept:	This forms a kind of *crossroad*—different directions join up.[81]
	Crossroads have something special about them—strange things happen there—probably because different directions come together. Union of opposites?
	In the first church, the coming together of below and above was emphasized; here, it's the crossing of different directions on a plane. The connection of these two would then result in three-dimensionality, i.e. reality, perhaps?
The transept runs into a pathway:	so it is *open* to the outside; it transitions directly into life— not separated from it, unlike the other, more medieval church.

---

80 Ulrich Zwingli (1484–1531): founder of the Swiss Reformed Church. His reform movement was joined in his lifetime by the city of Zurich and also by Schaffhausen, Emma Jung's childhood city. "Zwingli-style" refers to the simple, unadorned church architecture favored in Swiss Reformed tradition.

81 *EJ*: In contrast to the other church, this one does not have such a striking sanctuary[?], rather … [Incomplete sentence, deleted by author.]

was converted to passage:

Reconstruction—to Bauholzweg?[82] Passage to what? the Christian church is a sort of passage to heaven—this one, a passage to the world? To everyday life—

Does it also correspond to the feminine, that religion is not practiced separate from everyday life but *in* everyday life? Both churches therefore on the Bahnhofstrasse? Or does it point to a completely different religious attitude—another *stand*point (new shoes!), not turned away from the world, but connected to it.

---

82 As above, the name means, literally, "Building Timber Way."

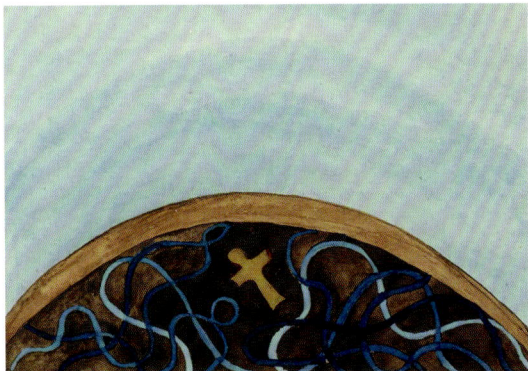

7.1.

7.2.

7.3.

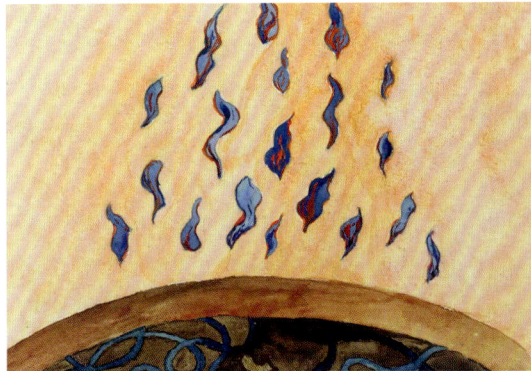

7.4.

FIGURES 7.1–7.9.
[Death and rebirth of
the world]. Series of
paintings by Emma
Jung, September–
November 1917.

FIGURE 7.1.
What is buried in
the depths—how
may it reach the light?
12 September 1917.

FIGURE 7.2.
Look, the fire spirits
are approaching.
13 September 1917.

FIGURE 7.3.
From below, flames
blaze up to earth.
14 September 1917.

FIGURE 7.4.
From heaven, like
rain, fire is falling.
15 September 1917.

FIGURE 7.5.
The whole world is in
flames. 17 September
1917.

7.5.

7.6.

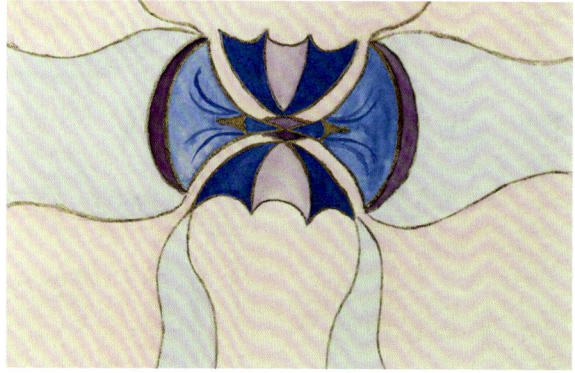

7.7.

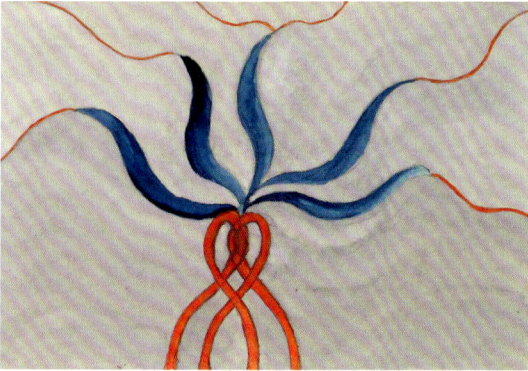

7.8.

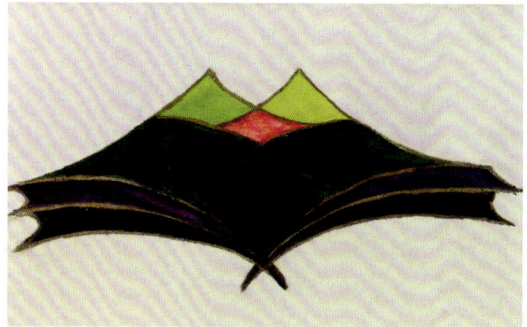

7.9.

The fire died, the
smoke drifted away,
the world collapsed
into ash. And now?

FIGURE 7.6.
A flower rises from
the waters. 18 September 1917.

FIGURE 7.7.
And a second, called
the Crystal Flower.
19 September 1917.

FIGURE 7.8.
And a third, whose
name is "Connected
to the All." 20 September 1917.

FIGURE 7.9.
Also a butterfly, which
brings a message
from flower to flower.
This is the new world.
21 November 1917.

The System:
A Cosmology

Introduction

STARTING IN THE spring of 1915, in collections of writings and drawings, Emma Jung elaborated certain wide-ranging cosmological questions and imaginative proposals concerning the emergence not only of the physical creation but also of the human psyche. Through dream analysis and amplification, using subjective responses, drawn images, archetypal associations, scientific concepts, and symbolic reasoning, she explored the images and questions that arose for her in a group of dreams and a compelling fantasy.[1]

The author left these cosmological writings untitled, except for one significant reference to "the System," which provides the chapter title here. Handwritten in the marbled book, above a dream text dated May 1915,[2] we find this notation, apparently a reminder from the author to herself: "(related ideas partly carried over into the System)."[3]

On first glance, the author's use of "System" seems puzzling, but an explanation is available. There is reason to think that in 1915 the term was familiar within the Jung household in a cosmological sense. By the middle of that year, Carl Jung had completed the text of his *Liber Novus*.[4] In the fifth of his *Black Books*, he drew his first mandala, calling it "*Systema mundi totius*" (The structure of the whole world).[5] At about the same time, Emma Jung used the German term, *System*, in reference to her writings about creation.[6]

---

1   The author frequently engaged with her dream materials and products of the unconscious, using an analytic method developed by C. G. Jung, now commonly called "active imagination." (See "Reader's Guide," volume introduction, 73ff.; also Chapter V, 241 and note.) At the beginning of the twentieth century, when the term "active imagination" was not yet current, Emma Jung generally called such writings "fantasies" or, less often, "imaginations." Consistent with the author's usage, the editors of this volume treat the term "fantasy" as equivalent to "active imagination."

2   This untitled dream is discussed below, 319ff., under the working title, "Dream of the house of Virgo."

3   "Related ideas" probably include the vortex and spiral found in this dream (322), which the author copied into her black notebook (333). The "System" mentioned by the author is printed here as System I, 330ff.

4   Cf. Shamdasani, "Introduction," in Jung, *The Red Book*, 202ff., and "Editorial Note," ibid., 225.

5   The German word *System* is a cognate of the ancient Greek term, σύστημα (*systema*). Jung used this term in the title of his first mandala, recorded on 16 January 1916 (Jung, *Black Book V*, 169). Ulrich Hoerni writes: "Jung himself nowhere provided a translation of the image title *Systema Mundi Totius*. It is a combination of the Greek word '*systema*', which can be translated as 'composition' or 'structure', and the genitive singular of the two Latin words '*mundus*' and '*totus*' (translated as 'world' and 'whole' respectively)" (Hoerni, "Images from the Unconscious," *The Art of C. G. Jung*, 16, note 7).

6   We cannot determine which spouse first used the terms *systema* and *System*. Both knew Greek; and at this time each was engaged in creating a personal cosmology.

The materials for Emma Jung's System come from four handwritten sources. One notebook, which the author called "Night Voices," contains a record of her fantasy and dreams dated April and May 1915, accompanied by extensive commentaries. These materials consist of a cluster of contemporaneous dreams and active imaginations, which the author amplifies and analyzes, referring back and forth between them as if they were parts of a single, complex communication from the psyche.

Unless otherwise identified, passages quoted in this chapter introduction are from "Night Voices."

The second source, an undated, black notebook, constitutes Emma Jung's first organized compilation of these raw materials. This version of the System, probably written in about 1915 or 1916, is printed below as System I. It begins with an exposition of key elements from "Night Voices," then enters a new arena. Inspired by her drawing of a large color wheel, whose many, finely graded segments are organized in her own imagination, she produces a lengthy text containing further questions and discoveries about the mystery of creation.

The third source, an illustrated text found in a brown leather notebook, is printed below as System II. In this concise synthesis, apparently written in 1918–1919,[7] the author advances beyond certain questions that she left open in System I. Her basic concepts are reorganized and to some degree reconceptualized. Most of the personal associations are removed, and ideas are presented mainly in abstract and universal terms, producing a text that can rightly be called systematic. Many drawings from System I are faithfully repeated but freshly interpreted in System II. Certain drawings, appearing there for the first time, are also prominent in the painting that concludes her work on the System.

The fourth source for the System is the marbled book.[8] Some dream and fantasy texts related to the System are recorded there, in versions slightly revised from those in "Night Voices" and without the author's commentaries. Most important for the present chapter, this notebook contains the painting we are calling "Image of an emerging world" (361),[9] probably created in 1919, which harmonizes essential symbols of the System into a coherent whole.[10]

---

7 The first page of the brown leather notebook states that its entries cover the dates "February 1915–June 1924." An extended middle section, lacking dates, is devoted to Emma Jung's second version of her System, printed here as System II. Dated texts before and after those pages make it evident that they were written between 1918 and 1919.

8 See "Reader's Guide," volume introduction, 93, note 72.

9 Emma Jung may have chosen the pages of the marbled book for this painting because she reserved that notebook for finished versions of her work. The untitled painting, called here "Image of an emerging world," represents a synthesis of symbols belonging to the System. Located halfway through the marbled book, the painting is followed by several blank pages, on which the author may have intended to add further text.

10 Originally in color, this image was later published in Jung's *Collected Works* as a black-and-white

Taken together, Emma Jung's cosmological writings and drawings represent a daring thought experiment, one so vast and complex that the author herself exclaims at one point, "Must I actually write a treatise on physics?[11] Or what should that even be?"

FIRST TEXT AND DRAWINGS

Commentary on dream of the miraculous city. The creation of the System apparently began with the author's commentary on her April 1915 dream and fantasy of the miraculous city.[12] In "Night Voices," we find the author's first copy of this dream and fantasy, together with many pages of commentary and drawings pertaining to the System. In the fantasy's final scene, the central figure finds herself waiting alone in a dark forest,[13] where she has the shattering feeling that she has lost her identity:

> So I sat for a long time and thought about all sorts of things—how I had actually got to this forest, what I wanted here, where I came from, and above all, who I really was. In truth, I had no idea who I really was. What kind of being was sitting here under the pine tree? Well, let's see. I had believed that this being was "I," that this "I" was a person, a woman. "I" spoke about "I" and "me" and had a certain notion about this being.—And now, how strange! "I" no longer means anything, no longer says anything to me.
>
> What is that actually, "I"? Was it ever anything at all, and what lies at the root of it? What kind of a sound is that, "I"? It seems so familiar, and yet I haven't the faintest idea what it means. What agony, not to find it![14]

---

reduction (*CW* 9.i, §550, figure 2). There the image, redrawn, is attributed to a former woman patient and dated 1916. The actual date of the painting, based on textual evidence, was probably 1919.

11 Emma Jung's mention of "a treatise on physics" is not as hyperbolic as it sounds. Passages in System I and System II (342, 353 and notes) show that she was aware of Einstein's theory of the equivalence of energy and matter.

12 The version of this dream and fantasy printed in Chapter VI (268ff.) was taken from the marbled book. Up to and including the final scene, it is a verbatim copy of the text found in "Night Voices."

13 The dark forest is a recurring theme in Emma Jung's writings. In "Do you see the sea?" (Chapter III, 179ff.), brother and sister are tragically driven together by a storm in the woods at night. In "Night Voices" she refers to a book, *Au coeur sombre de la forêt verte* (In the dark heart of the green forest), whose theme, the innocent discovery of sexuality, had fascinated her as a girl. The dark forest is a motif in medieval and Renaissance literature, e.g., the opening lines of Dante's *Divine Comedy*. This motif also appears in Wagner's operas, with which Emma Jung was well acquainted.

14 This scene occurs in both "Night Voices" and the marbled book. When the author entered this text in the marbled book, however, instead of following it with commentary, she rounded it out with a poem (Chapter VI, 272).

In "Night Voices," this final scene leads immediately into an exploration of related sensations, questions, thoughts, and drawings, representing the author's first steps toward her System:

> But something is here—What—Hard? What can it be?—Something does this (VII.1) this ... something does this. (VII.2) It's called an egg.

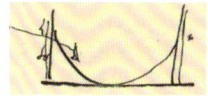

VII.1.

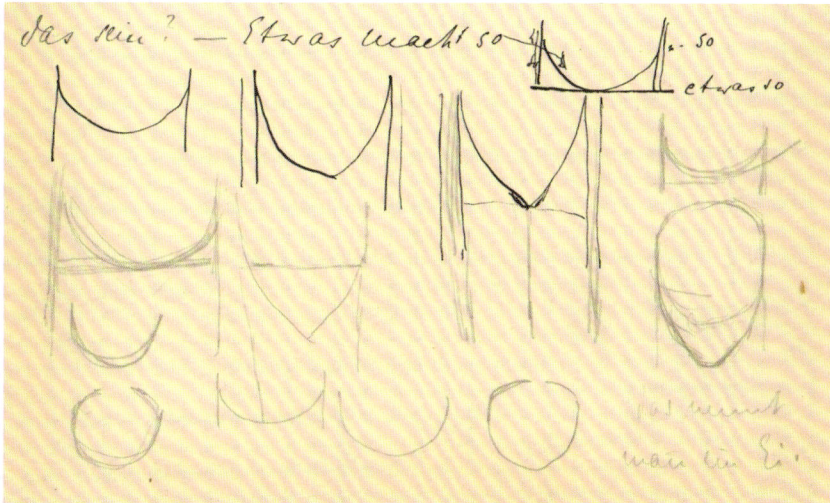

VII.2.

> What can all this mean? My first clear feeling, like this, (VII.3) is something like sucking, taking in, pulling in. At the same time there's another feeling. I can show both of them best this way. (VII.4) The second goes out until it finds an obstacle. (VII.5)

VII.3.

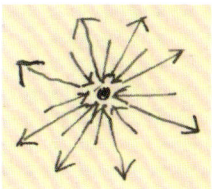

VII.4.

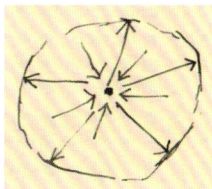

VII.5.

> The one strives together to a point, the other spreads out on all sides into boundlessness, that is, as far as it can without encountering resistance, which will be the case sooner or later. And with this resistance, that which wants to spread out is captured into a form, which saves it from dispersing into the All. [...] This restriction brings about the separation of space—the creation of space, as it were—by the fact that there are now two: space and a *form*, which is

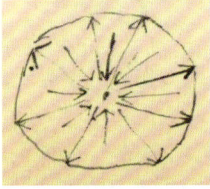

VII.6.

VII.7.

VII.8.

VII.9.

contained within it and yet different from it. And what did the form come from? From *movement*, which is the first sensation of matter, the feeling of sucking in, then the feeling of spreading out, the feeling of being overpowered by the obstacle, which is simultaneously a feeling of pleasure and maybe also of pain.

Now we would have space and form, (VII.6) but what else? (VII.7)

Before my eyes I see an undefined mass in streaming, circular motion, (VII.8) roughly in spiral form or in concentric circles. (VII.9)

Dream image: Falling into the mill. Emma Jung does not trust her rational process to shed light on the questions that have arisen. Instead, she turns to a dream fragment, which allows her to seek answers through a process involving both conscious thoughts and images from the unconscious:

There would probably be a lot to think about, but that wouldn't be much use. Must I go back to a dream?—One fragment says: an accident had happened to Marianneli. She had somehow got into a kind of mill that ground her into it, and she didn't reappear.

This image of a daughter, Marianne, lost in the mill, brings physical sensations, visual images, and a train of thought:

VII.10.

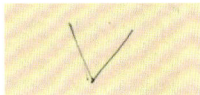

VII.11.

In the dream of Marianneli I have the strong sensation of being sucked down into the mill through the funnel. Rather than seeing it, I feel the pulling in— maybe it's part of what was described above, that went like this: (VII.10) It's strange, though, that nothing more appears—in the dream I can't understand that my child should simply have disappeared. Here I must come back to the first drawing, the emergence of the egg. (VII.11) There, too, what is pulled in sinks into the depth, and as it goes, it weighs down what is curved inwards to form a pointed sack, while simultaneously stretching out the sides until they close at the top.

The sensation of being contained and suspended, of needing to reach the ground, is a recurring theme for the author.

Here the first movement (VII.12) imposes itself again, and with it the way out—indeed, there is an "above"! But if only for once I had solid ground!

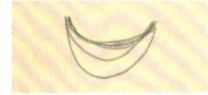

This theme of suspension may be related to the author's besetting concern, discussed below, about the relationship between spirit (light) and the physical world (matter).

Dream of the house of Virgo.[15] A related dream now comes into consideration, one that came soon after the dream of the mill, and which the author treats as belonging to the same series. It is long and episodic, beginning with the discovery of a naked infant in the street of an Italian city. The dreamer tries to wrap the infant in thin fabric, then calls out for warmer material. But when a piece of fabric is thrown down from a window, it merely floats in the air and does not reach the ground.

In the next episode, the dreamer is driven around the city in a small, horse-drawn cart. The coachman, a trusted friend, Dr. K.,[16] symbolizes for her *der Mensch* (the person, the whole human being). Her comment reads:

> *Dr. K*: I have a special fondness for him. He appeared in an earlier dream as a symbol of the "*human being*."[17] He seems to me a particularly good person. He must therefore be steering the chariot of the new sun.

As the dream unfolds, the carriage ride leads to a house where Dr. K. has work to do. They pass the birthplace of the dreamer's youngest child; then they drive through a thunderstorm. At the height of their drive, above a ring of hills, the dreamer enters a house painted black and white, where Dr. K. will do "the work of the new person." The dreamer waits in a bedroom that seems empty of personality until she sees some hair ornaments left on a washstand, which show her that someone is indeed living here. These ornaments are shaped like vortices and spirals. In reflecting on the dream, she recognizes vortex and spiral as symbols with meaning for the System.

In the dream's final episode, Dr. K. has disappeared. The dreamer descends from the hilltop and meets a curious-looking man, Herr Wünschmann (Wish-man), "all blue and violet," who is surprised that she is in mourning. She protests that she

---

15 Elements in this unnamed, episodic dream provide essential material for the System. The "house of Virgo" (so identified by the author in her commentary) is the high point of the dream journey. It is where the coachman, "Dr. K.," does his work. Here, too, the dreamer finds a pair of symbols—vortex and spiral—central to her System.

16 In a related passage, the author identifies this figure as Dr. Adolf Keller, a Swiss pastor-analyst and family friend. (See Chapter I, "On Guilt," 131, note 1.)

17 *ein Symbol des "Menschen"*: The German term *der Mensch* (person, human being) here carries moral connotations of integrity and honor.

is not; her dress is both white and black. Herr Wünschmann then goes on ahead, saying he will prepare the onions.[18]

Later, remembering this dream encounter, she reflects that she may indeed be in mourning, either for her daughter lost in the mill or for the infant in the street, whom she had wrapped from head to toe in a thin fabric that could be either a diaper or a winding sheet. In the author's reflection on these dream figures, the polarities of life and death coexist and shift places. Each child image may signify either death or the renewal of life.

> Mourning—probably pertains to the lost child and the shroud. But it is only half-mourning: white is resurrection. Something has died—a child—and something is resurrected or born—also a child, the one wrapped in the swaddling cloth.

Similarly, the daughter lost in the mill may have died, or she may have been translated to heaven.

This insight comes when Emma Jung employs astrology to amplify the symbols of her dream.[19] She notes that the house to which Dr. K. drives her is directly across the circle from the one where her youngest daughter, Helene, was born. Reading "house" as an astrological term, she writes that Helenli was born in Pisces; so the opposite house must be Virgo:[20]

VII.13.   VII.14.

> So now I'm there with my sun chariot, and the house opposite is "Virgo." That is Marianneli's sun position (VII.13) *discrimination*—(VII.14) chaos, undifferentiation.

These reflections on the contrasts between Pisces and Virgo help resolve two of the author's questions. First, she realizes that there is a reason why, in her earlier dream, Marianne does not appear below the mill funnel: it is because she has been translated to heaven, signifying the "sublimation of M's characteristics." She is now

---

18   The dreamer thinks he will prepare an onion tart for the family. In System I, see the author's symbolic drawing of a cut onion (facsimile page, 338).

19   Astrological symbols and references feature prominently in Emma Jung's work. Interest in astronomy had been passed on to the author by her mother (see "Emma Rauschenbach: Portrait of Her Childhood and Youth," volume introduction, 3 and note). Carl and Emma Jung's shared interest in astrology seems to have started around the time of their psychoanalytic work with Freud, as documented in a letter from Jung in 1911 (Freud and Jung, *The Freud/Jung Letters*, 254 J, p. 421). (See also Greene, *Jung's Studies in Astrology*.) On 23 February 1911, in order to establish her natal chart, Emma Jung asked for the exact time of her birth at the register office (civil status office), Schaffhausen. Her birth was confirmed for 10:45 a.m. on 30 March 1882. The certified time and date of birth of Emma Rauschenbach are found at the Jung Family Archive.

20   Although Virgo—associated with order, form, and an untouched state—is not the dreamer's sun sign, in some sense the house seems to be hers, as well. It is painted black and white, like her dress. She comments: "Now I'm also wearing the quality of the house."

TABLE 7.1 *Astrological symbols in Emma Jung's System*

♍	♓	≈	♈
VIRGO	PISCES	AQUARIUS	ARIES

above. If the characteristics of Pisces are sublimated in Virgo, the author reflects, this not only makes possible the emergence of form and space; it also supports differentiation, a basic element of human consciousness:

> In the dream this is apparently also indicated through the established goal of Virgo—*discrimination*. As the opposing sign to Pisces, Virgo is thus the pinnacle of what the Pisces-fish point to: *form* and the *gift of differentiation*, which imply each other. Once a form and a space exist, this creates the possibility and the need to *differentiate*.

The actions of Dr. K., symbolizing the human person, become especially significant when the author reflects that he does his work in Virgo, where the characteristics of Pisces are sublimated. His work has personal meaning for the creator of the System, who counsels herself to hold this insight steadily in awareness:

> Dr. K's business thus takes place in the sublimated Pisces-sign—Virgo. The work of the new person is done there. In everything that follows, this must be kept in mind.

This interpretation points toward the overall sense of the dream. "The work of the new person" is nothing less than the creation of the individual, that is, the process of individuation.[21]

If Virgo is the sublimation of Pisces, the author now realizes, then the opposite-aiming fish no longer symbolize only chaos and formlessness; instead, one can see in them the essential psychological principle of inward and outward orientation. In the physical creation, too, she notes, fish represent the start of evolution:

> That striving of the Pisces-fish in two directions no longer seems merely problematic; rather it expresses something elementary, in the same way as inward and outward striving seemed to me the most elementary of feelings. "Fish" are the first manifestation of what has evolved into plants, humans and animals. It is the beginning of creation.

---

21 Individuation is a key concept in Jungian psychology. See "Reader's Guide," volume introduction, 81, note 38.

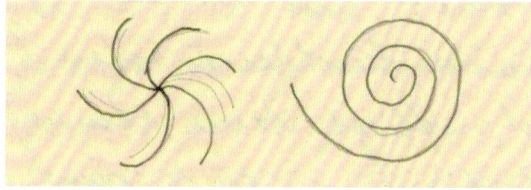

A major pair of symbols emerging from this dream are the vortex and spiral, found in the form of hair ornaments, signs of human presence that the dreamer discovers in an otherwise impersonal room. In her commentary, the author explores the meanings and dynamic qualities of these shapes, which belong together as a pair of complementary opposites. (VII.15)

She discovers that the vortex has masculine characteristics:

> The blazing, radiating, grasping vortex, is there something masculine about it?

In contrast, she determines,

> the spiral motion is calmer. It lacks the flaming, swift, grasping, radiating aspect of the *vortex*. Something about it is receiving, more *welcoming* than *capturing*, and it has the sense of wrapping around—enveloping—something maternal. Its movement does not return to its starting point—rather it starts at one point and circles to another, located further ahead. Thus, it represents the quality of becoming.

Connecting the symbols to each other through their patterns of motion, she now arrives at a theory that unites the opposites. The vortex, whipping its arms around "rather like tentacles," captures what is outside and delivers it to the spiral. The spiral then guides what has been captured, conducting it further into its orbit, and thus into the depths.[22] From this reflection, she observes,

> It is the first connection of the two principles—outward, inward. It is no longer this feeling of two entirely different things, existing side by side and having nothing to do with each other, but rather a connection has emerged (copulation?). A place where the motion of one acts upon the other.

Having described the symbolic union of the masculine and feminine images, she finds a third, the child that belongs to this archetypal constellation. Her episodic

---

22 This dynamic interplay between the masculine vortex and the feminine spiral is illustrated identically in System I, 333 (VII.37) and System II, 352 (VII.97).

dream ends with the scene of the dreamer's encounter with Herr Wünschmann, who offers to go ahead and prepare the onions for the evening meal. Wünschmann (wish-man) is renamed Wunschkind (desired child):

The child goes before us "to prepare the way."[23]

The image of the onion also suggests to her the principle of childhood and becoming:

Onion—is characteristic in the layering of skins. It especially clearly depicts enveloping, wrapping. Here is growth—enveloping with ever new skins.[24] In its round form it also shows physicality very well and brings to mind the shape of the earth. The longed-for child, which has emerged three-fold, is thus to be consumed in the onion meal.

Grail dream and analysis. Next in "Night Voices," after the author's commentary on her first series of dreams, we find a draft of her "Dream of the Grail," together with many pages of associated analysis.[25] The dream begins with a summer heath-land in the mountains, where the dreamer is alone. It then shifts to a mountain snow scene, in which her mother and children descend toward her on a sled. It ends indoors, in a magnificent house, where the presence of the Grail is honored by a community, including children.

In the author's analysis, images in the dream are amplified with material from other dreams, poems, childhood reading, and adult memory. The first scene, a mountain heath where a red-and-black bird sits on a rectangle of pressed-down grasses, evokes significant moments in the author's adult life, then a medieval love-poem, and finally a favorite story from adolescence. The grassy rectangle reminds her of the first lines of a famous love-poem by a medieval Minnesänger, in which a woman fondly describes the broken flowers and grasses "under the linden, on the heath, where we two had our bed."[26] Continuing to explore these associations, Emma Jung writes:

---

23 Quoted from Isaiah 40:3, Matthew 3:3, and Mark 1:3.

24 In System I, under a colored-pencil diagram of an onion in cross-section, the caption reads: "*Vereinigen der 2 Prinz. Bewegung u. Wachstum*"—"Uniting the two principles, movement and growth" (336 and facsimile page, 338).

25 *Analyse* is the author's heading for these pages. A slightly revised version of the dream text is printed in full above (Chapter VI, 273). Dated May 1915 in the marbled book, the revised version omits the author's analysis.

26 First lines of a famous love-poem by medieval poet Walther von der Vogelweide. The original text reads: "Under der linden / án der Heide / dâ unser zweier bette was / dâ muget ir vinden / schône beide / gebrochen bluomen unde gras" (Neumann, ed., *Deutscher Minnesang*, 78). The bird who stands in the rectangle in Emma Jung's dream is associated for her with the literal meaning of *Vogelweide*: "bird-meadow."

The bed makes me think of the bridal bed in the field or the forest, in nature in any case, which was once a favorite fantasy of mine. Union in nature—(union in the Mother?). That book *Au coeur sombre de la forêt verte*,[27] where two "children," completely shut off from the world, discover love and sexuality for themselves, corresponded to just this fantasy[28]—including the "state of being unspoiled"—it was "*forêt vierge*,"[29] cf. my previous dream with the house of Virgo. The heath, too, is "*terre vierge*."[30]

Once again, the author's commentary contains elements for her System. The feather she finds in the grassy rectangle leads her to speculate about the relationship between plant and animal life:

VII.16.

I pick up a small, red feather that I find. Feather: the golden feather in the fairy tale.[31] Why do feathers have such magical significance,[32] e.g., for the Mexicans?

It is actually like a leaf or a grass-seed head—in the middle the shaft, with fibers spreading out from it, like rays or feelers—it's like fingers. (VII.16) In plants, where these fine ramifications serve to let in air and light, they are channels and create larger surfaces, so that more air can be absorbed? Like pine trees, for example? Is the feather part of the pine forest? Oddly, the feather principle reminds one of plants—one thinks of the theory of unification—it is a symbol of two worlds, plant and animal, for although it belongs to the animal realm, it brings to mind the realm of plants. Two worlds are united here—flora and fauna.

She goes on to ask a philosophical question, which is developed further in System I: "But is the union of two worlds creative? Is it even possible?"[33]

Significantly, a central concept, "emergence of a world," arises here in the word *Weltwerdung*:[34]

---

27 French: In the dark heart of the green forest. (No book by this title is found now in Emma Jung's library.)

28 Perhaps this book was one source for the theme of marriage between brother and sister (Chapter III, 179).

29 French: virgin forest.

30 French: virgin land.

31 Cf. Emma Jung's lecture, "The Tale of the Two Brothers," Chapter I, 100. She may be referring here to that fairy tale, or to another well-known tale by the Brothers Grimm, "The Golden Bird."

32 A loose slip of paper, inserted here, shows drawings of red-and-black feathers. In one feather the colors are divided vertically, in the other horizontally (273, 339).

33 The question is paraphrased in System I (339).

34 "*Weltwerdung*": Rendered here "emerging world," the word means literally "world-becoming." A term used by cabalistic and neoplatonic writers since the seventeenth century to refer to the divine act of creation.

The heath of Pontresina[35] gave me the very strong impression of the "initial stage," the first life after the glacial period. [...] Here I really had the feeling of being able to sense the "emerging world" and primeval times.

The scene depicting her mother and children coming toward her on a sled raises questions in the realms of both physics and psychology. For example, she draws small diagrams representing the mountain slope on which she fears being swept away by the sled bearing her mother and children. With these diagrams we find two penciled questions:

Is this the way into the depths?
   More likely it means the *reversal* (overcoming) of nature (culture)/individu-ation? Fear and dizziness belong to these.[36]

She speculates: What physical laws determine the downhill speed of a sled? Are diz-ziness and a fear of heights really a fear of depth? Is fear of water a fear of expanse? In exploring these questions she arrives at new ideas for her System, some closely related to images, others philosophical and archetypal. Among the latter: What is meaningful about the four directions? When animals eat plants, is that a form of union? If so, she adds, their union would involve nourishment and growth, "thus more the motherly principle."

DEVELOPMENT OF THE SYSTEM

In the pages of "Night Voices," it is clear that images and ideas for Emma Jung's System arose initially from her inner life. Later entries in the same notebook show that her writing about the System quickly evolved, always remaining symbolic but becoming more objective and abstract. Kernels of the whole system are present, however, in the earliest texts.

---

35 Pontresina: a mountain village in the Engadine, in the Canton of Graubünden, where Emma and Carl Jung had visited together. In the summer of 1914, a few months after Helene's birth, Emma Jung went there alone for a rest in the mountains. This may have been her opportunity to ponder the primal character of the glaciated landscape. The custom of spending a few weeks in the mountains "for a cure" (*zur Kur*) was common at the time, among women of Emma Jung's social standing. She went to the Alps or a spa resort almost yearly in the period of 1910 to 1930, sometimes alone, some-times with one of the children when they were young. During her 1914 stay in Pontresina, Carl Jung and Hans Schmid-Guisan each visited her, separately, for a couple of days. The following year, 1915, during her stay in Klosters, another Alpine village, she studied Schopenhauer's *The World as Will and Idea* (145, note 30).

36 When commenting on her dream of "The blue flower" (Chapter VI, 260), Emma Jung records similar thoughts about nature and culture.

In April 1915, as discussed above, she writes about the anguish of losing her identity, her sense of being "I" (316). Returning to this theme just two months later, in a passage dated 13 June 1915, she uses philosophical language, "our nothingness in the totality of the world," and asks whether this universal, human situation could be related to the flow of time and the law of change:

> It seems a grand thought—and if one becomes aware of our nothingness within the totality of the world, it is crazier still to want to believe that the human being could be something of and for himself.—And yet—Has a certain law for a process already been laid down for every creature, one that would be connected with the essence of time—a certain impossibility to remain the same, because every moment is different, and no moment can be retrieved and relived.

Emma Jung's cosmogonic reflections underwent a similar process of transformation in the successive versions of her System, moving from the personal toward the universal. She begins with image and narrative, draws from it a general principle, and arrives at an abstraction. For example, a thought about the beginning of the world starts with this image from her Grail dream:

VII.17.

> The mountain basin again suggests this form (VII.17)—movement has become form—solidified movement!

A related thought appears in System I as an epigram, echoing the first verse of the Fourth Gospel:[37]

> Maybe the verse should say: *"In the beginning was movement."* […] Is this conceivable? A world that is only movement and not yet at all physical? (334)

Later in System I, still speculating about the formation of a physical world, the author capitalizes her term "Solidified Movement" (*Erstarrte Bewegung*), as if naming a philosophical concept (346). This speculative concept becomes a certainty in System II, where movement is identified as an *Urelement*, a primal factor in creation, preceding both chaos and form: "Movement is overpowered by form" (350).

A shift away from personal experience, toward philosophical or archetypal abstraction, is also illustrated by comparing the last paragraph of the author's initial Grail dream analysis with its later recensions. Pondering the opening scene, in which she expects to be swept away by a descending sled, she draws diagrams representing the rise and fall of anxiety. This emotional experience is represented

---

37 This passage may also allude to a scene in Goethe's *Faust I*, in which the aged doctor experiments with alternative phrasings for the biblical verse "In the beginning was the Word" (John 1:1). (Goethe, *Faust, Erster Teil*, "Studierzimmer," ll. 1224–37.) References to Goethe's works often appear in Emma Jung's writings.

first as a shallow inverted V, which she labels simply "crescendo-decrescendo." Next comes a slightly more complex image, labeled "rising" and "falling" with a plateau between them. The resulting diagram, resembling a flat-topped mountain, reminds her of another recent dream, where the breasts of an adolescent girl appeared, "half horrible, half interesting," like a pair of volcanoes topped with flames. She records this image in a new diagram: a pair of mountains with flattened tops, surmounted by rising, wavy lines. (VII.18)

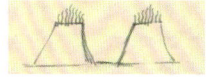

VII.18.

This image of paired volcanoes (or breasts) is included in System I (339, VII.64), although without reference to the dream of an adolescent girl.

In System II, a diagram of two mountains illustrates not only the rise and fall of anxiety but also a more universal phenomenon, the waxing and waning of intensity as such, understood in relation to the two pleromas[38] of movement and matter:

> The two *pleromas* would correspond by and large to oscillations of intensity, (VII.19) except that here the high and low points are really extreme, whereas within every individual the differences are relatively minor. (354, VII.107)

VII.19.

MATTER AND SPIRIT

The author's recurring questions about movement and matter led to a remarkable evolution in her thinking about the creation of the material world. In "Night Voices," and again in System I, we find a comment on the shapes she discovered in her dream of the house of Virgo:

> In the dream, both of these are found: vortex and spiral. With this, depth has also been found. For the spiral goes from one level to another, while the vortex stays on the surface. (333)

In System II, revisiting this idea, the author recognizes that depth is essential to material reality:

> The converging currents arrange their particles in a spiral. Due to the concentration at the center, an impossible state is created, and as a result the spiral moves *into the depths*. A third dimension emerges—physicality. (351)

---

38 *Pleroma*, meaning the infinite, uncreated realm, is a term C. G. Jung adopted from Gnosticism, where it contrasts with *creatura*, meaning the universe of created things. When Emma Jung uses the term in her cosmology (353ff., 358, *et passim*), it has the same sense that Jung gave it in 1916, in his *VII Sermones ad Mortuos*. There he writes: "Nothingness is the same as fullness. … A thing that is infinite and eternal hath no qualities since it hath all qualities. This nothingness or fullness we name the PLEROMA" ("Septem Sermones ad Mortuos," appendix V, translated by H. G. Baynes, in *Memories, Dreams, Reflections*, 379). Jung included "Seven Sermons to the Dead" in *The Red Book*, where this passage on the pleroma is found on 346ff. (see also note 82).

Accompanying the author's focus on physicality is her struggle to explain how immaterial forces, such as light, air, or spirit, are related to the material world. In System I, when struggling to imagine how materiality emerged, she speculates that it may have been a solidified form of light or the divine. Her first attempt to answer the question leads to an impasse:

> Light as "that which differentiates"—to be taken figuratively, as well—light must have an effect on matter? (Does Virgo belong here?) [...] But where does matter come from? Was it also once light? Or was light once matter?—But then, where did that come from? For heaven's sake? (343)

After six months she reaches again for an answer. What now comes to mind seems borrowed from mysticism; and yet her question is still not fully resolved:

> Half a year later: In the end, could light be that from which physicality as such emerged, not only because it illumines bodies, but because something in the *rays* actually enables the demarcation from space and the formation of matter?
> See the first drawing,[39] where the body actually emerges out of rays—although the Something on which the rays fall remains unexplained. It would be condensed divinity—matter. (343)

When she writes System II, the author's question about the creative role of light has evidently been laid to rest. In this later version, the word "light" appears only in the first paragraph, in a statement that suggests a new perspective. Reflecting on the division of "the all" into two parts and thence into many, she writes, "The second is the yellow = light or *heat*." Based on this definition, she continues:

> But the yellow cannot come from outside, since there is nothing there; it must therefore be produced from within. (349)

This statement, that the yellow (the light) must be "produced from within," is enigmatic, until we see, later in System I and again in System II, passages that are probably related. At the end of System I, she writes:

> Special consistency of matter—so-called latent matter—suspended matter. Corresponding to energy of motion and potential energy, one could speak here of matter that is latent in motion—living matter, from dead matter/material. (348)

---

39 Apparently referring to the first of the four "egg" drawings in System I, 330, and System II, 349. The original "egg" drawings occur at the beginning of the System material in "Night Voices" (cf. chapter introduction, 317).

And in System II, she writes:

> One may assume that *matter is quasi dissolved in motion* (latent), in the same way that energy may be latent in matter (static and kinetic energy) (living matter?) (353)

These passages point to the author's grasp of Albert Einstein's new theory about the equivalence of energy and matter.[40] Since energy is now known to arise from the material world, her question about the source of yellow (light) is answered: it is latent within the stuff of creation. On the other hand, consistent with her understanding of movement as a primary element, she grasps the paradoxical reverse side of the equation: matter is also latent in energy. These thoughts finally lead her to see spirit and matter no longer as contradictions but as complementary opposites, mutually related and even able to transform into each other. At the end of System II, she draws two columns to be incorporated into her final painting, captioning them, respectively, "Materialization" (356) and "Spiritualization" (357).

Emma Jung's texts and drawings of her System are presented below in their entirety. In approaching these texts, it is helpful to keep in mind that objective and subjective meanings are interwoven in them, as are the outer and inner dimensions of cosmology. Whatever she writes about *Weltwerdung*—an emerging world—also implicitly concerns individuation, the psychological emergence of the individual. Her System arose, to begin with, from an experience of the near-annihilation of personal identity. The symbolic texts and drawings that follow are phrased in terms of the physical cosmos; but always, at the same time, they address the mysteries of consciousness, the relationship of spirit and matter, and the very existence of the human psyche.

---

40 In 1905, Albert Einstein published four groundbreaking papers, one of which argued for the equivalence of matter and energy ($E = MC^2$). Emma Jung recorded System I about ten years after this turning point in physics, and she wrote System II three or four years later. Indirect allusions to Einstein's theory appear in both versions (below, 342, 349, 353). The author had opportunities to talk with the physicist when he visited the Jungs at home. One of C. G. Jung's letters mentions that, in the early years of the century, before Einstein left Zurich, he was occasionally the Jungs' dinner guest (Jung to Carl Seelig, 25 February 1953, *Letters II*, 108ff. and note). And in a letter to Freud, dated 18 January 1911, Jung wrote: "Last Sunday I invited Bleuler over to my place. … We spent the whole evening talking with a physicist about something far removed from our ordinary concerns—the electrical theory of light" (Freud and Jung, *The Freud/Jung Letters*, 230J, p. 384). The physicist, again, was Albert Einstein. Although she is unnamed in her husband's letter, Emma Jung was probably present for this conversation.

[System I][41]

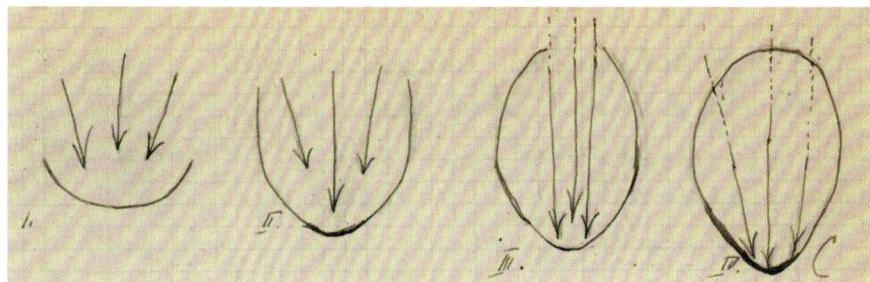

VII.20.

1. Movement of absorbing or sucking in.[42] Whatever is taken in from above has a certain weight, on account of which the cavity becomes deeper and deeper. The deeper it gets, the more the thing closes together at the top, until finally the lines or walls on either side collide, but then the contact with the "outside" is interrupted or suspended. (VII.20)

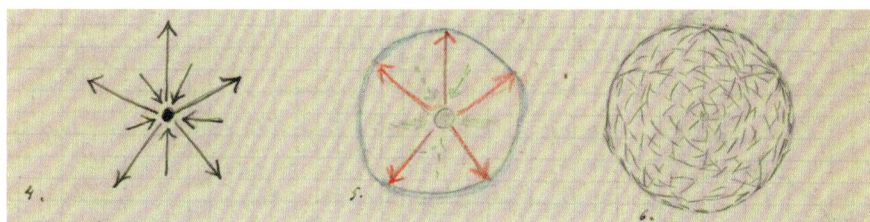

VII.21.

4.[43] Currents directed outward and inward. (VII.21)

5. The outward-directed streams encounter a resistance that forces them to flow backward. Through this resistance a form arises—a thing that is limited in space and distinct from it.

6. The outward currents have a strong propulsion (tension?) but are not strong enough to break through the resistance, so at first they move along its edge, which defines the *form* even more sharply; then within the form they move confusedly in all directions, creating an unruly swarm (felt psychologically as *anxiety*, caused when powerful currents are enclosed in a limited space).

---

41 The author's first formulation of the System, found in the black notebook, was composed in 1915–16. In the present edition, this untitled text is called System I.

42 This paragraph applies to the four "egg" drawings above. A rough version of these drawings is found at the start of Emma Jung's commentary in "Night Voices" (chapter introduction, 317). The same sequence of four ovals reappears in System II, with a revised heading (349).

43 In the handwritten text, this and the following drawings are misleadingly numbered "4, 5, 6," etc. Corresponding drawings in System II are correctly numbered, "5, 6, 7," etc. (350).

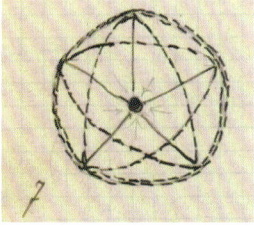

VII.22.

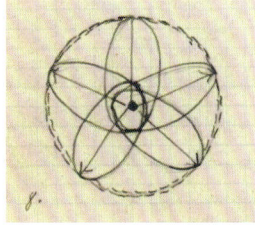

VII.23.

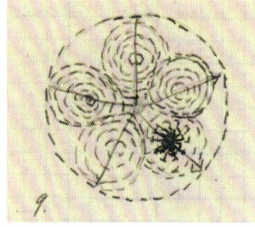

VII.24.

7. In time, there is a little more order in the swarm, perhaps because the tension has dissipated somewhat? The particles move in fixed orbits; yet the circular motion is still frenzied, inexorable. (VII.22)

8. The orbits become smaller and organize themselves into ellipses around each of the five axes. As yet, the primal swarm has no order; it is chaotic. Here it begins to become regulated, due, in fact, to the separation of space and form. (VII.23)

9.[44] In the general circling, one of the particles has suddenly come to a stop or slowed down. A second and third have collided with it and unified into a solid whole.[45] (At first, it is below and to the right. In the color wheel,[46] this is also the location of the "physical," the solidity of the earth-color.) It's as if this fixed point exerted a kind of attraction on the circling particles. (VII.25) They no longer remain parallel but turn toward the central point, forming vertical rays around it. The circling continues inside. (VII.24)

VII.25.

But what are the inward, converging rays doing? A dream in which Marianne falls into a mill funnel and no one knows where she's gone[47] gives me the insight that I am missing a dimension—that of depth—with its corresponding, characteristic feeling of perplexity—the way we feel while awake, confronted by the fourth dimension.[48] Since we do not know it yet, and have no sense organ for it, we cannot

---

44 *EJ*: "On 9: Confusion leads to anxiety—anxiety leads to pulling in and holding on—conglomeration of many small particles—a fixed point emerges (diagram B)." [This penciled note is squeezed onto the preceding page. It evidently refers to the diagram the author numbered 9.]

45 In System II, where the same diagram appears (numbered "10"), the attached text reads: "Modification of the orbits (by reciprocal influence?). Following the collision of two particles that remain stuck together, and whose movement is stopped or slowed by this, a new center of activity (*Wirkungscentrum*) emerges" (350f.).

46 See author's discussion of her color wheel, 340.

47 This dream, discussed in "Night Voices" (318), is part of the author's 1915 dream series.

48 In "Night Voices," when pondering her daughter's disappearance in the mill, the author writes: "In a sense, then, she is transposed to heaven—contrary to all expectations, which had to assume that she would somehow come out again below the mill. So here once again the word is 'above'—as before, where the currents that are drawn in are supposed to have come from *Above*." A few pages later, commenting on the signs of Pisces and Aquarius, she writes: "Aquarius who comes before [in the zodiac] and pours out water—*from above* (the currents that come from above) stands

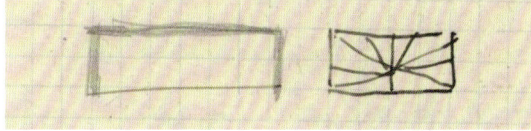

VII.26.

work with it. The diverging currents belong to a plane—they move along the surface into infinity, but they cannot move from one plane to another. It's highly embarrassing to have no depth dimension—two-dimensional—incorporeal, but striving toward the infinite. (VII.26)

VII.27.

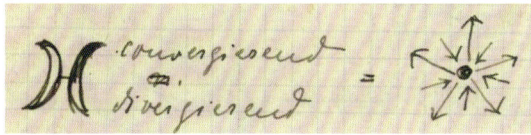

VII.28.   VII.29.

I would like to know how the converging currents look. (VII.27)—
b. is mill-funnel converging (VII.28) = diverging (VII.29)

VII.30.

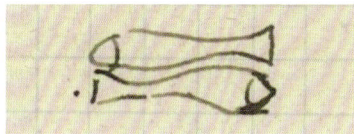

VII.31.

   (VII.30) is also the symbol of Pisces in the zodiac, (VII.31) which also indicates different directions, but not parallels. Opposing currents would equate to the first *precondition of life*. Precisely this precondition or primal cause is indicated in Pisces.

---

apart—transcendent—unknown—divine—superordinate."

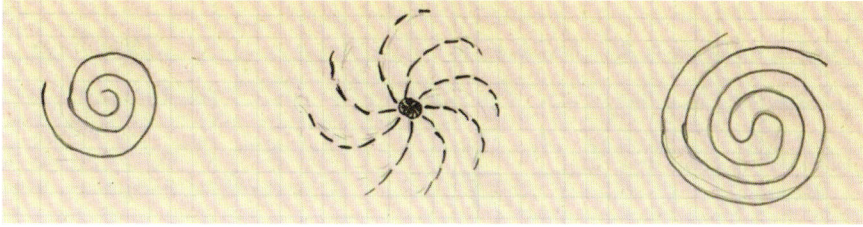

VII.32.

VII.33.

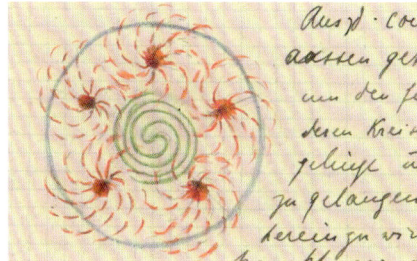

VII.34.

In the dream, both of these are found: vortex and spiral.[49] With this, depth has also been found. For the spiral goes from one level to another, while the vortex stays on the surface. (VII.32)

The converging currents arrange themselves in a spiral around the central point and thereby penetrate into depth. This is how physicality emerges. (VII.33)

From the concentric circling of the outward-moving currents, vortices have formed around the fixed point. Their circling movement is now able to reach beyond the boundary and capture external elements, whirling them inward toward the center, where they are absorbed into the spiral movement that carries them further on its path—that is, a body is built up—Life becomes possible.[50] (VII.34)

Chaos and form emerge together

How does order emerge out of chaos? A question. By form being delimited in space. But how does form arise? By the movement of the currents colliding with a resistance which, at first, they cannot overcome—they are captured by it—but this has also brought chaos into existence.

Accordingly, chaos would not have to come first, *but rather the directional currents*. Chaos emerges only through the confinement into form, for then the streams

---

49 Images of vortex and spiral appear originally in the long, episodic dream described in "Night Voices" (319ff.). They are essential symbols for the author, found again in System II (351) and in her painting of an emerging world (361).

50 This image appears in System II with a revised explanation (352).

have left their direction and must find it again, as shown in the drawings. Creation would therefore be this progression from the chaotic to the orderly. It follows, then, that God preceded chaos.

But how does form emerge? The same way as the resistance.

Where do the streams come from?

Maybe the verse should say: *"In the beginning was movement."*[51] That's how it is here, first movements are sensed or assumed. Is this conceivable? A world that is only movement and not yet at all physical? And where did movement come from? We have a better idea of where it goes—together and apart.[52] (VII.35)

VII.35.

In directions of movement?
Primal source of the cosmos
Primal currents converging and diverging (VII.36)

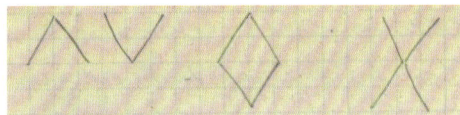

VII.36.   VII.37.

Diamond or cross = symbols for the primal source of the cosmos.

This cross, too, represents the two directions; the feather likewise. (VII.37)

The currents in the (VII.38) have a different angle than in the (VII.39). What does that mean? Or does it mean nothing?

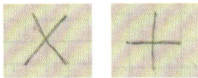

VII.38.   VII.39.

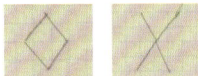

VII.40.   VII.41.

The four arms of the cross also bring to mind the four rivers of Paradise.[53] Again, the primal source of the world.

Do the currents come from one point and flow back into one point, as with the (VII.40), or do they come from two points into a single point, and separate again from there, like this? (VII.41) These arrangements presuppose, however, that time already exists.

Or do the currents exist side-by-side? Like this? (VII.42)

VII.42.

---

51 Cf. chapter introduction, 326 and note.

52 At the end of System II, this description of a converging/diverging pattern of motion is related to an element in the author's final painting (356, 361).

53 In legend, the four rivers of the Garden of Eden are Pison, Gihon, Hiddihel, and Euphrates.

They could be simultaneous. Here two parallels intersect in infinity; but that hardly brings a world into existence. For that to happen, the two systems must somehow *cross*, (VII.43) or *merge into one*. (VII.44)

VII.43.   VII.44.

But then, who is to say that the currents (VII.45) run parallel. Is there one path, one space, and one form?

VII.45.

Perhaps it is all mixed up, running in different directions? (VII.46)

VII.46.

A reciprocal effect can then occur, a kind of short-circuit, that can also create a world. Thus the Aquarius sign (VII.47) would actually be even more primordial than the (VII.48) or (VII.49) (significantly also the monogram for Christ).

VII.47.

Indeed, in this way it is also a kind of zodiac. More original and also more comprehensive, designating *infinity* (two parallels, [...][54]). There is still no outward or inward—that is already a value judgment, like the knowledge of good and evil. In contrast (VII.50) is absolutely beyond good and evil. Therefore, our age is also more comprehensive than the Christian (VII.51) age. (VII.52) = indigo.[55]

VII.48.   VII.49.

VII.50.   VII.51.   VII.52.

The question of how form comes into being is still dark. Where resistance may come from—Heat must play a part in it—light, color, and heat are added by the unconscious—But how—by differing wave motion or length?

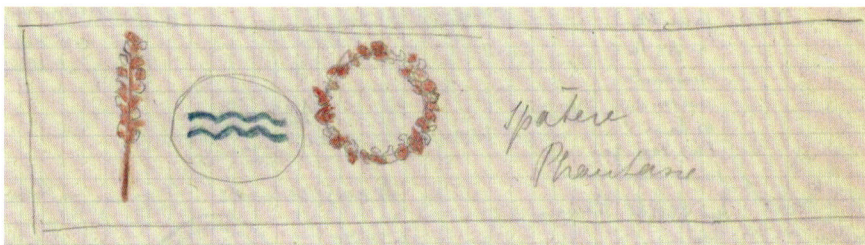

VII.53.
later fantasy[56]

VII.53.

---

54 Illegible in manuscript: two letters.

55 See color drawing of "later fantasy," above. In System I and System II, the blue Aquarius symbol is captioned "infinity/being/(pleroma)" (347, 353).

56 Apart from these drawings, the content of her "later fantasy" is not described.

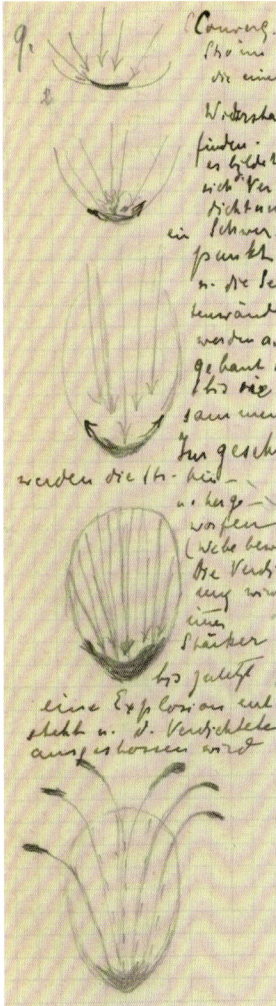

VII.54.

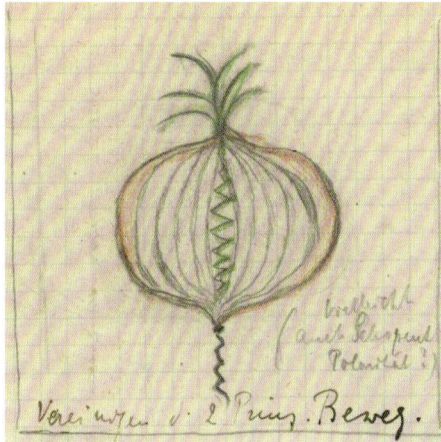

VII.58.

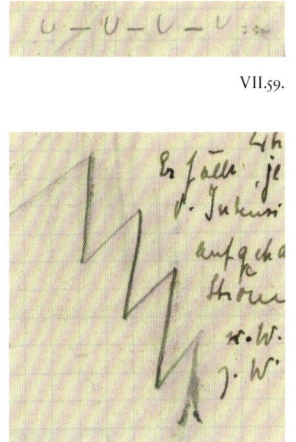

VII.59.

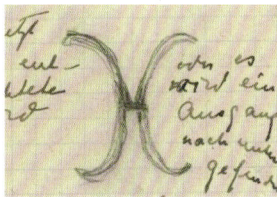

VII.55.

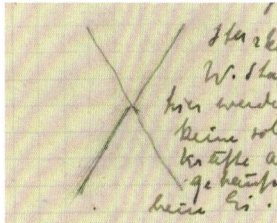

VII.56.

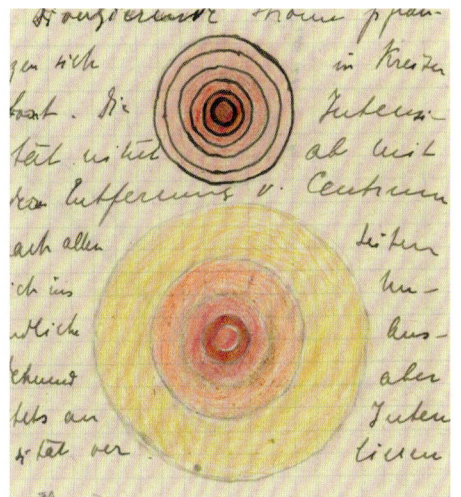

VII.61.

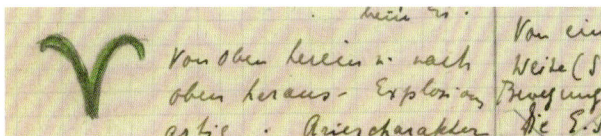

VII.57.

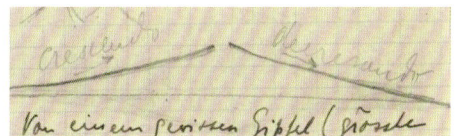

VII.62.

VII.60.

(VII.54) Converging currents that find a resistance. A center of gravity is formed through compression, and the side walls are built up until they collide.[57] In the enclosed space the currents are thrown back and forth (weaving motion). The compression becomes stronger and stronger until finally an explosion occurs, and the compressed matter is expelled (VII.55) or it finds a place to escape below, (VII.56) where the resistance is less strong. No such forces accumulate here, compared to the egg.

(VII.57) Coming in and going out through the top—like an explosion.
Aries-style.
Extraversion of the explosion. Everything moving upwards. Predominantly intellectuals.

(VII.58) Perhaps also Schopenhauer's polarity?)[58]
Union of the two principles, movement and growth

(VII.59) Extraverted current repelled by the resistance

(VII.60) Depending on the intensity of the arrested current, it falls from one resistance to the other.

(VII.61) Diverging currents expand in circles. As the distance from the center to all sides diminishes, the intensity diminishes; it extends into infinity, but with a perpetual loss of intensity.

(VII.62) From a certain high point onward—greatest width (diffusion?)—again the opposite movement.
Broken movement or direction.
The extraverted rays reach a certain climax, and then diminish again?

---

57 See text and drawings at the beginning of System I (330) and again, somewhat revised, in System II (349).

58 In "Night Voices," under the heading "Klosters, 30 July 1915," the author's reflections about Schopenhauer's *The World as Will and Idea* include an extended comment on the concept of polarity (see chapter introduction, 325).

Converg.
Strömungen die einen

Widerstand
finden, es bildet
sich Ver-
dichtung
ein schwer
punkt
u. die Sei-
tenwände
werden an-
gebaut
bis sie zu-
sammenstossen

Im geschl. Raum
werden die th. hei-
n. herge-
worfen
(stehe beweg)
die Verdicht-
ung wird
immer
stärker
bis zuletzt
eine Explosion ent-
steht u. d. Verdichtete
ausgeschossen wird

oder es
wird ein
Ausgang
nach unten
gefunden
bei wenige
starken
W. stand
hier werden
keine solch
Knötchen auf-
gehäuft
hier sie

Von oben herein u. nach
oben heraus. Explosion
artig. Rriescharakter
Exhavers. d. Explos. Alles n. Oben
vorrig Fehlelcekluda

Vorbeugen v. 2 Prinz. Beweg.
v. Wachstum

Strömungen erhalte Strömen pflan-
gen sich
fort. Die
teil wirkt
den Entfernung v. Centrum
nach allen
sich ins
endliche
dehnend
stets an
w tat ver

in Kreise
Intens.
ab mit
Centrum
leiten
un-
aus-
aber
Intens
liessen

Von einem gewissen Gipfel (grösste
Weite (Strenung?) wieder ausgezogeschte
Bewegung. Gebrochene Bewegung od.
die E Strahlen gehen bis zu einem
gewissen Hochpunkt dann wieder
abzukehren?

Vom Widerstand zurückge-
worfen
∪—∪—∪—∪—∪
Erh. Strom
er fällt je nach
d. Intensität d.
aufgehaltenen
Strömung
n. W. stand
z. W stand

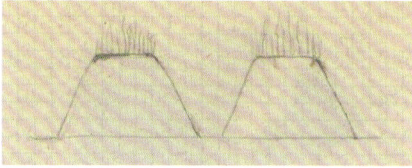
VII.64.

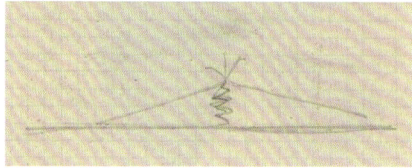
VII.65.

VII.66.

VII.67.

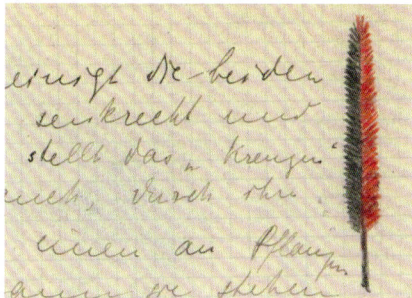
VII.68.

(VII.64) is that = (VII.65)

(VII.66) Should the *wave* motion of the extraverted rays and the *winding* motion of the introverted rays be united here? (later: longitudinal and transverse waves)

(VII.67; VII.68) The feather unites the two directions, vertical and horizontal. It represents "crossing." Equally, in its structure reminding one of plants, it can stand for the union of the two worlds, flora and fauna. It is also significant that flying animals have this thing, so that in this way the union of the two worlds and "flying" (overcoming gravity) belong together.—I wrote in the other notebook, "is the union of the two worlds even creative?"[59] Not for flora and fauna but perhaps nurturing—therefore maternal, so that generativity must be sought elsewhere. In this connection, "sneezing" comes to mind (VII.69)—tension, explosion—The generative principle must have to do with that.[60]

VII.69.

---

59 Paraphrased. The original question in "Night Voices" reads: "But is the union of two worlds creative? Is it even possible?" (chapter introduction, 324).

60 In "Night Voices," discussing sneezing, the author adds: "The word 'repulsion' occurs to me. Also ejaculation."

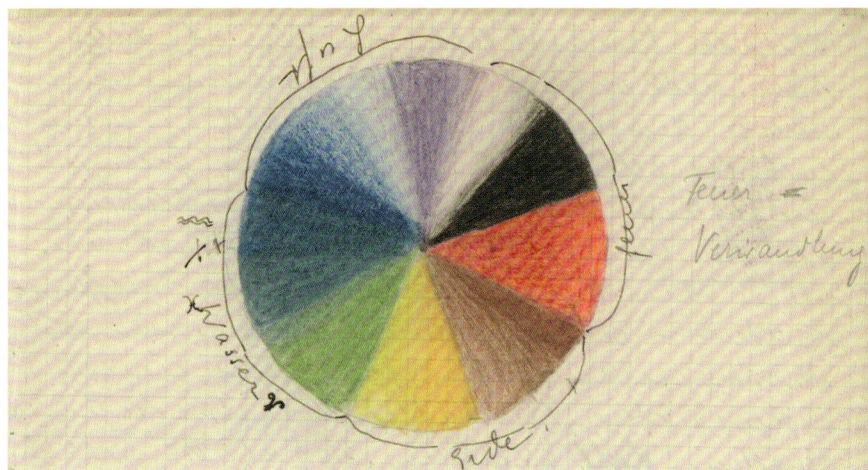

Fire = transformation (VII.70)

The color wheel[61] begins either with x or with xx. Red-brown (x) was the first one that came to me visually; then violet—and in such a way that red-brown had to be at the bottom right, and violet at the top center. Between them, red, black—all the other colors arranged themselves according to feeling, in the above arrangement. Starting on the left with blue-green—corresponding to water or the primal element, the darker blue-green to the sign (VII.71), the lighter to (VII.72)—from this comes green—i.e., growth, hope for the future, the sign (VII.73)—and after that comes yellow, as if little by little all the blue had faded out (sucked out, or radiated?) and only yellow were left. But at the same time, yellow is something absolutely different from the blue-green sequence (i.e., as blue-green already contains yellow—the sun). It is as if it introduced new possibilities. It has something of the essence of the sun—in any case, an essentially different quality than green. Above all, light and heat. Has it completely absorbed the blue-green water quality? Now something new emerges—red-brown. *Emergence of solid matter*: Red—color of conflagration—transformation. And with that, the greatest physicality—fullest life—red-brown is the color of the earth—connected through yellow (the sun) with green (water), or perhaps separated from it (differentiated). Into the light quality of yellow, red is added—life—movement; and in this way all earthly life emerges. Everything that is biological or in any way earthly—

Then red—the color of love—passion—The physical and earth-bound is inundated by the burning red—It is as if the *heavy, earthly*, physical were more and more displaced by the *fiery, blazing*, and much less physical. For the human, in addition

VII.71.

VII.72.   VII.73.

---

61 Emma Jung also drew this color wheel in pencil on a slip of paper, which she inserted loose inside the back cover of the "Night Voices" notebook. Here, in System I, she treats it as an inspiration for scientific and symbolic reflections. At the end of System II, the identical drawing occurs without textual commentary (359).

to purely biological drives and instincts, a new thing arrives here: love—but still in an elementary form—that has an all-consuming effect—which is why *black*—death—directly follows.[62] For this red cannot last long, and life's highest intensity must change immediately into the blackest night of death—

Yet night also gradually relents, and black changes into grey—then this is also gone—entirely white—but only for a brief moment, which can scarcely be grasped—then comes a very delicate, barely visible pink—a residue of the glowing red that outlasted the blackness of death and now emerges from night, purified. Now here, once again, a new element is added: *blue*, that is, *air*. Together with pink, it creates violet. Air is also the spiritual. Through "death" or purification, the earthly has become the spiritual, which continues to become more and more pure—red disappears entirely—only blue remains, which constantly deepens. Everything earthly has now vanished—so the "spiritual" becomes the divine (religious-mystical). Nothing physical is left, but everything is dissolved into air—spirit. Gradually, however, there is a growing density—spirit condenses and finally transforms again into water, from which we began.

Thus, the physical world arises again from the divine spirit—and in fact, the god creates it from himself—while the world and its life arise from the fact that (always a new element is added to it) the elements have a reciprocal effect—the divine is there, where an element is purest and everything else has evaporated. Aquarius represents the point where the divine has become dense enough to fall again upon the earth as water—for which reason (VII.74), too, is an "air" sign—only (VII.75) is watery—god engenders from himself—Worldly procreation arises from two different principles that together create a new life.

VII.74.

VII.75.

I'm greatly concerned with how yellow winds up like this at the bottom, between green and brown, since yellow is the color of the sun and has little to do with water and earth.[63] Only the body *reflects*. With yellow, I always tend to think of Taurus, which is also associated with the sun.—In green (combining *yellow* and blue) and in blue, indeed, there is probably the primal element that arose from the condensation of the divine—but in green, too, are the first possibilities, beginnings, promises, perhaps an explosive breaking out of an Individual New Thing.—That is present also in (VII.76), which well represents this green quality. There the primary role is taken by what is above; the base actually comes up short. For the (VII.77) individual, the intellect stands in the foreground, which also means the nonphysical: thoughts, plans, concepts, hopes. But nothing to do

VII.76.   VII.77.

---

62 Beside this sentence, faintly penciled in the margin of the page: "Sch … er [*illegible name*] acute oxidation process." Reference unclear. The author appears to be exploring an amplification for this symbolic sequence in her color wheel, by comparing it to a chemical or, by extension, a psychological phenomenon.

63 In writing about her color wheel, the author repeatedly ponders the paradoxical relationship of yellow (light) to its adjacent colors, representing earth and water. The same question is restated a few paragraphs below (343). When she wrote System II, however, she had apparently resolved her concern about this relationship.

with genuine physicality is fully realized here. For that one probably needs to add Taurus, which, as a bull, of course, is a primal image of physicality. Thus, in order for the earth to emerge, with life upon it, something else must have emerged or come into being first, other than the divine water, which only possesses and nourishes possibilities and germinal beginnings. I would like to call the new thing—the yellow—light and heat—so something quite unrelated to everything watery and airy, i.e., that stems from another source. Light comes from neither air (light and heat, see *power*—water—*matter*) nor water; rather it is genuinely *transcendent*, for it comes from another world, the *sun*.

Water and air belong to our world—they are both physical in a certain sense, and both are actually just different states of the same "divine." But from water and air alone nothing new arises; they only alternate in the eternal cycle. For the new to arise, light and heat are needed. Light—heat—yellow and red are the colors of the sun and the earth. Light and heat expand outward in the form of waves (thus in the form of extraversion, the pleroma). But water and air? What other laws of motion do they have? Perhaps the spiral motion or introversion—What confusion—I'm lost. (Later: the laws of *matter*, not of power.)

Is there even an essential difference, or not?

Can one say that all elements are different states of one and the same thing? Fire a state of earth—earth a state of water, water a state of air, and air a state of fire? (In any case, a state of *matter*?)[64]

And why could it not be so, actually—Then there would be no essential difference at all; it would all be one.

An example of the way a solid transforms into something nonphysical would be, e.g., radium or anything radioactive.

But then why the "enmity" between the elements—water and fire, or earth and water? Elements that consume each other? But perhaps this shows precisely the original sameness, that identical things strive together, wanting to change again into one—is that affinity? Perhaps it's like that for human beings, too—enmity and friendship arise because entities that are the same stream together and merge with each other?

Usually what results from this is a new, third thing. This would also explain *regression* in the face of a new achievement, actually it is a dissolution of an existing state, or a breakthrough, a mutual concession; and, depending on the point at which the two entities meet, as they strive for dissolution or depletion, what emerges is something different, or nothing at all.

---

64 In this passage, and in the mention of radioactivity that follows, the author may be referring indirectly to Einstein's theory of the equivalence of matter and energy. In System II (353), she again refers implicitly to his theory, which seems to have helped her conceptualize the relationship of the material with the immaterial.

Resistance must also play a role here somewhere. If I throw water into fire or vice versa, either the fire is doused or the water is consumed by the flame. In either case, nothing comes into being, i.e., water becomes smoke—thus, air—and fire becomes ash, thus a body—They assume a different state, but no life is generated (but perhaps a sublimation in the transformation). When, for example, vaporized water encounters resistance, it works as a *force*—in this way, *power* is generated. Does this then explain Sexual Resistance, since without resistance, no new, living thing is generated? (*No power.*)

Can power be conceived of in general without resistance? In any case, it can only act as such against a resistance—Aren't power and matter even different by nature?

Power also arises from the demarcation of space—only through its limitation does resistance arise. Doesn't it also require power to demarcate space?

(And then, what about time and light? Are they also one in the end?)

Light is also differentiating—one of the first separations[65] was that between bright and dark—light and darkness—day and night! Maybe because light is a *force*. But perhaps light only works to differentiate one thing from another. For example, we can distinguish things with light. But we don't sense ourselves because we see ourselves, and we distinguish ourselves from space through matter. Light leaves no traces perceptible to the senses (or only not tangible? sight is also a sense)—But it helps make things perceptible to the senses. Again, this would be the same reason why (yellow) light is located between *earth* (solid) and water—it serves to differentiate.—But is that true only for our eyes, or is there something in light, as such, that really creates differentiation? (E.g., like the polarity in electrical bodies?) As is true, for example, with heat—which sucks water out of the earth—thereby separating air and earth?

Light as "that which differentiates"—to be taken figuratively, as well—light must have an effect on matter? (Does Virgo belong here? After *fiery* Leo, the *light* phase of Virgo.) But where does matter come from?[66] Was it also once light? Or was light once matter?—But then, where did that come from? For heaven's sake?

Half a year later:

In the end, could light be that from which physicality as such emerged, not only because it illumines bodies, but because something in the *rays* actually enables the demarcation of space and the formation of matter?

See the first drawing,[67] where the body actually emerges out of rays—although the Something on which the rays fall remains unexplained. It would be condensed divinity—matter.

---

65 In the biblical account of creation: "And God separated the light from the darkness" (Genesis 1:4).

66 The author's search for the origin of matter (*der Stoff*) and its relationship with the immaterial—viewed variously as movement, light, power, energy—occupies her repeatedly. See also System II, 353f.

67 A reference to the first "egg" drawing, chapter introduction, 317, 330; see also System II, 349.

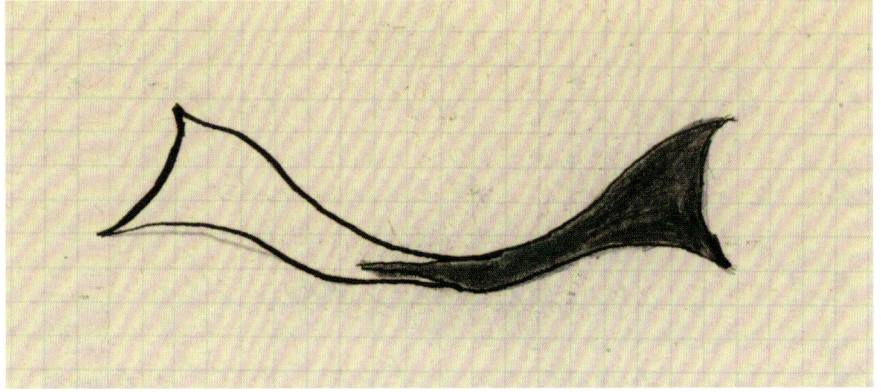

Horns.

For the comfortable feeling-tone, like a child's toward sexuality. An inescapable law of nature must be found here. Thought: *Death is swallowed up in victory.*[68] (VII.78; VII.79)

---

68 Biblical quotation: 1 Corinthians 15:54. Several pages follow in the black notebook, containing a variety of drawings, three of which are reproduced below: two flower-like versions of the color wheel (for example, see viii, figure XX) and a linear sequence of colors that perhaps anticipates the reduced color wheel in the final painting. Other drawings are either unrelated to the text or are printed elsewhere. Unrelated drawings include geometric angles and diagrams, progressive zigzags, the Greek letter Phi, a cellular pattern in color, and a black-and-white sketch of the human eye. Printed elsewhere in this volume: color drafts of the Coral Tree (292), images of the "flying face" (276), parallel waves (353), and pencil sketches of the "drops" (349).

VII.80.

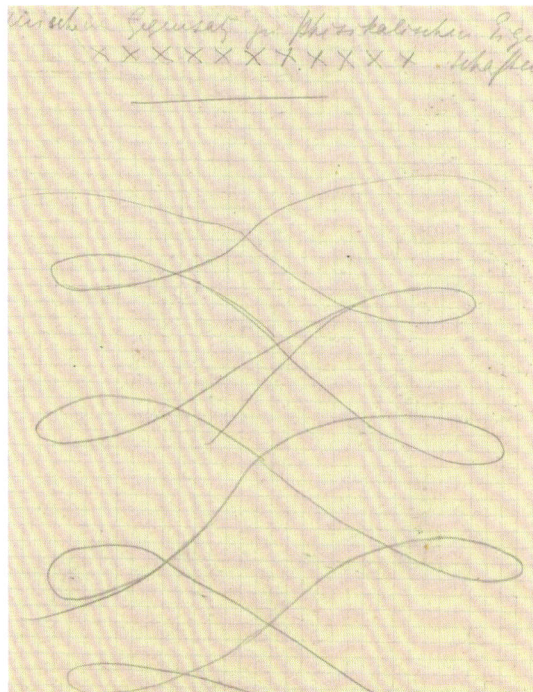
VII.82.

VII.81.

(VII.80) *Color* seems to represent inner qualities—those that are differentiated by light are brought into prominence, in contrast to the others, or principles of motion.

(VII.81) Chemical as opposed to physical properties

(VII.82) *Association:* Two currents move toward each other and exercise an attraction upon each other. But the living force is stronger than the attraction, so that the currents go on until the living force is exhausted; then they are subject again to the attraction. That is, they are each pulled toward the other, as well as by the earth; therefore the *advancing line*

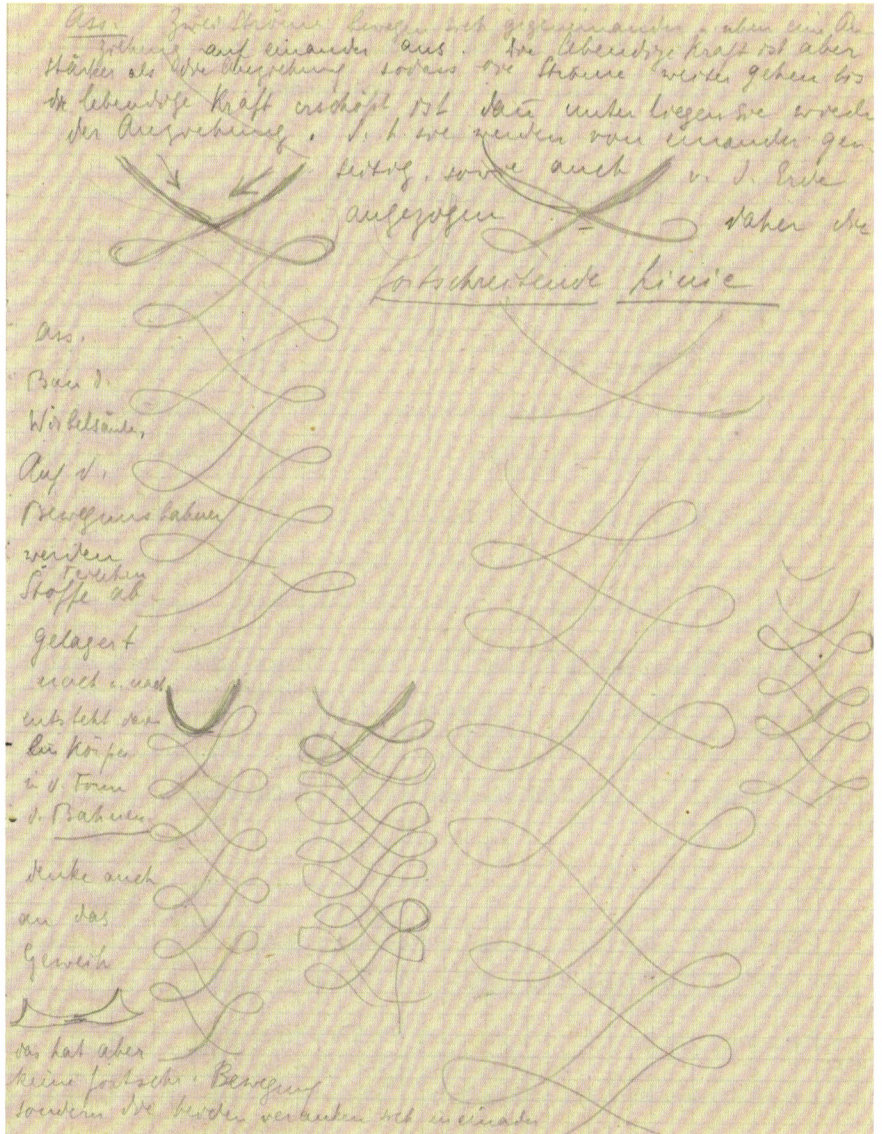

VII.83.

VII.84.

(VII.83) Association: Construction of the spine. In the pathways of movement, bits of matter (particles) are deposited; out of this, a body gradually develops in the form of the pathways. Think also of the horns. (VII.84)—only they have no progressive movement, rather both are anchored in each other.

Everything that comes into existence would be Solidified Movement,[69] deposited particles that retain the form of the pathways—as the flesh in human beings arranges itself around the skeleton! Or as, in the embryo, the pathways are already

---

69 See "Night Voices," chapter introduction, 326.

indicated and just become more and more pronounced. Every different pathway would correspond to a different part of the organism—in a sense, different types of vibrations, which act differently—like light, heat, sound, etc. Perhaps the earth is a sphere because it always moves in a circle! Is that consistent with other bodies, e.g., comets?

On its way, the earth would absorb solar material,[70] contained in the rays that it passes through, which would be deposited on the earth. (Plants need *light* for growth. Only up to a certain stage, growth without light is possible.) So the earth would have grown little by little, like an avalanche. Perhaps, as it traveled, it absorbed materials from various stars that were already there; for material is also always deposited in the fixed pathways. Once the density is great enough, it consolidates into a whole; and the greater the mass, the greater is the attraction on other particles. In the drawing of the *swarm*,[71] [this is] the moment when a nucleus is formed through attraction, out of which various orbits gradually organize themselves.

One can also *imagine a swarm* as the beginning of the world, which however *presupposes* an enclosed *space*, because otherwise the tension is not attained. Then space would not be a category of our thinking, but an *a priori*.[72]

A sort of atmosphere of solar matter would have to be deposited all around the sun—*emanations*, which would be absorbed by the earth and other planets. The planets nearest the sun would be most similar to the sun; the most distant would only be composed of the materials with the greatest radius of action.

Important points of assimilation [would be] places where various orbits intersect.—Every other world system would then occupy a unique space.

(VII.85) Symbol of the infinite. (Pleroma)[73] Two parallels intersect in the infinite: *Being*. The condition for this: parallel directional movement. Motion back and forth/the same orbit—no distinctions—

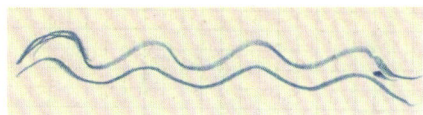   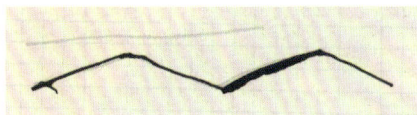

VII.85.   VII.86.

---

70 This concept, the growth of the earth through contact with interstellar material, may have been under discussion between Carl and Emma Jung at the time of writing (chapter introduction, 329 and note).

71 See above, 330.

72 "category of our thinking … *a priori*": Epistemological concepts, developed by Immanuel Kant in his *Critique of Pure Reason* (*Kritik der reinen Vernunft*, 1781). Kant was a German philosopher highly respected by C. G. Jung. Six of his major works are presently found in the Jung family library. (Curiously, *Kritik der reinen Vernunft* is not among them.)

73 This drawing of the Aquarius sign, in blue, reappears in System II (353) and in the final painting (361). In the present passage and later, the author no longer identifies it with Aquarius but with the unbounded Pleroma.

back = forth.

Special consistency of matter—so-called latent matter—suspended matter. Corresponding to energy of motion and potential energy, one could speak here of matter that is latent in motion—living matter, from dead matter/material.

Through an extraordinarily fine suspension of matter, only motion remains present, as it were—*very fast*

(VII.86) The increasing and decreasing rhythm = rhythm of intensity.[74]

Perhaps alternating intensity, between greater materiality and greater motion.

VII.87, VII.88 These drawings, which follow the pages of System I, contain elements of the final painting, Figure 7.13.

---

74 The diagram representing "the increasing and decreasing rhythm of intensity" reappears in System II (354). There a second drawing recalls the author's earlier diagram of volcanoes. In "Night Voices," the drawing of two volcanoes is related to the author's personal experience of rising and falling anxiety (chapter introduction, 326f.). Here, in System I, the drawing resembles drawing VII.19 (327) in "Night Voices," but the author's personal associations are omitted.

[System II] [75]

By *combining only with itself*, the One, *undivided* All or Nothing has reached a state of highest saturation, thereby creating a tension that leads to the expulsion or detachment of a piece. With this Divided One there is also now simultaneously a Second—which causes further division: thus, *with the Two, the Many*. The second is the yellow = light or heat.[76] This produces differentiation. But the yellow cannot come from outside, since there is nothing there; it must therefore be produced from within. Since the only, i.e., the most distinct quality of the divided drop is the motion created by the tension, further differentiation must be caused by this.—Thus the yellow would differ from the blue in the way it moves.

(VII.89) *Drops*: By being contained within itself, the "blue" has become so pure and blue, so *dense*, *intense*, that a tension arises and a piece becomes detached. It is separated by the yellow into smaller, individual units, which tend to repeat the same process.[77]

In addition to the tendency to taper off to infinity, there is also the tendency to pass from a more dense to a less dense state, which means that the units that are formed strive to move away from each other: *Radiation*. (VII.90)

VII.89.

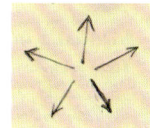

VII.90.

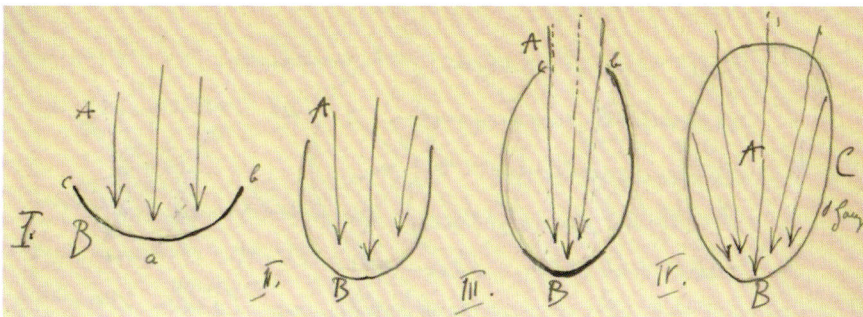

VII.91.

Movement of sucking in, absorbing, contracting (VII.91)

That which moves from above to below collides with something moving in another direction, which presents resistance to its continued movement. The direction of both currents is changed by the collision. On the one hand, the horizontally flowing current, the resistance, yields (side a), which causes, on the other hand, an approximation (sides b c). Through this continued yielding and approximating,

---

75   Emma Jung's second formulation of the System was written in 1918–1919. In the present edition, this untitled text is called System II.

76   This passage signals the author's resolution of her earlier concern about the relationship of yellow (light) with the adjacent colors of blue (water) and red-brown (earth). (System I, 341 and note.)

77   The following statement is crossed out by the author: "The motion does not remain constant, but tends to become slower."

the individual currents, which were formerly parallel, are guided together more and more toward a single point. Through this reciprocity, B encloses A more and more, while c and b approach each other and finally meet. A is fully enclosed in B.

The nature of the collision's impact suggests that the two currents had not only different directions but also different velocities and different strengths; and indeed that B was far less strong than A.

The nature of C, the product of this process, depends on the angle at which the two currents intersect and the ratio of the velocities.

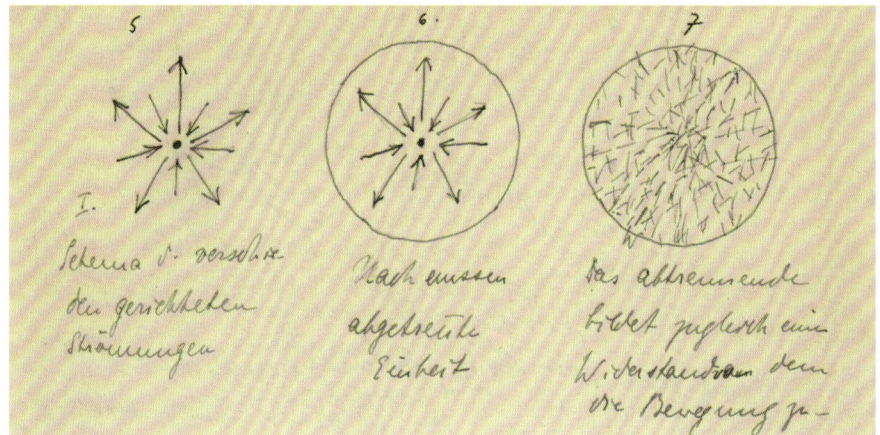

VII.92.

Diagram of the variously directed currents

Unit separated toward the outside

That which separates forms a resistance, which throws the movement back.

This creates a wild confusion of individual particles, *chaos, together with form. Movement is overpowered by form.* (Pleasure and pain are experienced together. The enclosed currents are perceived psychologically as anxiety.)

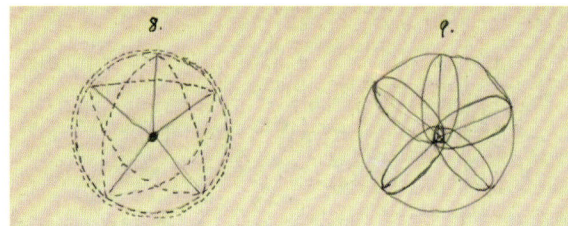
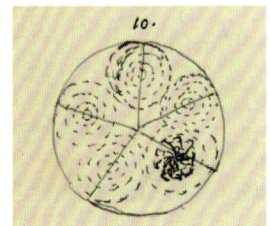

VII.93.   VII.94.

In time, certain primary orbits develop around the original directional axes. As a result of delimitation, regularity emerges. (VII.93)

Modification of the orbits (through reciprocal influence?). (VII.94)

Following the collision of two particles that remain stuck together, and whose movement is stopped or slowed by this, a new center of activity emerges. This central point exerts a force of attraction upon the surrounding particles, which no longer remain concentric and parallel, but rather bend at one end toward the center, so that they are perpendicular, radiating toward it. The circular motion continues.

The quintile structure probably indicates that five systems (or another number) are available and undergo development in this construction. (Five senses, fingers, limbs and head; nervous system, respiration, circulation, digestion, and sexual system.)

Representatives of each of the above-named developmental stages should be found in nature.

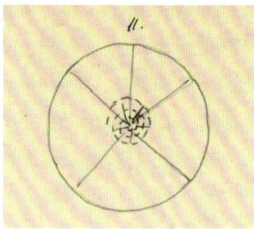

VII.95.

The converging currents arrange their particles in a spiral. Due to the concentration at the center, an impossible state is created, and as a result the spiral moves *into the depths*. A third dimension emerges—physicality. (VII.95)

Through the cooperation of these two kinds of movement, a more complicated organism. (VII.96)

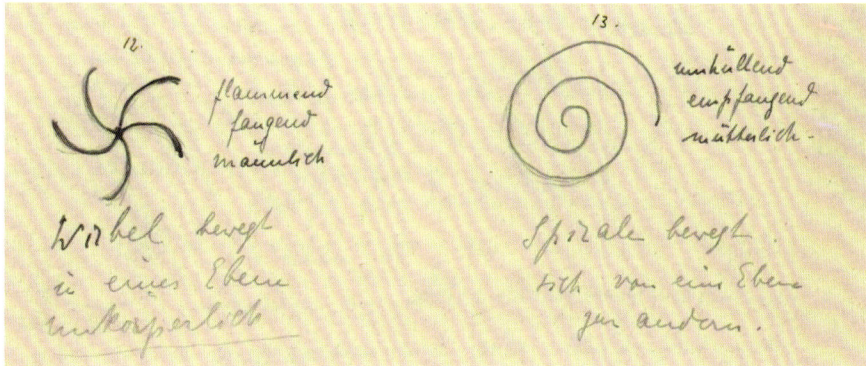

VII.96.

Vortex moves on a plane *nonphysical*	flaming grasping masculine	Spiral moves from one plane to the other	enveloping receiving maternal

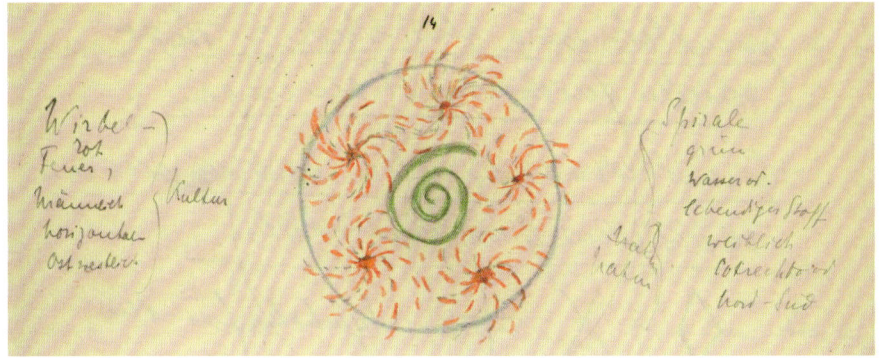

Vortex— red fire, masculine horizontal east-west	} culture	~~nature~~ nature	Spiral— green water or living matter feminine vertical or north-south

Vortices have developed from the diverging particles, a spiral from the converging ones. Thanks to their rapid motion, the vortices can reach out beyond their limit and bring in some of the external element (primal element, pleromatic matter). This is taken up by the spiral and carried further on its path, so that a physical body emerges. (The colors designate different qualities; here, for example, different velocities.) (VII.97)

The quality of the vortex is masculine; that of the spiral, feminine. Thus, a typical difference between the sexes is a different movement of libido.

Differently directed currents are the basic condition of all development. Different speeds, different rhythms, are the basic condition of all differentiation.

 Symbols for the *primal source of development* (VII.98).

VII.98.

(Cf. the four rivers of Paradise, the magical significance of the cardinal points for primitives.)

The astrological symbol of the fishes, at the same time the *vernal equinox*, also represents the primal source of (natural) evolution[78] of the two diversely directed currents. (VII.99)

But the same sign also points to another kind of development than the one described above (or rather, a failure). What emerges is not a system (egg); rather, due to overly great power differences in the currents, one is disrupted, divided into two, so that what comes out of the All above simply goes through and rejoins the All below. In the grand scheme of things, it seems that life occurs in such a transition, which is a sort of transformation. (VII.100)

VII.99.

VII.100.

---

78 *des (Natur)Werdens*: The original manuscript shows *(Natur)* written above the line, between the article and the noun.

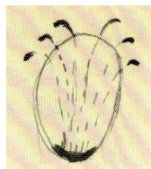
VII.101.

(VII.101) Another process is the one in which the particles gather together, perhaps because there is more substance than motion in them. The motion is minimal—not chaotic and circling, but back-and-forth. An increasing density and tension emerges, which finally makes room for itself by breaking out—in fact, in the *upward direction*.

(VII.102) The Aries sign opens above, thus, whereas (VII.103) is open on both sides. (VII.104), as a symbol of natural evolution, is like a bed for a river. (VII.105) = a transformer, where the original direction is not only changed but immediately reversed. In contrast to the natural direction (falling), it could mean the *cultural direction*, which in the symbol of *fire* also has the aspect of explosion, and is likewise, in a certain sense, characteristic of the direction opposite to nature. Furthermore, in fire, as in culture, there is the element of energy being liberated from matter (spiritualization), whereby (through sacrifice) the new direction is achieved.

VII.102.

VII.103.

VII.104.

VII.105.

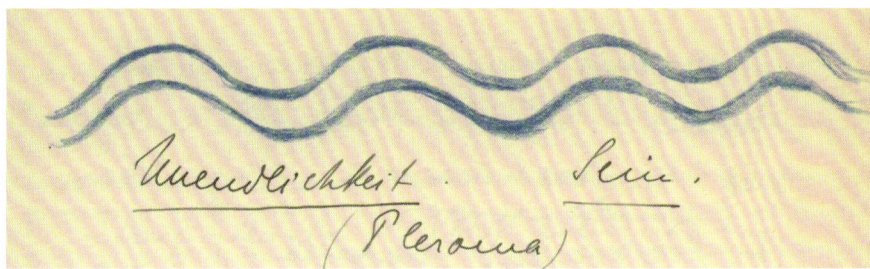

Infinity.

(Pleroma)

Being.

VII.106.

(VII.106) characterized by movements in a parallel direction, in contrast to movements in many directions, which are the condition of *evolution*. It is like a back-and-forth motion (oscillation) that constantly remains the same (between two points?). Neither beginning nor ending—or every point is identical and equivalent to every other.

Movement is not conceivable without something being moved.—In the pleroma it is united, meaning that moving, it is moved, and moved, it is moving = *Perpetuum mobile*.[79]

One may assume that *matter is quasi dissolved in motion* (latent), in the same way that energy may be latent in matter[80] (static and kinetic energy) (living matter?)

The motion must be tremendously fast, therefore the element of motion must be absolutely dominant; this is only possible with the greatest speed and the

---

79 Latin: perpetual motion.

80 Apparently another reference to Einstein's theory of the equivalence of energy and matter. (See above, System I, 329 and note.)

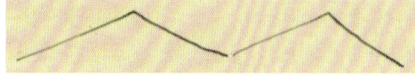

VII.107.

VII.108.

smallest mass. When the motion slows, the matter condenses. This is also when differentiation begins.

The motion has a certain rhythm (VII.107) i.e., increasing and decreasing intensity. Where it is most intense, the material factor/element is most latent (most suspended). Where it is least intense, the material element is densest. If it attains a state of excessive density (perhaps at two adjacent points) (VII.108), a kind of short-circuit may occur, and thereby a detachment and increasing materialization and slowing of the motion.

The saturation comes about when (through combustion) more and more new suspended particles achieve a parallel direction (i.e., a pleromatic character), and the element of motion dominates in relation to matter.

Therefore in the pleroma, so to speak, everything is motion. As this lessens, materialization increases. That is, motion gradually condenses, as it were, into matter, which finally absorbs it fully and is entirely dominant.

This state is like a second pleroma (*below*), or a pleroma of matter.

VII.109.

The two *pleromas* would correspond by and large to oscillations of intensity (VII.109), except that here the high and low points are really extreme, whereas within every individual the differences are relatively minor.

Liberation from this material state is then achieved when the latent elements of motion are once again freed from matter. This can primarily occur through processes of combustion.—Under certain conditions (the state of reciprocity?) the energy of motion is increased or set free (chemical affinity), which then results in an increasing dissolution of matter and transformation into motion.

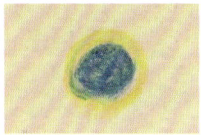

VII.110.

(VII.110) Immediately after falling away from the pleroma, the differentiation into two different elements or principles—yellow = another motion (much faster than blue)—can perhaps be explained thus: *yellow* would correspond to the element of motion, as *blue* would to that of matter.

Particles of both the faster-moving and the more material phase are caught up in the short-circuit.[81] They retain the character of their movement at the moment of detachment and arrange themselves accordingly.

Or one may assume that the whole pleroma consists in progressive movement, and in such a way that individual parallel currents are present, going in opposite directions.

If particles of various currents then come together and unite as a consequence of the short-circuit, they bring with them different *directional elements*.

---

81 *Kurzschluss*: In the manuscript, this word replaces *Explosion*, which is crossed out by the author.

CHAPTER VII

The non-parallel directions that are required for *evolution* would then be present. Thus we would have four primal elements/factors or principles (a four-fold current!): two factors of intensity (intensity and extensity), and two (or more) *directional factors*. (VII.III)

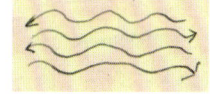

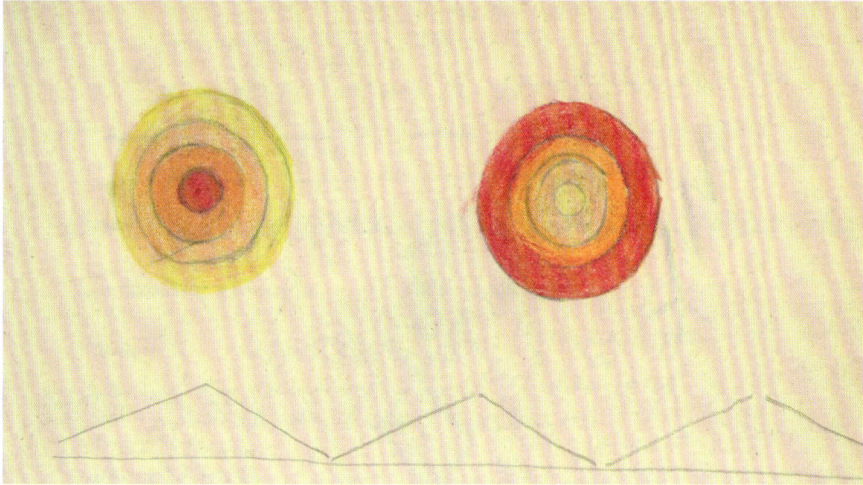

VII.112.

Diagram of movements in the pleroma. Rhythmic increase and decrease of intensity. (VII.112)

VII.113.

VII.114.

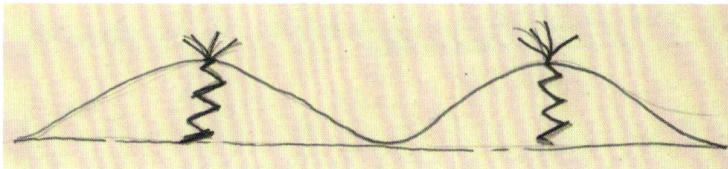

VII.115.

Irregular (syncopated?) rhythm of the explosion or the short-circuit, i.e., occurring between two parallel levels or currents. (VII.113; VII.114)

Combination of the two types of movement and rhythm. (VII.115)

Abtrennung v. Pleroma u. zunehmende Ver-
stofflichung.

Die Bewegung gleicht einem Fall. (Abfall i. Seele!)
2 stoffliche Kompo- nenten (grün u. braun)
nenten die losgelösten Pleroma tropfen die noch
vorwiegend aus Bewegung bestehen auf u. geleiten
die weiter unter zu- nehmende Verstoff-
lichung? (die eiag- schlossen Räume d. be-
schriebenen Flächen vergrössern sich!

möglicher weise sind grün u. braun Ströme die schon
älter sind u. dahen schon weiter verstoff-
licht sind als gelt u. blau. Möglicher-
weise Stellt es auch einfach die sofort
mit d. Abfall ein- setzende Spaltung in
die Gegensätze dar: blau u. gelt = Bewegung,
(auch himmlisch!) grün u. braun = Materie
(irdisch.)

Diese Spaltung die Gegensätze. tritt auch
in dem Auseinander u. gegen einander gehen
zu Tage, im Gegensatz i. Pleroma, wo d. Parallele
herrscht.

Befreiung vom Stoff. (Vergeistigung)

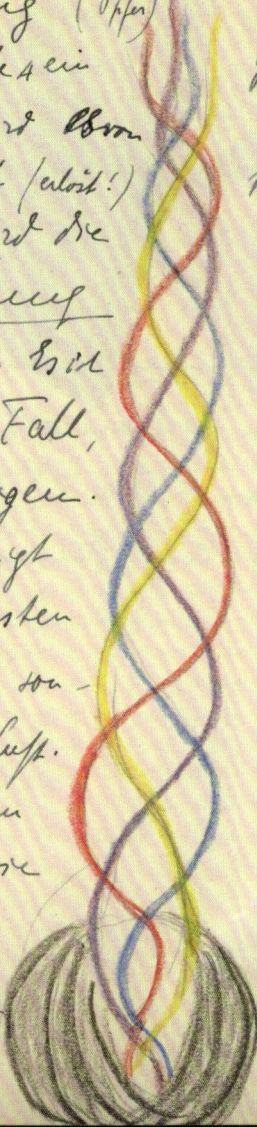

Durch Erhitzung (Opfer)
ks in d. Schale + ein
geschlossenen und aus
Stofflichen gelöst (erlöst!)
u. zugleich wird die
Gesamtrichtung
umgekehrt. Es ist
nicht mehr ein Fall,
sondern ein Steigen.
Was da aufsteigt
hat keinen festen
Körper mehr son-
dern ist wie Luft.
Es sind dieselben
4 Elemente wie
drüben, aber
durch den durch-
gemachten

Prozess der Entstofflichung
gereinigt; jedes stellt
ein Wesen in unge-
trübter Reinheit dar
Blau ist nicht mehr
grünlich - wässrig
rot nicht mehr bräun-
lich u. irdisch - das Gelbe,
Lichte ist lichter ge-
worden u. violett ent-
spricht dem Grünen
auf der andern Seite.
Dieses bezeichnet dort
das Leben u. hier
ebenfalls, nur das dem
aufsteigenden Prozess
angehörige - Jenes das
org Stoffliche, dieses das
geistige Leben. (Beide
sind im Farbenverbindung

(Fig 7.11) The movement resembles a fall (falling away of the soul!). Two material components (green and brown) take up the separated pleroma-drops, which still consist mainly of motion, and guide them further as materialization increases: *the enclosed spaces or described surfaces grow larger!*

Possibly green and brown are currents that are already older and therefore further materialized than yellow and blue. Possibly it also simply represents the splitting into opposites that begins immediately with the falling away: blue and yellow = movement (including heavenly!), green and brown = matter (earthly).

This splitting of the opposites can also be seen in the pattern of moving apart and back together, contrary to the pleroma, where the parallel reigns.

LIBERATION FROM MATTER. (SPIRITUALIZATION)

(Fig 7.12) By heating (sacrifice) of what is contained in Vessel A, it is freed (redeemed!) from materiality, and at the same time *the whole direction is reversed*. It is no longer a falling, but a rising. What rises up no longer has a solid body but is like air. Here are the same four elements as on the other side, but purified by the completed process of dematerialization; each one presents its essence in unclouded purity. Blue is no longer *greenish-watery*, red no longer *brownish-earthy*; yellow, light, has become *lighter*. Violet corresponds to green on the other side. There the color designates *life*; here the same, only belonging to the rising process—green for material life, violet for spiritual.

Both are a combination of colors: *green from yellow and blue*, the two pleromatic components that together compose material life. *Violet* from *red* and *blue*, i.e., from the combination of a material and a pleromatic element, thus, a union of the two worlds, below and above. Through *combustion* the elements are purified and brought back to the pleromatic state. The complex turns into single entities, the alloyed becomes pure.

This color wheel
follows the text of
System II without
commentary.

FIGURE 7.13. [Image of an emerging world]. Painting by Emma Jung, 1919. This untitled painting, here called "Image of an emerging world," was executed in gouache, probably in 1919, on a page in the marbled book. Several blank pages follow it there, suggesting that at one point the author intended to add comments. The painting unites many symbols in Emma Jung's cosmology, including a simplified color wheel, vortex and spiral, yellow-and-blue drops, and the blue waves indicating Aquarius or pleroma. The Pisces sign and egg symbol are suggested at the base of the left- and right-hand columns, respectively. As explained by the author, the columns signify "materialization" and "spiritualization."

Emma Jung's "Grail" Abstracts, 1940 and 1944

"Stories of the Grail"

THIS FIRST PART[1] gives a general overview of the Grail legends, their origin and their various versions, almost all of which were written at the turn of the thirteenth century. Two types can be distinguished: the search for the Grail, focusing on the experiences of the heroes Perceval or Galahad, and the history of the Grail and its guardians. Among the former are Chrétien de Troyes's *Conte del Graal* and Wolfram von Eschenbach's *Parzival*; among the latter are Robert de Boron's *Estoire du Saint Graal*, *Petit Saint Graal*, and a similar work attributed to Walter Map called *Grand Saint Graal*. Almost all of these versions point toward a preexisting story, which however cannot be verified. According to some reports, the story may have originated in the eighth century and been already well-known at that time.

In the form it has come down to us, the legend is part of the so-called Contes Bretons, the stories that formed around King Arthur and his Round Table, in which fairy tales and legends, especially of Celtic, but also of Eastern or ancient origin, were fused with tribal stories of ancient Britain and material from Christian legends. While the various versions are similar in many respects, they also differ, not only in their embellishment of the events that take place, but also in the fact that while some have a distinctly fairy tale character, others have a more religious-legendary quality. Interpretations also vary as to what the Grail actually is: an undefined vessel; a bowl containing the blood of Christ collected by Joseph of Arimathea; or (according to Wolfram von Eschenbach) a stone endowed with miraculous power. The word Grail has also undergone various interpretations. The most convincing is that it comes from the Latin word *gradale* = plate or recessed

---

1   Previously untranslated author's abstract, originally printed under the title "Frau Emma Jung: Die Graalserzählungen," in *Inhaltsangabe der Vorträge im Geschäftsjahr 1940/41* (Contents of lectures in the business year 1940/41), annual report of the Psychology Club Zurich, 15–20.

bowl. In some texts, it is associated with *gratus* = pleasant or pleasing, because of the gracious effects emanating from the Grail. Initially denoting something mysterious and sacred, the meaning of the word changed over time, until finally Grail simply meant the occasion or place of noisy revelry. Even the legend fell increasingly into oblivion and was only brought to light again in the Romantic era.

The Breton fairy tale of Peronik that is cited as an example of a popular form of the Perceval legend is the story of a poor boy called Peronik who, after many adventures, succeeds in obtaining the talismans, "*La lance qui tue et le bassin qui vivifie,*"[2] guarded by a magician in a castle that is difficult to reach.

The second lecture reviews the contents of the Conte del Graal according to Chrétien de Troyes and the versions that followed it. The story of Perceval's youth falls into the category of so-called simpleton tales, in which it is always the youngest or most stupid one who succeeds in accomplishing the great deed or attaining the difficult-to-get treasure. Being fatherless, Perceval grows up alone in a wild, lonely forest with his mother, who wants to protect him from the perils of knighthood. A chance encounter with knights prompts him to go out into the world to become a knight himself. Stricken with grief over his departure, his mother dies. After receiving some initial instruction in the art of arms and the knightly virtues from Gornemant de Goort, Perceval's further journey leads him to the besieged castle of Belrepeire, for whose chatelaine, the beautiful Blancheflur, he fights and prevails. As his reward, she pays him with her love. Soon, however, he sets forth again to search for his mother, and, following the directions of a fisherman he meets along the way, he arrives at the Grail Castle. He is led to the lord of the castle, who is ill and invites Perceval to sup with him.

After Perceval has been presented with a sword, and a sumptuous table has been ceremoniously set, a page enters the hall while the meal is underway, bearing a lance dripping blood; a maiden follows with the hallowed Grail set with precious stones; another enters bearing a silver platter. As the procession passes and then departs, Perceval watches without asking the meaning of it all. Once the meal is over, everyone retires. In the morning, the castle is deserted and Perceval has no choice but to leave through the open gate. Outside, he meets a maiden lamenting over a dead knight. From her, he now learns more about the castle and the ailing lord of the castle, who is called the Fisher King, and whom he could have redeemed if he had asked about the Grail. He also learns that he was to blame for the death of his mother, who died of grief over his departure. The girl turns out to be Perceval's cousin, who had been brought up in his mother's house. The boy now suddenly remembers his previously unknown name. Saddened by his failure and conscious of his guilt, Perceval continues his journey, resolved not to rest until he has once again found the now vanished castle and has asked the truth about the lance and the Grail.

---

2   French: The lance that kills and the bowl that brings to life.

After many wanderings, he comes to a hermit who similarly reproaches him for not having put the question to the Grail King, and for being responsible for the death of his mother. Then follows another long series of adventures, some of which are undertaken by Perceval and some by Gauvain, who is a sort of a double of Perceval. Gauvain's most notable act is the disenchantment of the so-called Castle of Marvels or Castle of Damsels. After countless battles and trials, in which fairy-like maidens play an important role, Perceval finally reaches the sought-after castle once more and asks the question, thereby redeeming the king and all of the enchanted Grail Kingdom.

The Grail Castle is interpreted as being in the realm of dreams, i.e. in the unconscious, and Perceval's visit there as a dream, namely an initiation dream, in which the hero is shown the treasures guarded by his ancestors (the Grail Kings), and in which, in the Grail Bearer, he also encounters the archetype of the anima.

Perceval is shown four things primarily: sword, lance, Grail, and platter (the latter only in one version) or table, that is, four archetypal objects that are universally recognized as such in both mythology and legend.

The *sword*, a masculine symbol, signifies strength, instrumental in overcoming hostile forces; as a tool to cut and separate, it figuratively signifies discernment, understanding and intellect.

The *lance*, too, is a masculine symbol, suited to taking aim and striking; understood psychologically, it can mean being aware of one's goal and striving to achieve it.

As a vessel that "contains," the *Grail* is a feminine, specifically a maternal symbol, because, precisely as the Grail vessel, it has both a nourishing and a life-giving power. As the bowl that received the blood of Christ, the Grail is seen as a mystical vessel, often even as the cup of the Last Supper.

As mentioned above, for Wolfram von Eschenbach the Grail is not a vessel but a stone. Because the text states that the host which was brought from heaven was placed upon it, it has also been thought of as an altar stone or portable altar. This idea leads to the fourth object, *the table*, which likewise has a feminine-maternal significance. The Grail table is also important because it symbolizes the table at which Christ took the Last Supper with His disciples.

The quaternity often appears as an expression of becoming conscious. Conceiving of the world in the image of a quaternity seems to have been particularly fitting, perhaps arising from the original orientation toward the four cardinal points.

Becoming conscious, understanding the world, and culture all go hand in hand, and therefore lend themselves to being expressed through symbols of a fourfold nature. That Perceval's story is concerned with a process of becoming conscious emerges clearly as the story unfolds. At first he is depicted as a foolish youth. Impulsively, unconsciously, he goes out into the world; he arrives at the Grail Castle without any conscious reflection; and only after he is expelled from there does he awaken, know his name, and become aware of his guilt and his quest. All of this occurs because of a conversation he has with a girl to whom he is related, whom he meets after leaving the Grail Castle and who is interpreted as the anima.

His *guilt* is that he caused the death of his mother and failed to ask the question about the Grail that would have redeemed the ailing king and the wasted land. His *task* is to make up for his mistakes and bring about the king's healing.

The king's affliction is explained differently in the various versions. Either it is mere old age, or punishment for disobeying the law of the Grail; or it is the consequence of a treacherous attack on the Grail king or his brother by an evil enemy. In this instance, redemption is brought about when revenge for the past wrongdoing is taken upon its perpetrator. Another explanation, especially for the wasted state of the land, can be found in the so-called "Elucidation," a prehistory of Perceval, where it is said that there were once fairy maidens in the Land of Logres who refreshed tired wanderers with food and drink, but who disappeared after a certain King Amangons ravished them. Along with them, the castle of the Fisher King, who was learned in magic, also disappeared, and the land became barren. Arthur's knights took it upon themselves to search for the castle and protect the maidens. Perceval found them and was thereby able to redeem the land from the spell under which it had been cast.

Thus, it is an "offence against the feminine" that is behind the country being laid to waste, just as it is the guilt Perceval bears for his mother's death that is behind his initial forfeit of the Grail. The theme of an offence against the world of the mother or the fairy world, i.e. against nature, is also connected with becoming conscious; for, from the standpoint of the unconscious, becoming conscious appears to be some kind of offence. If, however, the realm of the Grail is interpreted here as the unconscious itself, and it is ailing—an ailment that is cured by the hero asking a certain question and thereby gaining knowledge in some way—one may conclude that there is a readiness on the part of the unconscious to communicate its contents to consciousness. One could then see the impetus for illness as a failure on the part of consciousness to heed contents that are ripe for integration. In this sense, Perceval would be an antitype to Adam, a redeemer who expiates the old offence through some new achievement.

A further related psychological aspect is the masculine approach toward the feminine, particularly a man's attitude toward his own feminine side. Gauvain's redemption of the Castle of Marvels or Castle of Damsels fits in here, a clear parallel to Perceval's redemption of the realm of the Grail. Even if it seems that there was little reason to emphasize the "offence against the feminine" at a time when women were being venerated, it must be remembered that subsequently, witch hunts became the order of the day, that the Reformation ousted women, i.e. the Mother of God, from the Church, and that with the Renaissance, the age of science and technology dawned, an age that concerned itself not with the veneration of nature, but rather with having dominion over it, indeed with exploiting and raping it. As life becomes more and more mechanized, there is, in equal measure, a loss of soul. If, then, in our story, the offence against the feminine is described as having such serious consequences, it made good sense with a view to future developments.

When the Grail King dies shortly after his healing, as he does in most versions, and Perceval takes his place, this apparently means that what is old, which has actually already outlived itself, must continue to lead an illusory existence until what is new has reached the point where it can take the place of the old. The developmental process of this new person is depicted in the various adventures and battles of the Grail hero. The latter, after becoming conscious of his own self and his guilt, finds helpers and advisors in the anima and the wise old man (the hermit). As a final task, he must do battle with an opponent who is his equal—psychologically speaking, with the shadow. Only after this confrontation does he reach his goal.

The search for the Grail can thus be viewed as a human developmental process, as a process of becoming conscious, and as a path of individuation. The first stage on this path is Perceval's experience at the Grail Castle, perceived as a dream or vision, that directs the hero toward his future goal. Achievement of the latter becomes his life task, which consists of connecting this world with the world beyond, that is, in a union of the unconscious with consciousness and in the integration of the personality, expressed through the fourfold symbol.

"Le Roman de l'estoire dou Graal by Robert de Boron"

The Grail legend by Robert de Boron[3] was written around the same time as Chrétien de Troyes wrote his poem on Perceval, discussed in an earlier lecture. It is made up of three parts: "Joseph of Arimathea," "Merlin," and "Perceval." Part One tells how, at the descent from the Cross, Joseph of Arimathea collected the blood of Christ in a vessel, and how, during his subsequent forty years of imprisonment, he was kept alive by this very vessel that Christ conferred upon him. It forms a sign or symbol of Christ's death; and, corresponding to the Holy Trinity, it is to be entrusted to three successive guardians. Christ tells Joseph that there will come a time when tables will be erected upon which his body will be sacrificed, and he imparts to him secret words to be passed on from one guardian of the Grail to the next. He further explains that the table signifies the Cross upon which he died, and the sacrificial vessels the tomb in which he was laid.

After being liberated by Vespasian, Joseph and some followers set out to preach Christianity. After a time, they encounter difficulties, and Joseph learns through the voice of the Holy Spirit that these are caused by the sins of some of his companions.

---

3   Previously untranslated author's abstract, originally printed under the title "Frau Emma Jung: 'Le Roman de l'estoire dou Graal' des Robert de Boron" (The Romance of the story of the Grail by Robert de Boron), in *Inhaltsangabe der Vorträge im Geschäftsjahr 1944/1945* (Contents of lectures in the business year 1944/1945), annual report of the Psychology Club Zurich, 28–31.

He is told to set up a table similar to that of the Last Supper, to place the Cup upon it, and to take his place around the table with his followers. When they do, there is an empty space between Joseph and his brother-in-law, Brons, which proves to be a "*siège périlleux*";[4] for the person who sits there uninvited is swallowed up by the earth. The power of the vessel is proven by the fact that it fills with grace those who are good, while those who are evil, who are unable to approach the table, feel nothing and are sent away. It is the effect of this grace that gives the Grail its name, and from now on a service—the Grail Service—is held daily.

The story ends with Joseph giving the Grail to his brother-in-law Brons, who is to head west with it, to Britain, while Joseph stays behind.

The interpretation strives to show the archetypal foundation upon which the legend is based. Images that play a primary role in Robert de Boron's work, apart from the archetypal images of the vessel and the table, are the primordial ideas of "blood" as the seat of the soul and the substance of life, and the "grave" as the place of transformation and resurrection, as well as the place of non-being or emptiness, associated with the emergence of the Self. Related to this is the idea of a hidden treasure that awaits redemption along with its guardian, which in turn leads to the idea of a paradise lost and found, and the figure of the archaic human being awaiting redemption. This story, which provides valuable insight into the medieval psyche, seems important as an attempt to make Christian doctrine accessible to the laity.

The second part of the story takes us to Britain. Merlin, as the son of a devil and a pious girl, is gifted with supernatural powers, by virtue of which he becomes advisor to the British kings, Uther Pendragon and Arthur. At Merlin's instigation, the famous Round Table is inaugurated as the third of three tables, once again corresponding to the Holy Trinity: the table of the Last Supper, the table of the Grail, and King Arthur's Round Table. He also foretells the arrival of the Grail in Britain, and later the search for it and its discovery by Perceval.

As the son of a devil, Merlin appears to be meant as a kind of Antichrist; in his capacity as seer and sorcerer, on the other hand, he represents the figure of the ancient sage. Simultaneously, as a kind of natural being, he represents the pagan spirit of Britain waiting to be converted by Joseph and the Grail. In this context, Part Two explains how the configuration of the Grail legend can be understood as an expression of the process by which Christianity is assimilated.

The third part describes Perceval's experiences while searching for the Grail. With the exception of an epilogue and some significant deviations, his experiences are similar to those of Chrétien de Troyes's Perceval. One deviation, for example, is the "*siège périlleux*," which plays a significant role here but does not appear in de Troyes's version. On his first visit to Arthur's court, Perceval wants to sit on this seat, but because he is not yet worthy of occupying the seat, the stone splits. This

---

4   French: perilous seat.

marks the beginning of the search for the Grail. Once it is found and the Grail King—here Perceval's grandfather—is redeemed, the stone repairs itself with a loud roar. When the Knights of the Round Table hear that Perceval has become the Grail King, renouncing his knighthood, there is great sorrow and a decision is made to go on a crusade to the Continent, with disastrous consequences. When Arthur is betrayed by his nephew and deputy and forced to turn back, a bloody battle ensues in which all the Knights of the Round Table perish, and Arthur, seriously wounded, is brought to Avalon. Merlin also retires from the world and builds a dwelling in the forest, near the Grail Castle, where he will live and prophesy forever.

In this part of the story, the Grail that is being searched for corresponds to the hidden treasure that needs to be found, and whose condition of "not being found" is related to the state of enchantment over the land and the suffering of the Grail King. This state of needing redemption leads in turn to the idea of paradise lost. The hero's act of redemption is a twofold one: on the one hand, it is a matter of insight, i.e. of becoming aware, and on the other, of making amends.

The path that leads Perceval to the Grail is interpreted as the path of individuation, the goal of which is wholeness, including the integration of the shadow. This motif is taken up in the Epilogue which, with its tragic conclusion, leads to the problem of "evil" foreshadowed in the "*siège périlleux*," the seat of Judas. A solution does not come about, however; for, instead of making the Round Table complete by taking his place on the "*siège périlleux*," Perceval withdraws from the knighthood. Wholeness, then, has not been achieved. It would appear that this task could not be accomplished by the medieval mind. It remains unfinished, as seems indicated in the figure of Merlin, who unites the opposites within himself, living hidden outside the gates of the Grail Castle, and who is at the same time the embodiment of that original human being whose redemption, perhaps, our age is called to further.

Emma Maria Jung-Rauschenbach (1882–1955)

Dates in Her Life

1882	Born on 30 March in Schaffhausen, Switzerland, in the parental home, "zum Rosengarten," on the banks of the river Rhine.
Parents:	Johannes (known as Jean) Rauschenbach (1856–1905, Schaffhausen industrialist and factory owner) and Bertha Schenk (1856–1932, art sponsor and supporter of writers and musicians), married in 1881.
1883	7 July, birth of sister Berta Margaretha (called Marguerite).
1888–1893	Elementary school Schaffhausen.
1893–1898	Secondary school (Mädchenrealschule Schaffhausen). Father denies Gymnasium and further university studies. Emma becomes an avid reader and letter writer.
1894	Father goes blind, probably as a consequence of a syphilitic illness. The two sisters are now raised with the help of a governess, Anna Stokar von Neuforn.
1896	First encounter with twenty-one-year-old medical student Carl Jung, who pays a courtesy visit to Bertha Rauschenbach at the "Haus zum Rosengarten."
May 1898–April 1899	After finishing secondary school, spends a year in Paris with Madame Lavater, taking classes in French, Italian, English, history, literature, and piano. During summer vacation in 1898 travels to Normandy and the Channel Islands.
End of 1898	The Rauschenbach family moves into their newly built home, Villa Oelberg, on a small hill overlooking Schaffhausen.

1899   In summer, beginning of a regular correspondence with Carl Jung, who recommends various readings in psychological literature and philosophy.

1901   Secret engagement to Carl Jung.

1902   Assists her fiancé in the research of French and English literature for his doctoral dissertation *Zur Psychologie und Pathologie sogenannter Okkulter Phänomene* (On the psychology and pathology of so-called occult phenomena).

   1 May official announcement of engagement to Carl Jung.
   In autumn Carl Jung leaves for a study semester in Paris and London.

1903   14 February, wedding ball followed by a church wedding in Schaffhausen two days later. Honeymoon in Paris, London, and trip to Madeira, Gran Canaria, and Tenerife.

   26 April, the couple moves into their own apartment at Zollikerstrasse 198 in Zurich. Carl Jung returns to work at the Burghölzli clinic. Director Eugen Bleuler and his wife, Hedwig Bleuler-Waser, encourage principal physicians' wives to engage as volunteers in the clinic's work. Emma assists her husband in the new experimental researches on diagnostic association studies.

   7 November, sister Marguerite marries Ernst Homberger, director of Georg Fischer Company in Schaffhausen, into which the Rauschenbach factories are later incorporated in 1921.

1904   Carl Jung becomes deputy director at the Burghölzli, and the couple moves to the senior physician's apartment at the clinic, where their first daughter, Agathe Regina (Agi), is born on 26 December (married Niehus, †1998).

   The clinic doctors and their wives explore the new psychoanalytic method of dream interpretation, according to the theory of Sigmund Freud, by mutual dream analysis and observing each other's complexes.

1905   2 March, death of father Jean Rauschenbach. Bertha and the two daughters Emma and Marguerite become heirs to the two companies he had owned, Rauschenbach Machine Factory and the International Watch Company (IWC).

1906   8 February, daughter Anna Margarethe (Gret) is born (married Baumann, †1995)

1907   3–6 March, first personal encounter with Sigmund Freud, while accompanying her husband and Ludwig Binswanger, assistant physician at the Burghölzli, on a visit to Vienna.

1908   Carl Jung engages in a relationship with his former Burghölzli patient Sabina Spielrein, now a medical student at Zurich University.

18–21 September, second encounter with Sigmund Freud, on the occasion of his return visit to the Jungs at their Burghölzli apartment.

28 November, son Franz Carl is born (married Jung-Merker, †1996).

1909   25 May, move into the newly built home at Seestrasse in Küsnacht.

September 1909 to January 1910, first attempt at psychoanalysis with her husband, to address marital problems.

1910   8 March, stepping in for her husband, who is on an unanticipated journey to see a wealthy patient in the United States, begins a personal correspondence with Sigmund Freud, concerning organizational issues for the second Psychoanalytic Congress in Nürnberg, Germany, held on 30 and 31 March.

20 September, daughter Marianne (Nannel) is born (married Niehus, †1965).

September, first encounter of Carl Jung with Toni Anna Wolff (1888–1953), as a patient.

1911   Maria Johanna Moltzer (1874–1944), former nurse specializing on the psychological causes of physical problems in children, becomes an analyst in private practice and close collaborator of Carl Jung. Rumors of an extramarital relationship.

Emma encounters Albert Einstein, physicist and originator of the theory of relativity (1905/1915), who was the Jungs' dinner guest on several occasions.

Assists her husband in preparation of *Die Wandlungen und Symbole der Libido* (Transformations and Symbols of the Libido), published in two parts 1911/1912.

16–19 September, Sigmund Freud is guest at the Jungs' house in Küsnacht.

21–22 September, participation in the third Psychoanalytic Congress held in Weimar, Germany.

Fall, short period of analytical work with Leonard Seif.

Attempts to mediate between her husband and Sigmund Freud in their conflict over libido theory.

1912   Translates Ernest Jones's contribution, "Some Cases of Obsessional Neurosis," into German for the *Jahrbuch für psychoanalytische und psychopathologische Forschungen* (Yearbook for psychoanalytic and psychopathological research), part 2, 1912, IV/1.

1913   Participates as a layperson in the meetings of the local Zurich Psychoanalytic Association.

Prepares her first paper and presentation on psychological motifs in the Grimms' fairy tale "The Two Brothers."

Carl Jung resumes contact and subsequently engages in an intimate relationship with Toni Wolff, who becomes his close confidante in the experiment with his unconscious, leading to the creation of *The Red Book*.

1914   18 March, daughter Emma Helene (Lill) is born (married Hoerni, †2014).

Beginning of longer analytical work (training analysis) with Hans Schmid-Guisan.

Begins recordings of important dreams, fantasies, and images in the marbled book.

Joins the newly named Association for Analytical Psychology in Zurich, after the local group of psychologists and physicians officially splits off from the International Psychoanalytic Association.

28 July, outbreak of World War I, general mobilization of the Swiss army.

30 October and 13 November 1914, presents her first paper to the Association for Analytical Psychology ("The Tale of the Two Brothers").

1915   First elements to the "System," a personal cosmology, documented in an active imagination in a notebook named "Stimmen der Nacht" ("Night Voices").

1916   26 February, founding of the Psychology Club Zurich. Emma Jung is elected its first president, until resignation in 1919.

17 June, first lecture delivered to the Psychology Club, *"Über die Schuld"* (*"On Guilt"*).

1915–1918   Longer absences of Carl Jung from home due to military service during World War I: 5 January–10 March 1915 in Olten and

19 October–2 December 1916 in Herisau as commander of a medical company; 11 June–10 October 1917 and 2 November–14 December 1918 as commander of the British military internee camps in Château d'Oex and Mürren.

1919 Finalizes the image of an emerging world in the marbled book, synthesis of her "System" cosmology.

1920 27 September, first presentation on the symbolism of the Grail legend in the framework of Carl Jung's Seminar at Sennen Cove in Cornwall, UK.

New Year's holiday in Zuoz in the Engadine with fifteen Zurich Psychology Club members, including Toni Wolff, Emilii Medtner, Edith McCormick, Hans and Susi Trüb, the Jung children, and Emma Jung's sister and family.

1921 7 May, first women's evening at the Psychology Club, initiated by Emma Jung, Erika Schlegel, and Susi Trüb.

June, visit of Jungs, Emilii Medtner, and Toni Wolff, with the family of Hans and Susi Trüb, on the Laui-Alp in Toggenburg.

1922 August, joint summer vacation of the "sextet" (the Jungs, Trübs, Wolff, and Medtner), camping out and sailing together on an uninhabited island in the upper Lake of Zurich, followed by a September visit to the village of S'charl and hiking in the Lower Engadine.

7 November, reads "Reflections on a Passage by Meister Eckhart" to the Psychology Club women's circle.

17 November, Carl and Emma Jung temporarily withdraw from the Zurich Psychology Club (until 1924) after a conflict with the new president, Hans Trüb, over its orientation and guiding principles.

1923 Building of the initial Bollingen Tower retreat, where Emma Jung adorns the window frieze of her upstairs room with symbols of the "System."

1924–1926 Extensive travels by Carl Jung: mid-December 1924 to January 1925 to the Pueblo Indians of New Mexico, with Jaime de Angulo; the following year from October 1925 to end of February 1926 to the Elgonyis in eastern Africa (Bugishu-Expedition), with Helton Godwin (Peter) Baynes and George Beckwith.

1925–1929 Regular secretarial and editorial work for Carl Jung.

1926 Writes the ironic drama "Mystère de la Croisade" ("Mystery of the Crusade") in French *vers mêlés*.

1929   Emma and Carl Jung sell their active shares in the Rauschen-
        bach Machine Factory (by now part of Georg Fischer Corpora-
        tion) and IWC to Ernst Homberger, sister Marguerite's husband
        and the companies' managing director.

        Emma Jung's first documented patient, Elisabeth Heusler. As of
        1930, works regularly as an analyst with patients.

1931   21 November, Club lecture *Über das Wesen des Animus* ("On
        the Nature of Animus").

1932   16 March, death of mother Bertha Rauschenbach.

        21 April, death of Hans Schmid-Guisan.

        July, presentation of "On the Nature of Animus" in French to
        Le Gros Caillou Psychology Club in Paris.

        September, presentation of "On the Nature of Animus" in
        English to the Analytical Psychology Club in London.

1934   First publication under the title of "Ein Beitrag zum Problem
        des Animus" (On the problem of the animus), in *Wirklichkeit
        der Seele* by Carl Jung.

1937–1938 December 1937 to February 1938 Carl Jung is absent from home,
        traveling through India with Harold Fowler McCormick Jr.

1939   1 September, outbreak of World War II. Many of the Jungs'
        foreign acquaintances leave Zurich; only a few U.S. and British
        citizens remain in neutral Switzerland for the period of the
        war. Contacts across borders are interrupted, notably with Ger-
        man colleagues and friends, and correspondence to all Europe-
        an territories occupied by the Axis powers becomes subject to
        censorship of letters.

        Daughter Gret Baumann-Jung and children from Paris come
        to live at the Jungs' house at Seestrasse in Küsnacht; son-in-law
        Fritz Baumann joins them in summer 1940 after the occupation
        of France by Nazi Germany.

1940   2–29 March, four lectures on the subject of the Grail theme
        delivered to the Psychology Club Zurich: "Die Graalser-
        zählungen" (Stories of the Grail), including a psychological
        commentary.

        End of May, after occupation of Belgium, the Netherlands,
        France, and Norway by German forces, warnings of an immi-
        nent German invasion of Switzerland reach the Jung house-
        hold. Emma Jung and her daughters and daughter-in-law
        with eleven grandchildren retreat to safety near Saanen in

the Bernese Oberland for several months, behind the defense perimeter line defined by the Swiss army command. Carl Jung moves back and forth between Küsnacht, Saanen, and Bollingen.

1941   "On the Nature of Animus," translated by Cary Baynes, appears in the newly founded journal *Spring* of the Analytical Psychology Club of New York.

1942   Emma Jung celebrates her sixtieth birthday among immediate family members; her son, Franz, and three of her daughters' husbands are absent for military service.

1944   16 November–2 December, three lectures on Robert de Boron's Grail story delivered to the Psychology Club Zurich under the title "Die Geschichte vom Graal nach Robert de Boron" (The story of the Grail according to Robert de Boron).

1948–1955   Lecturer and training analyst at the newly founded C. G. Jung Institute Zurich. Vice president of the Curatorium, the Institute's governing body, as of 1950. Teaches courses in English on the Grail legend, dream interpretation, and the psychology of animus and anima; lectures in German "On the Problem of the Anima."

1952   October, honorary member of the Psychology Club Zurich.

1955   "Die Anima als Naturwesen," her second contribution on the subject, appears in Festschrift for the eightieth birthday of C. G. Jung (translated into English by Hildegard Nagel as "The Anima as an Elemental Being," 1957).

27 November, Emma Jung-Rauschenbach passes away after severe illness in her home at Seestrasse in Küsnacht.

1957   *Animus and Anima: Two Essays* is first published in book form. The German edition of *Animus und Anima* appears ten years later in 1967.

1960   *Die Gralslegende* is published posthumously, coauthored by Marie-Louise von Franz, assembling the main writings on the Grail theme left by Emma Jung at her death. (Translated into English by Andrea Dykes and published as *The Grail Legend* in 1970.)

BIBLIOGRAPHY

Works Published by Emma Jung

Jung, Emma. "Ein Beitrag zum Problem des Animus." In C. G. Jung et al., *Wirklichkeit der Seele: Anwendungen und Fortschritte der neueren Psychologie*. Mit Beiträgen von Hugo Rosenthal, Emma Jung, W. M. Kranefeldt. Zurich: Rascher, 1934, 296–354.

["On the Nature of the Animus." Translated by Cary F. Baynes. In *Animus and Anima: Two Essays*. New York: Spring, 1957, 1–43.]

———. "Die Anima als Naturwesen." In *Studien zur Analytischen Psychologie C. G. Jungs*, vol. 2. Festschrift zum 80. Geburtstag von C. G. Jung. Edited by the C. G. Jung Institut Zürich. Zurich: Rascher, 1955, 78–120.

["The Anima as an Elemental Being." Translated by Hildegard Nagel. In *Animus and Anima: Two Essays*. New York: Spring, 1957, 45–94.]

———. *Animus und Anima*. Zurich: Rascher, 1967.

[*Animus and Anima: Two Essays*. Translated by Cary F. Baynes ("On the Nature of the Animus") and by Hildegard Nagel ("The Anima as an Elemental Being"). New York: Spring, 1957.]

———. "Frau Emma Jung: Die Graalserzählungen, Autoreferat." In *Jahresbericht des Psychologischen Clubs Zürich 1940/1941*. Library of the Psychology Club Zurich, 1941, 15–21.

. "Frau Emma Jung: 'Le Roman de l'estoire dou Graal' des Robert de Boron, Autoreferat." In *Jahresbericht des Psychologischen Clubs Zürich 1944/1945*. Library of the Psychology Club Zurich, 1945, 28–31.

Jung, Emma, and Marie-Louise von Franz. *Die Graalslegende in psychologischer Sicht*. Zurich and Stuttgart: Rascher, 1960; Düsseldorf and Zurich: Walter, 1980/1991; Stuttgart: Patmos, 2001.

[*The Grail Legend*, 2nd ed. Translated by Andrea Dykes. Princeton: Princeton University Press, 1970.]

Works Cited by Emma Jung

Translations used in the English edition are listed, within square brackets, directly after the German titles to which they correspond.

Aeschylos. *Der gefesselte Prometheus*. Translated by Alexander von Gleichen-Russwurm. Jena: Dietrichs, 1912.

["Prometheus Bound." In *Aeschylus*, vol. 1. Translated by Herbert Weir Smyth. London: Heinemann; Cambridge, MA: Harvard University Press, 1963.]

Bin Gorion, Micha Josef, ed. *Von der Urzeit: Jüdische Sagen und Mythen*. Frankfurt a. M.: Rütten & Loening, 1913.

Deussen, Paul. *Die Geheimlehre des Veda: Ausgewählte Texte der Upanishad's*. Leipzig: Brockhaus, 1909.

[*Sixty Upanisads of the Veda*, vol. 2. Translated by V. M. Bedekar and G. B. Palsule. Delhi: Motilal Banarsidass Publishers, 1980.]

[Hume, Robert Ernest, ed. and trans. *The Thirteen Principal Upanishads*, 2nd ed., revised. Oxford: Oxford University Press, 1931.]

Eckhart, Meister. *Meister Eckhart*. Translated and edited by Franz Pfeiffer. Leipzig: Göschen, 1857.

Esser, Gerhard, ed. *Tertullians apologetische, dogmatische und montanistische Schriften*. Translated by Karl Adam Heinrich Kellner. Kempten: Kösel, 1915.

Frazer, James George. *The Dying God*. London: Macmillan, 1911.

———. *The Magic Art and the Evolution of Kings*. Vol. 1. London: Macmillan, 1911.

———. *Taboo and the Perils of the Soul*. London: Macmillan, 1911.

Goethe, Johann Wolfgang. *Faust, Erster Teil*. In Werke: Vollständige Ausgabe letzter Hand, vol. 12. Stuttgart: Cotta, 1829.

[*Faust, Part One*. Translated with an introduction by David Luke. Oxford: Oxford University Press, 1987.]

———. *Faust, Zweiter Teil*. In Werke: Vollständige Ausgabe letzter Hand, vol. 12. Stuttgart: Cotta, 1829.

[*Faust, Part Two*. Translated with an introduction by David Luke. Oxford: Oxford University Press, 1994.]

———. "Prometheus." In "Vermischte Gedichte," Werke: Vollständige Ausgabe letzter Hand, vol. 2. Stuttgart & Tübingen: Cotta, 1827.

———. *Wilhelm Meisters Lehrjahre*. In Werke: Vollständige Ausgabe letzter Hand, vol. 18. Stuttgart: Cotta, 1808.

[*Wilhelm Meister's Apprenticeship and Travels*, vol. 1, book 2. Translated by Thomas Carlyle. New York: Lovell, Corvell & Co., 1882.]

Harding, Mary Esther. *Women's Mysteries, Ancient and Modern*. London: Longmans, 1935.

Hesiod. "Theogonie," "Hauslehren, oder Werke und Tage." In *Hesiod's Werke verdeutscht im Versmasse der Urschrift*." 2nd ed. Translated by Eduard Eyth. Stuttgart: Krais & Hoffmann, 1865, 25–28, 67–69. [Reprinted in Langenscheidtsche Bibliothek sämtlicher griechischen und römischen Klassiker in neueren deutschen Muster-Übersetzungen, vol. 2: *Äsop, Hesiod, Quintus*. Berlin: Langenscheidt, 1855–85.]

["Works and Days" and "Theogony." In *The Homeric Hymns and Homerica*, edited, translated, and with introduction by Hugh G. Evelyn-White. Cambridge, MA: Harvard University Press; London: William Heinemann Ltd., 1964, 2–64, 78–154.]

Homer. *Iliade*. 2 vols. Edited by J. U. Faesi. Leipzig: Weidmann'sche Buchhandlung, 1853.

———. *Ilias*. Translated by Thassilo von Scheffer. Munich: Georg Müller, 1913.

———. *Odyssee*. 2 vols. Edited by J. U. Faesi. Leipzig: Weidmann'sche Buchhandlung, 1853.

———. *Odyssee*. Translated by Rudolf Alexander Schröder. Leipzig: Insel, 1911.

van der Hoop, Johan. "Die Bedeutung des Golem." Lecture delivered to the Psychology Club Zurich, 1 January 1917. Unpublished typescript, Library of the Psychology Club Zurich.

Hubert, Henri, and Marcel Mauss. *Mélanges d'histoire des religions*. Paris: Alcan, 1909.

Jensen, Peter. *Das Gilgamesch-Epos in der Weltliteratur*. Vol. 1. Strassburg: Trübner, 1906.

Jeremias, S. A. *Das alte Testament im Lichte des alten Orients: Handbuch zur biblisch-orientalischen Altertumskunde*. Leipzig: Hinrichs, 1906.

Jung, Carl Gustav. *Wandlungen und Symbole der Libido: Beiträge zur Entwicklungsgeschichte des Denkens*. Leipzig and Vienna: Franz Deuticke, 1912. Reprinted: *Wandlungen und Symbole der Libido*, foreword by Lutz Niehus. Munich: Deutscher Taschenbuch Verlag (DTV), 1991.

[*The Psychology of the Unconscious: A Study of the Transformations and Symbolisms of the Libido, A Contribution to the History of the Evolution of Thought*. Translated by Beatrice Hinkle. Supplementary vol. B of the *Collected Works of C. G. Jung*. Princeton: Princeton University Press, 1991. (Original publication 1916.)]

Keller, Gottfried. *Der grüne Heinrich*. Berlin: Hertz, 1889.

[*Green Henry*. Translated by A. M. Holt. London: Calder, 2010.]

von der Leyen, Friedrich, ed. "Das Märchen von den Zwei Brüdern." In *Kinder- und Hausmärchen gesammelt durch die Brüder Grimm*, vol. 1. Jena: Diederichs, 1912, 12–32.

Mannhardt, Wilhelm. *Antike Wald- und Feldkulte aus nordeuropäischer Überlieferung*. Vol. 2. Berlin: Borntraeger, 1877.

———. "Die lettischen Sonnenmythen." In *Zeitschrift für Ethnologie*, vol. 7. Berlin: Dietrich Reimer Verlag, 1875, 281–329.

Nietzsche, Friedrich. "Vom Weg des Schaffenden." In *Also sprach Zarathustra: Ein Buch für Alle und Keinen*. Leipzig: Naumann, 1901.

["The Way of the Creator." In *Thus Spake Zarathustra: A Book for All and None*. Translated by Thomas Common. Revised by Oscar Levy and John L. Beevers, with an introduction by Oscar Levy. London: Allen & Unwin, 1909.]

Nork, Friedrich. *Der Mystagog oder Deutung der geheimen Lehren, Symbole und Feste der christlichen Kirche*. Leipzig: Wilh. Alex. Künzel, 1838.

Pfeiffer, Franz, ed. *Meister Eckhart*. Leipzig: Göschen, 1857.

Preuschen, Edwin, ed. *Antilegomena: Die Reste der ausserkanonischen Evangelien und urchristlichen Überlieferungen*. Giessen: Ricker, 1901.

Roscher, Wilhelm Heinrich, ed. *Ausführliches Lexikon der griechischen und römischen Mythologie*. Vol. 3. Leipzig: B. G. Teubner, 1897–1902.

Schmid, Hans. "Tristan." Lecture delivered to the Psychology Club Zurich, 6 May 1916 and 19 May 1916. Unpublished typescript, Library of the Psychology Club Zurich.

Schopenhauer, Arthur. *Die Welt als Wille und Vorstellung*. Vol. 1. Leipzig: Philipp Reclam Jr., 1891.

[*The World as Will and Idea*. Vol. 1. Translated by R. B. Haldane and J. Kemp. London: Kegan Paul, Trench & Trübner, 1891.]

———. "Preisschrift über die Freiheit des Willens." In *Die beiden Grundprobleme der Ethik*. Sämtliche Werke in zwölf Bänden, vol. 7. Introduction by Rudolf Steiner. Stuttgart: Cotta, c. 1890.

[*"Prize Essay on the Freedom of the Will."* In *The Two Fundamental Problems of Ethics*. Edited and translated by Christopher Janaway. Cambridge: Cambridge University Press, 2009.]

Schultze, Fritz. *Psychologie der Naturvölker: Entwicklungspsychologische Charakteristik des Naturmenschen in intellektueller, ästhetischer, ethischer und religiöser Beziehung: Eine natürliche Schöpfungsgeschichte menschlichen Vorstellens, Wollens und Glaubens*. Leipzig: von Veit, 1900.

Seligmann, Siegfried. *Der böse Blick und Verwandtes: Ein Beitrag zur Geschichte des Aberglaubens aller Zeiten und Völker*. Vol. 1. Berlin: Barsdorf, 1910.

Spitteler, Carl. *Imago*. Jena: Diederichs, 1910.

———. *Prometheus und Epimetheus: Ein Gleichnis*. Jena: Dietrichs, 1881/1906.

Talbot, P. Amaury. *In the Shadow of the Bush*. London: Heinemann, 1912.

Tertullian. *Tertullians apologetische, dogmatische und montanistische Schriften*. Edited by Gerhard Esser. Translated by Karl Adam Heinrich Kellner. Kempten: Kösel, 1915.

[*The Apology of Tertullian*. Translated by William Reeve. London and Sydney: Griffith, Farran, 1889.]

———. *Tertullians private und katechetische Schriften*. Edited by Karl Adam Heinrich Kellner. Kempten: Kösel, 1912.

[*De Idololatria, Critical Text, Translation and Commentary*. Edited and translated by J. H. Waszink and J.C.M. van Winden. Leiden: Brill, 1987.]

Wagner, Richard. *Parsifal: Ein Bühnenweihfestspiel*. Mainz: Schott, 1912.

Wolfram von Eschenbach. *Parzival*. Edited by Wilhelm Hertz. Stuttgart: Cotta, 1911.

[*Parzival*. Translated by A. T. Hatto. Middlesex: Penguin, 1984.]

Works Consulted by the Editors

Abraham, Hilda. *Karl Abraham: Sein Leben für die Psychoanalyse*. Munich: Kindler, 1976.

Augusti, Brigitte. *Im Banne der freien Reichsstadt*. Leipzig: Ferdinand Hirt & Sohn, 1886.

Augustine of Hippo, Saint. "Eighth Homily on I John 4:12–16." In *Augustine: Later Works*. Selected and translated by John Burnaby. Library of Christian Classics, vol. 8. Philadelphia: Westminster Press, 1955, 320–28.

Bair, Deirdre. *Jung: A Biography*. London: Little Brown, 2003.

Bashkoff, Tracey, ed. *Hilma af Klint: Paintings for the Future*. New York: Guggenheim Museum Publications, 2021.

Bauriedl, Thea, and Astrid Brundke, eds. *Psychoanalyse in München—Eine Spurensuche*. Giessen: Psychosozial-Verlag, 2008.

Baynes Jansen, Diana. *Jung's Apprentice: A Biography of Helton Godwin Baynes*. Einsiedeln: Daimon Verlag, 2003.

Beeg, Marie. *Lust und Leid der Kinderzeit: In Wort und Bild*. Stuttgart: Wilh. Nitzschke, c. 1879.

Bernet, Brigitta. *Schizophrenie: Entstehung und Entwicklung eines psychiatrischen Krankheitsbildes um 1900*. Zurich: Chronos Verlag, 2013.

Bernhart, Josef, ed. and trans. *Meister Eckhart: Reden der Unterweisung*. Munich: Beck, 1922.

Böldl, Klaus, and Katarina Yngborn, eds. *Ritter und Elfen, Liebe und Tod: Nordische Balladen des Mittelalters*. Munich: Beck, 2011.

Bourget, Paul. *L'étape*. Paris: Librarie Plon, 1902.

Bridges, Robert Seymour, trans. "O sacred head, sore wounded." In *The Hymnal 1982, according to the use of the Episcopal Church*. New York: Church Hymnal Corporation, 1985, #168, #169.

Brunner, Cornelia. "Auszüge aus dem Buche *Die ewige Frau* von Gertrud von Le Fort—mit anschliessendem Kommentar." Lecture delivered to the Psychology Club Zurich, 11 December 1943. Unpublished typescript, Library of the Psychology Club Zurich.

Bundesamt für Statistik, ed. *Eidgenössische Volkszählung 1990: Bevölkerungsentwicklung 1850–1990—Die Bevölkerung der Gemeinden*. Bern, 1992.

Burdach, Konrad. *Vorspiel: Gesammelte Schriften zur Geschichte des deutschen Geistes*. Vol. 1: *Mittelalter*. Halle: M. Niemeyer, 1925.

C. G. Jung Bibliothek. "Literatur zum Graal." In *C. G. Jung Bibliothek: Katalog*. Küsnacht-Zürich: privately printed, 1967, 109–17.

von Chamisso, Adelbert. *Peter Schlemihls wundersame Geschichte*. Bern: Alfred Scherz, 1813.

Clark-Stern, Elizabeth. *Out of the Shadows: A Story of Toni Wolff and Emma Jung*. Carmel, CA: Genoa House, 2010.

Clay, Catrine. *Labyrinths: Emma Jung, Her Marriage to Carl and the Early Years of Psychoanalysis*. London: William Collins, 2016.

Covington, Coline, and Barbara Wharton, eds. *Sabina Spielrein: Forgotten Pioneer of Psychoanalysis*. Hove and New York: Brunner-Routledge, 2003.

Dostojewski, Fjodor. *Raskolnikow's Schuld und Sühne*. Translated by Hans Moser. Berlin: O. Janke, 1891. [Dostoyevsky, Fyodor. *Crime and Punishment*. Edited and translated by Michael R. Katz. New York: Norton, 2019.]

Eckermann, Johann Peter. *Gespräche mit Goethe in seinen letzten Jahren des Lebens*. Vols. 1–3. Leipzig: Reclam, 1835. [*Conversations with Goethe in the Last Years of His Life*. Translated by Margaret Fuller. Boston: Hilliard, Gray & Co., 1839.]

Fierz, Linda. "Ein Beitrag zum Animusproblem." Lecture delivered to the Psychology Club Zurich, 14 February 1931. Unpublished typescript, Library of the Psychology Club Zurich.

———. "Einige Gedanken über die natürliche Einstellung der Frauen zum Leben." Lecture delivered to the Psychology Club Zurich, 3/5 July 1941. Unpublished typescript, Library of the Psychology Club Zurich.

———. "Mutterliebe." Lecture delivered to the Psychology Club Zurich, 22 October 1932. Unpublished typescript, Library of the Psychology Club Zurich.

Finiello Zervas, Diane. *"Enchanting the Unconscious": C. G. Jung, Great Britain, and His English Seminars, 1919 and 1920*. London: Routledge Taylor & Francis Group, forthcoming.

Fischer, Thomas, and Bettina Kaufmann. "C. G. Jung and Modern Art." In *The Art of C. G. Jung*. Edited by the Foundation of the Works of C. G. Jung. Translated by Paul David Young and Christopher John Murray. New York: W. W. Norton, 2019, 19–31.

Fischer, Thomas, and Christfried Tögel. "Der Briefwechsel zwischen Emma Jung und Sigmund Freud." In *Luzifer-Amor: Zeitschrift zur Geschichte der Psychoanalyse*, Heft 73 (36. Jg., 3/2023).

Flammarion, Camille. *L'Inconnu et les problèmes psychiques*. Paris: Ernest Flammarion, 1900.

Flournoy, Théodore. *Des Indes à la Planète Mars: Étude sur un cas de somnambulisme avec glossolalie*. Paris and Geneva: F. Alcan/Ch. Eggimann & Cie, 1900.

Forel, Auguste, and Albert Mahaim. *Crime et anomalies mentales constitutionelles: La plaie sociale des déséquilibrés à responsabilité diminuée*. Geneva: Kündig, 1902.

Förster-Nietzsche, Elisabeth. *Das Leben Friedrich Nietzsches*. Vols. 1–3. Leipzig: Naumann, 1896–1904. [*The Life of Nietzsche*. Translated by Anthony M. Ludovici and Paul Victor Cohn. New York: Sturgis & Walton, 1912–15.]

Foundation of the Works of C. G. Jung. *The Art of C. G. Jung*. Edited by Ulrich Hoerni, Thomas Fischer, and Bettina Kaufmann. Translated by Paul David Young and Christopher John Murray. New York: Norton, 2019.

Frauenfelder, Reinhard. *Siebzig Bilder aus dem alten Schaffhausen*. Schaffhausen: Lempen & Cie, 1937.

Freud, Sigmund, and Eugen Bleuler. *Sigmund Freud—Eugen Bleuler: "Ich bin zuversichtlich, wir erobern bald die Psychiatrie," Briefwechsel 1904–1937*. Edited by Michael Schröter. Basel: Schwabe Verlag, 2012.

Freud, Sigmund, and Sándor Ferenczi. *The Correspondence of Sigmund Freud and Sándor Ferenczi*, vol. 1, 1908–1914. Edited by E. Brabant, E. Falzeder, and P. Giamperi-Geutsch. Cambridge, MA: Harvard University Press, 1993.

Freud, Sigmund, and Ernest Jones. *The Complete Correspondence of Sigmund Freud and Ernest Jones, 1908–1939*. Edited by Andrew R. Paskauskas. Cambridge, MA: Harvard University Press, 1993.

Freud, Sigmund, and Carl Gustav Jung. *The Freud/Jung Letters: The Correspondence between Sigmund Freud and C. G. Jung*. Edited by William McGuire. Translated by Ralph Manheim and R.F.C. Hull. London: Hogarth Press and Routledge & Kegan Paul, 1974.

Gaudissart, Imelda. *Emma Jung, Analyste et écrivain*. Lausanne: Editions L'Age d'Homme, 2010.

Goethe, Johann Wolfgang. *Faust, Erster Teil*. Aarau: Sauerländer, 1950.
[*Faust, Part One*. Translated with an introduction by David Luke. Oxford: Oxford University Press, 1987.]

———. *Faust, Zweiter Teil*. Aarau: Sauerländer, 1947.
[*Faust, Part Two*. Translated with an introduction by David Luke. Oxford: Oxford University Press, 1994.]

Greene, Liz. *Jung's Studies in Astrology: Prophecy, Magic, and the Qualities of Time*. Oxford: Routledge, 2018.

Hannah, Barbara. *Jung: His Life and Work*. Wilmette: Chiron Publications, 1997. [Original publication 1976.]

———. "On Esther Harding's Book: *Women's Mysteries: Ancient and Modern*." Lecture delivered to the Psychology Club Zurich, 29 June 1935. Unpublished typescript, Library of the Psychology Club Zurich.

———. "The Writings of the Brontë Sisters: An Early Victorian Manifestation of the Problem of Modern Woman." Lecture delivered to the Psychology Club Zurich, 19 November 1938. Unpublished typescript, Library of the Psychology Club Zurich.

Harding, Esther. "The Spiritual Problem of Women." Lecture delivered to the Psychology Club Zurich, 26 June 1936. Unpublished typescript, Library of the Psychology Club Zurich.

Hartmann von Aue. *Gregorius, der gute Sünder*. Middle High German text from the edition by Friedrich Neumann. Translated by Burkhard Kippenberg. Afterword by Hugo Kuhn. Stuttgart: Reclam, 1959.

Hauff, Wilhelm. *Das kalte Herz: Ein Märchen*. Berlin: Holzinger, 2016.
["The Marble Heart." In *Tales of the Caravan, Inn and Palace, by William Hauff*. Translated by Edward L. Stowell. Chicago: Jansen, McClurg and Co., 1882.]

Healy, Nan Savage. *Toni Wolff and C. G. Jung: A Collaboration*. Los Angeles: Tiberius Press, 2017.

Hensch, Traute, ed. *Sabina Spielrein, Tagebuch und Briefe: Die Frau zwischen Jung und Freud*. Giessen: Edition Kore im Psychosozial-Verlag, 2003.

Hesse, Hermann. *"Die dunkle und wilde Seite der Seele": Briefwechsel mit seinem Psychoanalytiker, Josef Bernhard Lang, 1916–1944*. Edited by Thomas Feitknecht. Frankfurt a. M.: Suhrkamp, 2006.

Heusler, Elisabeth. "Ein kleiner Abstieg in mein Mutterland." Lecture delivered to the Psychology Club Zurich, 18 May 1935. Unpublished typescript, Library of the Psychology Club Zurich.

Hoerni, Ulrich. "Images from the Unconscious." In *The Art of C. G. Jung*. Edited by Ulrich Hoerni, Thomas Fischer, and Bettina Kaufmann. Translated by Paul David Young and Christopher John Murray. New York: Norton, 2019, 10–16.

van der Hoop, Johan. "Die Bedeutung des Golem." Lecture delivered to the Psychology Club Zurich, 1 January 1917. Unpublished typescript, Library of the Psychology Club Zurich.

Hubschmied, Renata. *Frauen, Macht, Geschichte: Frauen- und gleichstellungspolitische Ereignisse in der Schweiz 1848–1998*. Edited by Eidgenössische Kommission für Frauenfragen. Bern: Eidgenössische Kommission für Frauenfragen, 1998.

Jaffé, Aniela, ed. *C. G. Jung: Word and Image*. Translated by Krishna Winston. Princeton: Princeton University Press, 1997.

Jensen, Ferne, and Sidney Mullen, eds. *C. G. Jung, Emma Jung and Toni Wolff: A Collection of Remembrances*. San Francisco: Analytical Psychology Club of San Francisco, 1982.

Joël, Karl. *Philosophenwege, Ausblicke und Rückblicke*. Berlin: Gaertner, 1901.

Jones, Ernest. "Einige Fälle von Zwangsneurose." In *Jahrbuch für psychoanalytische und psychopathologische Forschung*, IV/1. Edited by Sigmund Freud and C. G. Jung. Leipzig: Franz Deuticke, 1912, 563–606.

Joris, Elisabeth. "Geschlechtshierarchische Arbeitsteilung und Integration der Frauen." In *Etappen des Bundesstaates: Staats- und Nationsbildung der Schweiz 1848–1998*. Edited by Brigitte Studer. Zurich: Chronos, 1998, 187–201.

Jost, Hans Ulrich. *Die Reaktionäre Avantgarde: Die Geburt der Neuen Rechten in der Schweiz um 1900*. Zurich: Chronos, 1992.

Jung, Carl Gustav. "Approaching the Unconscious." In *Man and His Symbols*. New York: Doubleday, 1964, 18–102.

———. *The Black Books 1913–1932: Notebooks of Transformation*. Vol. 1. Edited by Sonu Shamdasani. New York: W. W. Norton, 2020.

———. *C. G. Jung Letters*. Vol. 2: *1951–1961*. Selected and edited by Gerhard Adler in collaboration with Aniela Jaffé. Translated by R.F.C. Hull. Princeton: Princeton University Press; London: Routledge, 1975.

———. *C. G. Jung Speaking: Interviews and Encounters*. Edited by William McGuire and R.F.C. Hull. Princeton: Princeton University Press, 1977.

———. *The Collected Works of C. G. Jung* (*CW*). 20 vols. Edited by Herbert Read, Michael Fordham, and Gerhard Adler; executive editor (from 1967), William McGuire. Translated by R.F.C. Hull, except as otherwise noted. New York: Pantheon Books for Bollingen Foundation, 1953–60; Bollingen Foundation (distributed by Pantheon Books, a Division of Random House), 1961–78 (Bollingen Series XX). London: Routledge & Kegan Paul, 1953–78. (The New York and London editions are identical except for title pages and binding. Reprintings vary.)

- *Collected Works*, vol. 2, *Experimental Researches*, translated by Leopold Stein in collaboration with Diana Riviere, 1973. [First part, §1–497. Originally published in several parts: C. G. Jung and Franz Riklin, *Experimentelle Untersuchungen über Assoziationen Gesunder* (Diagnostische Assoziationsstudien I), in *Journal für Psychologie und Neurologie*. Leipzig: Verlag Johann Ambrosius Barth, 1904–5.]
- *Collected Works*, vol. 5, *Symbols of Transformation: An Analysis of the Prelude to a Case of Schizophrenia*, 1956/1967. [Original publication: *Wandlungen und Symbole der Libido: Beiträge zur Entwicklungsgeschichte des Denkens*. Leipzig and Vienna: Franz Deuticke, 1912.]
- *Collected Works*, vol. 6, *Psychological Types*, 1971. [Original publication 1921.]
- *Collected Works*, vol. 7, *Two Essays on Analytical Psychology*, 1953/1966. [First essay originally published 1917/1926/1943. Second essay originally published 1928. Appendix: 1912, 1916, 1966.]
- *Collected Works*, vol. 9.i, *The Archetypes and the Collective Unconscious*, 1959, 1968. [Original publication 1934–55.]
- *Collected Works*, vol. 9.ii, *Aion: Researches into the Phenomenology of the Self*, 1958, 1968. [Original publication 1951.]
- *Collected Works*, vol. 10, *Civilization in Transition*, 1964, 1970. [Original publication 1918–59.]
- *Collected Works*, vol. 11, *Psychology and Religion*, 1958, 1969. [Original publication 1932–54.]
- *Collected Works*, vol. 12, *Psychology and Alchemy*, 1953, 1968. [Original publication 1944.]
- *Collected Works*, vol. 13, *Alchemical Studies*, 1968. [Original publication 1929–54.]
- *Collected Works*, vol. 15, *The Spirit in Man, Art, and Literature*, 1966. [Original publication 1929–50.]

———. "Die Ehe als psychologische Beziehung." In *Das Ehebuch: Eine neue Sinngebung im Zusammenklang der Stimmen führender Zeitgenossen*. Edited by Graf Hermann Keyserling. Celle: Niels Kampmann Verlag, 1925, 294–307.
["Marriage as a psychological relationship," *CW* 17, §339–45.]

———. "Die Frau in Europa." In *Europäische Revue*, Jg. 3, Heft 7, 1927, 481–99. [In *CW* 10, §236–75.]

———. *Erinnerungen, Träume, Gedanken*. Recorded and edited by Aniela Jaffé. Zurich: Rascher, 1962.
[*Memories, Dreams, Reflections*. Recorded and edited by Aniela Jaffé. Translated by Richard Winston and Clara Winston. New York: Vintage Books, 1965.]

———. "Foreword." In Daisetz Teitaro Suzuki, *An Introduction to Zen Buddhism*. New York: Philosophical Library; London: Rider, 1949, 9–29.

———. "Historische Beiträge zur Typenfrage." Lecture delivered to the Psychology Club Zurich, 3 June 1916. Unpublished typescript, Library of the Psychology Club Zurich.

———. *The Red Book: Liber Novus*. Edited with an introduction by Sonu Shamdasani. Translated by Mark Kyburz, John Peck, and Sonu Shamdasani. New York: Norton, 2009.

———. "The Relations between the Ego and the Unconscious." In *CW* 7.2, §266–406.

———. *Seminar in Analytical Psychology: Human Relationships in Relation to the Process of Individuation*, 14–27 July 1923, Lecture XIV. Notes by members of the class, 92; Notes by Dr. W. B. Crow, 22; Notes by Dr. Esther Harding, 26ff. Princeton: Princeton University Press, forthcoming.

———. *VII Sermones ad Mortuos. Die sieben Belehrungen der Toten. Geschrieben von Basilides in Alexandria, der Stadt, wo der Osten den Westen berührt*. Übersetzt aus dem griechischen Urtext in die deutsche Sprache. Printed for private circulation by the author, 1916.

[*VII Sermones ad Mortuos. The Seven Sermons to the Dead. Written by Basilides in Alexandria, the City Where the East Toucheth the West*. Translated by H. G. Baynes. Printed for private circulation. Edinburgh: Neill, 1916, 1–28.]

["Septem Sermones ad Mortuos." Translated by H. G. Baynes. Appendix V in *Memories, Dreams, Reflections*. Recorded and edited by Aniela Jaffé. New York: Vintage Books, 1965, 378–90.]

———. "The Structure of the Unconscious." In *CW* 7, undated, §442–521.

———. "Über das Selbst." In *Eranos-Jahrbuch 1948*. Zurich: Rhein-Verlag, 1949, 285–315.

———. *Wandlungen und Symbole der Libido*. Munich: Deutscher Taschenbuch Verlag (DTV), 1991. (Reprint of original edition, 1911, 1912.)

———. *Wirklichkeit der Seele: Anwendungen und Fortschritte der neueren Psychologie*. Mit Beiträgen von Hugo Rosenthal, Emma Jung, W. M. Kranefeldt. Zurich: Rascher, 1934.

Jung, Carl Gustav, and Wilhelm Hauer, Heinrich Zimmer, and Mircea Eliade. *Jung and the Indologists: Jung's Correspondences with Wilhelm Hauer, Heinrich Zimmer und Mircea Eliade*. Edited by Giovanni Sorge. Princeton: Princeton University Press, forthcoming.

Jung, Carl Gustav, and Aniela Jaffé. *Jung's Life and Work, as Told to Aniela Jaffé: The Original Protocols for Memories, Dreams, Reflections* [provisional title]. Edited by Sonu Shamdasani, with consulting editors Thomas Fischer and Robert Hinshaw. Princeton: Princeton University Press, forthcoming.

Jung, Carl Gustav, and Hans Schmid-Guisan. *The Question of Psychological Types: The Correspondence of C. G. Jung and Hans Schmid-Guisan, 1915–1916*. Edited by John Beebe and Ernst Falzeder. Princeton: Princeton University Press, 2013.

Jung, Emma. "Die Anima als Naturwesen." In *Studien zur analytischen Psychologie C. G. Jungs*. Edited by the C. G. Jung-Institut, Zurich. Festschrift for the 80th Birthday of C. G. Jung, vol. 2. Zurich: Rascher, 1955, 78–120.

["The Anima as an Elemental Being." In *Animus and Anima*. Translated by Hildegard Nagel. New York: Spring, 1957, 45–94.]

———. "Die Geschichte vom Graal nach Robert de Boron." Lectures delivered to the Psychology Club Zurich, 16 November, 18 November, and 2 December 1944. Unpublished typescripts, vol. 7 (1943–47), Library of the Psychology Club Zurich.

———. "Die Graalserzählungen." Four lectures delivered to the Psychology Club Zurich, March 1940. Unpublished typescripts, Jung Family Archive, Küsnacht.

———. "Ein Beitrag zum Problem des Animus." In C. G. Jung, *Wirklichkeit der Seele: Anwendungen und Fortschritte der neueren Psychologie*. Mit Beiträgen von Hugo Rosenthal, Emma Jung, W. M. Kranefeldt. Zurich: Rascher, 1934, 296–354.

———. "Frau Emma Jung: Die Graalserzählungen." In *Inhaltsangabe der Vorträge im Geschäftsjahr 1940/41*. Library of the Psychology Club Zurich, 15–20. [In the present volume: "Stories of the Grail." Appendix A: "Emma Jung's 'Grail' Abstracts," 363–67.]

———. "Frau Emma Jung: '*Le Roman de l'estoire dou Graal*' des Robert de Boron." In *Inhaltsangabe der Vorträge im Geschäftsjahr 1944/1945*. Library of the Psychology Club Zurich, 28–31. [In the present volume: "*Le Roman de l'estoire dou Graal* by Robert de Boron." Appendix A: "Emma Jung's 'Grail' Abstracts," 367–69.]

———. "Über das Wesen des Animus." Lecture delivered to the Psychology Club Zurich, 21 November 1931. Typescript, Jung Family Archive, Küsnacht. [Published under the title "Ein Beitrag zum Problem des Animus" in C. G. Jung, *Wirklichkeit der Seele*, 1934.]

———. "Wie wirkt sich der psychologische Typus in den Beziehungen zu andern Menschen aus?" Talk delivered to the Psychology Club Zurich, 1943. Unpublished typescript, Jung Family Archive, Küsnacht.

Jung, Joseph. *Das Laboratorium des Fortschritts: Die Schweiz im 19. Jahrhundert*. Flawil: NZZ Libro, 2019.

Keller, Tina. "Vom Animus zum Führer: Innere Erlebnisse während der Analyse." Lecture delivered to the Psychology Club Zurich, 7/8 February 1938. Unpublished typescript, Library of the Psychology Club Zurich.

———. *Wege inneren Wachstums für eingespannte Menschen: Aus meinen Erinnerungen an C. G. Jung.* Erlenbach and Bad Homburg: Bircher Benner Verlag, 1972.

Kiraly, Ursula. "Das Clubproblem, 1920–1924." Lecture delivered to the Psychology Club Zurich, 7 November 2020. Unpublished typescript, Library of the Psychology Club Zurich.

Kunz, Emma. *Neuartige Zeichnungsmethode: Gestaltung und Form als Mass, Rhythmus, Symbol und Wandlung von Zahl und Prinzip.* Self-published, 1953.

Landsberg, Hans. *Friedrich Nietzsche und die deutsche Literatur.* Leipzig: Seemann, 1902.

Lang, Gertrud. "Die Frau—Ausschnitte aus Sage, Geschichte und Gegenwart." Lecture delivered to the Psychology Club Zurich, 27 February 1943. Unpublished typescript, Library of the Psychology Club Zurich.

Ljunggren, Magnus. *The Russian Mephisto: A Study of the Life and Work of Emilii Medtner.* Stockholm: Gotab, 1994.

Loewenfeld, Leopold. *Somnambulismus und Spiritismus.* Wiesbaden: Bergmann, 1900.

Lothane, Zvi. "Tender Love and Transference: Unpublished Letters of C. G. Jung and Sabina Spielrein (with an addendum/discussion)." In *Sabina Spielrein: Forgotten Pioneer of Psychoanalysis.* Edited by Coline Covington and Barbara Wharton. Hove and New York: Brunner-Routledge, 2003, 191–226.

Loti, Pierre. *Pêcheurs d'Islande.* Paris: Calmann-Lévy, 1886.

Luther, Martin, trans. *Die Bibel oder die ganze Heilige Schrift des Alten und Neuen Testaments, nach der deutschen Übersetzung D. Martin Luthers.* Stuttgart: Privileg. Württemberg Bibelanstalt, 1954.

Maeder, Alphonse. "Hodler und die Typenfrage in der Kunst." Two lectures delivered to the Analytical Association, February 1915. Unpublished typescripts, Library of the Psychology Club Zurich.

McGuire, William. *Bollingen: An Adventure in Collecting the Past.* Princeton: Princeton University Press, 1982.

Meillet, Antoine. *Introduction à l'étude comparative des langues indo-européennes.* Paris: Hachette, 1903.

Mensendieck, Otto. "Die Gral-Parzivalsage." Lecture delivered to the Analytical Association, 16 May 1913. Unpublished typescript, Library of the Psychology Club Zurich.

———. "Die prospektive Tendenz des Unbewussten in Wagners erstem Worttondrama über den Parsifal." Lecture delivered to the Analytical Association, 5 December 1913. Unpublished typescript, Library of the Psychology Club Zurich.

Meyrinck, Gustav. *Der Golem.* Leipzig: Kurt Wolff, 1915.

Möbius, Paul Julius. *Über das Pathologische bei Nietzsche.* Wiesbaden: Bergmann, 1902.

Moltzer, Maria. "The Relation between the Zurich School and the Club." Lecture delivered to the Psychology Club Zurich, 1 September 1917. Unpublished typescript, Library of the Psychology Club Zurich.

Mösli, Rolf, ed. *Eugen Bleuler: Pionier der Psychiatrie.* Zurich: Römerhof, 2012.

Müller, Sabina. "Schlussbericht zu Emma Jungs Gralsmaterial." Unpublished typescript, 2013. Archive of the Foundation of the Works of C. G. Jung, Zurich.

Muser, Friedel Elisabeth. "Zur Geschichte des Psychologischen Clubs von den Anfängen bis 1928." Lecture delivered to the Psychology Club Zurich, 25 June 1983. Offprint, *Annual Report of the Psychology Club Zurich*, 1984.

Neri, Nadia. *Oltre l'Ombra: Donne intorno a Jung.* Rome: Edizione Borla, 1995.

Neumann, Friedrich, ed. *Deutscher Minnesang (1150–1300).* Nachdichtung von Kurt Erich Meurer. Stuttgart: Reclam, 1954.

Nietzsche, Friedrich. *Also sprach Zarathustra: Ein Buch für Alle und Keinen.* Leipzig: Naumann, 1901.

[*Thus Spake Zarathustra: A Book for All and None.* Translated by Thomas Common. Revised by Oscar Levy and John L. Beevers. Introduction by Oscar Levy. London: Allen & Unwin, 1909.]

———. *Schopenhauer als Erzieher.* Leipzig: E. W. Fritzsch, 1874.

[*Schopenhauer as Educator*. Translated by Adrian Collins. Gloucester: Dodo Press, 2009.]

Peglau, Andreas. "Sigmund Freud in Weimar: A Photo from the Year 1911—and a Snapshot of the Psychoanalytic Movement." In *Weimar-Jena: Die grosse Stadt—Das kulturhistorische Archiv* 5, no. 3 (2012): 228–38.

du Prel, Carl. *Der Spiritismus*. Leipzig: Reclam, 1893.

von Rhoden, Emmy. *Der Trotzkopf*. Stuttgart: Stuttgarter Verlag, 1885.

Riklin, Franz. *Wunscherfüllung und Symbolik im Märchen: Schriften zur angewandten Seelenkunde*. Vol. 2. Edited by Sigmund Freud. Leipzig and Vienna: Franz Deuticke, 1908.

[*Wish-fulfillment and Symbolism in Fairy Tales*. In The Nervous and Mental Disease Monograph Series, no. 21. Translated by William A. White. New York: The Nervous and Mental Disease Publishing Company, 1915.]

Schär, Hans. "Rede von Herrn Pfarrer Prof. Dr. Hans Schär an der Abdankungsfeier in der Kirche Küsnacht, 30. November 1955." In *Emma Jung-Rauschenbach (30. März 1882–27. November 1955)*. Jung Family Archive, Küsnacht, 5–15.

Schlegel, Erika. "Rahel Varnhagen." Lecture delivered to the Psychology Club Zurich, 8 June 1922. Unpublished typescript, Library of the Psychology Club Zurich.

Schmid-Guisan, Hans. *Tag und Nacht*. Foreword by C. G. Jung. Zurich: Rhein-Verlag, 1931.

Schoenl, William. *C. G. Jung: His Friendship with Mary Mellon and J. B. Priestley*. Asheville: Chiron Publications, 1998.

Serina, Florent. "C. G. Jung's Encounter with His French Readers: The Paris Lecture (May 1934)." *Phanês: Journal for Jung History* 1 (2018): 112–37.

Shalit, Erel, and Nancy Swift Furlotti, eds. *The Dream and Its Amplification*. Skiatook, OK: Fischer King Press, 2013.

Shamdasani, Sonu. *Cult Fictions: C. G. Jung and the Founding of Analytical Psychology*. London: Routledge, 1998.

———. *Jung and the Making of Modern Psychology: The Dream of a Science*. Cambridge: Cambridge University Press, 2003.

———. "Toward a Visionary Science: Jung's Notebooks of Transformation." In C. G. Jung, *The Black Books 1913–1932: Notebooks of Transformation*, vol. 1. Edited by Sonu Shamdasani. New York: W. W. Norton, 2020, 11–112.

Steiner, Rudolf. "The Evolution of the World and Man." In *An Outline of Occult Science*. New York: Anthroposophic Press, 1922.

Stiftung C. G. Jung Küsnacht, ed. *The House of C. G. Jung: The History and Restoration of the Residence of Emma and Carl Gustav Jung-Rauschenbach*. Wilmette, IL: Chiron, 2009.

von Sury, Elisabeth. "Die psychologische Wirkung der Frau." Lecture delivered to the Psychology Club Zurich, 5 May 1928. Unpublished typescript, Library of the Psychology Club Zurich.

Suzuki, Daisetz Teitaro. *Die grosse Befreiung—Einführung in den Zen-Buddhismus*. Geleitwort von C. G. Jung. Leipzig: Weller, 1939.

[*An Introduction to Zen Buddhism*. Foreword by C. G. Jung. New York: Philosophical Library/London: Rider, 1949.]

Tolstoi, Lew. *Auferstehung*. Translated by Wladimir Czumikow. Halle a. d. S.: Verlag Otto Hendel, c. 1900.

[Tolstoy, Leo. *The Awakening (The Resurrection)*. Translated by William E. Smith. New York: Street & Smith, 1900.]

Viebig, Clara. *Das tägliche Brot*. Berlin: Fontane, 1901.

[*Our Daily Bread*. Translated by Margaret L. Clarke. London: John Lane, 1909.]

Weber, Nadir. "Vom Selbst zur Welt: Zur intellektuellen Biographie von Hans Trüb." In *Hans Trüb, Welt und Selbst: Bausteine einer modernen Psychotherapie*. Edited by Nadir Weber. Gevelsberg: EHP Verlag, 2020, 171–206.

Wieser, Annatina. "Zur frühen Psychoanalyse in Zürich, 1900–1914." Inaugural dissertation, 2001. Unpublished typescript, Universität Zürich. https://www.luzifer-amor.de/extras/downloads/wieser-psychoanalyse-in-zuerich.

Wolff, Toni. "Einige Gedanken zum Individuationsprozess der Frau." Lecture delivered to the Psychology Club Zurich, 12 May 1934. Unpublished typescript, Library of the Psychology Club Zurich.

Zimmer, Heinrich. "Abenteuer zweier Artusritter (Gawain und Owain) als Individuationssymbole des Artuskreises." Lecture delivered to the Psychology Club Zurich, 25 June 1938. Unpublished typescript, Library of the Psychology Club Zurich.

Archival Sources

JUNG FAMILY ARCHIVE, KÜSNACHT
Emma Jung papers collection.
Private family correspondences.

STIFTUNG DER WERKE VON C. G. JUNG, ZURICH
Working archive.

PSYCHOLOGY CLUB ZURICH ARCHIVES
Protokoll der Vorträge des Vereins für Analytische Psychologie I, 1913–16.
Protokolle Psychologischer Club, vols. 1–10, 1916–55.

ETH ZURICH UNIVERSITY ARCHIVES
C. G. Jung papers collection.

UNIVERSITÄTSBIBLIOTHEK BASEL
Nachlass 335 (Lucie Heyer-Grote), C2 45, 1.

ZENTRALBIBLIOTHEK ZÜRICH
Nachlass Kranefeldt, Ms Z II 395.

SAMMLUNG FELIX NAEFF, BASEL
Wolff/Trüb/Naeff correspondences.

SAMMLUNG RALI NEUMANN, JERUSALEM
Erich Neumann–Emma Jung correspondence.

SAMMLUNG CORINA FISCH-SCHLEGEL, FRAUENFELD
Tagebuch Erika Schlegel.

INDEX

Page numbers in *italics* indicate figures and tables.

conscience, 132, 133, 135; German word for, 132n5; Latin derivation in English and French, 132n5
constancy of character, 141
Conte del Graal (Troyes), 363
converging currents, 336, 337
Conversations with Goethe in the Last Years of His Life (Eckermann), 12
"Coral Tree, The": color drafts, 344n68; dream and fantasy of, 85, 292–93, painting of, 76, 292
cosmology: day and night, 104; Emma Jung's theme, 93–94; personal, of Emma and Carl Jung, 38–39. *See also* System
creative person, 172
creative work: concepts and methods, 67–79; amplification, 70–71; archetypes, 68–70; concept of the unconscious, 72–73; dream series, 78–79; fantasy (active imagination) in, 73; objective and subjective levels of meaning in, 71–72; psychological typology, 79; symbolic imagery, 74–77
Crime et anomalies mentales constitutionelles (Forel), 12
cross, 334, 335
cross and scorpion, painting by Emma Jung, *176*
crossing, 339
cultural direction, 353
currents, 350, *350*; arrested, 336, 337; association, 345; converging, 351, *351*; diverging, 336, 337; extraverted, 336, 337
Cyrano de Bergerac (Rostand), 11

dancer, fantasy, 261–64
darkness, light and, 343
death and rebirth of the world, painting series by Emma Jung, *310, 311*
"death is come upon me, A" (Emma Jung), 239, 241
de Boron, Robert, Grail version, 55, 96
dependence of God on human beings, theme, 87
devil, dream of, 286
diamond, 334, 335
differentiation, gift of, 321
Dioscuri, 103, 103n9, 104
directional elements, 354–55
directional factors, 355
discrimination, 320, 321
Don Giovanni (Mozart), 85
doubling (Verdoppelung), Emma Jung's theme, 83, 266n14
"Do you see the sea?" 82, 84, 179, 316n13; narrative poem, 181, 183, 185, 187, 189, 191, 193
dragon fight, 121, 123, 126

dream(s): animal enclosure, 287–88; bear goddess (Ursanna), 88–89; blue flower, 260; Carl and an eagle, 300; Coral Tree, 292–93; devil, 286; figure of Christ, 274; the gatekeeper, 299; girl in red, 275; goddess and bear, 88; Grail, 273, 323–25; house of Virgo, 319–23; image of falling into the mill, 318–19, 331; meeting Aranû, 279–83; miraculous city, 268–72; seeking Undine, 276–78; series, 78–79; of Schaffhausen, 231n1; swan and star, 258; temple of Ursanna, 88–89; two churches, 301–9; two pictures, 259; world turned upside-down, 289–91. *See also* fantasies/fantasy
"Dream and Fantasy of the Coral Tree," 85, 292–93
dream interpretation: Emma Jung's lectures on, 57; objective and subjective levels of meaning in, 71n14, 71–72; psychoanalytic method of, 31
du Prel, Carl, Carl Jung on, 12

Eabani (Enkidu), 109, 109n41, 116
earth: creation of, 342; destruction of, in paintings, *310*; as "Erde," segment of color wheel, *340*; enmity with water, 342; as microcosm of universe, 38; as opposite to heaven, 15, 69, 80, 87, 104, 145, 203, 205, 207, 211, 215, 219, 223, 227; relationship to light, 341n63, 342, 343, 349n76; signified by red-brown, *340*, 331, *340*, 349n76; sun and, 69, 145n30, 259, 289, 341, 341n63, 347, 347n70
Eckermann, Johann Peter, Carl Jung on, 12
Einstein, Albert, 329, 329n40; Emma Jung and, 373; guest of Carl and Emma Jung, 329n40, 373; theory of equivalence of energy and matter, influence on Emma Jung's System, 316n11, 329, 329n40, 342n64, 353, 353n80
Eitingon, Max, 60
"Elucidation," 366
emanations, 347
emergence of a world, concept of, 324; Emma Jung's painting of, *361*
emergence of solid matter, 340
"Emergence of the star-bird," painting series by Emma Jung, 228
energy: archetypes as potential forms of, 69; equivalent to matter (Einstein), 316n11, 329, 329n40, 342n64, 353n80; liberated from matter, 353, 357; libido and, 80n35; of motion, 328, 348, 354
Engadine: Jungs vacationing in, 62; title of dream painting, 259; villages in, 251n10, 325n35
Enkidu. *See* Eabani
Epimetheus, Prometheus and, 142, 144, 151

"Goddess and Bear" (dream), 88
goddess: Mary as, 221; Themis, mother of Prometheus, 142; Ursanna (bear goddess in dream), 88–89
Goethe, Johann Wolfgang von: *Faust I*, 117n62, 283n33, 326n37; *Faust II*, 166n29; song from *Wilhelm Meister*, 131
golden bird, fairy tale figure, 107
Golem, Der (Meyrinck), 166, 166–67n36
good and evil, 132–33, 135
"Goose Girl, The" (fairy tale), 117
Gospel, Christ and, 122–23
Götterdämmerung (twilight of the gods), Emma Jung's theme, 86–88; Nietzsche's term, 158n5, 265n10
Grail: books in Emma Jung's library, 56, 56n168; castle, 119, 364–67; dream, 273; dream and analysis, 70, 273n24; 323–26; king, 125, 129, 365, 367; Kundry as servant of, 53–54, 117, 117n64; presentations on theme of, *xxiv*, 53–56, 54n154, 54n160, 57, 59, 96, 375, 376, 377. *See also Parsifal*; *Parzival*; Perceval
"Grail Abstracts" (Emma Jung), *xiii*, 363–69; "*Le Roman de l'estoire dou Graal* by Robert de Boron," 367–69; "Stories of the Grail," 363–67
Grail Legend, The (Emma Jung and von Franz), 51, 53–56, 96; Emma Jung's lifelong work on, 53; von Franz's contribution to, *xiii*, 53n148
Grand Saint Graal (Map), 54, 363
gratitude, by animals, 114–15
"great eye has opened, The," painting by Emma Jung, 297
green: associated with spiral, 352, 352; associated with water, 281, 340, 341, 352; in color wheel, 340; of forest (nurturing), 84, 84n45, 179n3, 268n18, 316n13; signifying growth, hope, 340, signifying material life, 358
green linen notebook, *xvii*, 294n47
"Grief" (Emma Jung), 237
Gros Caillou, Le, Psychology Club, Paris, 47
grüne Heinrich, Der (Keller), 110–11
Guardian of the Valley, The, painting by Thoma, 15
guilt: in Adam and Eve, 147–49; concept of, 132, 135; in fairy tales, 140; feelings of, 134–35, 154; in Grail story, 151–53, 364–67; in myth of Prometheus, 142–44, 146–48; in primitive peoples, 136–37; psychological definition of, 134; relative and absolute, 45, 147, 153–55, 170. *See also* "On Guilt" (lecture by Emma Jung)

Hannah, Barbara; analysis with Emma Jung, 49n129
"Hansel and Gretel" (fairy tale), 108, 140

Harding, Esther: Emma Jung and, 71, 71n12; *Women's Mysteries*, 71, 89
harlequin figure, painting by Emma Jung, 76n27, 77
heat, 328, 335
Heintze, Ilse; analytical training with Emma Jung, 47n137
Hesiod, 96, 143n26, 143–44, 149
Heusler, Elisabeth, Emma Jung and, 50
Hinkle, Beatrice, 60; translator of *Wandlungen und Symbole*, 34n31, 80n35, 116n60
Hochheim, Eckhart von. *See* Meister Eckhart
Hoerni-Jung, Helene (Lill), *xvi*, 3n5, 27, 243n5, 259n2; birth of, 19, 36, 53n153, 100n1, 259, 320, 325n35; in dream commentary, 320; family memories of, *xxiv*, 3n6, 7n16, 18n65
Homberger, Ernst, 18, 18n64, 372; Jungs and, 376
Homberger-Rauschenbach, Marguerite, 371, 372; in dreams, as Emma Jung's shadow, 71, 79, 79n34, 84, 301, 303; Emma Jung and, 2, 4, 18, 18n66, 22
Homberger, Rudolf, Psychology Club Zurich, 62
horns, *344, 346, 348*
horoscope, 287
house of Virgo, dream of, 319–23
Howes, Elisabeth B., 51n139; Emma Jung and, 51
human being(s), 171, 319; characteristics of, 155; development of, 113
hunter(s): Adonis, 125n87; Apollo, 121; brothers in fairy tale, 100–103, 111, 113, 121, 125, 127; in "Little Red Riding Hood," 111; Nimrod-Gilgamesh, 116; Odin, 112; Orion, 112; Parzival, 111; Siegfried, 111, 125n87; Tristan, 111
hunting: ancient human skill, 111; characteristic of heroes, 111–13; loss of soul while, 124; signifying mastery of libido, 81, 113
Hymns of Avesta, 121, 121n74

idolatry, 120, 150–51, 155; of monsters, 120
Iliad, The (Homer), 104
image(s): of the animus, 85, 87, 223, 225, 227; archetype(s) as, 69n5, 70, 105; eternal, 80; feminine, 88–92; of god/God, 86n52, 86–88 157, 158n5, 201, 205; as imago, 150; of a mouse, 265; otherworldly, 92–93, 175; "primordial," 69; symbolic reading of, 74–77; worship of (idolatry), 150–51. *See also* archetypes
"Image of an emerging world," 315; painting by Emma Jung, *361*
imagination: term, 73. *See also* active imagination; fantasies/fantasy
Imago (Spitteler), 125
imago, 150, 151

individual psyche, 105

individuation: distinct from Adlerian and Freudian theory, 161; in Jungian psychology, 34–35, 81n38; sacrifice and, as Emma Jung's theme, 81–82; term, 82n41

infinity, 335, 353, 353

inner development, symbolic depiction of, 120

insane asylum Burghölzli, 8, 8n23

International Psychoanalytical Association, 30n7, 160n1, 160–67

International Watch Company (IWC), 2

introversion, 106, 107, 122; forest as symbol of, 125–26

intuition, 79n32, 79n33; as Emma Jung's inferior function, 79, 79n34, 260, 260n7, 303, 304. *See also* sensation

"Iron John" (fairy tale), 108, 109, 110, 115

Janet, Pierre, Carl Jung and, 15, 15n58

Jones, Ernest, 60, 374; Emma Jung's translation of his 1912 paper, 34, 34n32; letter to Sigmund Freud, 33n26

Joseph of Arimathea, 367–68

"Journey to the Underworld," fantasy, 87–88, 294–98

Judaism, 150

judgment, 152

Jung, Agathe. *See* Niehus-Jung, Agathe (Agi)

Jung, Carl Gustav: active imagination, 314n1; Burghölzli and first years of marriage, 16–18; common interest in art with Emma, 15–16; on death of wife Emma, 21, 21n75; dissertation, 13; early marriage years, 25; Emma and, vacationing, 63; engagement to Emma Rauschenbach, 13, 24, 372; family photograph, 26; as a figure in Emma's dreams, 71n14, 72, 84, 85, 86, 260, 289, 300; Freud and, 31–33; meeting Emma Rauschenbach, 7–11; name change from Karl, 8, 8n18; photographs with Emma, 27, 28, 61, 62, 64, 66; recommending readings for Emma, 11, 12–13; relationships outside marriage, 20, 20n71, 33, 33n22, 33n23, 33n24, 373, 374; separation from Sigmund Freud, 70, 70n10; texts and images from the unconscious, 37–39. *See also Wandlungen und Symbole der Libido* (C. G. Jung)

Jung, Emilie, 7, 8, 8n21, 19

Jung, Emma, 60: analysis with Schmid-Guisan, 36n40, 36–37; analysis with Seif, 35n26; birth of Agathe (Agi), 372; birth of Franz, 373; birth of Helene (Lill), 19, 320, 325n35, 374; birth of Margarethe (Gret), 372; birth of Marianne (Nannel), 19, 32, 373; Burghölzli and first years of marriage, 16–18; Carl and, vacationing, 63; Carl enriching life of, 20;

childhood photographs, 22, 23, 25; concepts and methods in creative work of, 67–79; cosmological questions and proposals, 314–61; death of, 21; early marriage photograph, 25; family photograph, 26; Grail legend, her work on, 51, 53–54, 54n154, 56; honeymoon photograph, 25; letters with Freud, 32, 32n18; meeting Sigmund Freud, 31–33; photograph at masked ball, 61; photographs at Eranos, 64, 65; photographs at Seestrasse house, 65, 66; photograph at Weimar Psychoanalytic Congress, 60; photographs with Carl, 27, 28 61, 62, 64; as pioneer, 58–59; president of Psychology Club Zurich, 29, 40–44; "*Le Roman de l'estoire dou Graal* by Robert de Boron," 367–69; sources for her System, 315–16; starting a family and building a house, 19–21; "Stories of the Grail," 363–67; work as an analyst, 49–52; work at C. G. Jung Institute, 56–58. *See also* creative work: concepts and methods; dreams; fantasies/fantasy; lecture(s); notebooks of Emma Jung; paintings by Emma Jung; poems (Emma Jung); System

Jung, Franz, 3n5

Jung, Helene. *See* Hoerni-Jung, Helene (Lill)

Jung, Margaretha. *See* Baumann-Jung, Margaretha (Gret)

Jung, Marianne. *See* Niehus-Jung, Marianne (Nannel)

Jung, Paul Achilles, 7; pastor of church of Laufen, 14n53

Jung-Rauschenbach, Emma Maria, chronology of, 371–77

Keller, Adolf, 60, 131n1, 161, 161n9; figure in dream ("Dr. K."), 319, 319n16, 319n17

Keller, Gottfried: on adolescent influx of love, 110–11; author, *Der grüne Heinrich*, 110

Keller, Tina, 43–44n88; Emma Jung and, 43–44

Kerényi, Karl, Emma Jung and, 56n166

Kerner, Justinus, Emma reading, 11

Keyserling, Hermann, 49n126; Darmstadt School of Wisdom, 49

King Arthur's Round Table, 363, 368

knife, thrusting a, 118, 119

Kranefeldt, Hanna, Emma Jung and, 50

Kranefeldt, Wolfgang, 46n106; Emma Jung and, 46, 49–50, 52; Psychology Club Zurich, 50n136

Künstlerhaus, 15

Kunz, Emma, Emma Jung and, 39

Kutonagua Indians of British Columbia, 120

Lady from the Sea, The (Ibsen), 160

lance, 365

steinere Gast," 252; "The Stone Guest," 253; "The Stranger," 255; "Trauer," 236; "The Wall," 231; "Was ist anders der Mensch als ein Kampfplatz," 131n4, "Weite," 234; "We Stand at the Gateway," 251; "What is the human being but a battleground," 131n4; "Wir stehen an den Pforten," 250; "Wunder," 246

Polytechnic University, Dresden, 2

portfolios, Jung Family Archive, *xii*

positive feminine image, 88–90

power, 343

precondition of life, 332

Preiswerk, Helene, Carl Jung's dissertation and, 13

prejudice, 152

"primitive": expression, in Emma Jung's writing, *xxiv*, 95; word, 104, 104n17

"Problem of the Animus, On the" (Emma Jung), 49, 54, 57, 85; Emma Jung's lectures on, at the Jung Institute, 377; included in *Wirklichkeit der Seele*, 85

Prometheus and Epimetheus (Spitteler), 142

Prometheus myth, 142–44, 146–48, 151

Psychoanalytic Association of Zurich, 35

Psychoanalytic Congress in Weimar, photograph of, 34, 60

Psychological Study Group, Munich, 47

Psychological Types (C. G. Jung), 47, 73

psychological typology, 79

Psychologie der Naturvölker (Schultze), 133, 133n9, 136

Psychology Club Zurich, 18, 19, 374, 375, 376; activities of, 41–42, 62; Emma Jung as first president of, 29, 40–44, 59; formation of, 40; lecture for twentieth anniversary of, 160–67; masked ball for members of, 41n77, 61; women's gatherings at, 85, 167n37

Psychology of the Unconscious, The, Beatrice Hinkle's translation of *Wandlungen und Symbole der Libido*, 34n31, 80n35, 104n21, 108n39, 116n60

"Puss-in-Boots" (fairy tale), 115

radiation, 349, *349*

"Rapunzel" (fairy tale), 108

Rauschenbach (née Schenk), Bertha, 1, 3, 7–9, 18, 22

Rauschenbach, Conrad, 2

Rauschenbach, Emma Maria: background and childhood of, 1–5; engagement to Carl Jung, 13, *24*, 29; illness of her father, 5; making acquaintance of Carl Gustav Jung, 7–11; philosophy and psychology interests, 11–13; photograph, 22; photograph as bride, *24;* photograph at age 17, *23;* religious point

of view and meaning of life, 13–15; sharing interest in art with Carl, 15–16; sitting in the sun photograph, 25; year abroad in Paris, 6–7. *See also* Jung, Emma

Rauschenbach, Johannes (1815–81), 2

Rauschenbach, Johannes (1856–1905) (Jean), 1–3, 371; illness of, 5; illness and death of, 17–18; photograph, 22

Rauschenbach, Marguerite, 6, 6n13, 18, 371; photograph, 22

Rauschenbach Machine Factory, 2, 3, 18, 376

red: of Aranû in visions, 87, 282, 295–96; clothing of girl in dream, 88, 275; as color of love, 340–41; in color wheel, 340; coral tree in dream, 292; feather(s) in dream, 273, *273,* 324, 324n31, 339; flowers in dream, symbolizing biological life, 82, 260; of god-image in dream, 274; symbolizing fire and transformation, 340; in vortex drawing, 352, *352*

Red Book, The (C. G. Jung), 37, 83n43, 374

red-brown: in color wheel, 340, 349n76; color of pot and castle in dream, 281

redemption of world, Schopenhauer on, 146

"Reflections on a Passage by Meister Eckhart" (lecture, Emma Jung), 156–59

regression, 342

resistance: in creation of form, 317, 330, 333–35, 349, 350; in generation of power, 337, 341; psychological, 82, 164; sexual, 343

resurrection, 124

Résurrection (Bataille), 16; adapted from Tolstoy's *Auferstehung*, 16n60

rhythm, 355

rhythm of intensity, 348

Rig-Veda, The, 121

Riklin, Franz, 30n7, 60, 160, 160n1; Carl Jung and, 30–31, 34; International Association, 35

Rockefeller, Edith, 162n13, 162–64, 166

Roman de l'estoire dou Graal, Le (de Boron), 367–69

Rome (Zola), 13

Roscher, Wilhelm, on Orion, 111–12

sacrifice, 81n39, 113; Christ, 145; mythology and legends, 120–21

sacrifice and individuation, Emma Jung's theme, 81–82

sacrificial meal, custom of, 114

"Sapphire shield amid the clouds of becoming," painting by Emma Jung, 98

Schär, Hans, pastor of Reformed Church, 58n178, 58n179, 58–59

Schaffhausen: Astronomical Society of, 3n5; city view of, 23; dream of, 23n11; history of Rauschenbach family in, 2, 2n4, 7n15, 371